# The Long Peace

# THE LONG PEACE

## Inquiries Into the History of the Cold War

John Lewis Gaddis

OXFORD UNIVERSITY PRESS
*New York    Oxford*

**Oxford University Press**
Oxford   New York   Toronto
Delhi   Bombay   Calcutta   Madras   Karachi
Petaling Jaya   Singapore   Hong Kong   Tokyo
Nairobi   Dar es Salaam   Cape Town
Melbourne   Auckland

and associated companies in
Berlin   Ibadan

First published in 1987 by Oxford University Press, Inc.,
200 Madison Avenue, New York, New York 10016

First issued as an Oxford University Press paperback, 1989

Oxford is a registered trademark of Oxford University Press

Library of Congress Cataloging-in-Publication Data

Gaddis, John Lewis.
The long peace.

Includes index.
1. United States—Foreign relations—Soviet Union.
2. Soviet Union—Foreign relations—United States.
3. United States—Foreign relations—1945–
I. Title.
E183.8.S65G33   1987       327.73      86–33334
ISBN 0-19-504336-7
ISBN 0-19-504335-9 (PBK)

2  4  6  8  10  9  7  5  3

Printed in the United States of America

*For*
*John and Elizabeth Baker*
*Peacemakers*

# Preface

This book shows what happens when curiosity and serendipity combine with shameless opportunism. The curiosity grew out of my sense that an earlier and conceptually more ambitious analysis of postwar United States national security policy* had nonetheless left certain questions unresolved: What exactly had Americans found threatening about Soviet behavior at the end of World War II? Did Washington really want a sphere of influence in postwar Europe, or did it not? How was it that the Truman administration endorsed, but then almost immediately backed away from, a strategy of avoiding military commitments on the Asian mainland? Why did the United States refrain from using nuclear weapons during the decade in which it was immune to any possibility of a Soviet retaliatory attack? Did American officials really believe in the existence of an international communist "monolith"? How did Russians and Americans fall into the habit of not attempting to shoot down each other's reconnaissance satellites? And, most important, why, given the unprecedented levels of super-power tension that have existed since 1945, has World War III not occurred?

The serendipity came in three forms: First, the progress of declassification brought about the release, in vast quantities, of once-secret American and British documents that made it possible to begin to answer these questions. Second, it has been my good fortune to have participated in a series of conferences and symposia—in locations as diverse as Kiev, Beijing, Oslo, Palo

* *Strategies of Containment: A Critical Appraisal of Postwar American National Security Policy* (New York: 1982).

Alto, and Mount Kisco—which provided opportunities to present findings, test hypotheses, and secure the always valuable (if not always followed) suggestions of colleagues in my own and related fields. Third, as a consequence of having prepared papers for these occasions, I found myself in the surprising but pleasing situation of having written a book without quite having set out to do so.

The opportunism resides in the fact that I am, to an extent, republishing myself. Three of the essays included in this volume have already appeared in slightly different versions as articles in journals or conference volumes; three others are to be published in that latter format at some point in the future. The difficulty with such publications, though, is that what appears in them necessarily stands apart from what one has published on related topics elsewhere and is not, therefore, easily connected with one's wider concerns. If that sounds like a flimsy excuse for reworking old material, I will not wholly deny the charge. But I can plead in my defense the established ecological soundness of the principle of recycling, together with the fact that I am not, I believe, the first historian to have discovered it.

My intention in pulling these essays together in one place is to make several interconnected points: that the sources now exist for producing carefully documented studies in "contemporary history"—that is, the period that falls in between what journalists write about and what history textbooks teach; that what is contained in these sources modifies, at times in striking ways, our perception of the recent past; and that an awareness of how recollections of "what happened" differ from "what actually happened" can provide new and at times valuable angles of vision from which to comprehend, and perhaps even to attempt to modify, the present.*

I should like here to express my gratitude to those who made possible the occasions upon which these essays in their original form were presented: specific individuals and organizations are identified at the beginning of each chapter. None of them, I hasten to add, is to be held responsible for what resulted. I am indebted as well to the librarians, archivists, and editors without whom we who write about the recent past would be totally adrift: in particular, to those at the Office of the Historian in the Department of State, which produces the indispensable series, *Foreign Relations of the United States*; the Diplomatic and Modern Military Branches at the National Archives; the Public Record Office, London; the Harry S. Truman and Dwight D. Eisenhower Libraries; the Seeley G. Mudd Library at Princeton University; and, not least, the Ohio University Library, where the staff have long since learned to brace themselves when they see me coming.

Publishing with Sheldon Meyer and the Oxford University Press has become a pleasant habit, not only for me but for several of my colleagues in the History Department at Athens. I am particularly grateful this time around

* For an engaging and thoughtful elaboration of this last point, see Richard E. Neustadt and Ernest R. May, *Thinking in Time: The Uses of History for Decision-Makers* (New York: 1986).

to Leona Capeless for a superlative job of copy-editing. For permission to use previously-published material under their copyright, my thanks as well to the Norwegian University Press (Chapter Three), and the Columbia University Press (Chapter Four).

Barbara, Michael, and David have tactfully pointed out to me that readers who remember nothing whatever about the substance of my books nonetheless tend to recall, years afterward and with unnerving precision, what I write in prefaces about my family. Lest I mark them all for life, therefore, I will say here only that all are well and happy, thank goodness, and (as our Finnish friends say) send regards.

Two people who deserve special credit for this book are Richard Barr, of Vere Smith Audio-Visuals, who patiently introduced me to the multiple benefits of word processing, and Robert Martin, of Martin Builders, who with great care and competence constructed the study in which most of it was composed, and in which the all-important computer now resides.

The dedication is my way of paying respect—and expressing gratitude—to two individuals whose long, full, and fruitful lives have greatly enriched the town in which I live and the university in which I teach, but whose vision extends to much wider things as well.

*Athens, Ohio*                                                                 J. L. G.
*February, 1987*

# Contents

# The Long Peace

# 1

# Legacies:
# Russian-American Relations
# Before the Cold War

THE HISTORY of Russian-American relations* is of sufficient duration, complexity and ambiguity that it is capable of sustaining remarkably different interpretive perspectives. The first full-length account of that relationship to be published in the United States, that of Foster Rhea Dulles, which appeared at the height of wartime cooperation in 1944, concluded that there existed no permanent basis for hostility between the two countries: "They have had no grounds for conflict that have involved them in war against each other, and they should be able to continue to live together in harmony."[1] But by 1950, another American historian, Thomas A. Bailey, had drawn from roughly the same set of experiences the conclusion that "Czarism was about as antipathetic ideologically to democracy as is present-day Stalinism." Coexistence, for Americans, required keeping "our heads clear, our nerves steady, and our powder dry."[2] Nor is this phenomenon of deriving differing conclusions from the same body of evidence limited to historians in the United States: Soviet

This paper was originally prepared for the Fifth Colloquium of Soviet and American Historians, co-sponsored by the Soviet Academy of Sciences and the American Historical Association, and held in Kiev in June, 1984. It is a distillation of certain themes developed in my 1978 book, *Russia, the Soviet Union, and the United States,* but it has not been previously published in this form.

* Throughout much of this chapter I shall use, purely for reasons of convenience, the term "Russian-American relations," fully cognizant of the fact that neither "Russia" nor "America" are accurate or wholly satisfactory appellations for the countries and peoples involved.

historians have had their own firmly held viewpoints on this subject, and these have at times differed markedly from those of their American counterparts.[3]

That this is so should not be at all surprising. Historians bring to the writing of history a considerable quantity of intellectual baggage, made up not only of their own personal experiences and their own understanding of the past but also of the political and social context from which these derive. When that context differs as much as it does in the case of the Soviet Union and the United States, it becomes "no accident," as the Russians like to say, that we view history from such different perspectives. Certainly that has happened in the area of Russian-American relations in which I concentrate my own work—and on which this book concentrates—the period of the Cold War.

But relations between Russia and the United States did not begin with the Teheran Conference, or with Yalta, or even with Harry S. Truman's famous confrontation with Soviet Foreign Minister Vyacheslav Molotov less than two weeks after Franklin D. Roosevelt's death. Americans and Russians have been dealing with one another, at various levels, and with varying degrees of amicability and hostility, since the latter part of the 18th century. If we are to understand the relationship that has so preoccupied us during these past four decades, then we ought not to cut ourselves off from the eighteen or so decades of Russian-American contacts that preceded them.

# I

There is, in fact, a long tradition of Russian-American "friendship," although unfortunately it manifested itself more during the early history of our relations than during the latter. It began with Francis Dana's unsuccessful mission to St. Petersburg in 1780 in search of recognition for the new American republic, and ended shortly after the sale of Russian-America, or Alaska, in 1867. The Soviet historian N. N. Bolkhovitinov, whose work on the first half of this period has not been surpassed in either of our countries and is not likely to be, has reminded us that we should not "present an idealized picture and create an impression that no disagreement or antagonism existed between Russia and America." For him, the lesson of early Russian-American relations "consists not in the absence of differences and conflicts, but in the fact that history testifies to the possibility of overcoming them."[4]

Cynics might find this platitudinous. Given the infrequency of contacts between Russia and America in the 19th century, they might observe, the "friendship" that existed between these two countries was about as remarkable as that which prevails today between, let us say, Swaziland and Iceland: there just were not that many opportunities for antagonism in the first place.

But that is a narrow view. There were potential areas of conflict: one thinks of the ideological challenge to monarchism posed by the first successful republican revolution in modern history; or rivalries over territory and fishing rights in the Pacific Northwest; or the threat of Russian support for the restoration of European colonial rule in Latin America; or even the possibility of small but critical "tilts" in the balance of power at delicate moments during the Crimean War or the American Civil War. There were, in addition, recurring irritations over the treatment of each other's citizens and diplomatic representatives, as well as complaints over what appeared in each other's press. It is worth inquiring how these 19th-century antagonisms were managed in such a way that they had so little impact upon the relatively cordial relations that existed between Russia and the United States for so many years.

The principal explanation, to borrow from a more recent terminology, was a mutual willingness to tolerate the coexistence of states with differing social systems. As the late Professor Nikolai Sivachev has observed, one could hardly have found a more striking disparity between the political organization, class structure, and ideological orientation of the United States under Andrew Jackson and Russia under the Tsar Nicholas I.[5] And yet, upon arriving in St. Petersburg in 1832, American minister James Buchanan found that "the Emperor is very willing to be upon good terms with the most free people upon earth, and . . . is still more gratified at their disposition to cultivate his friendship." One reason for this, Buchanan reported, was the American tradition "of attending to our own affairs, and leaving other nations to do the same," a way of doing things that "has had the happiest influence upon our foreign relations."[6] Indeed, Americans of that era did feel little compulsion to attempt to alter—or even to comment officially upon—political or social conditions inside other countries. Foreign policy, for diplomats of that generation, was a means of promoting the interests of own's own state, not an instrument for seeking to reform others.

But Buchanan's dispatch hinted at another reason as well for the relative absence of conflict in early Russian-American relations: this was the realization on Russia's part that "Europe is at this time a vast magazine of gun powder," that "the first spark applied to it will probably produce an explosion which may shake all it's [sic] thrones to their centre," and that, "in such contest, she is well aware, that England and France must be arrayed against her."[7] Americans of that era—or at least their leaders—were hardly innocents when it came to world politics. Fully sensitive to the workings of the international balance of power, they did not make the mistake of assuming that geography had exempted the United States from its effects; within the limits of their capabilities, they were determined to make use of that balance to promote American interests. What this meant, insofar as relations with St. Petersburg were concerned, was cooperation with the Russians where this could be expected to counterbalance the threats both nations saw from the British and the French.

Thus it was that these two very different countries offered modest help to one another in the course of major crises encountered by each during the mid-19th century. The Americans, during the Crimean War, maintained a benevolent neutrality toward the Russians that caused noticeable uneasiness in London.[8] More significantly, the Russians, during the American Civil War, refused to cooperate with Great Britain and France in imposing a mediated settlement advantageous to the Confederacy.[9] It may well be that one fruit of this subtle cooperation was the amicable transfer of Russian-America in 1867; one could hardly have expected that Alaska would not eventually come under the influence of the United States, but this might not have happened so soon or with such ease had relations between Washington and St. Petersburg been cooler. Certainly that episode reflects yet a third tendency that can be said to have facilitated friendly relations during that period: the Russian government's realism in recognizing its own inability to compete for influence with the Americans in any part of the Western hemisphere.*

Professor Bolkhovitinov is right: we ought not to romanticize the early 19th-century Russian-American "friendship," for it was really not that at all, but rather a relationship of mutual advantage, based upon non-intervention in the internal affairs of the two countries and upon a joint recognition of common external dangers. One senses how important these principles were when one looks at the thoroughness and rapidity with which Russian-American relations deteriorated, late in the 19th and early in the 20th century, in their absence.

# II

The responsibility for this deterioration of relations prior to 1917 rests to a considerable degree with the government—and the people—of the United States. The attitude of the Russian government toward Washington did not change all that much during the fifty years that separated the purchase of Alaska from the overthrow of the Tsar. Nor is there evidence that the traditional ambivalence with which Russian observers had always viewed the United States had evolved toward perceptibly greater hostility by the turn of the century.[10]

But American policies and attitudes had changed, in two very important ways. First, technological developments, together with the existence of a power vacuum in East Asia, had by 1900 tempted the United States into an assertion of authority well beyond its borders in such a way as to bring it into conflict with the perceived geopolitical interests of the Russian Empire. Second, the United States government during this period had gradually abandoned its traditional view that the internal character of other states should have no bearing upon the external relations it maintained with them. A new approach to diplomacy had set in, based upon an assumed linkage between domestic institutions and foreign policy and particularly upon the view that autocracy at home was inconsistent with the practice of tolerance, restraint, and mutual cooperation in the world at large.

* Similar considerations had led the Russians not to make an issue of American claims in the Pacific Northwest at the time of the proclamation of the Monroe Doctrine in 1823.

Because the first of these developments has been adequately—though not recently—dealt with,[11] it is not necessary to say a great deal about it. One might note only the curious coincidence in the way new technologies simultaneously brought Russians and Americans into conflict in Northeast Asia at the beginning of the 20th century: first by giving the Russians the means, through the Trans-Siberian Railroad, to project significant economic and military power into that part of the world; and then by encouraging the United States to use its new naval strength, along with other major European states and Japan, to compete with the Russians for influence in an arena left vacant by the decline of Chinese political authority. It would not be the last time technological innovation would lead the two countries to discover previously unsuspected vital interests, or to assume that if quick action was not taken to guard them, some ill-defined harm would result.

Washington's response, of course, was the Open Door policy, as clear an example of the pursuit of self-interest through the proclamation of disinterest as we have in our history. One may differ, as American historians have, over whether that strategy reflected naive idealism or crafty calculation—there may have been some of both in it.[12] But there can be no question that this assertion of an American interest in economic access to and in the territorial integrity of China ran up against the sphere of influence the Russians had constructed through their own arrangements with the Chinese dating from 1896, arrangements they had unilaterally expanded upon four years later in the wake of the Boxer Rebellion.

Another important consequence of the Open Door was its implied alignment of American interests with those of Great Britain. Here, too, historic trends had been reversed. One of the constants in earlier Russian-American relations had been shared antipathy for the British: this common adversary had bound the two countries together throughout most of the 19th century in a loose but nonetheless perceptible congruence of interests. But the Open Door Notes reflected the rapprochement that had taken place between Britain and the United States since 1895; that trend would evolve all the more to Russia's disadvantage when Britain with President Theodore Roosevelt's tacit approval signed an alliance with Japan in 1902, and when the outbreak of war between Russia and Japan two years later left St. Petersburg diplomatically isolated. Roosevelt's intervention on behalf of the Russians at the Portsmouth peace conference grew out of his determination to maintain a balance of power that could have been threatened either by unchallenged Japanese dominance in Northeast Asia or by social disintegration inside Russia itself, but it did not reflect any particular sympathy with, or affinity for, the Russian Empire.[13] It remained for Roosevelt's successor, William Howard Taft, to alienate both Russia and Japan through his ill-considered schemes for promoting American economic influence in Manchuria:[14] as a result, the geopolitical ties that had linked Russian and American interests in the past had, by the outbreak of World War I, almost wholly disappeared.

The change in American attitudes toward the internal structure of the

Russian Empire is something that has been much less adequately studied. What it involved was nothing less than a shift from the view that Americans could coexist with states of differing social systems to the conviction that this might no longer be possible. There had always been, in the United States, a keen awareness of the extent to which that nation's domestic system differed from that of most others. There had always been a great deal of pride in that system, and a belief that other states, in time, might come of their own accord to emulate it. But at no point before the late 19th century did the United States embrace as a matter of fundamental national interest the idea that it had an obligation to try to change the internal systems of other countries: indeed, precisely such coercion, it was thought, could corrupt the system Americans were trying to preserve, based as it was upon the principle of freedom of choice.[15] It is significant that despite its sympathies the United States made no formal efforts to intervene on behalf of national independence movements in Latin America and Greece in the 1820's, or the liberal movements in Europe that were crushed in the revolutions of 1848.[16] As late as 1863, Secretary of State William H. Seward could refrain from official expressions of support for an uprising in Poland because of Washington's geopolitical interest in maintaining the Russians' good will.[17]

All of this changed in the last decades of the 19th century. By the 1880's, the United States had begun to protest persecution, not just of Jews traveling in Russia on American passports, but of Jews inside Russia itself.[18] By the 1890's, there was widespread pressure for Washington to speak out on the issue of political prisoners in Russia—pressure instigated in no small part by the books and lectures of the first George Kennan.[19] By 1903, the Roosevelt administration had publicly condemned the Tsarist government for the pogrom at Kishinev, and by 1911, bowing to overwhelming public and Congressional pressure, the Taft administration had abrogated a commercial treaty with the Russians that dated back to the mission of James Buchanan in 1832. By 1915 President Woodrow Wilson had come to share the view of his personal confidant, Colonel Edward M. House, that a German defeat might pave the way for the domination of Europe by an autocracy at least equally inimical to American interests, that of the Russian tsar.[20]

This was a striking change in the American government's position, and we really do not know as much as we should about what caused it to occur. There are several possible explanations: the expansion of public education and literacy; the rise of a mass-circulation publishing industry; the growth of travel and of interest in it; and the emergence of what the historian Norman Saul has called "a concerned core of individuals, whose mission was to improve public knowledge . . . , some simply as a profession, others with the zeal of socially concerned critics."[21] These new sources of information about Russia began to flourish in the United States just in time to chronicle the repression that followed the assassination of Alexander II in 1881: one has the impression that the cheap newspapers, popular magazines, and well-attended lectures of that day had something of the same effect in sensitizing Americans to the nature of autocracy as television reporting from Vietnam did years later in bringing home the brutality of war.

But we must go beyond the question of how information was disseminated to explain the change in attitudes toward Russia: one must also take into account shifts in the structure of American politics. Certainly there was nothing new, in the late 19th century, about the habit of exploiting foreign policy for domestic political purposes. This was an old and distinguished tradition that extended back at least to debates between the Federalists and their Jeffersonian rivals in the 1790's. For reasons related both to the psychological satisfaction of rebelling against one's elders and to the presence within the United States of a substantial number of Irish immigrants, this tendency to play politics with diplomacy had been directed chiefly against the British throughout most of the 19th century. But by its later decades, millions of immigrants from Russia and Eastern Europe had made those parts of the world tempting targets as well; reinforcing this trend was the fact that one of the groups most discriminated against in Russia—Jews—now had co-religionists in powerful positions within the American political and economic establishment. It was almost certainly in deference to these groups that Roosevelt formally protested the pogroms at Kishinev;[22] similar considerations led the Taft administration in 1911 to yield to pressures—of which the late Senator Henry Jackson would have thoroughly approved—to abrogate the 1832 commercial treaty.[23]

There is reason to think, as well, that the rise of the progressive reform movement in the United States had something to do with this new and less friendly attitude toward Russia. The relationship between reform movements and foreign policy, although much debated, is not well understood. Still, it seems clear that the progressives attached a high priority to certain qualities—efficiency, honesty, order, social justice—that were not prominent features of life in tsarist Russia. It is significant that Roosevelt privately denounced the Russians during the Portsmouth peace negotiations for being not only "treacherous" "tricky," and "shifty," but also "corrupt," "incompetent," and "inefficient."[24] From him, this was the supreme indictment.

Professor Sivachev suggested, in his recent analysis of these events, that it really did not make much difference whether American "monopolists" were displeased about conditions in Russian prisons, or for that matter whether the Tsar was upset by the lynching of blacks in the United States. The real rivalries, he argued, were economic in character, and they focused primarily upon East Asia.[25] Here I must respectfully enter a dissent. Without questioning the importance of the competition for influence in that part of the world, it seems to me of critical importance to grasp the nature of the change in American attitudes toward internal conditions in other states that took place during these years. From a tradition of coexistence among states of differing social systems we fell into the habit of trying to reform such systems along lines congenial to ourselves. We did so at considerable cost and with little success; not only Taft's experience with Russia but Wilson's with China, Mexico, Central America, and the Caribbean amply testifies to this. And in each of these cases intervention for purposes of reform quite often worked against prevailing and potential economic interests, which is precisely why the Republican administrations of the 1920's abandoned such policies.

We will not advance very far toward understanding the nature of American foreign policy—or, for that matter, of the American people—unless we grant that both are, from time to time, motivated by more than considerations of mere profit; that the "humanitarian" instinct in American dealings with the rest of the world is real, however misguided, impractical, or self-interested it may at times seem; and that this, along with a considerable number of other factors of which economic interest is unarguably one, must be taken into account if we are to explain the puzzling behavior Americans so often exhibit to the rest of the world.

# III

But if candor compels acknowledgment of United States responsibility for the deterioration of Russian-American relations prior to World War I, and if we can attribute this development in large part to the ineffectual efforts of Americans to reform the Russian Empire, then it seems fair to say that after 1917 a different pattern of events began to emerge. To be sure, the United States and its allies in the months following the October Revolution intervened more directly and more purposefully in Russian internal affairs than ever before. That intervention has been the subject of extended comment among scholars in the West, and even more so in the Soviet Union. Few historical topics have been approached from so many different angles; few have occasioned explanations that swing as wildly as these do between extremes of complexity on the one hand—that Wilson was out to promote self-determination in Russia, or to monitor the behavior of his allies, or to defer to his allies' wishes, or to rescue embattled Czechs, or that he was the victim of diplomatic preoccupations, poor communications, and deteriorating health[26]—and utter simplicity on the other—that he hated Bolshevism and all its works and was determined from the first to do it in.[27]

This debate over the motives for intervention misses an important point, though, which is that Wilson and his allies saw their actions in a defensive rather than an offensive context. Intervention in Russia took place in response to a profound and potentially far-reaching intervention by the new Soviet government in the internal affairs, not just of the West, but of virtually every other country in the world: I refer here, of course, to the Revolution's challenge—which could hardly have been more categorical—to the very survival of the capitalist order.

Soviet historians have argued, to be sure, that there was nothing inconsistent about calling for the overthrow of capitalism throughout the world while simultaneously advocating "peaceful coexistence."[28] But it is a bit much to expect this subtlety to have filtered through to a group of Western statesmen who, in the course of desperately fighting a total war, found an important ally suddenly in the control of a small band of revolutionaries bent not only on negotiating an immediate peace but on promoting international class warfare. Such a situation would have tried the patience of statesmen of almost any political complexion; it is not at all surprising that Wilson, Lloyd George, and Clemenceau reacted in the way that they did. Representatives of old orders, however enlightened they may be, do not normally respond with warmth and enthusiasm to efforts by revolutionaries to overthrow them.

And yet, Soviet historians in their writing about these events—like some key Soviet officials at the time—appear to have found it shocking, unnatural, and even a violation of the legal norms that should exist between nations that the United States and its allies should have taken the October Revolution seriously and reacted to it in this wholly predictable manner.[29] One cannot have it both ways. One could not complain vigorously—as the Soviet government did—about Western and particularly American intervention in the internal affairs of Russia, and yet expect placid acquiescence and an eagerness for "business as usual" when the most profound revolutionary challenge of the century was mounted against the West. Human nature just does not work that way.

From this perspective, the interesting question regarding Western intervention in Russia after the Bolshevik Revolution is why it was such a half-hearted, poorly planned, and ulitmately ineffectual enterprise, given the seriousness of the threat it sought to counter. Here one might cite all the standard reasons: the distractions of fighting a major war and then negotiating a difficult peace; the erosion of Wilson's political authority in the face of resurgent domestic isolationism; the failure of the various forces fighting the Bolsheviks to unite in any meaningful way; the ability of the Bolsheviks themselves to rally popular support. All of these have merit.

But there is one other explanation as well that bears looking at: this has to do with Wilson's own profound ambivalence about revolutions and how to deal with them. Fairness obliges us to recognize that he was himself a revolutionary in the sense of seeking to overturn the existing structure of international relations: indeed, no single individual in this century has come closer to accomplishing just that. He manifested as well a greater degree of sympathy for revolutionary movements inside other countries than any other modern American president with the possible exception of Franklin Roosevelt. He had learned from painful experience in Mexico something of the counterproductive effects of intervention;[30] he was determined above all else to secure self-determination in Russia, and supported intervention only when convinced—however precariously—that such action would enhance the prospects for achieving it.

One ought not through these arguments to try to excuse the intervention, which was from the start ill-conceived, as Wilson himself recognized. But it may not be out of place to suggest that Wilson's own reservations about the actions he ultimately sanctioned had something to do with their failure: that his surprising reluctance to authorize anything other than a very limited use of force grew in part from his own recognition of how counterproductive such intervention usually is. From this perspective, Wilson was not so much an enemy of revolutions as a manipulator of them: a statesman who sought to channel revolutionary energies into safe—which, for him, meant democratic—directions.

Here one can see the linkage between Wilson's policy and what preceded and followed it. Wilson represented more clearly than anyone else the mentality that had grown up in the United States in the late 19th and early 20th century: that authoritarianism within a state produced aggressive behavior toward other states. This was a fundamental departure from the traditions of 18th- and 19th-century American diplomacy, but it has been a persistent element in American thinking about foreign affairs since Wilson's time. The combination of "democratic centralism" with "proletarian internationalism," however Lenin and the other founders of the Soviet state may have understood these concepts, came across in the West as precisely a confirmation of the relationship that had been thought to exist between authoritarianism and aggression. It is hardly surprising that the response was less than cordial.

This brings up another point worth thinking about in the context of our current difficulties. One of the perpetual irritants in Soviet-American relations has been each side's tendency to take the other's rhetoric literally. Americans listened for years to Moscow's revolutionary exhortations to "proletarians in all countries," and eventually took them seriously, despite subsequent assurances that all that was meant was that the proletarians should organize a revolution themselves, without outside help. Russians in turn listened for years to American rhetoric about the "evils" of communism and eventually took it seriously, despite subsequent indications that these outbursts were intended chiefly for domestic audiences and were not meant to challenge the legitimacy of the Soviet state. Sophisticated observers in both countries may know enough to apply to such rhetoric the discount it deserves, but policy is not always made by sophisticated observers.

# IV

Another recurrent theme in Russian-American relations has been the connection—or, to be more precise, the absence of a connection—between political and economic policy. The pattern originated during the years 1914–1917, a period that American scholars have almost entirely neglected—although Professor R. Sh. Ganelin has contributed substantially to our understanding of it from the Soviet side.[31] The years that separated the outbreak of the war from the overthrow of the tsar witnessed a coolness in political relations that approximated a much more recent time, and for some of the same reasons, notably American concern about human rights inside Russia. It is an indication of how bad relations were that the tsarist government rejected the first two ambassadors President Wilson sought to send to St. Petersburg, though probably with good reason given the quality of Wilson's early diplomatic appointments. And yet trade between Russia and America flourished as never before, as the tsarist government placed orders for war materials in the United States and as American financiers, working indirectly through the British and the French, made those purchases possible. At a time when political relations were frozen as they had rarely been, United States factories were providing about two-thirds of all outside military assistance received by the Russian Empire.[32]

This pattern of disconnection between political and economic relations became even more obvious in the 1920's, much to the surprise of the early Soviet leadership. Lenin and his colleagues were not prone to make sharp distinctions between political and economic matters: they had hoped to use economic incentives to bring about an end to intervention and the establishment of normal diplomatic relations with the West. Washington's persistent refusal to take up such offers puzzled Soviet leaders because it failed to fit their assumptions about the primacy of economic motivation in human affairs. As Foreign Minister Georgii Chicherin noted in 1922: "It would seem that everything should urge [the United States] towards meeting our desire for a *rapprochement* and for entering into close economic relations. . . . Up to the present the new American administration has not fulfilled these hopes."[33]

The economic incentives the new Soviet government offered were considerable. With or without Washington's approval, many Americans took advantage of them in the 1920's and early 1930's, to such an extent as to come close to fulfilling Lenin's prophecy that the capitalists would provide the means necessary to consolidate Soviet power.[34] And yet, the Republican administrations of Harding, Coolidge, and Hoover repeatedly rebuffed Moscow's attempts to build a political relationship upon this promising economic base long after other Western countries had granted diplomatic recognition. It is worth asking why this disconnection between political and economic relations persisted, why the United States failed to link the two together in the way Soviet leaders had anticipated.

The answer, it appears, is that purely economic considerations did not then, anymore than they do now, drive American foreign policy. Whatever the potential profits involved, Washington officials were still too concerned about what they perceived to be the Soviet ideological threat—a threat they saw as the ultimate form of intervention in the internal affairs of other countries—to seek to capitalize directly upon those economic opportunities. As Joan Hoff-Wilson has pointed out, ideology prevailed over economic self-interest.[35]

But if the principle of noninterference by foreigners in the internal affairs of the United States could be used to justify non-recognition, so too could the equally weighty principle of non-interference by government in the private affairs of individuals be used to justify the remarkable level of trade and investment with the Soviet Union that had developed by the end of the 1920's. Here we see the workings of the American *laissez-faire* tradition. For although foreign policy fell within the unquestioned responsibility of the government, its scope was narrowly defined. Issues of trade and investment remained matters for individual businessmen to decide according to traditional standards of profit and loss. Government might provide information and assist businessmen in carrying out their decisions, but the idea that government should tell businessmen where to invest and with whom to trade was distasteful in the extreme.

As a result, the Republican administrations of the 1920's avoided the political risks of recognizing—and thus appearing to sanction—what was, to them, a repugnant ideology. But at the same time they left the way open for American business to exploit the very considerable economic opportunities made possible through Soviet industrialization. As the journal *Business Week* put it in 1930: "the common-sense proceeding seems to be to sell the misguided fanatics all they are willing to pay for—business being what it is just now."[36]

The establishment of formal diplomatic relations between the United States and the Soviet Union has received more than ample treatment by historians,[37] and needs no further elaboration here. But this phenomenon of disconnection between political and economic policy does come up again in the immediate wake of recognition, and is worth making brief reference to. One is struck by the fact that American exports to the Soviet Union as a percentage of total American exports reached their highest level during the depression year of 1931—4.2 percent—and then dropped off precipitously, to the point that in the first full year of diplomatic relations, 1934, they came to less than one percent. At no point before the beginning of World War II would exports rise to the level they had attained during the final years of non-recognition.* Joan Hoff-Wilson has suggested that establishing diplomatic relations may actually have impaired economic relations by linking the provision of credits to the old issue of the Provisional Government's war debt.[38] Certainly the Roosevelt-Litvinov agreements created expectations on both sides—not just with regard to economic but strategic cooperation as well—that neither was prepared to fulfill. The formalization of relations may well, in this case, have contributed to their deterioration.

The point is that economic relations do not always run neatly along the channels into which political leaders seek to direct them. Surely this is what Lenin meant when he said, quite accurately as it turned out, that whatever the attitudes of their governments, the capitalists would provide the means to

---

* Exports to Russia as a percentage of total U.S. exports were as follows: 1929: 1.54%; 1930: 2.89%; 1931: 4.24%; 1932: .78%; 1933: .53%; 1934: .70%; 1935: 1.08%; 1936: 1.36%; 1937: 1.28%; 1938: 2.07%; 1939: 1.81%; 1940: 2.16%. [Based on U.S. Department of Commerce, *Statistical Abstract of the United States: 1933, 1937, 1941* (Washington: 1933, 1938, 1942).]

industralize and to feed Russia. This phenomenon is not unknown even in our own time. But the evidence of the 1920's and 1930's suggests that the reverse side of the equation holds up as well: politics do not always run neatly along the channels determined for them by economic interests. Soviet attempts to use economic incentives to influence American foreign policy have turned out no more successfully than American attempts to impose political controls on the activities of businessmen. Economics and politics, it would appear, occupy discrete spheres, and coordinating the connections between them is often more difficult than statesmen assume.

# V

There is yet another area as well where the Soviet Union and the United States have found it difficult to coordinate their interests: this has to do with the larger international environment in which they exist. Not the least of the ironies surrounding the events of 1933 was the sharp deterioration, not just in the economic sphere but in relations at all levels, that immediately followed recognition. This development was all the more surprising given the joint interest both nations had in containing the rising power of Germany and Japan. After all, common threats had produced complementary responses at various times in the earlier history of Russian-American relations; they would do so again, most emphatically, less than a decade hence. And we now know from Soviet documentation what the American sources had previously only hinted at: that in their private discussions Roosevelt and Soviet Foreign Minister Maxim Litvinov gave at least as much attention to the geopolitical as to the economic justifications for recognition.[39]

And yet, such cooperation was not forthcoming: a whole decade was lost in which the international balance of power was allowed to shift against both Soviet and American interests, without either Washington or Moscow doing anything effective to halt the process. The reasons have largely to do with the subordination, in both countries, of "external" to "internal" concerns.

For Franklin D. Roosevelt, the chief priority during his first years in office was to secure the legislation necessary to bring about domestic recovery. However sensitive he was in private to external geopolitical considerations—and the evidence suggests that he was in fact very sensitive to them[40]—he could not exhibit in public the slightest inclination to involve the United States in overseas responsibilities without dissipating the domestic coalition necessary to sustain the New Deal.[41] His discussions with Litvinov regarding Soviet-American cooperation against Germany and Japan reflected his private geopolitical musings, but no viable basis for public policy. There was, accordingly, less than met the eye in his pronouncements: internal concerns, for Roosevelt, remained predominant.

Precisely for that reason, there was more than met the eye in the President's somewhat casual handling of the question of debts and Comintern activities inside the United States. Litvinov no doubt got the impression that these issues were window-dressing, brought out to satisfy domestic constituencies but not likely to stand in the way of the geopolitical and economic cooperation the Soviet Union primarily wanted. The President, though, could no so easily dismiss them: Congress and the public took the question of debts very seriously indeed, and they were apt to look with even less favor upon indications that Moscow was not honoring its pledge, made as part of the agreement on recognition, to forgo support for the Communist Party of the United States.

One can only sympathize with Litvinov in his negotiations with F.D.R. When one is dealing with a man who is casual about everything, it is difficult to know when to take him seriously and when not to. Still, it ought not to have required too extensive a study of American domestic politics to realize that the President might have had difficulty making good on his implied promises of joint cooperation against the aggressors, and that he might have found it difficult to compromise on such issues as debts and Comintern activities. There was here a tendency, repeated more than once in the subsequent history of Soviet-American relations, for Moscow to attribute too much power to the president of the United States, and to neglect the domestic constraints under which he operates.

There is no reason to doubt the Soviet Union's desire for cooperation with the United States and the other Western democracies to counter growing German and Japanese power. But internal constraints operated in that country too, and one cannot ignore the effect they had in undercutting the prospects for such cooperation. One of these had to do with the simple physical treatment of diplomats inside the Soviet Union. Despite the fact that there was historically little that was new about this phenomenon, Americans who served in Moscow after 1933 could not help but be affected by the officially sanctioned suspicion of foreigners, a suspicion that took the form of surveillance, travel and currency restrictions, and the discouragement of informal contacts with Soviet citizens. This is hardly the place to speculate on the reasons for such treatment, but its effects were clear enough: a whole generation of career diplomats whose training had inclined them to question the possibility that the United States might have interests in common with the Soviet Union[42] had those preconceptions thoroughly reinforced.

The inconveniences suffered by diplomats had little immediate effect, though, upon public, Congressional, or administration attitudes toward the U.S.S.R., all of which had become more favorable in the wake of recognition. What did affect those attitudes, and very much for the worse, were the purge trials of the mid-1930's. That series of events shocked Americans, but in a way that reflected more upon the nature of the Soviet system than upon the threat with which those trials were supposed to be dealing. Old suspicions about correlations between autocracy and aggression resurfaced, sustained now by a fear of communism as well.[43]

Roosevelt did not give up on his efforts to improve Soviet-American relations in the light of these difficulties, as his appointment of the relentlessly uncritical Joseph E. Davies as ambassador in 1936 indicates. Nor did the Soviet government lose interest in the possibility of some form of military cooperation with the United States, a fact made clear by Stalin's remarkable—and little-known—efforts between 1936 and 1939 to have American shipyards construct warships for the Soviet Navy.[44] But the internal impediments to this pursuit of a common external interest were, in the end, too great. Both nations witnessed the outbreak of World War II from positions of hostility toward one another; it would take the efforts of Adolf Hitler himself to overcome this mutual suspicion and make possible the joint geopolitical enterprise Roosevelt and Litvinov had so optimistically discussed almost a decade before.

# VI

World War II confirmed an important—and, these days, too easily forgotten—characteristic of the Russian-American relationship: that for all their mutual suspicions, the United States and the Soviet Union have never been such bitter rivals as to blind themselves indefinitely to the emergence of common threats, or to the necessity of devising cooperative means by which to oppose them. Admittedly, that principle was not immediately apparent as the war began: Stalin, with what appeared to be cold-blooded realism but in fact was one of the most astonishing displays of naiveté in the history of diplomacy, took it upon himself in August of 1939 to extend a most uncharacteristic quality—trust—to a most unlikely recipient—the German Fuehrer—in the hope of purchasing Russian immunity from the impending conflagration. Roosevelt, too, hoped to keep the United States out of the fighting, but not at the price of neutrality: he was prepared from the spring of 1940 to risk war in order to ensure an outcome consistent with American interests, and unlike his Soviet counterpart he did not exclude the possibility of cooperation between Moscow and Washington in that effort.[45]

It took nothing less than Germany's invasion of the Soviet Union in June, 1941, to bring home to Stalin the dangers of relying on trust alone to guarantee national security: one has the impression that neither he nor his successors ever made that mistake again.[46] But Hitler's attack also opened the way for alignment with the United States. American military assistance began to flow to the Soviet Union even before Pearl Harbor; once the United States had joined that country and Great Britain as an active belligerent in December, 1941, there quickly evolved the most potent great-power alliance in modern history, one whose creation could hardly have been anticipated on the basis of the previous relationship between those three states.

The "lessons" of 1939–41, though, also limited the cordiality—and, ultimately, the durability—of that relationship. Stalin was at no point prepared to assume on the part of his British and American allies the same good faith he had so mistakenly perceived in Hitler: the result was an oddly asymmetrical coalition that saw two of its partners—Roosevelt and Churchill—develop the most intimate relationship between heads of government in this century, while Stalin remained a distant and by no means trusting third party. The Soviet leader was determined as well to retain the gains, territorial and otherwise, of his pact with Hitler: his insistence on that point did nothing to facilitate more cordial ties with his Western allies, or to simplify the problem of reconciling his war aims to theirs.

Still, it has to be recognized that, with all these difficulties, the Grand Alliance did hold together for four difficult years: long enough, as it turned out, to vanquish with unprecedented thoroughness the threat that had brought it together. However much the Cold War experience may have caused Russians and Americans to romanticize or to patronize their World War II cooperation—and it has had both of those effects—it is still worth recalling that we have, at least once within living memory, encountered dangers and overcome threats we both saw as posing greater risks to our respective national interests than those we ourselves have become accustomed to posing to each other.

# VII

Are there patterns that emerge from this review of Russian-American relations during the century and a half when that relationship was *not* the most critical issue in world politics? One, in particular, seems to stand out:

Where Russians and Americans have pursued interests that derive from their respective positions in the world at large, there have been remarkably few conflicts. Despite profound differences in internal systems, common threats have forced cooperation, whether against Britain throughout most of the 19th century, or against Germany twice in the first half of the 20th, or, by somehow managing to preserve the peace since 1945, against the very real threat of mutual annihilation. We may not have found this cooperation easy to arrange or to sustain. There have been times when one might have wished for cooperation in different forms, or with different results. But the fact is, we have cooperated when we have had to, and that fact alone says something about where our ultimate interests lie.

Antagonism between our two countries has most often arisen, not so much from our internal differences, substantial though those have been, but rather from attempts by one side somehow to change the internal system of the other. Both sides have made such efforts in the past: the United States in the form of a generalized concern with human rights; the Soviet Union in the form of a generalized call for world revolution. Neither side has been successful, or is likely to be, in achieving those ambitious objectives. But we have managed, through these outward manifestations of internal preoccupations, to make action in pursuit of common interests at the level of world politics more difficult than it might otherwise have been.

One need not go into detail to make clear the extent to which this tendency persists to this day. One can only hope that the pendulum will, in time, swing back toward a greater awareness of what history has shown to be our joint responsibilities, and away from our unfortunate mutual habit of letting the distractions that come from trying to change one another get in the way.

# 2

# The Insecurities of Victory:
# The United States and the
# Perception of the Soviet Threat
# After World War II

THE COLD WAR, whatever else one might say about it, has been a remarkably durable phenomenon. It has already exceeded in length the Peloponnesian War, the First and Second Punic Wars, the Thirty Years' War, the Wars of the French Revolution and Napoleon, and what Winston Churchill called the second Thirty Years' War that began with an assassin's gunshot at Sarajevo and ended with mushroom clouds over Hiroshima and Nagasaki.[1] Almost half of the 20th century has now been taken up by one aspect or another of that conflict, a rivalry made all the more striking by the fact that at no point in its long history have its major antagonists actually come to blows.

*"De quoi s'agit il?"* Marshal Foch used to ask his subordinates in World War I. "What is it all about?" The passage of time has made this no easy question to answer. The great antagonism between the United States and the Soviet Union has become encrusted, over the years, with successive layers of routine, custom, tradition, myth, and legend. Few of the men who shaped the affairs of nations at its outset are still alive; fewer still are able to recall with any precision what impelled them to act as they did at that time. Documents on the origins of the Cold War abound in Western archives—though almost none are available in the Soviet Union—but these sources provide no guaran-

This essay was originally prepared for the Harry S. Truman Centennial Symposium at the Woodrow Wilson International Center for Scholars, Washington, D.C., September 7–8, 1984. It is to be published, in a somewhat different form, in a forthcoming volume containing the proceedings of that conference. I am indebted, for helpful comments, to Alonzo Hamby, Michael Hogan, Michael Lacey, and Vojtech Mastny.

tee that those who use them will be able to reconstruct the past "as it actually happened." Historians, like most other people, are prone to see what they seek; they do not always take care to insulate their accounts of what transpired from their concerns with what is transpiring.

To recapture what was in the minds of Western leaders as the Cold War began requires, in addition to traditional methods of historical research, something of an imaginative leap. One must get a sense of how things looked at the time. One must free one's vision from the accumulated impressions of the more recent past, from the tyranny of knowing what came next. One must avoid at all costs imposing a contemporary frame of reference upon those who were in no position to anticipate the contemporary world. There are standards of judgment in history, but they should be standards derived from a range of historical experience that goes beyond what happened last month, or last year, or even in the last decade.

What follows is an attempt, in the spirit of this approach, to answer a single simple question: what was there in the behavior of the Soviet Union immediately after World War II to convince American statesmen that the security of the United States was once again in danger, as it had been in 1917 and again in 1940–41? Of the fact that they were so convinced, there can be no doubt: alarm, when projected so widely and when sustained for so long, would be difficult to feign. The reasons for that alarm, though, are not at all clear at this distance. It is necessary to reconstruct them if we are to understand.

# I

Early in November, 1945, subscribers to *Life* picked up their copies of the magazine to find depicted there, in lurid detail, a mushroom cloud rising over Washington, a view from space of rockets raining down on other American cities, an anti-ballistic missile system responding to the attack while retaliatory rockets were launched toward enemy targets from underground silos, an invasion of the United States by gas-masked airborne troops equipped with infrared goggles, and, finally, after the successful American counterattack, a depiction of weary technicians checking for radioactivity in front of the New York Public Library's marble lions, the only recognizable feature of the city left intact amid the rubble. The occasion for this apocalyptic vision was General Henry H. Arnold's final wartime report of Army Air Force activities, a document that pointedly looked as much to future dangers as to past victories.[2] The successful conclusion of the war had brought with it no guarantee of lasting security, both Arnold and the editors of *Life* seemed to be saying: it was as if the United States had finally assumed a decisive role in world affairs, only to find that the price of preeminence is vulnerability.

This sense of vulnerability is basic to an understanding of how Americans perceived their interests—and potential threats to them—in the postwar world. Prior to World War II, the dominant view had been that the security of the United States required little more than insulating the Western hemisphere from outside influences. This "continentalist" vision arose from several sources: traditional American isolationism, reinforced in the 1920's by disillusionment with the results of World War I; an assumption of economic self-sufficiency, intensified in the early 1930's by a self-centered preoccupation with economic recovery; and, by the mid-1930's, the fear of new conflicts in Europe and Asia in which Americans appeared to have no visible stake.[3] It is an indication of the strength of this attitude that Franklin D. Roosevelt, who never wholly shared it, felt obliged nonetheless consistently to defer to it during his first two terms in office.[4]

The fall of France and the Japanese attack on Pearl Harbor provided a painfully abrupt education on the inadequacies of "continentalism." Isolationist arguments that events overseas would never imperil the security interests of the United States could hardly have been more thoroughly discredited. In their place, there arose a new "globalist" consensus among opinion-shapers both within and outside government: that the primary American postwar interest now lay, not just in securing the Western hemisphere, but in keeping its Eastern counterpart as well free from control by a single potentially hostile power.

The idea, of course, was hardly a new one. Such a strategy of denial had formed the basis of England's policy toward Europe since at least the days of the Spanish Armada, and as early as 1904 the British geopolitician Sir Halford Mackinder had extended the concept to imply that the world balance of power depended upon preserving Eurasian "rimlands" free from domination by the Eurasian "heartland."[5] What was new in the 1940's was the conversion of influential Americans to this viewpoint, with all that it implied for a more active postwar role by the United States in world affairs.

"The most important single fact in the American security situation is the question of who controls the rimlands of Europe and Asia," Frederick Sherwood Dunn, Director of the Yale Institute of International Studies, wrote late in 1943. "Should these get into the hands of a single power or combination of powers hostile to the United States, the resulting encirclement would put us in a position of grave peril, regardless of the size of our army and navy."[6] Dunn's colleague at Yale, Nicholas John Spykman, had provided the earliest and most thorough statement of this argument in his 1942 book, *America's Strategy in World Politics*, and in a second shorter volume, *The Geography of the Peace*, published in 1944 shortly after his death. Drawing on Mackinder's insights, Spykman pointed out that North and South America were in effect islands, possessing slightly over a third of the Old World's land area but only a tenth of its population. Throughout its history the United States had depended for its security upon the maintenance of a balance of power in Europe and Asia. Previous challenges to that balance had elicited Anglo-American cooperation to restore it—tacitly at the time of the Monroe Doctrine in 1823, overtly in 1917. World War II had again called the balance into question: its outcome would determine "whether the United States is to remain a great power with a voice in the affairs of the Old World, or become merely a buffer state between the mighty empires of Germany and Japan."[7]

Spykman's professorial arguments refuted continentalism effectively enough, but not at a level likely to reach a mass audience. That task was left to Walter Lippmann, whose brilliant 1943 popularization of the Mackinder-Spykman thesis, *U. S. Foreign Policy: Shield of the Republic,* became one of the most influential books published during the war. With characteristic disdain for his own previous Wilsonianism, Lippmann now found support in the writings of the Founding Fathers for a strategy based on an explicit recognition of power realities. "[L]ike the idle rich who regard work as something for menials," Americans had too easily come to believe "that a concern with the foundations of national security, with arms, with strategy, and with diplomacy, was beneath our dignity as idealists." In fact, "the first concern of the makers of foreign policy in a sovereign national state must be to achieve the greatest possible security." This required the projection of power beyond national borders: "the strategic defenses of the United States are not at the three-mile limit in American waters, but extend across both oceans and to all the trans-oceanic lands from which an attack by sea or by air can be launched." It also required allies, because "[t]o be isolated is for any state the worst of all predicaments."[8]

This new determination to base foreign policy upon the facts of power implied no necessary rejection of the campaign to commit the United States to membership in a new collective security organization after the war;[9] indeed "internationalists" and "realists" emphatically shared the goal of undercutting isolationism, whatever their differences as to the nature of the postwar world. But the new geopolitics did insist upon the continuing importance of power in international affairs, however effective the new world body might turn out to be.[10] And, indeed, architects of the United Nations themselves seemed to acknowledge the point by building into the structure of that organization explicit provision for permanent big-power membership on the Security Council, with the right of veto guaranteed.[11]

President Roosevelt himself had always been at least as sensitive to considerations of power as his more forthright colleagues in the Grand Alliance, Churchill and Stalin. Despite his deference to isolationist opinion in the 1930's, F.D.R. had never accepted the argument that events in the Old World had no bearing upon the security of the New. As early as January, 1939, he had privately described the "first line of defense" for the United States as requiring the continued independence of those European states not then under German control and denial to Japan of islands from which that nation might seek to dominate the Pacific.[12] By 1941, Roosevelt was discussing a postwar settlement based upon joint action by the "Four Policemen"—the United States, Great Britain, the Soviet Union, and China—to keep the peace.[13] Although the President would later incorporate his "Four Policemen" concept into a collective security framework acceptable to Wilsonian idealists, he never lost his own insistence upon the importance of power relationships. "We cannot deny that power is a factor in world politics," he noted in his last State of the Union address in 1945, "any more than we can deny its existence as a factor in national politics."[14]

Military planners too moved during the war toward a recognition of global responsibilities. The Navy, under the influence of Alfred Thayer Mahan, had never questioned the importance of overseas bases, especially in the Pacific, an attitude now strongly reinforced by Pearl Harbor and the loss of the Philippines.[15] Of greater significance was the conversion of Army strategists, who in the interwar period had been prepared to deny the existence of vital American interests in both Europe and Asia, to an active concern with the balance of power in these areas. "General Eisenhower . . . does not believe that it would be in our interest to have the continent of Europe dominated by any single power," the American Embassy in Paris reported late in 1944, "for then we would have a superpowerful Europe, a somewhat shaken British Empire and ourselves." The Joint Strategic Survey Committee had reached similar conclusions about Asia a year earlier.[16] Intelligence analysts agreed with these assessments: as an Office of Strategic Services study put it in the summer of 1944, "our interests require the maintenance of a policy designed to prevent the development of a serious threat to the security of the British Isles (and of the United States), through the consolidation of a large part of Europe's resources under any one power."[17]

But the most persuasive arguments in favor of a global rather than a continental perception of postwar interests came from the Army Air Force, which to the irritation of its ground- and sea-based counterparts was not hesitant to stress the strategic implications of the new technology of warfare. "Bombers can now range the world," General Arnold pointedly noted in his final report that so impressed the editors of *Life;* moreover, improved versions of the German V-2 rocket capable of reaching the United States from Europe or Asia were not at all impractical. The V-2 "is ideally suited to deliver atomic explosives because effective defense against it would prove extremely difficult." It was entirely possible, Arnold concluded, "that the progressive development of the air arm, especially with the concurrent development of the atomic explosive, guided missiles, and other modern devices, will reduce the requirement for or employment of mass armies and navies." But it would also create permanent vulnerability, because even with existing equipment an enemy air force could, "without warning, pass over all formerly visualized barriers or 'lines of defense' and . . . deliver devastating blows at our population centers and our industrial, economic or governmental heart."[18]*

---

* Curiously, Arnold coupled his vision of future warfare with an enthusiastic account of Army Air Force experiments in the field of hydroponics. These had produced, without soil, gratifying quantities of "tomatoes, radishes, lettuce and cucumbers." [*The War Reports of General of the Army George C. Marshall, General of the Army H. H. Arnold, Fleet Admiral Ernest J. King* (Philadelphia: 1947), pp. 465–66.]

The demonstrated feasibility of atomic weapons, together with the long-range bombers and—in the not too distant future—the rockets necessary to carry them, created a security problem for postwar planners that went beyond concern for the Eurasian balance of power: it involved nothing less than the physical safety of the United States itself. No longer, it appeared, would Americans enjoy the luxury of mobilizing their strength after threats had materialized; military force now would have to be maintained on a permanent basis, and in a manner that would make possible its quick use. As Arnold put it in his report: "real security against atomic weapons in the visible future will rest on our ability to take immediate offensive action with overwhelming force. It must be apparent to a potential aggressor that an attack on the United States would be immediately followed by an immensely devastating air-atomic attack on him."[19]

All of this seemed to confirm, then, the wisdom of a postwar strategy based on denying control of the Eurasian continent to any potentially hostile power. As the experiences of 1917 and 1941 had shown, it was a strategy with deep—if not always clearly perceived—historical roots. Nor was it inconsistent with the objectives for which Americans liked to think of themselves as fighting: after all, maintaining a balance of power could only enhance the opportunities for self-determination, liberal trading policies, and collective security called for in the Atlantic Charter and in innumerable other wartime justifications for the wielding of military force. Americans, it appeared, could respond to their new-found preeminence in world affairs by following the designs of both Wilson and Mackinder at the same time.[20]

# II

"The most important political development during the last ten years of localized and finally global warfare," columnist C. L. Sulzberger noted in the *New York Times* a week after Japan's surrender, "has been the emergence of the Union of Soviet Socialist Republics as the greatest dynamic and diplomatic force on the vast Eurasian land mass which stretches from the Atlantic to the Pacific oceans."[21] No one could quarrel with the conclusion, which had been foreseen for some time. Nor could there be any doubt that this situation carried with it profound implications for the future of American foreign policy, given the widespread consensus that the security of the New World now depended upon what happened in the Old. Interestingly, though, this concern with the postwar balance of power did not automatically translate into a conviction that the Soviet Union posed the most likely threat to it.

The danger in World War II, after all, had come from the Germans and the Japanese, not the Russians; it is significant that in 1943 Mackinder himself had modified his thesis, pointing out the hazards of "rimland" domination of the "heartland" and not the other way around.[22] American geopoliticians, noting Moscow's vigorous participation in the war against Germany and potential assistance against Japan as well, followed his lead. As Spykman himself put it: "The heartland [has become] less important than the rimland and it is the co-operation of British, Russian, and United States land and sea power that will control the European littoral and, thereby, the essential power relations of the world."[23]* Lippmann agreed, pointing out that the primary American interest was to allow no *European* power to become capable of committing aggression *outside* of Europe. "Therefore our two natural and permanent allies have been and are Britain and Russia."[24]

Certainly this was the viewpoint of the Roosevelt administration. "I personally don't think there's anything in it," F.D.R. commented early in 1944, when asked about rumors that the Russians were out to dominate all of Europe. "They have got a large enough 'hunk of bread' right in Russia to keep them busy for a great many years to come without taking on any more headaches."[25] Roosevelt had built his whole strategy upon the expectation that the wartime alliance would survive the end of the war. He had sought to ensure this through public deference to Soviet security interests, mixed with subtle behind-the-scenes pressures to encourage Moscow's cooperation. Although concerned during the last months of his life about the increasing frequency of misunderstandings with the Russians, he at no point sought to contest the substantial expansion of Soviet influence in Europe and Asia that the end of the war would bring. Rather, he hoped to maintain a balance of power by convincing the Russians that security could best be attained through cooperative rather than unilateral efforts to counter potential threats.[26]

Despite obvious differences in personality and style, Harry S. Truman continued Roosevelt's policy upon coming into office. A more dedicated Wilsonian than his predecessor, the new Chief Executive held high hopes that the United Nations would provide workable mechanisms for resolving world tensions. During his first months in office he firmly rejected proposals from Winston Churchill and from some of his own advisers that would have denied the Russians previously agreed-upon occupation zones in Central Europe and Northeast Asia.[27] "I was having as much difficulty with Prime Minister Churchill as I was having with Stalin," the new President noted in May of 1945. As late as the fall of that year, both Truman and his new Secretary of State, James F. Byrnes, were still relying upon the establishment of a personal relationship with Stalin as the best way to overcome the difficulties that had already begun to emerge in the Soviet-American relationship.[28]

The State Department followed this lead, though from a somewhat different perspective. Still very much under the influence of the recently retired Cordell Hull, it saw potential threats to world order as arising, not specifically

---

* Although Spykman in 1942 had raised the possibility that the United States and Britain might seek to preserve some form of German power to balance Soviet influence in Europe, because "a Russian state from the Urals to the North Sea can be no great improvement over a German state from the North Sea to the Urals." [Nicholas John Spykman, *America's Strategy in World Politics* (New York: 1942), p. 460.]

from Soviet ambitions, but from spheres of influence in general. Any such perpetuation of power politics could set off new international rivalries, weaken the United Nations, and, worst of all, provoke a disillusioned American public into a reversion to isolationism like the one that had followed the First World War. These dangers could arise as easily from British as from Russian activities, the Department warned in July, 1945: any attempt by London to lure Washington into supporting a spheres of influence settlement in Europe would "represent power politics pure and simple, with all the concomitant disadvantages. . . . Our primary objective should be to remove the *causes* which make nations feel that such spheres are necessary to build their security, rather than to assist one country to build up strength against another."[29]

Military planners too saw the United States more as a mediator between Britain and Russia than as a permanent ally of either one of them.* The Joint Chiefs of Staff had noted in the spring of 1944 that Soviet influence in postwar Europe would far exceed that of the British: indeed, the shift in power was more comparable "with that occasioned by the fall of Rome than with any other change occurring during the succeeding fifteen hundred years."[30] But the Chiefs did not draw from this the conclusion that the United States itself should step in to redress the balance. Intelligence estimates tended to downplay the likelihood of Soviet hostility even as they acknowledged the probability of Soviet hegemony: however repugnant it might be for those on the receiving end, the expansion of Russian influence would be taking place more for defensive than offensive reasons. Moreover, overt attempts to build countervailing power in Europe might have the effect of a self-fulfilling prophecy, reinforcing the Kremlin's suspicions and perpetuating its inclination toward unilateralism.[31]† Since public opinion seemed likely to insist in any event upon the withdrawal of American forces from Europe after the war, there seemed to be few means by which the United States could expect to challenge the Russians on the ground there, even if it should become desirable to do so.[32]

Nor did Moscow appear to possess the potential to threaten the United States directly. Concern about the new technology of warfare had the paradoxical effect of reassuring American military planners about the Russians because they had so little of it: their navy was little more than a coastal de-

---

* President Truman himself was publicly describing the United States as an "umpire" between Great Britain and the Soviet Union as late as April, 1946. [Press conference, April 18, 1946, *Public Papers of the Presidents: Harry S. Truman, 1946* (Washington: 1962), pp. 211–12.]

† For evidence that American military planners did not begin thinking seriously about trying to secure permanent bases on the European continent until the summer of 1945, see Elliott Vanvelnter Converse III, "United States Plans for a Postwar Overseas Military Base System, 1942–1948" (Ph.D. Dissertation, Princeton University, 1984), pp. 90–98, 137–38, 151–54. As late as December, 1945, General Eisenhower informed the War Cabinet that "a General Zhukov [had] told him that Russia was determined to make friends with the United States, to raise its standard of living, and to live up to every agreement made." [War Council minutes, December 3, 1945, Robert P. Patterson Papers, Box 23, Library of Congress].

fense force; their air force had no capability for long-range bombing; and there seemed to be no imminent prospect of their building an atomic bomb.* "Our Allies of today may be leagued against us tomorrow," an Army Air Force study had cautiously concluded in 1944, but it might well take from 20 to 100 years for "an Eurasian nation to grow into an aggressive-minded power."[33] As late as July, 1945, General Arnold himself, the most visible alarmist on the subject of technological vulnerability, could rule out the Russians as a serious threat because of the primitive nature of their military power.[34] The next war, Pentagon planners assumed, would be much like the last, with the danger more likely to come from a resurgent Germany or Japan than from a defensive and technologically backward Soviet Union.[35]

It is true that military planners attached a high priority to the acquisition and indefinite retention of overseas bases. But there is reason to think that these postwar base requirements were determined more by a generalized sense of vulnerability (and perhaps as well by the need to justify a large peacetime defense establishment) than by any specific perception of the Soviet Union as an immediate threat.† The locations chosen for these bases suggested a concern with defending the east and west coasts of the United States and maintaining a sphere of influence in the Pacific, but little apparent interest in the fact that the shortest air route to and from the U.S.S.R. lay to the north, or in the potential advantages of having bases in Europe and the Near East. Not until the summer of 1945 did consideration of the Russians as likely adversaries begin to influence the actual selection of bases, and even then interservice disagreements, the anticipation of tight postwar budgets, and delays in the negotiation of base rights severely retarded the process of acquisition.[36]‡

But the main reason both diplomatic and military planners failed to foresee the full implications of the shift in the balance of power that World War II was bringing about was precisely the fact that the war was still on, that the Soviet Union was still an ally, and that its cooperation was still needed to assure victory over Germany and Japan. Common enemies constituted the glue that held the Grand Alliance together, and until they had been laid low, the presumption in relations between Washington, London, and Moscow had

---

* General Leslie R. Groves, never one to be complacent about the Russians, thought it would take them up to twenty years to develop an atomic bomb. [Gregg Herken, *The Winning Weapon: The Atomic Bomb in the Cold War, 1945–1950* (New York: 1980), pp. 98–99.]

† Similar considerations led Air Force planners to give enthusiastic support to the concept of a postwar international police force, administered by the United Nations, that would depend heavily on air power to keep the peace. [Perry McCoy Smith, *The Air Force Plans for Peace, 1943–1945* (Balitmore: 1970), pp. 43–51.]

‡ Converse argues that the Air Force was fully aware of the strategic importance of the polar regions, but did not push for bases there because of the technical difficulties of operating at such latitudes. ["United States Plans for a Postwar Overseas Military Base System," pp. 71–74, 204–11.]

to be in favor of cooperation rather than competition. Too candid a consideration of possible postwar antagonisms could impair prospects for victory in the war that was going on at the time; no one was yet prepared to let long-term geopolitical realities overwhelm the immediate necessity of victory.

# III

Wartime lack of concern over the powerful position the Soviet Union would occupy in the postwar world had been predicated upon the assumption that the Russians would continue to act in concert with their American and British allies. So long as the Grand Alliance remained intact, Western statesmen could assure each other, Moscow's emergence as the dominant Eurasian power would pose no threat. But during the final months of the war, there began to appear unsettling indications of a determination on Stalin's part to secure postwar interests without reference to the corresponding interests of his wartime associates. It was these manifestations of unilateralism that first set off alarm bells in the West about Russian intentions; the resulting uneasiness in turn stimulated deeper and more profound anxieties.

"I am becoming increasingly concerned," Secretary of State Hull warned Ambassador W. Averell Harriman early in 1944, "over the . . . successive moves of the Soviet Government in the field of foreign relations." Hull went on to observe in this message, drafted by Soviet specialist Charles E. Bohlen, that whatever the legitimacy of Moscow's security interests in Eastern Europe—"and as you know we have carefully avoided and shall continue to avoid any disputation with the Soviet Government on the merits of such questions"—unilateral actions to secure those interests "cannot fail to do irreparable harm to the whole cause of international collaboration." The American people would not be disposed to participate in any postwar scheme of world organization which would be seen "as a cover for another great power to pursue a course of unilateral action in the international sphere based on superior force." It was "of the utmost importance that the principle of consultation and cooperation with the Soviet Union be kept alive at all costs, but some measures of cooperation in relation to world public opinion must be forthcoming from the Soviet Government."[37]

This document reflects as well as any other the point from which American statesmen began to develop concerns about the postwar intentions of the Soviet Union. The United States had not challenged Moscow's determination to retain the boundaries it had secured as a result of Stalin's unsavory pact with Hitler in 1939, nor had it questioned the Russians' right to a postwar sphere of influence in what remained of Eastern Europe. It was prepared to grant similar concessions in East Asia in return for eventual U.S.S.R. participation in the war against Japan. But because the Roosevelt administration had justified American entry into the war as a defense of self-determination, and because it had committed the nation to participation in a postwar world collective security organization as a means of implementing that principle, it required from the Soviet Union a measure of discretion and restraint in consolidating these areas of control. Unilateral action seemed likely to endanger the balance of power, not by allowing the Russians to dominate areas beyond their borders—that domination was assumed—but rather by weakening the American capacity for countervailing action in the postwar world by provoking, first, public disillusionment and then, as a consequence, a revival of the isolationism the President and his advisers had fought so long and so hard to overcome.[38]

The Russians, to put it mildly, were less than sensitive to these concerns. As their armies moved into Eastern Europe in 1944 they immediately set out to undermine potential sources of opposition, not just in the former enemy countries of Rumania, Bulgaria, and Hungary, but most conspicuously of all in Poland, which had been, after all, an ally. The callousness with which the Red Army allowed the Germans to decimate the anti-communist resistance in Warsaw late that summer shocked Western statesmen; meanwhile British and American representatives on Allied Control Commissions in the Balkans found themselves denied any significant influence in shaping occupation policies there as well.* Moscow had interpreted Western restraint as a sign of weakness, Harriman reported in September: "Unless we take issue with the present policy there is every indication that the Soviet Union will become a world bully wherever their interests are involved. . . . No written agreements can be of any value unless they are carried out in a spirit of give and take and recognition of the interests of other people."[39]

Franklin Roosevelt made valiant efforts at Yalta to make Stalin aware of the need to observe the proprieties in Eastern Europe, but these proved unsuccessful almost at once when the Soviet leader interpreted agreements made to hold free elections there as in fact license to impose still tighter control on Poland and Rumania. "Averell is right," Roosevelt complained three weeks before his death. "We can't do business with Stalin. He has broken every one of the promises he made at Yalta."[40] F.D.R. had not been prepared, on the basis of these difficulties, to write off all possibilities of postwar cooperation with the Russians. But Soviet unilateralism does appear to have convinced him, by the time of his death, that efforts to win Stalin's trust had not worked; and that future policy toward the Soviet Union would have to be based on a strict *quid pro quo* basis.[41]

Harry S. Truman emphatically agreed. Although the new Chief Executive had had no direct experience in the conduct of foreign affairs, he could hardly have believed more firmly in the importance of keeping one's word. "When I say I'm going to do something, I do it," he once wrote, "or [I] bust my insides trying to do it." It was characteristic of him that he did not believe in divorce because "when you make a contract you should keep it."[42] Convinced

---

* Although, on this point, the Russians could with some justice claim only to be following the precedent set by the Americans and British in refusing to grant the Russians any substantial role in the occupation of Italy after the surrender of that country in 1943.

that the Yalta agreements on free elections in Eastern Europe were in fact contracts, determined to demonstrate decisiveness in an awesome and unexpected position of responsibility, Truman resolved—probably more categorically than Roosevelt would have done—to hold the Russians to what they had agreed to. It was this determination that occasioned the new President's sharp rejoinder to Soviet Foreign Minister V. M. Molotov after less than two weeks in office: "Carry out your agreements and you won't get talked to like that." A month later he complained again that the Russians were not honoring their agreements: they were, he told Henry Wallace, "like people from across the tracks whose manners were very bad."[43]

The experience of meeting Stalin personally at Potsdam seems to have modified the President's attitude somewhat. The Soviet autocrat evoked memories of the Kansas City political boss Tom Pendergast, a man with whom deals could be made because he had always kept his word.* "I can deal with Stalin," Truman noted in his diary at Potsdam. "He is honest—but smart as hell." Disturbed by rumors of the dictator's ill health, the President worried about what would happen "if Joe suddenly passed out" because his potential successors lacked sincerity.[44] For several years afterward, there persisted in Truman's mind the notion that difficulties with the Russians reflected Stalin's internal political problems—interference from a recalcitrant Politburo was the most frequent explanation—rather than any personal desire on the Soviet leader's part to violate his word.[45]

But deals had to be honored if they were to work, and with the return of peace instances of Soviet unilateralism began to proliferate. Reasonably free elections took place in Hungary and Czechoslovakia, but only in those countries: Moscow's grip on Poland, Rumania, and Bulgaria remained as tight as ever.[46] The Russians joined the French in resisting central economic administration of occupied Germany; they also arbitrarily transferred a substantial portion of that country's eastern territory to Poland.[47] Attempts to reunify another divided nation, Korea, came to naught as the Russians refused to tolerate anything other than a satellite government there.[48] The Soviet Union rejected participation in the World Bank and the International Monetary Fund, institutions American planners regarded as critical for postwar economic recovery.[49] And Stalin was showing strong signs, as 1945 ended, of exploiting the presence of Soviet troops in northern Iran to carve out yet another sphere of influence there.[50] He was "trying to find a basis for an understanding which would give him confidence that an agreement reached with the Russians would be lived up to," Truman told his advisers in December, 1945. He had such

---

* "People have stored within memory a wide collection of 'personae,' or cognitive structures representing the personality characteristics of stereotypical characters—the hooker with a heart of gold, the truck-stop waitress, the 'urban cowboy,' Archie Bunker. Often people assimilate casual acquaintances or public figures to these stereotypical characteristics, on the basis of a superficial resemblance. Influenced by the Pendergast persona, Truman expected Stalin—a revolutionary who had never visited the West—to understand American public opinion." [Deborah Welch Larson, *Origins of Containment: A Psychological Explanation* (Princeton: 1985), p. 178.]

confidence in dealing with the British, the Dutch, and the Chinese (though not the French), "but there is no evidence yet that the Russians intend to change their habits so far as honoring contracts is concerned."[51]*

The Chief Executive's initial inclination had been to regard these difficulties simply as failures of communication;[52] with that explanation in mind, he had authorized Secretary of State Byrnes to make one more effort to settle them at a hastily called meeting of foreign ministers in Moscow in December. By that time, though, public and Congressional impatience with Soviet unilateralism had considerably intensified. Sensitive to these pressures, irritated by Byrnes' eagerness to reach agreements without consulting him, Truman early in 1946 proclaimed to himself—if not directly to Byrnes, as he later claimed—his intention to stop "babying" the Soviets: "Unless Russia is faced with an iron fist and strong language another war is in the making. Only one language do they understand—'how many divisions have you?' I do not think we should play at compromise any longer."[53]

There was, in fact, no compromise when the Russians failed to meet their agreed-upon deadline for removing their troops from Iran: instead the administration confronted Moscow publicly in the United Nations Security Council and forced a humiliating withdrawal.[54] Truman drew the appropriate conclusions: "Told him to tell Stalin I held him to be a man to keep his word," he noted in his appointment book after a meeting with the newly designated ambassador to the Soviet Union, Walter Bedell Smith, on March 23. "Troops in Iran after March 2 upset that theory."[55]† By June, he was writing to the author Pearl Buck that "the United States has performed no unfriendly act nor made a single unfriendly gesture toward the great Russian nation. . . . How has Russia met our friendly overtures?"[56] The following month, after New York Times correspondent Brooks Atkinson had published a series of articles highly critical of the Russians, Truman pointedly invited him to the White House.[57] That same day he told his advisers that he was "tired of our being pushed around," that "here a little, there a little, they are chiseling from us," and that "now is [the] time to take [a] stand on Russia."[58]

It was in this spirit that the President authorized the first comprehensive study of Soviet-American relations to be carried out within the government.

* For a recent—and considerably less critical—reassessment of the Soviet record on keeping agreements during this period, see Melvyn P. Leffler, "Adherence to Agreements: Yalta and the Experiences of the Early Cold War," *International Security*, XI (Summer, 1986), 88–123.

† Career Foreign Service officer Elbridge Durbrow noted the implications of the new tough line: "It is the general feeling here that it has been finally realized all across the board that the only way to have really good relations with the Soviet Union is to stand by our guns when we feel we are right. If we can hold this fort all along the line from Korea to Timbuktoo, we may start to get somewhere. . . . General Smith has got the proper attitude and will, in all probability, impress the boys profoundly that we are not just talking through our hats to hear our own voices." [Durbrow to Charles W. Thayer, April 11, 1946, Charles E. Bohlen Papers, Box 1 "Personal (CEB) 1946," Diplomatic Branch, National Archives.]

Compiled under the direction of his Special Counsel, Clark M. Clifford, and written after consultations with the Departments of State, War, Navy, the Joint Chiefs of Staff and the Director of Central Intelligence, the report acknowledged that agreements between nations were at times susceptible to differing interpretations. Nonetheless, it argued, there existed a persistent pattern on Moscow's part of either unilaterally implementing such agreements in such a way as to serve Soviet interests, or encouraging satellites to do so. "[T]here is no question," the report emphasized, "where the primary responsibility lies."

The implications could only be that the Soviet Union had no intention of cooperating with the West to maintain the existing balance of power; that it sought to expand its own influence as widely as possible without regard for the security requirements of its former allies; and that, when circumstances were right, it would be prepared to risk war to attain that objective. American policy could no longer be based upon the assumption of shared interests, therefore; priorities henceforth would have to be directed toward the accumulation of sufficient military strength to deter war if possible and to win it if necessary, while at the same time keeping open possibilities for dealing with the Russians should a change of heart in the Kremlin eventually occur. "[I]t is our hope," the report concluded, "that they will eventually change their minds and work out with us a fair and equitable settlement when they realize that we are too strong to be beaten and too determined to be frightened."[59]

President Truman received the Clifford report on September 24, four days after he had fired Henry Wallace from the Cabinet for publicly advocating a more conciliatory policy toward the Soviet Union. There is no question that he agreed with its general conclusions: on the day before he dismissed Wallace he had complained in his diary about

> Reds, phonies and . . . parlor pinks [who] can see no wrong in Russia's four and one half million armed forces, in Russia's loot of Poland, Austria, Hungary, Rumania, Manchuria. . . . But when we help our friends in China who fought on our side it is terrible. When Russia loots the industrial plant of those same friends it is all right. When Russia occupies Persia for oil that is heavenly.[60]

But Truman chose not to use the Clifford report, as he might have, to justify increased military appropriations; instead he ordered all copies to be locked in the White House safe, where they remained for the duration of the administration.[61] "There is too much loose talk about the Russian situation," he had written former Vice President John Nance Garner on the day after Wallace's dismissal. "We are not going to have any shooting trouble with them but they are tough bargainers and always ask for the whole earth, expecting maybe to get an acre."[62]

The President's cautious reaction to the manifestations of Soviet unilateralism catalogued in the Clifford report reflected a desire to avoid hasty and ill-considered action, but certainly no continuing assumption of common interests.

Repeated demonstrations of Moscow's callousness to the priorities and sensibilities of its former allies had by this time virtually drained the reservoir of good will toward the Russians that had built up during the war. American leaders had been inclined, for many months, to give the Kremlin the benefit of the doubt: to assume, despite accumulating evidence to the contrary, that difficulties with Moscow had arisen out of misunderstandings rather than fundamental conflicts of interest. But such charitableness could not continue indefinitely, as Winston Churchill pointed out in the summer of 1946: "The American eagle sits on his perch, a large strong bird with formidable beak and claws. . . . Mr. Gromyko is sent every day to prod him with a sharp sickle, now on his beak, now under his wing, now in his tail feathers. All the time the eagle keeps quite still, but it would be a great mistake to suppose that nothing is going on inside the breast of the eagle."[63]*

# IV

In fact, a good deal was going on inside the breast of the eagle, all of it related in one way or another to attempting to explain the motivation for Moscow's puzzling behavior. Throughout the period of wartime cooperation there had lingered in the minds of most Americans latent but persistent suspicions about Russia, suspicions that extended back to, and even beyond, the Bolshevik Revolution. These grew out of the fact that the Soviet Union combined— as no other country in the world at that time did—two characteristics that Americans found particularly objectionable: arbitrary rule and ideological militancy. As long as the direct Axis threat remained, Americans had been willing to overlook these shortcomings, even to hope that in time they would disappear.[64] But after 1945, with no common foe to compel unity, with ample evidence that the Russians intended to proceed on their own rather than in concert with their former allies to consolidate postwar interests, the predisposition to assume the worst about Moscow's intentions came out into the open once again.

Americans had not always found cooperation with authoritarian regimes to be impossible: the Russian-American relationship itself had been friendly throughout most of its early history, despite the vast cultural and political dif-

---

* Former ambassador Joseph E. Davies, one of the Soviet Union's most sympathetic interpreters, commented early in 1946: "I know of no institution that needs a high pressure 'public relations' organization as much as the U.S.S.R. They do not seem able to get their case across, even when, as it happens sometimes, they have a good case." [Davies to Clarence Dykstra, January 8, 1946, Joseph E. Davies Papers, Box 22, Library of Congress.] For other indications of the extent to which Soviet behavior alienated even those inclined to give the Russians the benefit of the doubt, see Jonathan Evers Boe, "American Business: The Response to the Soviet Union, 1933–1947" (Ph.D. Dissertation, Stanford University, 1979), pp. 235–37; and, on Eleanor Roosevelt, Joseph P. Lash, *Eleanor: The Years Alone* (New York: 1972), pp. 73–99.

ferences that separated the two countries. But toward the end of the 19th century a combination of circumstances—increasing repression within Russia, a keener American sensitivity to conditions inside other countries, growing rivalries between Washington and St. Petersburg over spheres of influence in East Asia—had produced in the United States the suspicion that a connection existed between autocratic rule at home and aggressiveness in foreign affairs.[65] Parallel concerns had accompanied the deterioration of relations with imperial Germany prior to World War I; certainly participation in that conflict, which Woodrow Wilson justified by stressing the linkage between autocracy and aggression, served powerfully to reinforce this idea.[66] Determination to remain aloof from European involvements caused Americans to worry less about such matters during the 1920's and early 1930's—indeed, the economic distress of the latter decade even produced in some circles a grudging respect for dictatorships[67]—but the experience of fighting Germany and Japan during World War II brought back repugnance for arbitrary rule with a vengeance. It would not take very many signs of aggressiveness on the part of totalitarian regimes in the postwar world—even totalitarian former allies—to convince Americans that the connection between domestic despotism and international expansionism still prevailed.[68]*

"If we fought Germany because of our belief that a police state and a democratic state could not exist in the same world," Rear Admiral Ellery W. Stone told Secretary of the Navy James Forrestal in July, 1946, then "it must necessarily follow that we could not afford to lie down before Russia."[69]† The simple fact that the Soviet Union was a totalitarian state raised suspicions that its foreign policy would proceed from priorities incompatible with those of the democracies—priorities now elaborately enshrined in the procedures the United Nations had established for settling international disputes. Totalitarian states, Americans assumed, relied upon force or the threat of force to secure their interests; such nations could hardly be expected to share Washington's aspiration to see the rule of law ultimately govern relations between nations. "[I]t

---

* Michael Sherry points out the tendency of Pentagon planners during the war to assume that the next war would be fought against a totalitarian power, without any clear idea of which nation that might be. [Michael S. Sherry, *Preparing for the Next War: American Plans for Postwar Defense, 1941–45* (New Haven: 1977), pp. 52–53.] See also, for a contemporary expression of this idea, William Liscum Borden, *There Will Be No Time: The Revolution in Strategy* (New York: 1946), pp. 181, 198. For further insights into the American tendency to connect totalitarianism with aggression, see Eduard Maximilian Mark, "The Interpretation of Soviet Foreign Policy in the United States, 1928–1947" (Ph.D. Dissertation, University of Connecticut, 1978), pp. 95–96, 326–29.

† "[I]t was not inconceivable," Forrestal himself noted in June, 1945, "that the real reactionaries in world politics would be those who now call themselves revolutionaries, because the dynamics of their philosophy all tended toward the concentration of power in the state, with the inevitable result of exploitation of the common man by the masses, or rather, by those who in such a system apply power over the masses—such as Hitler, Mussolini, Stalin and Hirohito." [Forrestal Diary, June 30, 1945, Walter Millis, ed., *The Forrestal Diaries* (New York: 1951), pp. 72–73.]

is not Communism but Totalitarianism which is the potential threat," publisher Arthur Hays Sulzberger pointed out. ". . . [O]nly people who have a Bill of Rights are not the potential enemies of other people."[70]*

The point, for Truman, was fundamental. "Really there is no difference between the government which Mr. Molotov represents and the one the Czar represented—or the one Hitler spoke for," he privately wrote in November, 1946.[71]† And, again, informally, in May, 1947: "There isn't any difference in totalitarian states. . . . Nazi, Communist or Fascist, or Franco, or anything else—they are all alike. . . . The police state is a police state; I don't care what you call it."[72] The President's public speeches during 1947 provided virtually a running commentary on the dangers of totalitarianism: "Freedom has flourished where power has been dispersed. It has languished where power has been too highly centralized." More than that, excessive concentrations of power produced temptations to use them. "The stronger the voice of a people in the formulation of national policies, the less the danger of aggression. When all governments derive their just powers from the consent of the governed, there will be enduring peace." There was no conflict between the requirements of justice and order: "The attainment of worldwide respect for essential human rights is synonymous with the attainment of world peace."[73]

It was no accident, then, that when the President in the most famous speech of his career characterized the world as divided between two ways of life, one reflecting "the will of the majority," the other based "upon the will of a minority forcibly imposed upon the majority,"[74] it was the distinction between democracy and totalitarianism to which he referred. By so doing, he implicitly linked his own justification of American action to restore the balance of power in Europe to those advanced by Franklin Roosevelt in the Atlantic Charter and by Woodrow Wilson in the Fourteen Points: in each case the assumption was the ultimate incompatibility of autocratic and democratic institutions. The fact that this particular autocracy also embraced the ideology of communism was, for Truman, relatively insignificant.

That certainly was not the case for most Americans, though. Nothing—not even totalitarianism—did more to arouse suspicion about the Soviet Union's

---

* "[I]t is becoming more and more evident to me," Secretary of War Henry L. Stimson noted in his diary while at the Potsdam Conference, "that a nation whose system rests upon free speech and all the elements of freedom, as does ours, cannot be sure of getting on permanently with a nation where speech is strictly controlled and where the Government uses the iron hand of the secret police." [Stimson Diary, July 19, 1945, Henry L. Stimson Papers, Yale University Library.]

† The implication here is that a surviving tsarist Russia would have posed as much of a threat, in the eyes of Truman and his advisers, as a communist one. The amount of attention given in the White House to a spurious "will" of Peter the Great bears this out. "Pete must have been a great guy," Admiral William D. Leahy commented. [Leahy to Clifford, September 21, 1946, Clark M. Clifford Papers, Box 14, "Russia: Folder 3," Harry S. Truman Library.] For an analysis of this document and its impact upon administration thinking, see J. Garry Clifford, "President Truman and Peter the Great's Will," *Diplomatic History*, IV (Fall, 1980), 371–85.

behavior than that country's long-standing and self-proclaimed intention to seek the overthrow of capitalist governments throughout the world. American hostility toward communism went back to the earliest days of the Bolshevik Revolution: to Russia's abandonment of the Allied cause in World War I; to the terror, expropriations, and executions that soon followed; to the postwar Red Scare, with its suggestion that even the United States might not be immune from the bacillus of revolution. The Soviet Union's commitment to communism had been the primary justification for Washington's refusal to recognize that country until 1933; and even after that date Moscow's claim to be the vanguard of world revolution had continued to plague relations with Washington.[75] Stalin implicitly acknowledged the corrosive effects of ideology upon his dealings with the West in 1943 when, eager for an Anglo-American commitment to establish a Second Front, he abolished the Comintern, Lenin's designated instrument for bringing about the world proletarian revolution.* But there could be no guarantee that such restraint would continue once Moscow's enemies had been defeated. As a Department of State memorandum put it in 1944, it was necessary to keep in mind the Soviet conviction that "there is an irreconcilable chasm between 'socialism' and 'capitalism' and that any temporary association in a common interest [is] an association of expediency for a specific purpose but with no underlying affinity of fundamental interest, civilization, or tradition."[76]

"I expressed it as my view that it would not be difficult to work with Russia provided we were dealing with her only as a national entity," James Forrestal noted in his diary during the summer of 1945. "[T]he real problem was whether or not Russian policy called for a continuation of the Third International's objectives, namely, world revolution and the application of the political principles of the dialectical materialists for the entire world."[77] Evidence that the Kremlin still harbored such ambitions arose from two sets of circumstances: the Russians' use of communist parties in Eastern Europe as instruments with which to create their sphere of influence there; and the increasing success of communist parties in Western Europe, the Eastern Mediterranean, and China. In retrospect, it is not at all clear that these phenomena were related: the popularity of communist parties outside the Soviet sphere grew primarily out of their effectiveness as resistance fighters against the Axis; in Eastern Europe the communists owed their prominence chiefly to Moscow's reliance on them to consolidate its control.[78] Nor was it obvious that the Soviet Union's use of foreign communist parties to promote its interests necessarily proved an ideological motivation for its policies.†

---

* At least Stalin's action was so regarded in the United States. [See John Lewis Gaddis, *The United States and the Origins of the Cold War, 1941–1947* (New York: 1972), pp. 47–49.] But Vojtech Mastny doubts that Stalin's primary motive was to improve cooperation with the West. [*Russia's Road to the Cold War: Diplomacy, Warfare, and the Politics of Communism, 1941–1945* (New York: 1979), pp. 94–97.]

† A State Department report, drafted late in 1945 by Charles E. Bohlen and Geroid T. Robinson, noted with unhelpful even-handedness that: "It is by no means to be expected

But these fine points were difficult to keep in mind as the end of the war brought increases in the militancy—and anti-American rhetoric—of all communist parties, not least that of the Soviet Union itself.* When combined with the indisputable evidence of Moscow's unilateral expansionism, when considered against the record of how Nazi Germany had used "fifth columns" before the war, it is not surprising that concern about the ideological dimension of the Soviet challenge should have surfaced as well. "The tendency is increasingly marked," the British Embassy in Washington reported in August, 1946, "to detect the Soviet mind or hand behind every move which seems to threaten or embarrass the United States or its friends, and to link events in one part of the world with those in another."[79] The editors of *Newsweek* put it more bluntly: "U.S. officials in the best position to judge fear they have confirmation that the Soviet Government has made up its mind that capitalism must be destroyed if Communism is to live."[80]†

Both the "totalitarian" and the "ideological" explanations of Soviet behavior had in common the assumption that one was dealing with a compulsive internally driven process, unresponsive to gestures of restraint or goodwill from the outside. There had been yet a third interpretation of Moscow's unilateralism, popular during the war, that had seen it as growing out of a quite understandable preoccupation with security capable of being alleviated by patient Western efforts to win the Russians' trust. President Roosevelt himself had made this "insecurity" theory the basis of his policy toward the Soviet Union, and it had remained very much alive—though under increasing challenge—during the first months of the Truman administration.[81] But theories require validation if they are to be sustained: however persuasive the "insecurity" model of Soviet behavior may be in retrospect, what struck most observers at the time was the utter imperviousness of Stalin's regime to the gestures of restraint and goodwill that emanated from the West during and immediately after the war.[82] Moscow's perceived failure to reciprocate these initiatives made it more and more difficult to sustain an interpretation of So-

---

that in the future the foreign policy of the Soviet leaders will be determined entirely by Marxian theory. This has never been the case since the establishment of the Soviet government. . . . Yet it would be very unsafe to assume, on the other hand, that the future attitude of the Soviet leaders toward non-Soviet states and toward the domestic forces and movements within those states will not be influenced in any degree by Marxian ideology." ["The Capabilities and Intentions of the Soviet Union as Affected by American Policy," December 10, 1945, as published in *Diplomatic History*, I(Fall, 1977), 395.]

* Particularly important in this regard was the Stalin "election" speech of February 9, 1946, which clearly gave the impression, whether intended or not, of a renewed ideological emphasis in Soviet policy. The impact of this speech is discussed in Hugh DeSantis, *The Diplomacy of Silence: The American Foreign Service, the Soviet Union, and the Cold War, 1933–1947*, pp. 172–73; but see also, for earlier indications of concern about ideology, Gaddis, *The United States and the Origins of the Cold War*, pp. 296–99.

† For an illuminating discussion of how John Foster Dulles had come, by the summer of 1946, to an almost entirely ideological explanation of Soviet behavior, see Ronald W. Pruessen, *John Foster Dulles: The Road to Power* (New York: 1982), pp. 276–87.

viet actions based on "insecurity," as Henry Wallace found out when he attempted, during the spring and summer of 1946, to revive it within the inner councils of the government.[83]* The "totalitarian" and "ideological" models were the obvious alternatives.

It is ironic that the individual most influential in discrediting "insecurity" as an explanation of Soviet unilateralism shared many of its basic assumptions. George F. Kennan had never been inclined to interpret Soviet behavior in either strictly totalitarian or ideological terms. As a keen student of Russian history and culture, he was fully aware of the lack of self-confidence that plagued the Stalinist government, and of the extent to which its unilateralism was defensively motivated.† But he emphatically did not share the view of Wallace and others that these attitudes could be modified from the outside. It was in an effort to bring official Washington to see that point that Kennan crafted the February, 1946, "long telegram," to this day the single most influential explanation of postwar Soviet behavior, and one which powerfully reinforced the growing tendency within the United States to interpret Moscow's actions in a sinister light.

The "long telegram" had the great influence that it did because it provided a way to fuse concerns about totalitarianism and communism in dealing with the Soviet Union. It portrayed that state as one in which an autocratic tradition had become incorporated within an ideological compulsion to treat the outside world as hostile. The conclusion was clear: no actions the United States or its Western allies could take would alleviate Stalin's suspicion; the best one could do was to look to one's own defenses—and to the strength and self-confidence of one's own society—and wait for the internal forces of change within the Soviet system to have their effect.[84]

There is a definite psychological satisfaction, when confronted with a phenomenon one does not understand, in finding a simple but persuasive explanation.[85] Whatever the actual intentions of its author,[86] the "long telegram" performed that function within the government in 1946; a similar analysis would

---

* Dulles's comment on Wallace is worth noting: "It is a good initial approach to say that if you pat the dog he will not bite you. If, however, after several times patting the dog he still nips you, then it is necessary to think of another approach. Wallace has been sitting behind the scenes and has not had to go through the experience of having his hand nipped." [Dulles to Irving Fisher, September 23, 1946, John Foster Dulles Papers, Seeley Mudd Library, Princeton University.]

† "Security is probably their basic motive," Kennan noted in the summer of 1946, "but they are so anxious and suspicious about it that the objective results are much the same as if the motive were aggression, indefinite expansion. They evidently seek to weaken all centers of power they cannot dominate, in order to reduce the danger from any possible rival." [Kennan paper, "Draft of Information Policy on Relations with Russia," July 22, 1946, Dean Acheson Papers, Box 27, "State Department Under Secretary Correspondence, 1945–7," Harry S. Truman Library.] Daniel Yergin's characterization of Kennan as an advocate of what he calls the "Riga axioms," an ideologically based explanation of Soviet behavior, strikes me as a considerable oversimplification. See his *Shattered Peace: The Origins of the Cold War and the National Security State* (Boston: 1977), pp. 27–28, 170.

find a wider audience the following year in the form of the famous "X" article in *Foreign Affairs*.[87] The "totalitarian-ideological" model of Soviet behavior provided a clear, plausible, and in many ways gratifying explanation of the Russians' failure to cooperate with their former allies in building a lasting peace: it absolved the United States of responsibility for the breakdown of wartime cooperation; it made any future relaxation of tensions dependent upon changes of heart in Moscow, not Washington. Americans did not welcome the onset of the Cold War. But the rationale they worked out to account for its appearance at least had the advantage of allowing them to approach the coming contest with a reasonably clear conscience.

# V

The Soviet Union's emergence as a potential adversary closed an obvious gap in Washington's thinking about the postwar world. A generalized sense of vulnerability, related both to historical experience and to technological change, had caused United States officials to regard preservation of a global balance of power as a vital interest even before specific challenges to that balance had manifested themselves. This situation of perceived vulnerability in the absence of apparent threat accounts for the failure of the United States to deploy forces and establish bases in the way one might have expected had the Russians been seen as the enemy from the beginning.[88] But Soviet unilateralism, together with the conclusions about the roots of Soviet behavior that unilateralism provoked, had by 1947 created a credible source of danger, with the result that American strategy now took on a clearer and more purposeful aspect.

Central to it was the defense of Western Europe, a priority so basic that it was more often assumed than articulated. "[It] is not a question of what men think now," the Joint Chiefs of Staff noted in the spring of 1947; "[it] is something that has been demonstrated by what we have had to do, though tardily, and therefore at greater risk and cost, in actual warfare in the past. . . . The entire area of Western Europe is in first place as an area of strategic importance to the United States."[89] And yet, American planners had given remarkably little thought to the means by which that part of the world might be secured against Soviet expansionism. Their assumption—again mostly unstated—had been that Great Britain would provide the necessary counter presence, and that the United States could concern itself with other matters.* It had done just that throughout 1946, concentrating on resisting Soviet pressures aimed at Iran and Turkey, consolidating its position in Japan and

---

* One of the best discussions of this point is still that of William Hardy McNeill, *America, Britain & Russia: Their Co-operation and Conflict, 1941–1946* (London: 1953), pp. 753–57, although the work of Sherry, Smith, and Converse, cited in the notes, makes it clear that McNeill somewhat exaggerated the eagerness of the American military to supplant British power.

southern Korea, mediating the Chinese civil war, and attempting to resolve the diplomatic stalemate over Germany.

The British decision to withdraw military assistance from Greece and Turkey in February, 1947, forced a reconsideration of these priorities, not because those two countries were of critical importance in and of themselves, but because of the way in which London's action dramatized the failure of Western Europe as a whole to recover from the war. A major consequence of that conflict had been, in Mackinder's terminology, a severe weakening of the "rimland" states surrounding the Soviet "heartland," leaving only the "world island"—effectively the United States—as a countervailing balance. But it was not until 1947 that Washington officials realized the full implications of that fact and set about taking corrective action.

At no point—despite references to the possibility of war in the 1946 Clifford report—did these officials seriously anticipate a Soviet military attack in Europe. Estimates of Moscow's intentions, whether from the Pentagon, the State Department, or the intelligence community, consistently discounted the possibility that the Russians might risk a direct military confrontation within the foreseeable future.[90] Several considerations contributed to that judgment, not least of which was the damage the Soviet Union itself had suffered during the war and the still relatively primitive character of its air and naval forces. But these estimates also suggested that the Russians would not need to use force to gain their objectives, because of the ease with which war-weakened neighbors could be psychologically intimidated. "[I]f the countries of the world lose confidence in us," General George A. Lincoln of the War Department General Staff told the Senate Foreign Relations Committee early in April, 1947, "they may in effect pass under the Iron Curtain without any pressure other than the subversive pressure being put on them."[91]*

American planners assumed a direct correlation between economic health, psychological self-confidence, and the capacity for defense. As a State–War–Navy Coordinating Committee report noted that same month: "[E]conomic weaknesses may give rise to instability and subsequently to political shifts which adversely affect the security of the U.S." This could happen through "boring from within" tactics or the threat of overwhelming external force, but in either event the outcome from the standpoint of American interests would be grim.[92] "Without further prompt and substantial aid from the United States," Under Secretary of State William Clayton argued, "economic, social and political disintegration will overwhelm Europe."[93]

A Soviet-dominated Europe would pose obvious military dangers, even if military means were not used to secure it. In a clear echo of the wartime Mackinder-Spykman analysis, the Joint Chiefs of Staff pointed out that the Western hemisphere contained 40 percent of the earth's land surface but only 25 per-

---

* "[T]he Soviets still do not want war," State Department adviser Harley A. Notter noted in July, "but believe that despite us they can gain their strategic objectives of control not only of the heartland of Europe and Asia but actually of the shores of those continents at every point of major vulnerability from sea and air." [Notter to Dean Rusk, July 14, 1947, U.S. Department of State, *Foreign Relations of the United States: 1947*, IV, 578.]

cent of its population. "The potential military strength of the Old World in terms of manpower . . . and war-making capacity is enormously greater than that of our area of defense commitments, in which the United States is the only arsenal nation." It was obvious, therefore, that in case of war "we must have the support of some of the countries of the Old World unless our military strength is to be overshadowed by that of our enemies." Western Europe was particularly important, not just because that region contained "almost all potentially strong nations who can reasonably be expected to ally themselves with the United States," but also because without access to the eastern shore of the Atlantic, "the shortest and most direct avenue of attack against our enemies will almost certainly be denied us."[94]*

The economic consequences of a European collapse were less clear. The Truman administration found it convenient to argue publicly that the effect on the American domestic economy, in terms of lost exports, would be little short of disastrous.[95] What strikes one in retrospect, though, is how self-sufficient that economy actually was. Exports as a percentage of gross national product did not rise above 6.5 percent between 1945 and 1950, a figure lower than had normally been the case before the Great Depression, when the government had adamantly resisted any kind of official aid for European reconstruction. American investment in Western Europe in the early postwar years was actually less than European investment in the United States. It seems likely that administration officials stressed the economic implications of the crisis not because these stood out above others, but because Washington had chosen economic assistance as the quickest and most effective way to respond to it. [96] It was easier to sell an unprecedented foreign-aid package as a program to ensure American prosperity than as a strategy for redressing the balance of power.

But it was the psychological implications of an extension of Soviet influence over Europe that probably most concerned American leaders. Although the term "domino theory" would not come into currency for another decade, administration officials worried deeply about the "bandwagon" effect that might ensue if the perception became widespread that the momentum in world affairs was on the Russians' side.[97] And despite the United States' own history of isolationism, despite its relative self-sufficiency, there was a very real fear of what might happen if the nation were left without friends in the world. In one sense, this fear grew out of the tradition of American exceptionalism: the United States had always viewed itself as both apart from and a model for the rest of the world; it could hardly have regarded with equanimity evidence that its example was no longer relevant.† But, in another sense, it was pre-

---

* Although for the purpose of launching a strategic bombing offensive, it is now clear that Pentagon planners regarded Middle Eastern bases as of primary importance. [Converse, "United States Plans for a Postwar Overseas Military Base System," pp. 211–19.]

† The British Embassy in Washington noted in March, 1947, that "[t]he missionary strain in the character of Americans . . . leads many of them to feel that they have now received a call to extend to other countries the blessings with which the Almighty has en-

cisely the unexceptional character of Americans in relation to the rest of the world that was at issue here: who was to say that, buoyed by success in Europe, the totalitarian instinct might not take hold in the United States as well? "There is a little bit of the totalitarian buried somewhere, way down deep, in each and every one of us," George Kennan reminded students at the National War College in the spring of 1947. "It is only the cheerful light of confidence and security which keeps this evil genius down. . . . If confidence and security were to disappear, don't think that he would not be waiting to take their place."[98]

The strategy of containment brought together the new American interest in maintaining a global balance of power with the perceived Muscovite challenge to that equilibrium in a part of the world that could hardly have been more pivotal—Western Europe. It sought to deal with that danger primarily by economic rather than military means; its goal was not so much the creation of an American hegemony as it was a re-creation of independent centers of power capable of balancing each other as well as the Russians.* This is hardly the place to evaluate the success of that strategy or to trace its subsequent mutations and incarnations: these subjects have received excessively lengthy treatment elsewhere.[99] Suffice it to say that the strategy could not have evolved without the perception of vulnerability brought about by the war, and the all-too-successful—if inadvertent—efforts of the Russians to give that abstraction an alarming reality.

# V I

Soviet historians have argued with unsurprising consistency through the years that the United States over-reacted to the "threat" posed by the U.S.S.R. in

---

dowed their own." But the following August it was reporting that "[i]n spite of all the exuberant confidence and bombast with which much of the public has embraced the new role of world leadership, Americans are genuinely afraid of standing alone." [Inverchapel to Foreign Office, March 13 and August 23, 1947, Foreign Office Records, FO 371/67035/R3482 and 61056/AN2982, Public Record Office, London.]

* "[B]asically the stability of international relations must rest on a natural balance of national and regional forces. . . . I would not hesitate to say that the first and primary element of 'containment' . . . would be the encouragement and development of other forces resistant to communism. The peculiar difficulty of the immediate post-hostilities period has rested in the fact that . . . Russia was surrounded only by power vacuums. At the outset, these could be filled . . . only by direct action on the part of this Government. This is admittedly an undesirable situation; and it should be a cardinal point of our policy to see to it that other elements of independent power are developed on the Eurasian land mass as rapidly as possible, in order to take off our shoulders some of the burden of 'bi-polarity.' To my mind, the chief beauty of the Marshall plan was that it had outstandingly this effect." [George F. Kennan to Cecil B. Lyon, October 13, 1947, Department of State Policy Planning Staff Records, Box 33 "Chronological—1947," Diplomatic Branch, National Archives.]

the wake of World War II.[100] During the late 1960's and early 1970's, a number of American students of the early Cold War expressed agreement with that conclusion, though not with the methods that had been used to arrive at it.[101] In an interesting inversion of Kennan's theory regarding Russian behavior, these accounts portrayed official Washington as having in one way or another fabricated the myth of a hostile Soviet Union in order to justify its own internally motivated drive for international hegemony. The difficulty with this argument was the impossibility of verifying it, for without access to Soviet sources there could be no definite conclusions regarding its accuracy: one cannot credibly assess responsibility when one can confirm the motives of only one side. The intervening years have brought us no nearer to a resolution of that problem, but they have witnessed the emergence of several new lines of historical interpretation that appear to call into question the thesis of American "over-reaction."

One of these involves a reconsideration of Stalin's policy by a new generation of scholars equally conversant, not only with the very limited number of Soviet and East European sources that are available, but with the overwhelming array of recently declassified American and British documents as well. The effect of this work is to confirm neither the "totalitarian" nor the "ideological" explanations of Stalin's actions that were popular during the early Cold War years, but rather to see that dictator as having followed an "imperial" model of expansion: a pattern of behavior motivated by insecurity and characterized by caution, to be sure, but one that was also incapable of defining the limits of security requirements and that sought, as a result, to fill power vacuums where this could be done without encountering resistance. The effect of this policy was twofold: to incorporate within the Soviet sphere what Vojtech Mastny has called "a cluster of sullen dependencies" that probably contributed to more than they subtracted from Moscow's nervousness; and to alarm, and ultimately alienate, the United States and its Western European allies, who saw Stalin's inability to define the full extent of his security requirements as likely to undermine their own.[102]

It may well be, as William Taubman has argued, that the West gave up on the possibility of cooperation with Stalin before Stalin gave up on the possibility of cooperation with the West. But Taubman points out that any such cooperation would have been on the Kremlin leader's terms and for his purposes: it would have been designed "to foster Soviet control of Eastern Europe whether directly (in the case of Poland, Rumania, and Bulgaria) or indirectly (in Hungary and Czechoslovakia) ; to expand Soviet influence in Western Europe, the Near East and Asia; to position the USSR for even greater gains when the next Western economic crisis struck; and to achieve all this while subsidized to the tune of at least six billion dollars in American credits."[103] Western statesmen may perhaps be pardoned for not having shared this particular vision of the postwar world.

Nor are they condemned, in the new historiography, for having resorted to a strategy of containment; indeed Mastny goes so far as to suggest that the West's responsibility for the coming of the Cold War lies more in the passive and dilatory character of its response than in its aggressiveness: "any Western policy likely to restrain [Stalin] would have had to follow a harder rather than a softer line; it would also have had a better chance to succeed if applied sooner rather than later."[104] Containment no doubt reinforced Stalin's suspicion of the West, but it can hardly be said to have created it; without containment, according to this new line of interpretation, the fears Western statesmen held at the time regarding Soviet expansionism might well have become reality.

Historians are also beginning to study the involvement of third parties in the early Cold War: this work sheds new light on the question of who saw whom as a threat. What emerges from it so far is the extent to which states along the periphery of the U.S.S.R. tended to share Washington's concern about Soviet intentions, and indeed to welcome American intervention in their affairs as a counterweight. The Norwegian historian Geir Lundestad has pointed out that Washington's influence actually expanded more rapidly than did that of the Russians in the postwar world, but he argues that this happened because the United States was *encouraged* to assert its power in order to balance that of the Russians.[105] Bruce Kuniholm has documented a similar pattern in the Near East: in 1946 the Iranian government was demanding not less but greater American interference in its internal affairs on the grounds, as the U.S. ambassador put it, that "[t]he only way they can think of to counteract one influence is to invite another."[106] But the clearest case of all is the policy of Great Britain, which as Terry Anderson and Robert Hathaway have demonstrated, amounted almost to a conspiracy to involve the United States more actively in world affairs.[107]

"If we cannot have a world community with the Russians as a constructive member," a British Foreign Office official minuted early in 1946, "it seems clear that the next best hope for peace and stability is that the rest of the world, including the vital North American arsenal, should be united in defense of whatever degree of stability we can attain."[108] This is as good a summary of London's early Cold War policy, under both the Churchill and Attlee governments, as one is apt to find. The British had come earlier than their American allies to the conclusion that cooperation with the Russians was not going to be possible; certainly they welcomed—and, at times, sought to reinforce—the increasing indications from Washington throughout 1946 and early 1947 that the Truman administration had come to share that view.[109] Their analysis of the reasons for Soviet unilateralism roughly paralleled that of the Americans;[110]* nor were they inclined to find fault—apart from some wincing at the rhetorical excesses involved—with the strategies Washington

---

* It is worth noting in this connection the similarity in the viewpoints of Kennan and Frank Roberts, the British chargé d'affaires in Moscow in early 1946. [See, on this point, Peter G. Boyle, "The British Foreign Office View of Soviet-American Relations, 1945–46," *Diplomatic History*, III(Summer, 1979), 310; also Robert M. Hathaway, *Ambiguous Partnership: Britain and America, 1944–1947* (New York: 1981), pp. 369–70.]

proposed to deal with that problem. Indeed, if anything, London's attitude was that the Americans were not doing enough: it was this conviction that led Foreign Secretary Ernest Bevin late in 1947 to propose to the United States a formal and permanent peacetime military alliance with Western Europe.[111]

It is, of course, easy to see self-serving motivations at work in the invitations the British government and its counterparts in Western Europe and the Near East extended to the United States to expand its influence in their parts of the world. It could be argued that had that desire for an American presence not existed, these "third party" assessments of Russian intentions might have been considerably less alarmist than they were. But that is missing the point, for it is also the case that had a credible Soviet threat not presented itself, these countries would not have been seeking the expansion of American power in the first place. "It has really become a matter of the defence of western civilisation," the British Foreign Office concluded early in 1948:

> [N]ot only is the Soviet government not prepared at the present state to co-operate in any real sense with any non-Communist . . . Government, but it is actively preparing to extend its hold over the remaining portion of continental Europe and, subsequently, over the Middle East and no doubt the bulk of the Far East as well. . . . [P]hysical control of the Eurasian land mass and eventual control of the whole World Island is what the Politburo is aiming at—no less a thing than that. The immensity of the aim should not betray us into believing in its impracticality. Indeed, unless positive and vigorous steps are shortly taken by those other states who are in a position to take them . . . the Soviet Union will gain political and strategical advantages which will set the great Communist machine in action, leading either to the establishment of a World Dictatorship or (more probably) to the collapse of organised society over great stretches of the globe.[112]

It is significant that this top-secret Foreign Office document, circulated only within the highest levels of the British government and declassified only after the passage of more than three decades, should have revealed an assessment of the Soviet threat more sweeping in character and apocalyptic in tone than anything in the record of private or public statements by major American officials at the time. The progression from Mackinder to Spengler, it appears, was easier than one might think,

# VII

History, inescapably, involves viewing distant pasts through the prism of more recent ones. The incontestable fact that the United States over-reacted more than once during the subsequent history of the Cold War to the perceived threat of Soviet and/or "communist" expansionism has, to an extent, blinded us to the equally demonstrable fact that in the immediate postwar years the behavior of the Russians alarmed not just Americans but a good portion of the rest of the world as well. How well-founded that alarm was— how accurately it reflected the realities that shaped Soviet policy—are issues upon which there are legitimate grounds for disagreement. But to deny that the alarm itself was sincere, or that Americans were not alone in perceiving it, is to distort the view through the prism more than is necessary. Fear, after all, can be genuine without being rational. And, as Sigmund Freud once pointed out, even paranoids can have real enemies.[113]

# 3

# Spheres of Influences: The United States and Europe, 1945-1949

A BASIC CONFLICT is . . . arising over Europe between the interests of Atlantic sea-power, which demand the preservation of vigorous and independent political life on the European peninsula, and the interests of the jealous Eurasian land power, which must always seek to extend itself to the west and will never find a place, short of the Atlantic Ocean, where it can from its own standpoint safely stop." This was George F. Kennan's depressing assessment of the situation that confronted the United States and its allies early in 1945, conveyed in a letter to his friend and fellow Russian expert, Charles E. Bohlen. Kennan went on to recognize the extent to which victory over Germany required the Soviet Union's military cooperation, even if this brought about an unprecedented projection of Moscow's influence into central Europe. "But with all of this, I fail to see why we must associate ourselves with this political program, so hostile to the interests of the Atlantic community as a whole, so dangerous to everything which we need to see preserved in Europe. Why could we not make a decent and definite compromise with it—divide Europe frankly into spheres of influence—keep ourselves out of the Russian sphere and keep the Russians out of ours? . . . And within whatever sphere of action was left to us we could at least . . . [try] to restore life, in the wake of the war, on a dignified and stable foundation."[1]

Bohlen received Kennan's letter at Yalta on the eve of Franklin Roosevelt's

This essay was originally prepared for the symposium on "European and Atlantic Defence, 1947-1953," organized by the Norwegian Research Centre for Defence History and held in Oslo in August, 1983. It appears, in slightly different form, in Olav Riste, ed., *Western Security: The Formative Years: European and Atlantic Defence, 1947-1953* (Oslo: 1985), pp. 60-91.

last meeting with Churchill and Stalin. In his hastily composed hand-written reply, he acknowledged as valid Kennan's assessment of Soviet intentions, but dismissed as "uttterly impossible" his recommendation for a division of Europe into spheres of influence. "Foreign policy of that kind cannot be made in a democracy," he continued. "Only totalitarian states can make and carry out such policies." Years later, in his memoirs, Bohlen elaborated: "The American people, who had fought a long, hard war, deserved at least an attempt to work out a better world. If the attempt failed, the United States could not be blamed for not trying."[2]

This exchange between the State Department's two most experienced Soviet specialists reflects the dilemma facing the United States as it contemplated the implications of a victory in Europe purchased at the price of an expansion of Soviet influence over Europe. Should the United States play by the Russians' rules and carve out for itself a sphere of influence over as much of the Continent as remained open to it? Or should it seek to persuade the Russians to change the rules: to build a new European order, based upon a rejection of power politics altogether? In the end, of course, Europe was divided, very much along the lines that Kennan had proposed. But Washington accepted this solution only slowly, and with considerable reluctance: Bohlen's idea of a postwar settlement based upon principles of self-determination and big power cooperation proved remarkably persistent. In its eventual decline and ultimate rejection can be traced the origins of a European settlement that has lasted, itself with remarkable persistence, down to the present day.

# I

Americans had not been much inclined, prior to World War II, to think about the balance of power in Europe, but events of the early 1940's had abruptly undercut earlier isolationist arguments that whatever happened on the Continent could not affect the security of the United States. In their place, there arose the conviction that the primary American interest in postwar international affairs would be to ensure that no single state dominate Europe.[3] As an Office of Strategic Service analysis put it in the summer of 1944: "our interests require the maintenance of a policy designed to prevent the development of a serious threat to the security of the British Isles (and of the United States), through the consolidation of a large part of Europe's resources under any one power."[4] Increasingly, as the end of the war approached, strategic planners in Washington became aware of the prospect that Germany's defeat would leave a power vacuum in central Europe into which only the Russians would be well-positioned to move. Great Britain, they noted, would be far too weak to provide a counter-balance.[5] But there was, as yet, no consensus that the United States should project its own influence into Europe to restore equilibrium.

Britain and the United States were following divergent policies in their efforts to deal with the inevitable expansion of Soviet influence into postwar Europe, another O.S.S. analysis pointed out in January, 1945: The British approach emphasized "the division of the problem areas into spheres of Soviet and non-Soviet predominance with a neutral zone between." Obviously, such a straightforward partition of the continent would be simple to accomplish, but it would be "a very primitive type of international compromise":

> [I]n its extreme form it implies that within each of the areas affected the interests of the Great Powers are essentially irreconcilable, and that the only practicable solution is to isolate geographically the fields where these interests are to operate. . . . Thus this system probably supplies each great power with the maximum of temptation and the maximum of opportunity for intervention in the domestic affairs of its neighbors. In the long run this might well lead to divergent trends of development in the Soviet and non-Soviet spheres and to a sharpening of the differences between "two worlds."

The American preference should be "to establish and maintain independent democratic regimes within both spheres and within the neutral zone. . . . In the absolute form, such a program would constitute a complete negation of the system of spheres of influence; and to the extent that it is realized in practice it will limit the authority of each Great Power within its sphere."[6]

To be sure, Washington never actually contemplated such a thorough rejection of spheres of influence. President Roosevelt's own cherished concept of a world settlement enforced by "Four Policemen"—the United States, Great Britain, the Soviet Union, and Nationalist China—clearly implied the existence of such spheres. Certainly the United States was not prepared to give up its own predominance in Latin America, or to deny itself new areas of influence in the Pacific after the war.[7] Nor was there a predisposition to challenge the Russians' obvious attempt to secure a dominant postwar influence along their western borders.[8]

But there was no great effort, as the end of the war approached, to position American forces in such a way as to counter Soviet strength in Europe: indeed it was at Yalta that Roosevelt in effect promised the withdrawal of American troops from the Continent within two years of Germany's surrender.[9]* Nor did Churchill's impassioned pleas to hold American forces in place after that event meet with a favorable response from President Truman.[10] As late as the Potsdam Conference in July, 1945, State Department planners were still worrying that the British might seek to lure the United States into supporting a spheres of influence settlement in Europe. Such a

---

* Admiral William D. Leahy, Chief of Staff to the Commander-in-Chief, had told the Combined Chiefs of Staff as early as February, 1944, that "he, personally, hoped that the United States forces in Europe would be withdrawn at the earliest possible date consistent with the stabilization of the peace." [Minutes, 144th meeting of the Combined Chiefs of Staff, February 4, 1944, Combined Chiefs of Staff Records, CAB 88/4, Public Record Office, London.]

solution, they concluded, would "represent power politics pure and simple, with all the concomitant disadvantages. . . . Our primary objective should be to remove the *causes* which make nations feel that such spheres are necessary to build their security, rather than to assist one country to build up strength against another."[11]

It requires something of an effort, at this distance, to reconstruct the reasons for Washington's aversion to spheres of influence in Europe, even in the face of what were clearly Russian efforts to create their own in that part of the world. Probably most important in the minds of Roosevelt administration officials, curiously enough, was the fear of a resurgent isolationism inside the United States. "Our boys do not want to fight to rule the world, isolationist Congressman Hamilton Fish warned, "or to divide it into three parts, like ancient Gaul, between Great Britain, Russia, and the United States."[12] The President and his advisers were keenly sensitive to such arguments. In the Atlantic Charter and other wartime pronouncements, they had resuscitated the vision of a Wilsonian peace, based on self-determination, economic multilateralism, and collective security, not because they believed such a settlement to be attainable in every respect, but as a means of overcoming the isolationism that had grown out of the failure to implement that kind of peace two decades before.[13] A peace based too obviously on spheres of influence might seem to many Americans to be no peace at all, and hence result, as had the settlement of 1919, in the withdrawal rather than the projection of United States authority.

It would be unfair, though, to write off the administration's idealism in this respect solely as a way to sanctify the wielding of power. There was, as well, a sincere sense among Roosevelt, his subordinates, and much of the public at large that the "old diplomacy" had failed, and that Wilsonian methods of collective security, tempered to be sure by a regard for practical circumstances, deserved to be given another try.[14] American officials did work overtime during this period to demonstrate, at times with creative ingenuity, how the benefits of a Wilsonian settlement would accrue not just to the United States but to the rest of the world as well. But these arguments were by no means wholly cynical: to have acknowledged openly spheres of influence would have been to admit the irrelevancy of the American domestic experience, upon which so substantial a portion of this new approach to world affairs was based.

There also still existed uncertainty as to the Russians' motives for seeking spheres of influence in the first place. Despite some worry over the ideological component in Soviet policy,[15] the prevailing wartime view in Washington was that the projection of Russian power into Europe was occurring for defensive rather than offensive reasons. If Moscow could be assured of the West's peaceful intentions, then its reasons for seeking spheres of influence, it was thought, would disappear.[16] An open attempt to build countervailing power in Europe might have the effect of a self-fulfilling prophecy, reinforcing the Kremlin's suspicions and perpetuating its inclination toward unilateralism. "[W]e must always bear in mind," a State Department analysis of Soviet-

American relations concluded in December, 1945, "that because of the differences between the economic and political systems of our two countries, the conduct of our relations requires more patience and diligence than with other countries." American interests had to be defended, to be sure. "On the other hand, in order to minimize Soviet suspicions of our motives we should avoid even the appearance of taking unilateral action ourselves."[17]

A year after his reply to Kennan's letter, Bohlen still considered spheres of influence an inappropriate solution to Europe's problems. It might be possible to reach a *modus vivendi* with the Russians on that basis, he acknowledged early in 1946. But such a settlement would

> reduce the United Nations organization to a façade with the real power concentrated in the hands of the United States, Great Britain, and the Soviet Union. While this policy would perhaps offer the best means of avoiding difficulties with the Soviet Union in the immediate future, merely to state it is to demonstrate its impossibility of adoption. . . . [I]t would constitute a great step backwards from the principle of a cooperative world and would never receive the support of the American people.

Moreover, Bohlen added, such a settlement "would merely temporarily postpone an eventual clash with the Soviet Union under conditions infinitely worse for the United States and Great Britain" since, as a dictatorship, the U.S.S.R. "would be able to consolidate into an absolute bloc its sphere of influence while the Western democracies by their very nature would be unable to do the same in theirs."[18]

For Bohlen and those who thought like him, the very nature of Western political systems precluded a spheres of influence settlement: democracies could not join with dictatorships to divide the world. There would have to be, instead, a compromise between the facts of power and the obligations of justice; only on that basis could American interests in Europe be satisfied. Even after reading Kennan's pessimistic "long telegram" on the roots of Soviet behavior, Bohlen saw no reason "why the two systems cannot peacefully coexist in the same world provided that neither one attempts to extend the area of its system by aggressive and ultimately forceable means at the expense of the other." The problem for the West was "(a) to convince the Soviet Union of this possibility and (b) to make clear well in advance the inevitable consequence of the present line of Soviet policy based on the opposite thesis."[19]

# II

For the next year, the Truman administration followed closely the dual approach Bohlen had recommended. On the one hand, there took place an

exhaustive effort—probably insufficiently appreciated, in retrospect—to convince the Russians that a comprehensive European settlement would be preferable to a cold-blooded division of the Continent into separate spheres. At
the same time, though, there was set in motion a program of gradual preparation for a division of Europe, as much in the hope that it would ward off
Soviet inclinations in that direction as from a desire actually to implement it.

There was little inclination in Washington in the early postwar months
to try to challenge directly the reality of Soviet hegemony in Eastern Europe.
Instead, American officials made an effort to try to "educate" the Russians
to the fact that outright domination would be both unnecessary and counter-
productive. In October, 1945, Bohlen had actually suggested recognizing
"legitimate" Soviet security interests in Eastern Europe if the Russians would
agree to show the same restraint regarding the internal affairs of that region
that the United States had demonstrated in Latin America.[20] Secretary of
State James F. Byrnes made this idea the subject of a public speech later
that month, pointing out that the disinterested and mutually beneficial Good
Neighbor Policy had evolved out of the self interested Monroe Doctrine:
"We surely cannot and will not deny to other nations the right to develop
such a policy."[21]

But Bohlen himself had seen the principal difficulty in this approach:
"from all indications the Soviet mind is incapable of making a distinction
between influence and domination, or between a friendly government and a
puppet government."[22] The report of the Ethridge Committee, a delegation
of American observers sent by Byrnes to Rumania and Bulgaria to report on
Soviet policies there, strongly reinforced this conclusion: "[T]o concede a
limited Soviet sphere of influence at the present time," it argued, "would be
to invite its extension in the future."[23] With public and Congressional opinion growing increasingly hostile to the idea of any further concessions to
the Russians on any grounds, it is not surprising that a consensus began to
emerge within the government early in 1946 against further efforts to "en-
lighten" Moscow as to the disadvantages of spheres of influence, and in favor
of tougher methods.[24]

The central issue here was the future of Germany. State Department
planners had argued virtually without exception that there could be no stability in postwar Europe if Germany remained divided. Experiences of the
interwar years had seemed to show that the Germans would never accept
permanent partition of their country; moreover, a unified Germany was
thought vital to the economic recovery of Europe as a whole.[25]

The failure to persuade the Russians to abandon their sphere of influence
in Eastern Europe brought the German question to the forefront in two important but contradictory ways: it made all the more urgent the need to
ensure that Germany could pose no threat to the Soviet Union in the future,
thereby removing the Russians' principal excuse for dominating Eastern Europe in the first place; but it also raised the need for the Western powers to
begin thinking about consolidating their own positions in Germany, in the

event agreement with the Russians proved impossible. The dilemma was that by weakening Germany to reassure the Russians the West would leave itself vulnerable, but by strengthening its position there it would confirm Soviet suspicions. It was in the effort to resolve this dilemma that the United States in the spring of 1946 undertook two new initiatives on Germany: the proposal, in the Council of Foreign Ministers, of a four-power disarmament treaty; and, simultaneously, movement toward the consolidation of Western occupation zones.

The idea of a treaty between the United States, the Soviet Union, Great Britain, and France to keep Germany disarmed had been discussed off and on in Washington for some time, both for the purpose of reassuring allies that the United States did not propose to abandon them after the war, and as a means of alleviating Soviet fears of a resurgent Germany that had provided the justification for imposing a sphere of influence in Eastern Europe.[26]* But by the spring of 1946 the proposed treaty had become a test of Soviet intentions as well: if the Russians accepted it, the argument ran, they would have no further need for spheres of influence. If they did not, then the division of Europe would have to be accepted as a fact and the West would have to begin consolidating its own sphere. It was with these alternatives in mind that Byrnes formally proposed a twenty-five year treaty to the Russians at the end of April, 1946.[27]

Moscow's negative response seemed to confirm the fears of those who had argued that its determination to impose spheres of influence reflected offensive rather than defensive intentions. There was as yet no unanimous acknowledgment in Washington that Europe had been divided into two spheres, James Reston noted in the *New York Times* early in May, "but even the most pro-Soviet members of Mr. Truman's Administration agree that the Administration is nearer to accepting this thesis today than it has been at any other time since the end of the war."[28] It was within this context that emphasis began to be given to the other element in American policy during this period: the consolidation of a defensible Western position in Germany in the event negotiations with the Russians failed.

Convinced that the division of Europe was inevitable in any event, Kennan had for some time been arguing in favor of this approach. The only acceptable alternative, he had written in March, 1946, was for the United States and its allies "to carry to its logical conclusion the process of partition which was begun in the east and to endeavor to rescue [the] western zones of Germany by walling them off against eastern penetration and integrating them into [the] international pattern of western Europe."[29] This in fact is what Washington began to do in the spring and summer of 1946, with the termination of reparations shipments from the American zone, the initiation of talks with

---

* Senator Arthur H. Vandenberg had originally suggested the idea of a German disarmament treaty in the famous speech announcing his "conversion" from isolationism, delivered on the floor of the Senate on January 10, 1945. [See the *Congressional Record* for that date, pp. 164–67.]

London looking toward a merger of American and British occupation zones, and, most important, Secretary of State Byrnes's assurance at Stuttgart in September that American troops would remain in Germany as long as the occupation forces of any other power did.[30]

It is important to note, though, that these decisions of 1946 did not constitute final American acceptance of the division of Germany. The consequences of such a division, both in economic and geopolitical terms, were sufficiently unsettling to keep American negotiators at work for another year in the effort to secure a German peace treaty. As late as December, 1947, Secretary of State George C. Marshall, who spent much of that year conducting these negotiations, was still emphasizing the need to make sincere offers to the Russians on Germany rather than simply gestures in the expectation of refusals. Marshall was "most anxious in regard to the general international situation to avoid a 'frozen front,' which was tragic to contemplate."[31]

But a German settlement that risked leaving the Soviet Union in a position of dominance in central Europe was an even more unsettling prospect, and by 1947 there had emerged a definite consensus in Washington that a negotiated reunification was not worth that price. "I think that it amounts to this," Kennan told students at the Air War College in April of that year:

> We insist that either a central German authority be established along lines that will make it impossible for the Soviet Union to dominate Germany . . . , or that we retain complete control over the western zones. . . . I think it may mean the partition of Germany, and we all admit that is undesirable. . . . I hope we won't shrink from carrying out that partition rather than giving the Russians the chance to dominate the whole country, though.[32]

If the fear of a Germany under Soviet control served to make the idea of a divided Europe more respectable in American eyes, so too did the prospect of a power vacuum in the Near East and Eastern Mediterranean brought about by the decline of British power there. American planners had been well aware of the fact that the war had weakened Britain's world position,[33] but even so the rapidity of the collapse came as a surprise. As late as April, 1946, Truman could still speculate publicly about the possibility of a contest for world influence between London and Moscow, with Washington acting as an impartial umpire.[34] But within less than a year, American opinion had shifted to the view, as an official in the British Foreign Office noted with grim satisfaction, "that no time must be lost in plucking the torch of world leadership from our chilling hands."[35]

The threat to the balance of power in the Near East had seemed, at first, something that could be handled simply by issuing statements aimed simultaneously at warning the Russians off and at arousing world opinion against them. Both the Iranian and Turkish crises of 1946 had been dealt with in this way, with Washington relying primarily upon the deterrent effect of pugnacious pronouncements.[36] The situation in Greece, though, was something else again. Here the danger to the balance of power came not so much from the possibility of external attack as from that of internal disarray, the effects of which, it was thought, would benefit the Russians without the risks of direct military involvement. As the State Department's Office of Near Eastern and African Affairs noted late in 1946, "[i]t is vastly to the interest of the U.S. that the recognized government [in Greece] be assisted in becoming strong enough *before the fact* to handle its internal problems without requiring a sudden increase in assistance *during* a state of actual or near civil war."[37]

The British decision to cut off economic and military aid to Greece and Turkey early in 1947 forced Washington to move beyond attempts to discourage Soviet expansion by rhetoric alone. Instead, it appeared, positive action would be required to reconstitute centers of resistance to the Russians in areas vulnerable to them. This new approach would require squeezing increased appropriations out of a Congress still much attracted by the budgetary advantages of isolationism: hence, the administration's all-too-successful effort, through the Truman Doctrine, to alarm legislators by raising the specter of a world divided between antipathetic ways of life.[38] But the new situation also stimulated serious thinking in Washington as to how the United States might most effectively use its resources, not just in Greece and Turkey but in Europe as a whole, to reconstitute the balance of power left unstable by the creation and feared expansion of Moscow's sphere of influence. The collapse of Council of Foreign Ministers discussions on a German peace treaty that April further heightened the sense of urgency.[39]

The result, of course, was the Marshall Plan, an ambitious attempt to reconstitute a political balance in Europe by economic means. The plan rested upon the assumption that the Russians were not prepared to risk war to extend their influence; rather, the danger was that they might successfully exploit European psychological demoralization resulting from war damage and the discouragingly slow pace of reconstruction, whether by means of external intimidation, internal subversion, or even the possibility that Europeans might vote their own communists into office through free elections.[40] The Marshall Plan also reflected, paradoxically enough, an awareness of limited capabilities: the United States could not afford to contain threats to the balance of power in all places by all means. Maintaining European equilibrium ranked first on Washington's list of priorities; of the limited instruments available for doing this, economic assistance seemed to provide the quickest and most effective way.[41]

Even so, the traditional aversion to spheres of influence still lingered in the United States: it was partly in deference to this sentiment that Marshall initially offered aid to the Soviet Union and its East European satellites as well, with a view to placing responsibility for the division of Europe squarely on Moscow's shoulders.[42] It was the Russians' refusal of this offer—after a disquieting initial hesitation—that reconciled American officials once and for all to the inevitability of a divided Europe. As career Foreign Service officer Burton Y. Berry put it at the end of July, 1947, it was time to "drop the pretense of one world."[43]*

It was left to Bohlen, who had originally so strongly resisted the idea of a divided Europe, to draft the most thoughtful analysis of the new situation:

> The United States is confronted with a condition in the world which is at direct variance with the assumptions upon which, during and directly after the war, major United States policies were predicated. Instead of unity among the great powers—both political and economic—after the war, there is complete disunity between the Soviet Union and the satellites on one side and the rest of the world on the other. There are, in short, two worlds instead of one. Faced with this disagreeable fact, however much we may deplore it, the United States in the interest of its own well-being and security and those of the free non-Soviet world must re-examine its major policy objectives. . . . The logic of the situation is that the non-Soviet world through such measures are open to it [should] draw closer together politically, economically, financially, and, in the last analysis, militarily in order to be in a position to deal effectively with the consolidated Soviet area. Only in this way can a free and non-Soviet world hope to survive in the face of the centralized and ruthless direction of the Soviet world.[44]

Or, as Secretary of State Marshall put it with characteristic brevity at a cabinet meeting in November: "Our policy, I think, should be directed toward restoring a balance of power in Europe and Asia."[45]

# III

"[T]he realisation is now widespread," the British embassy in Washington reported early in 1948, "that there is nothing reprehensible *per se* in the exercise of power. Whereas a year ago the phrase 'power politics' bore a sinister connotation in the American mind, it has since come to be accepted as a normal technical term."[46] Curiously, though, this willingness to think in "balance of power" terms did not produce a corresponding determination on the part of the United States to carve out a sphere of influence for itself in Europe, comparable to the one the Russians had imposed. Instead, Washington's preference was to try to reconstitute an *independent* center of power on the continent, strong enough to act on its own to maintain equilibrium there.

* Kennan, as it happened, had already anticipated this recommendation, as minutes for the Policy Planning Staff meeting of July 28, 1947, show: "Mr. Kennan undertook to prepare a paper setting forth the implications involved in the fact that we are presently faced with a two-world situation, whereas the UN Charter was drawn up in the hope of a one-world system." [Policy Planning Staff Records, Box 32, Diplomatic Branch, National Archives.]

As John D. Hickerson, Director of the State Department's Office of European Affairs, described it, the idea was to create "a third force which was not merely the extension of US influence but a real European organization strong enough to say 'no' both to the Soviet Union and to the United States, if our actions should seem so to require."[47]

"The idea of a United States of Europe has, of course, long appealed to Americans, who are always prone to accept the naive and uncritical assumption that ideas and institutions that have proved their value here can be exported to provide ready-made remedies for the ills of less fortunate areas of the world."[48] It was not unusual for British diplomats in Washington to take a slightly jaded view of American enthusiasms, and this dispatch, written in the spring of 1947, was no exception. But it would be a mistake to see the Truman administration's support for European integration—in preference to the overt extension of an American sphere of influence over Europe—as a simple-minded effort to transplant what had flourished at home to stonier and less fertile soil overseas. There were in fact good reasons for Washington's reluctance, even after acknowledging the reality of a divided Europe, to impose its own control there.

One reason was that American officials did not see themselves as possessing, at that time, either the resources or the domestic support necessary to dominate large portions of the world in order to deny them to the Russians. "[P]ublic and Congressional reaction to foreign affairs is still conditioned by two main factors," a British Foreign Office analyst observed in May, 1947: "fear and dislike of Russia and aversion to the responsibility, and more particularly to the cost, of preserving the world balance of power."[49] A country still wary of international commitments could not discard its traditions overnight; rather, administration leaders argued, there would have to be a gradual expansion of responsibilities, carried out with full awareness of the need to expend limited resources efficiently and alongside obvious and convincing demonstrations from its allies that the United States would not be the only nation carrying the resulting burdens.[50]

It followed from this that a multi-polar international system, with several independent centers of power sharing the burdens of containment, would best suit American interests. Certainly this was Kennan's view: "it should be a cardinal point of our policy," he wrote in October, 1947, "to see to it that other elements of independent power are developed on the Eurasian land mass as rapidly as possible in order to take off our shoulders some of the burden of 'bi-polarity.' " Kennan went on during the next year to develop the concept of keeping key power centers—notably Great Britain, the Rhine-Ruhr industrial complex, and Japan—from falling under Soviet control, not by extending American control over them, but rather by encouraging their development as independent forces with the strength and self-confidence necessary to defend themselves.[51] An American sphere of influence in Europe would undermine that strategy, to which Truman administration officials were generally sympathetic.[52]

Such a solution would also conflict with the still-cherished, if imperfectly observed, tradition of non-intervention. Despite the collapse of "one world-ism," American officials continued to pay deference to the principle of self-determination. "[I]t is not our intention to impose our way of life on other nations," Assistant Secretary of State Charles Saltzmann insisted in September, 1947. "That in itself would be undemocratic. Our only purpose is, in so far as possible, to give other nations the opportunity to decide these matters for themselves, free from coercion."[53] This was not simply boiler-plate rhetoric, intended for public consumption: the view in Washington persisted throughout the late 1940's that the viability of political systems depended in large part upon their autonomy, even spontaneity. For this reason, Americans were willing to tolerate a surprising amount of diversity within the anti-Soviet coalition: one of the more durable strains in State Department thinking between 1946 and 1948 involved the need to cooperate with the democratic Left in Europe, despite the fact that its programs of nationalization and social welfare were anathema to conservatives in the United States.[54] If one result of such flexibility was to make European governments better able to resist Soviet pressure because of their firm base of popular support, then that only confirmed the long-standing American view that principle and self-interest were not always irreconcilable.

It should be recognized as well, though, that the interests of the United States and non-communist Europe were largely congruent during this period, and that Washington as a consequence had little need to impose its will on potential allies. If there was ever a time when one nation was *invited* to extend its influence over another part of the world, then surely the experience of the United States in Europe after World War II came close to it.* "[W]e should be placed in an impossible position," Foreign Secretary Ernest Bevin reminded the Cabinet, "if the United States Government withdrew from Europe."[55] The governments of Greece, Turkey, and Iran all fervently applauded the growth of American influence in the Eastern Mediterranean and the Near East.[56] And certainly public opinion in Western Europe welcomed a more active American role there as well, given the alternatives at best of further economic deterioration, at worst of Soviet domination.[57] "It seems evident," Secretary of State Marshall commented in November, 1947, "that, as regards European recovery, the enlightened self-interest of the United States coincides with the best interest of Europe itself."[58]

There were other, more specific, reasons for promoting the idea of European integration. One involved the problem of what to do with Germany now that an agreement with the Russians had become unlikely. A Joint Chiefs of Staff analysis in April, 1947, summarized the dilemma: "Without German aid

* For more on this "expansion by invitation" thesis, see Chapter Two, above: also Geir Lundestad, "Empire by Invitation? The United States and Western Europe, 1945–1952," *Journal of Peace Research*, XXIII (1986), 263–77; and John Lewis Gaddis, "The Emerging Post-Revisionist Thesis on the Origins of the Cold War," *Diplomatic History*, VII (Summer, 1983), 182–83.

the remaining countries of western Europe could scarcely be expected to withstand the armies of our ideological opponents until the United States could mobilize and place in the field sufficient armed forces to achieve their defeat." Moreover, "the complete resurgence of German industry . . . is essential for the economic recovery of France—whose security is inseparable from the combined security of the United States, Canada, and Great Britain." But all indications were that the French would "vigorously oppose any substantial revival of German heavy industry." This was unfortunate, since "the German people are the natural enemies of the USSR and of communism." It followed that the American interest was to convince both the French and the Germans "that the emergence of a principal world power to the east . . . which they can successfully oppose only if both are strong and united . . . makes them interdependent just as France, England, Canada, and the United States are interdependent."[59] European integration might provide a way to incorporate Germany into a European system without leaving Germany in control of that system. As Kennan put it early in 1948: "Only such a union holds out any hope of restoring the balance of power in Europe without permitting Germany to become again the dominant power."[60]

Finally, it should be pointed out that Americans did not see the division of Europe as something that would last forever. To an extent that is only now coming to be fully appreciated, Washington planners throughout this period were quietly considering how the Soviet Union's Eastern European satellites might be detached from the Kremlin's control.* This had been one of the additional motives behind the offer of Marshall Plan aid to the satellites in the summer of 1947; a year later Kennan was making the point that "the door should be left open for everyone in Europe to come in at the proper time so that there could be a real unification of Europe and the development of a European idea."[61] Only a viable European union would exert this kind of attraction, William Clayton pointed out: "The Russian satellite countries would then feel the pull so much stronger from the West than from the East, that Russia would find it more and more difficult and in the end impossible to hold them."[62] "Our objective," Under Secretary of State Robert Lovett wrote to Averell Harriman in December of 1948, "should continue to be the progressively closer integration, both economic and political, of presently free Europe and eventually of as much of Europe as becomes free."[63]

"If the United States entertained any idea of extending American influence or domination over Europe," Secretary of State Marshall had commented in a public speech given a year earlier, "our policy would not be directed toward ending European dependency upon this country but toward perpetuating that relationship."[64] This statement can stand as an accurate reflection of how American officials saw their own *intentions* with regard to Europe during the early days of the Cold War. There was, as the British Embassy in Washington perceptively pointed out, a distinction between seeking a balance of power and a sphere of influence:

---

* For further details, see Chapter Six, below.

On a broad view, an analysis of its activities leads to the conclusion that what the United States most requires from candid observers abroad are not reproofs that it is abusing its giant power, but commendation for such wisdom and generosity as it has thus far displayed, along with encouragement bravely to persevere in the employment of its vast resources for its own and the general welfare. In the meantime, to those critics who accuse her of taking undue advantage of her own strength and of the weakness of others, America might well reply in the words of Clive when arraigned by a committee in the House of Commons for having exploited his unrivalled power in India for purposes of personal aggrandizement: "By God, Mr. Chairman, at this moment I stand astonished at my own moderation."[65]

But intentions are one thing; actual policy is something else again, as the events of 1948–49 made clear. The American vision of an independent, prosperous, and self-confident center of power in Europe proved to be more elusive than had appeared to be the case in 1947. Circumstances gradually compelled the United States to create its own sphere of influence in Europe, despite its own profound misgivings about that course of action.

# IV

It is evident, in retrospect, that Washington considerably underestimated the difficulties of establishing an independent "third force" in Europe. That concept had been based upon several precariously balanced propositions: that a Soviet threat existed awesome enough to compel Europeans to submerge ancient rivalries, but not so awesome as to prevent them from acting in a self-confident and decisive manner; that American economic assistance would stimulate self-reliance without encouraging dependency; that no further initiatives would be necessary to sustain a European order whose collective interests would be compatible with, though independent of, those of the United States. It did not take long for the shakiness of these assumptions to become apparent.

"It is curious that there is so little discussion of the strategic aspects of European integration," F. B. A. Rundall, of the British Foreign Office, noted in February, 1948. "One would imagine that Mr. Lippmann or a similar pundit would have taken up the point that, for the countries concerned, the economic decisions involved in integration are inevitably bound up with considerations of strategy and common defence in which the United States are no less involved. Yet perhaps this is a hare that no one wishes to start before the elections."[66] To the extent that domestic political considerations required a step-by-step approach to the expansion of American commitments overseas, Rundall was on target. Yet, one has the impression that American planners were genuinely surprised, quite apart from their concern about public and Congressional reactions, to have the issue of military security in Europe raised in the first place.

They themselves had consistently deprecated the probability of a Soviet military attack. "The Soviet effort in Europe is a *political* one, not a *military* one," Kennan had repeatedly argued. "The Soviet aim is not to undertake a military conquest which could only be followed by Red Army occupation of Western Europe. . . . The aim is rather to establish in that area a system of indirect control which will give them power without responsibility."[67] Admittedly, no one could rule out the possibility of war altogether. "[T]he threat of war, intended or unintended, will become greater in proportion to weaknesses in the economy, military force, and foreign policy of the United States," the Pentagon's Joint Intelligence Committee noted in February, 1948. But as long as reasonable American strength was maintained—and, in particular, as long as the deterrent power of the American atomic monopoly remained in existence—then the prospect of war in Europe by anything other than gross miscalculation on Moscow's part seemed very remote.[68]

Nevertheless, the whole point of the Marshall Plan had been to restore self-confidence, so that Europe would be in a position to defend itself. From this perspective, the European state of mind was at least as important as American intelligence estimates. It came as something of a shock, therefore, to have Ernest Bevin calling Washington's attention in January, 1948 to "the further encroachment of the Soviet tide" and the need to "reinforce the physical barriers which still guard our Western civilisation," in terms Dean Acheson might have found useful in prodding obdurate Congressmen toward a grudging acceptance of international responsibilities.[69] The Russians, with their usual deftness in producing responses opposite from those intended, punctuated Bevin's point dramatically by staging a coup in Czechoslovakia the following month: this event, together with warnings from other European leaders in addition to Bevin, was sufficient to convince many in Washington that the Marshall Plan alone would not restore self-confidence in Europe; some form of explicit military guarantee would be needed as well.[70]*

Such guarantees, though, would raise problems. There was no assurance that Congress would authorize a direct military commitment to the defense of Western Europe, or what the exact nature of that commitment would be.[71] There was the question of what countries would be covered by such a guarantee: for the United States to undertake to defend everyone would be to exceed American capabilities; for it to leave certain countries out might only invite aggression against them.[72] There was concern that such a guarantee

---

* The British Embassy in Washington had noted in September, 1947: "If it were not for the obstreperous behaviour of the Soviet Union, Marshall would never have made his suggestions, or, had he done so, they would have received almost no public support. The Soviet Union has not only succeeded in preventing the United States from retreating into its prewar isolationism but it is now ensuring that the United States will take an increasingly active part in the affairs of Western Europe." [Inverchapel to Foreign Office, September 6, 1947, Foreign Office Records, FO 371/61056, Public Record Office, London.]

might sap the Europeans' resolve to defend themselves in the first place. "If they are not willing to defend their national independence at this risk," Kennan argued in April, 1948, "then perhaps they would indeed be beyond helping. For there are very definite limits—which people here are constantly forgetting—on the ability of this country to shoulder alone the risks and responsibilities of keeping alive the hope for a continuation of civilization in large parts of this globe."[73]

Cautious negotiations with both allies and Congressional leaders over the next year solved some of these problems. The administration assured Congress that the proposed North Atlantic Treaty involved no obligation to go to war without its consent.[74] The problem of limited resources was addressed by stressing the extent to which an explicit commitment to defend Western Europe would in itself deter the Russians without more specific measures having to be taken; indeed, Secretary of Defense Louis Johnson even suggested that NATO might make it possible to *reduce* the American defense budget.[75] Washington carefully undertook no obligation to station additional troops in Europe, reviving instead the old pre-World War II concept of the United States as an "arsenal" supplying military hardware to the Europeans, who would themselves furnish the manpower. As John Hickerson put it late in 1948: "It is a question of committing, not forces now, but the potential of Pittsburgh and Detroit."[76]*

But the problem of reconciling self-sufficiency with reassurance was not so easily resolved. Despite official claims that the new alliance would facilitate more than it would impede European integration,[77] Kennan was quietly predicting to his colleagues that "this arrangement will come to overshadow, and probably to replace, any development in the direction of European union":

> Instead of the development of a real federal structure in Europe which would aim to embrace all free European countries, which would be a political force in its own right, and which would have behind it the logic of geography and historical development, we will get an irrevocable congealment of the division of Europe into two military zones: a Soviet zone and a U.S. zone. Instead of the ability to divest ourselves gradually of the basic responsibility for the security of western Europe, we will get a legal perpetuation of that responsibility. In the long run, such a legalistic structure must crack up on the rocks of reality; for a divided Europe is not permanently viable, and the political will of the U.S. people is not sufficient to enable us to support western Europe indefinitely as a military appendage.[78]

---

* The Americans were "only too ready to place a gun in the hands of any natural enemy of the Soviet Union," a confidential British political report had noted in the summer of 1948. "[W]ith 50% of the world's industrial capacity but only 7% of its population," the United States "must inevitably adopt a policy which the cynical might compare to the hiring of mercenaries." [Confidential Political Report #8, "Military Aid for Western Europe," June 26, 1948, Foreign Office Records, FO 371/68019.]

"The doubts and criticisms he raises regarding the Atlantic Pact . . . unquestionably have a certain validity," Bohlen wrote to Acheson early in 1949 in a memorandum which, while addressed to the views of James P. Warburg, could have applied to Kennan's as well. "It is, however, the same old story—while clearly expressing the objections to it, he does not seem to offer any feasible alternative. . . . I entirely agree with him that the primary danger is political and not military, but I do not think he fully values the intimate relationship between economic recovery, political stability, and a sense of security against external aggression."[79]

This was, in fact, the essence of the problem. A European "third force" could only be built upon a foundation of European self-confidence, a fact Kennan himself had recognized in supporting the Marshall Plan. But it was Europeans, not Americans, who would determine when the point of self-confidence had been reached, and what would be necessary to sustain it. If they concluded that self-confidence depended upon a formal American military commitment, then Washington, whatever its reservations about the effect this might have upon European self-reliance, was hardly in a position to argue. "I recognize fully that military alliances aren't worth a tinker's dam," Walter Bedell Smith noted with brutal candor in the summer of 1949, "yet those people do attach far greater importance to the scrap of paper pledging support than we ever have."[80]

If the issue of military security posed problems for the "third force" idea, so to did the awkward question of who should belong to it. Germany's position raised the most obvious difficulties. The collapse of talks with the Russians on a comprehensive German settlement late in 1947 pushed the United States, Britain, and France toward a consolidation of political and economic institutions in their three occupation zones, as much as a matter of administrative convenience as by subtle geopolitical design. By the summer of 1948, they had agreed, in what came to be known as the "London Conference" program, to allow Germans "those governmental responsibilities which are compatible with the minimum requirements of occupation and control and which ultimately will enable them to assume full governmental responsibility."[81] What this meant, as an internal State Department policy statement acknowledged, was the reconstitution of western Germany "as a political entity capable of participating in and contributing to the reconstruction of Europe."[82]

There was no escaping the fact, though, that a divided Germany would pose profound implications for the idea of a European "third force." No one was more sensitive to these than Kennan, who as late as 1947 had been prepared to contemplate the partition of Germany with equanimity.[83] What changed Kennan's mind was his growing preference for a multipolar over a bipolar postwar order, and the importance, in that scheme of things, of having an independent center of political, military, and economic power on the European continent. A permanently divided Germany, with each half the client of a rival non-European superpower, would not only ruin chances for a mutual withdrawal of Soviet and American forces and preclude any possibility of weaning away Moscow's East European satellites; it would also, by leaving a highly skilled and highly nationalistic people artificially separated, create a volatile and unstable political balance, subject to revanchist pressures from both sides of the line. With these considerations in mind, Kennan late in 1948 proposed an approach to the Russians looking toward a pull-back of occupation forces to specific garrison areas, and the establishment, after free elections, of an independent, demilitarized, neutral, but unified German state.[84]

Kennan's "Program A," as his proposal came to be known, raised fundamental questions as to where the American interest in Europe lay. Was the balance of power there to be maintained by accepting as permanent the division of the Continent, which in turn implied permanent Soviet and American spheres of influence there? Or was Europe to be reconstituted as an entity unto itself, with a unified but presumably "tamed" Germany at its core? The latter alternative—emphatically Kennan's own choice—was by no means rejected out of hand in Washington. Dean Acheson, upon becoming Secretary of State early in 1949, found Kennan's arguments persuasive enough to appoint him to chair a National Security Council steering group charged with formulating an American negotiating position should talks with the Russians on Germany eventually take place. After listening to one Kennan presentation on the subject, Acheson wondered out loud how the London Program looking toward a divided Germany had ever been agreed upon in the first place.[85]*

And yet, despite Acheson's intellectual sympathy for Kennan's approach, the hard reality was that Britain, France, and their smaller neighbors preferred the known risks of a Europe divided into Soviet and American spheres of influence to the imponderables of a unified "third force" that could conceivably fall under German or even Russian control. Bohlen had noted the difficulty when "Program A" was first proposed in the fall of 1948:

> [T]he one faint element of confidence which [the French] cling to is the fact that American troops, however strong in number, stand between them and the Red Army. If you add to that the strong fears to be generated with the prospect of returning power to Germans at the present juncture, I am sure that the general line of approach suggested . . . would have a most unfavorable reaction in France and probably in Holland and Belgium as well.[86]

These reservations became painfully clear when "Program A" was leaked to the press in May, 1949, just before the Council of Foreign Ministers was to take up the future of Germany. Ambassador David Bruce had to reassure the French "that we did not favor withdrawal of US forces or any disposition of

---

* "Kennan is, as you are aware, a powerful influence in the State Department," the British ambassador in Washington reported to the Foreign Office, "and I regard his mission to Germany [in connection with the steering group discussions] as likely to be of particular importance." [Sir Oliver Franks to Foreign Office, March 4, 1949, Foreign Office Records, FO 371/74160.]

those forces which would weaken our influence in [the] European scene."[87]

But the abandonment of "Program A" in no way lessened Washington's determination to end the occupation of Germany; what it meant, rather, was that if the integration of Germany as a whole into Europe as a whole was not possible, then its efforts would be directed toward integrating what remained of Germany into what remained of Europe. Even Kennan recognized the force of this logic: "Either the rest of Europe tries to work with the West German state, as it is now emerging, takes a sympathetic and constructive interest in it, and learns to regard its development as a European as well as a German responsibility, or there will be soon no Germany with which the rest of Europe can cooperate, and no possibility of real unity and strength in Western Europe."[88] It was in this connection that the North Atlantic Treaty interlocked neatly with the London Conference program. Acheson described the relationship early in 1949: "it was doubtful that, without some such pact, the French would ever be reconciled to the inevitable diminution of direct allied control over Germany and the progressive reduction of occupation troops; . . . a pact of this nature would give France a greater sense of security against Germany as well as the Soviet Union and should materially help in the realistic consideration of the problem of Germany."[89]*

There remained, though, the question of where Great Britain would fit into the postwar European order. London had no quarrel in principle with the idea of a "third force" in Europe: "We should use United States aid to gain time," the Cabinet had concluded in a secret session in March, 1948, "but our ultimate aim should be to attain a position in which the countries of western Europe could be independent both of the United States and of the Soviet Union."[90] At the same time, though, Britain had its own overseas responsibilities which the Americans, however much they might have railed against "imperialism" in the past, were reluctant to see too quickly liquidated. "It is essential for the British to take the lead in working towards closer European integration," Robert Lovett argued late in 1948. "However, at least at the present time it would be unwise both for them and for us were a position of strong European leadership to require a lessening of British ties with this country and the Dominions."[91]†

Mindful of these complexities, and with Bevin's approval, Gladwyn Jebb,

* Walter Lippmann made a similar point in a letter to Kennan on February 1, 1949: "The western anxiety about *our* leaving Europe and withdrawing across the Atlantic can be met by the North Atlantic Security Pact. In fact that is its chief advantage, that it supplies the juridical basis for remaining in Europe." [Kennan Papers, Box 28.]

† "[T]he trouble with the British," William Clayton wrote to Lovett in September, 1948, "is that they are hanging on by their eyelashes to the hope that somehow, or other with our help they will be able to preserve the British Empire and their leadership of it. . . . I think if we make it very clear to the British that, with complete cooperation on their part, we can possibly save them but that we cannot save their position as leader of the Empire bloc and do not intend to try, we will begin to see results in our Herculean efforts to pull Europe out of the hole." [Clayton to Lovett, September 17, 1948, Policy Planning Staff Records, Box 27, "Europe 1947–1948."]

British Assistant Under-Secretary of State for Foreign Affairs, wrote to Kennan in April, 1949, proposing informal consultations, not just on the position of Britain in Europe, but on the long-term prospects for European integration in general.[92] Coming at a time when developments with regard both to NATO and West Germany seemed to be undermining the "third force" idea, Jebb's suggestion met with a favorable response from Kennan. The real question, he told the Policy Planning Staff, was "whether the emergence of a united western Europe postulates the formation of a third world power of approximately equal strength to the United States and the Soviet Union. Another way of stating this question is whether there are to be two worlds or three."[93]

There ensued, in preparation for these discussions with the British, the most thorough analysis yet carried out in Washington on the question of what the United States really wanted in Europe: an independent, self-reliant aggregation of power comprising as much of Europe as possible, or a sphere of influence closely linked to Washington.

# V

"[W]e are getting here into very deep spheres of thought about the nature of ourselves as a nation and of the world we live in," Kennan told a group of consultants brought to Washington in June, 1949, to advise the Policy Planning Staff on how to answer Jebb's questions about the future of Europe.* The problem was more than just the achievement of peace and security: "It is a problem of man learning to manipulate his own nature in such a way as to handle effectively those sides of it which are apt to produce violence and degradation and to release in a far greater degree those sides of it which are capable of creating beauty and mastery of environment." The extent to which the United States, acting alone, could accomplish these ends was severely limited:

> [W]e must regard our role in world affairs in these coming years as a much more modest one than many of us are accustomed to think. . . . [W]e must concentrate, as all modest people must, on our own self-respect: on keeping ourselves and our friends above water amid the genuinely great dangers that modern civilization holds, on exercising as beneficial an influence as we can abroad without claiming that we have the insight or the power to effect any vast change of human institutions on a global scale, and meanwhile to try to shape the course of our internal life in such a way as to produce in later

* Among the consultants invited by Kennan to participate were Hans Morgenthau, J. Robert Oppenheimer, Arnold Wolfers, Reinhold Niebuhr, John McCloy, Walter Bedell Smith, and, interestingly, Robert W. Woodruff, Chairman of the Executive Committee of the Coca-Cola Company.

generations people who will be able to make a better and a greater contribution to the improvement of human life. Anything more ambitious than that, and anything that bears with it universal ambitions and pretensions, seems to me to be a form of arrogance and even intolerance based on a terrifying smugness and lack of historical perspective.

"I do not believe that our great moment as a factor in world affairs has yet arrived," Kennan added. "I fervently hope that it has not."[94]

Given this preoccupation with both the limited capabilities and limited wisdom of his countrymen, it is not surprising that Kennan continued to hope for the emergence of a "third force" in Europe, strong enough to maintain the balance of power against Soviet expansionism without an indefinite dependence upon American support. A unified Germany would be the nucleus of such a system, to be sure, but the system would also constrain the Germans by preventing any link-up with the Russians, on the one hand, and by reassuring Germany's western neighbors, on the other. Such a grouping might also attract the allegiance of Moscow's unhappy satellites in Eastern Europe; certainly it would encourage European self-reliance in the area of economic reconstruction. And it would fit within Kennan's larger geopolitical assumption that a world with power distributed among several centers would be more stable than one divided rigidly into two spheres.[95]

The problem, though, was how to keep the Germans from dominating such a grouping. One possibility would be to include Great Britain in it as a counterweight, and Kennan at first leaned toward that idea.[96] But as it became apparent that the British were not prepared to liquidate Commonwealth responsibilities in order to align themselves with the Continent, and as the extent of British financial difficulties became obvious with the devaluation of the pound, Kennan came instead to favor a purely continental grouping, with Britain linked instead to the United States and Canada.[97] Germany would be the dominant power in such a system, but one might hope that the experience of defeat and occupation would have moderated German ambitions.[98] Whether this was the case or not, though, the possibility of German hegemony had to be risked because the alternative—a permanently divided Germany—would leave Europe itself divided, incapable of playing the independent role Kennan had envisaged. There was a certain "horrifying significance" in the fact that the Germans would again "get a place in western Europe which is going to be very important," Kennan admitted to Dean Acheson. "But it often seemed to me, during the war living over there, that what was wrong with Hitler's new order was that it was Hitler's."[99]*

* "Mr. Kennan . . . said that he thought that we must decide whether we and our friends are strong enough as a group to hold the Russians and the Germans or decide that we are not strong enough to do so and therefore resign ourselves to the creation of a third force in Europe which might ultimately be dominated one way or another by the Germans. He added that he was inclined toward the second view and thought that EUR [Division of European Affairs] was in general inclined toward the first." [Minutes, PPS meeting of October 17, 1949, Policy Planning Staff Records, Box 32.]

Not surprisingly, this vision of a European "third force" dominated by Germany met with a less than cordial response in France when the British began circulating rumors there of this trend in American thinking. "It is not necessary to spell out in detail what the French think this would mean for them left alone on the continent to face Germany," Bohlen wrote Kennan from Paris in October, 1949. "[I]f it becomes evident that we are creating an Anglo–American–Canadian bloc as a political reality in our European policy we will not be able to hold on to the nations of Western Europe very long."[100] Bohlen's warning was reinforced later that month by a meeting of United States ambassadors in Western Europe, which concluded unanimously that "no effective integration of Europe would be possible without UK participation because of the belief (not without reason) held by western continental powers of potential German domination if such UK participation did not take place."[101]*

Interestingly, the British Foreign Office, which had taken care earlier in the year to disassociate Britain from participation in a continental bloc, now also questioned the viability of the "third force" concept. No possible combination of powers independent of the United States, Bevin told the Cabinet, was likely in the foreseeable future to develop the military, political, and economic cohesion necessary to resist the Russians: "The conclusion seems inescapable that for the present at any rate the closest association with the United States is essential, not only for the purpose of standing up to Soviet aggression but also in the interests of Commonwealth solidarity and of European unity." It was true that such a policy might well require the subordination of British and European interests to those of the United States. But despite "occasional violence of talk, American public opinion and the American Congress are both peace-loving and cautious, and more likely to err on the side of prudence than of rashness." If that should ever cease to be the case, "it may reasonably be expected that partnership with the United States in a Western system would increase rather than diminish the opportunities for the United Kingdom to apply a brake to American policy is necessary."[102]

"That you were right in your premonitions about the effects of talking to the British about European union I gladly concede," Kennan wrote Bohlen early in November. "The path of lesser resistance and lesser immediate trouble in this matter would have been to keep silent." Nor did he have any intention of challenging the collective opinion of the American ambassadors in Western Europe: "Even if the Secretary agreed one hundred percent with my view, I would not ask him to move in the face of such a body of opinion. Time will tell who is right." But the existing policy, Kennan warned:

(a) gives the Russians no alternative but to continue their present policies or see further areas of central and eastern Europe slide into

---

* John Hickerson had also expressed "grave doubts" as to "whether Germany can safely be absorbed in any association of nations in Western Europe to which the US and UK do not belong." [Hickerson to Kennan, October 15, 1949, Policy Planning Staff Records, Box 27, "Europe 1949."]

a U.S.-dominated alliance against them, and in this way makes unlikely any settlement of east-west differences except by war; and

(b) promises the Germans little more in the western context than an indefinite status as an overcrowded, occupied and frustrated semi-state, thus depriving them of a full stake in their own resistance to eastern pressures and forfeiting their potential aid in the establishment of a military balance between east and west.

"You may have your ideas where one goes from here on such a path and at what point it is supposed to bring us out on the broad uplands of a secure and peaceful Europe," Kennan added, with some bitterness. "If so, I hope you will tell the Secretary about them. . . . I find it increasingly difficult to give guidance on this point."[103]

Bohlen found Kennan's attitude less than helpful: "I had hoped we could profitably correspond on such subjects, but frankly I am not interested in polemics." "You know me well enough to take into account my polemic temperament," Kennan wrote back. But "I agree that there is no point in continuing the debate. A decision has fallen. . . . Perhaps it was the right one. None of us sees deeply enough into the future to be entirely sure about these things. But I find my estimate of my own potential usefulness here shaken by the depth of this disagreement . . . and I will be happier than ever if, as I hope, it will be possible for me . . . to subside quietly into at least a year or two of private life."[104]

# VI

It is curious that Kennan and Bohlen, who agreed so completely on the interpretation of Soviet behavior, should have disagreed so adamantly about the future of Europe, to the point that each had wound up by the end of 1949 defending precisely the opposite position on spheres of influence from the one each had advanced at the beginning of 1945. Kennan's initial advocacy of an outright division of the Continent had been modified by the evolution of his thinking on the advantages of multipolarity as a stabilizing force, by his awareness of the limits of American power, and by his growing conviction, as he recalled in his *Memoirs*, "that we were not fitted, either institutionally or temperamentally, to be an imperial power in the grand manner."[105] Bohlen's initial resistance to spheres of influence had been eroded by the failure of negotiations with the Russians, by the success of the Marshall Plan and NATO, and by the obvious willingness of Europeans themselves to welcome an American assertion of influence over them. Significantly, it was Bohlen whose views reflected at each point the mainstream of official thinking in Washington; Kennan, on this question at least, was the perpetual critic.

It is worth asking, though, why the Kennan vision of an autonomous "third force" in Europe, which at an earlier stage had had widespread support in Washington, failed to materialize. The reason, almost certainly, is that the Europeans themselves did not want it. Confronted by what they perceived to be a malevolent challenge to the balance of power from the east, they set about inviting in a more benign form of countervailing power from the west rather than undertake the costly, protracted and problematic process of rebuilding their own. The United States, with some reluctance, went along.

Time would indeed tell, as Kennan observed, whether the Europeans were wise in choosing this alternative; even the passage of four decades provides no clear answer to that question. What can be said is that the system that did come into being in Europe after World War II, however improvised, artificial and arbitrary, has proven to be far more stable and resilent than Kennan or anyone else could have foreseen at the time.[106] How long it will last is anyone's guess, but given all the accidents, irrationalities, and perversities of history, that uncertainty hardly lessens the necessity of being grateful for small favors.

# 4

# Drawing Lines:
# The Defensive Perimeter Strategy in
# East Asia, 1947-1951

ONE of the frustrations of being a statesman is that one's speeches are not always remembered for the reasons one wants them to be. Few have had better cause to acknowledge this difficulty than Dean Acheson, whose National Press Club speech of January 12, 1950, intended as the enunciation of a new East Asian strategy in the wake of China's "fall" to communism, has more often been recalled as having invited the North Korean attack on South Korea through its exclusion of that latter country from the American "defensive perimeter" in the Pacific. Acheson always insisted that his speech only reflected established policy and could not have had the effect attributed to it; still one wonders whether privately he may not have felt, as General J. Lawton Collins later suggested, "like a batter swinging at a bad ball [who] would have liked to have had that swing back again."[1]

Given presently available evidence, it is impossible to confirm or refute charges that Acheson's speech encouraged the North Koreans to attack.[2] Sufficient evidence does exist, though, to demonstrate that there was nothing casual or inadvertent about his proclaimed strategy of defending offshore islands while avoiding direct commitments on the Asian mainland. By the time Acheson spoke, this "defensive perimeter" concept had received endorse-

This essay was originally prepared for a conference on post-World War II Sino-American relations, sponsored by the East Asian Institute of Columbia University and held at Mount Kisco, New York, in June, 1978. It was subsequently published in Dorothy Borg and Waldo Heinrichs, eds., *Uncertain Years: Chinese-American Relations, 1947–1950* (New York: 1980), pp. 61–118, and appears here in a revised form.

ments from the Commander in Chief, Far East, the Joint Chiefs of Staff, the National Security Council, and the President of the United States. The product of no single individual or agency within the government, it had nonetheless come to be accepted, by early 1950, as the most appropriate strategic posture for the United States in East Asia.

But this consensus in support of the "defensive perimeter" proved to be remarkably fragile. Within six months, the Truman administration had reversed its own strategy: it had committed air, naval, and ground forces to the defense of South Korea, it had accelerated military assistance to the French in Indochina, and, by sending the Seventh Fleet to patrol the Taiwan Strait, it had involved the United States directly in the Chinese civil war. This abrupt turnabout reveals much about shifting perceptions of interests and threats in East Asia at the time; it is, as well, an illuminating commentary—as was Acheson's Press Club speech—on the gap between the intentions of statesmen and the consequences of their actions.

# I

"Today, so far as I can learn, we are operating without any over-all strategic concept for the entire western Pacific area." This warning, contained in a March, 1948, message from George F. Kennan, Director of the State Department's Policy Planning Staff, to Secretary of State George C. Marshall, did much to stimulate thinking within the government on American priorities in East Asia. With his recipient's background obviously in mind, Kennan apologized "for being so bold, as a civilian, to offer suggestions on matters which are largely military; but it is essential that some over-all pattern including military as well as the political factors be evolved." He then went on to propose the following as "the most desirable political-strategic concept for the western Pacific area":

1. While we would endeavor to influence events on the mainland of Asia in ways favorable to our security, we would not regard any mainland areas as vital to us. Korea would accordingly be evacuated as soon as possible.

2. Okinawa would be made the center of our offensive striking power in the western Pacific area. It would constitute the central and most advanced point of a U-shaped U.S. security zone embracing the Aleutians, the Ryukyus, the former Japanese mandated islands, and of course Guam. We would then rely on Okinawa-based air power, plus our advance naval power, to prevent the assembling and launching [of] any amphibious force from any mainland port in . . . east-central or northeast Asia.

3. Japan and the Philippines would remain outside this security

area, and we would not attempt to keep bases or forces on their territory, *provided* that they remained entirely demilitarized and that no
other power made any effort to obtain strategic facilities on them.
They would thus remain neutralized areas, enjoying complete political
independence, situated on the immediate flank of our security zone.

If Washington could accept this approach, then "we would have firm points
of orientation for our short-term policies in this area." Without some such
concept, "we cannot move at all." Kennan concluded: "I need hardly stress
the desirability of an early clarification of our policy in this area in view of
the trend of world events and the necessity of having all our hatches bat-
tened down for the coming period."[3]

Kennan found few objections to this strategy when he discussed it with
General Douglas MacArthur in Tokyo that same month.* MacArthur proposed a defensive line including the Aleutians, Midway, the former Japanese
mandated islands, Okinawa, the Philippines, Australia, New Zealand, and the
British and Dutch islands in the southwest Pacific. Okinawa, he stressed, was
the strongpoint: from it he could control each of the ports in northern Asia
from which an amphibious operation could be launched. He also agreed with
Kennan that it would not be desirable to retain United States troops permanently in Japan, although he did consider it necessary to hold on to Clark
Field in the Philippines.[4] For the next year and a half, MacArthur would repeatedly express the idea that as a result of World War II the American
strategic frontier had shifted from the West Coast to the Asian offshore island
chain, and that the security of the United States depended on keeping those
islands out of hostile hands.[5]

By the summer of 1949, the concept of a "defensive perimeter" had also
become widely accepted in Washington. A Central Intelligence Agency study
in May stressed the importance of the offshore islands in facilitating access
to the strategic raw materials of India and Southeast Asia, especially if the
Suez route should be closed.[6] The Joint Chiefs of Staff informed the National
Security Council in June that "from the military point of view, the ultimate
minimum United States position in the Far East vis-à-vis the USSR, one to
which we are rapidly being forced, requires at least our present degree of
control of the Asian offshore chain."[7] In November, an internal State Department memorandum cited Pentagon authorities in support of the proposi-

* Kennan had outlined an earlier version of the defensive perimeter concept before
leaving on his East Asian trip: "We should make a careful study to see what parts of
the Pacific and Far Eastern world are absolutely vital to our security, and we should
concentrate our policy on seeing to it that those areas remain in hands which we can
control or rely on. It is my guess . . . that Japan and the Philippines will be found to
be the corner-stones of such a Pacific security system and that if we can contrive to retain effective control over these areas there can be no serious threat to our security from
the East within our time." [PPS/23, "Review of Current Trends: U.S. Foreign Policy,"
February 24, 1948, U.S. Department of State, *Foreign Relations of the United States*
(hereafter *FR*) : *1948*, I, 525.]

tion that "our position is not directly jeopardized by the loss of China so long as the security of the islands continues to be maintained."[8] And a draft National Security Council paper concluded the following month that the "minimum position" required to defend Asia "against future Soviet aggression" would consist of "at least our present military position in the Asian offshore island chain, and in the event of war its denial to the Communists."[9]

Acheson was hardly breaking new ground, then, when he told the National Press Club that "this defensive perimeter runs along the Aleutians to Japan and then goes to the Ryukyus . . . [and] from the Ryukyus to the Philippine Islands." As he later recalled, "with the authority of the Joint Chiefs of Staff and General MacArthur behind me, it did not occur to me that I should be charged with innovating policy or political heresy."[10] But an examination of the assumptions that had led the State Department, the Joint Chiefs, and MacArthur to agree on this concept reveals striking disparities; these in turn suggest the unstable nature of the consensus upon which the "defensive perimeter" strategy rested and help to account for the rapidity of its demise.

# II

The State Department based its support of the "defensive perimeter" idea on a strong sense of pessimism regarding the ability of the United States to influence events on the Asian mainland. The frustrating outcome of General Marshall's mission to China just prior to his entering the Department had done much to generate this sense of discouragement; Marshall's own considerable influence as Secretary of State strongly reinforced it.[11] The Department did yield to Congressional pressures for a limited program of economic and military aid to Nationalist China in 1948, but it did so more for the purpose of defusing opposition to the European Recovery Program than from any conviction that aid to China might actually be effective.[12] Acheson, upon becoming Secretary of State, made no effort to conceal his own skepticism. In his August, 1949, letter transmitting the China "White Paper" to the President, he argued bluntly with reference to Chiang Kai-shek's defeat that "nothing that this country did or could have done within the reasonable limits of its capabilities could have changed that result; nothing that was left undone by this country has contributed to it."[13] United States assistance could be effective if it was the missing component in the situation, he noted in his National Press Club speech, but "the United States cannot furnish all these components to solve the question. It can not furnish determination, it can not furnish the will, and it can not furnish the loyalty of a people to its government."[14]

Reinforcing the Department's doubts about Washington's ability to shape events on the mainland was the conviction that China was not vital to the security of the United States in any event. This conclusion stemmed from a sharp awareness of the limits of American power, and of the need, as a consequence, to distinguish vital from peripheral interests.[15] It also grew out of a tendency to define interests primarily in terms of industrial war-making capacity: hence, Kennan's conclusion that there were only five vital centers of power in the world—the United States, the Soviet Union, Great Britain, the Rhine valley, and Japan—and that the task of containment was to see to it that the four not then under Soviet control remained free of it.[16] "If this is true," Kennan told an audience at the Naval War College in October,

> you do not need to hold land positions on the Eurasian land mass to protect our national security. If that is true, you can theoretically content yourself with permitting most of these land areas to be in the hands of people who are hostile to ourselves as long as you exercise that power of inhibiting the assembling and launching of amphibious forces from many Asian ports.[17]

Acheson set out the implications of this line of reasoning in executive session testimony before the Senate Foreign Relations Committee in May, 1950: "I think we have to start out with the realization that the main center of our activity at present has got to be in Europe. We cannot scatter our shots equally all over the world. We just haven't got enough shots to do that."[18]

Still another persistent theme in the State Department's thinking had to do with the need to be selective about allies. Progressive nationalism was the wave of the future in Asia, Department East Asian specialists believed; the United States, if it expected to retain influence in that part of the world, would have to accommodate itself to that trend.[19] This obviously meant avoiding commitments to support colonialism, as in the case of the French in Indochina or the Dutch in Indonesia; it also meant putting distance between the United States and what were perceived to be the reactionary nationalist regimes of Chiang Kai-shek in China and Syngman Rhee in South Korea.[20] Departures from this principle ran the risk not only of opposing irreversible forces in Asia but also of associating the United States with unpredictable clients whose interests, however impeccably anti-communist, did not always parallel its own.

Finally, there existed within the State Department the conviction that even if China should become a communist state, the Russians would not necessarily be able to dominate it. In his National Press Club speech and in other public pronouncements early in 1950, Acheson had hinted broadly at the possibility of differences between the Russians and the Chinese Communists.[21] Only with the opening of State Department and other official archives, however, has it become clear to what extent United States policy toward East Asia from 1947 had been based on that expectation.[22] As a Department memorandum put it in November, 1949:

> We anticipate the possibility that great strains will develop between Peiping and Moscow. These strains would not only work to our ad-

vantage but would contribute to the desired end of permitting China to develop its own life independently rather than as a Russian satellite.[23]

It was not always clear whether the Chinese people themselves would overthrow the Communists once their ties to the Russians had become apparent, or whether the Communists would follow Tito's example in Yugoslavia and repudiate Moscow's leadership. But since the Russians would control China in neither case, there was general agreement within the Department that the "loss" of that mainland area to communism would constitute no irreparable disaster for American security interests, and hence did not merit remedial action.

The Joint Chiefs of Staff also came to support the "defensive perimeter" strategy, but by a different route. Unlike the State Department, the Chiefs consistently took the position that the United States could influence events on the mainland through a selective and well-coordinated program of military aid. "The latent resources and manpower of China are such," they argued early in 1947, "that even small amounts of United States assistance to the National Government will materially strengthen its morale and at the same time weaken the morale of the Chinese communists."[24] Similar assumptions lay behind Lieutenant General Albert C. Wedemeyer's September, 1947, recommendation that the United States furnish the Nationalists with the material support necessary to prevent Manchuria from becoming a Soviet satellite, and Vice Admiral Oscar C. Badger's subsequent advocacy of limited military aid to anti-Communist regional warlords once it became apparent that Chiang Kai-shek's government was on the verge of collapse.[25]

The Joint Chiefs found it difficult as well to accept the view that significant differences could exist between the Chinese Communists and the Russians. "It is believed," a June, 1947, study pointed out, "that the Chinese communists, as all others, are Moscow inspired and thus motivated by the same basic totalitarian and anti-democratic policies as are the communist parties in other countries of the world. Accordingly, they should be regarded as tools of Soviet policy."[26] A victory for communism in China would, therefore, significantly affect the world balance of power, since it would make that country a satellite of the Soviet Union.[27] The Chiefs concluded:

> The United States must seek to prevent the growth of any single power or coalition to a position of such strength as to constitute a threat to the Western Hemisphere. A Soviet position of dominance over Asia, Western Europe, or both, would constitute a major threat to United States security.
>
> United States security interests require that China be kept free from Soviet domination; otherwise all of Asia will in all probability pass into the sphere of the USSR.[28]

But whatever the Chiefs' perception of the interests at stake in China, they shared with the State Department a keen sense of the limits on American resources and of the need to rank interests accordingly. It is significant that in

1947 they placed China thirteenth on a list of countries whose defense they considered vital to the national security of the United States.[29] By mid-1948, China had dropped to seventeenth place on a list of military aid priorities approved by the State–War–Navy–Air Force Coordinating Committee.[30] "[C]urrent United States commitments involving the use or distinctly possible use of armed forces are very greatly in excess of our present ability to fulfill them either promptly or effectively," the Joint Chiefs warned Secretary of Defense James Forrestal in November, 1948.[31] During the MacArthur hearings in 1951, General Marshall recalled that "we would literally have [had] to take over control of the country in order to insure that the [Chinese Nationalist] armies functioned with efficiency. . . . At that time . . . we had one and a third divisions in the entire United States."[32]

Moreover, mainland China did not appear to provide favorable terrain upon which to fight if war with the Soviet Union came. As early as July, 1945, a Joint Chiefs of Staff examination of postwar strategic requirements had defined as among "potentially critical operational zones" the offshore island chain, but no points on the Asian mainland.[33] "[In] the case of warfare with our ideological opponents," another study concluded in April, 1947, "China could be a valuable ally only if we diverted to her great quantities of food and equipment manufactured in this country. It is extremely doubtful that the end result would be any great assistance to our war effort."[34] The Joint War Plans Committee concluded two months later that while it might be desirable to hold certain areas around Qingdao for the purpose of aiding Chinese Nationalist forces and conducting strategic air strikes against the Soviet Union, "this course of action would be beyond Allied capabilities during the first phases of the war and . . . any U.S. forces in the area on D-Day should be withdrawn when their positions become untenable." East Asia itself, because of its distance from the centers of Soviet warmaking capability, was not "a feasible avenue of approach to the USSR."[35]

Nor did American strategic planners believe that the Russians would gain much by controlling that part of the world. "Soviet conquest of . . . Asia," the Joint War Plans Committee concluded in August, 1947, "would provide few military advantages and would not substantially increase their over-all military capability."[36] The Joint Staff Planners reiterated this conclusion in September, 1949: "The inability of the USSR to rapidly extend lines of communications, base development operations, and military and political control through the vast areas of Siberia and into Communist-dominated China appears to preclude military exploitation of this area, to our detriment, in the immediate future."[37] A comprehensive National Security Council study of Asian policy determined later that year that the United States possessed neither primary strategic interests nor the means to achieve its objectives in case of war on the Asian mainland. Accordingly, "the current basic concept of strategy in the event of war with the USSR is to conduct a strategic offensive in the 'West' and a strategic defense in the 'East.' " This meant the "minimum expenditure of military manpower and material" in such areas as would show "the most results in return for the United States effort expended."[38]

But the Joint Chiefs of Staff and the State Department were not the only significant shapers of strategy in East Asia. Of almost equal importance was General of the Army Douglas MacArthur, Commander in Chief of U.S. Forces, Far East, and Supreme Commander, Allied Powers, Japan. MacArthur, like the Joint Chiefs, saw possibilities for effective military aid to China, provided the United States concentrated on the issue of security and put aside its concern for internal reform. "Desirable as such reform may be," he wrote in March, 1948, "its importance is but secondary to the issue of civil strife now engulfing the land, and the two issues are as impossible of synchronization as it would be to alter the structural design of a house while the same was being consumed by flame."[39] Chiang Kai-shek might be on his way out, MacArthur commented in August, 1949, "but as long as he will fight I believe in helping him, as I would help anyone else who would fight the Communists."[40]

MacArthur came to this position, though, by a process of reasoning very different from that of the Joint Chiefs of Staff or the Department of State. For him, American strategic interests in the world were undifferentiated: "[I]f we embark upon a general policy to bulwark the frontiers of freedom against the assaults of political despotism, one major frontier is no less important than another, and a decisive breach of any will inevitably threaten to engulf all."[41] Victories of communism in China were those of the Soviet Union; the dangers they posed to United States security were no less than those created by the expansion of communism elsewhere in the world. As Senator H. Alexander Smith noted following a conversation with MacArthur in September, 1949: "He is violently against any form of communism wherever it shows itself and would back any of the anticommunist forces everywhere in the world."[42]

The General's well-known conviction that Asia was being neglected in favor of Europe grew logically out of this perception of undifferentiated interests. "It no longer appears realistic to consider the Far East as a static and secure flank in the military contest with Communism," he cabled General Wedemeyer in November, 1948.[43] By 1949, he was complaining vigorously about a "Europe first" mentality in Washington and a corresponding inclination to "scuttle the Pacific." He attributed these tendencies to the influence of Marshall and the "bright young men" around him, and to the inability of the Joint Chiefs to "understand" East Asia, a failing stemming from their concentration on European affairs during and since World War II.[44] What Washington failed to see, a study prepared by MacArthur's staff argued, was that the Soviet offensive had shifted from the European theater to East Asia, partly as the result of the success of containment in Europe. United States military planning had not shifted accordingly: as a consequence, Soviet utilization of the resources of East Asia, if linked with the industrial machine of Japan, "might prove ultimately decisive."[45]

But MacArthur was much less clear about how the United States should deal with this threat. He was fond of insisting that "anyone in favor of sending American ground troops to fight on Chinese soil should have his head examined,"[46] a point of view that would appear to have ruled out direct military assistance to Chiang Kai-shek. Moreover, MacArthur was extraordinarily sensitive to the self-defeating effects of prolonged military occupations (a characteristic he shared with Kennan).* One of his chief priorities after 1948 was to end the American occupation of Japan;[47] it seems unlikely that he would have welcomed similar responsibilities elsewhere. Given these circumstances, given the limited resources made available by Washington, it made sense from MacArthur's perspective to endorse the island perimeter concept as the most efficient way to retain a military presence in Asia without getting bogged down either in protracted war or in protracted occupation.

Hence, though the State Department, the Joint Chiefs of Staff, and MacArthur all came to support the "defensive perimeter" strategy, they did so for very different reasons. State saw the offshore island chain as a detached position from which to encourage Asian nationalism as a bulwark against Soviet expansionism. The Chiefs regarded it as a line capable of being held at minimal cost, should war come, while the strategic offensive proceeded elsewhere. MacArthur saw it as the nation's first line of defense and, more distantly, as a series of bases from which to launch offensive operations aimed at regaining the mainland, although he never made clear the nature and precise objectives of those operations. These differences in priorities and expectations became painfully clear as the Truman administration sought to apply the "defensive perimeter" strategy in three areas that did not easily fit it: Taiwan, Indochina, and Korea.

# III

There was never any question, whether in the Pentagon, the State Department, or the Far East Command, as to the strategic importance of Taiwan once it became apparent that Chiang Kai-shek could not retain control of the mainland. The prospect of a Taiwan dominated by "Kremlin-directed Communists," the Joint Chiefs concluded late in 1948, would be "very seriously detrimental to our national security," since it would give the Communists the capability of dominating sea lines of communication between Japan and Malaya, and of threatening the Philippines, the Ryukyus, and ultimately Japan itself.[48] A State Department draft report to the National Security Council early in 1949 argued that "the basic aim of the U.S. should be to deny Formosa and the Pescadores to the Communists."[49] MacArthur was particularly adamant on this point. He told Max W. Bishop, Chief of the State Department's Division of Northeast Asian Affairs, that "if Formosa went to the Chinese Communists

---

* MacArthur would call, in October, 1950, for the early withdrawal of U.S. forces from Korea once military operations had been completed "to the end that we may save . . . the Korean people from the undue impact of American troops upon the peaceful settlement of their internal affairs." [MacArthur to Truman, October 30, 1950, MacArthur Papers, Record Group 5, Box 1A, File 5.] For Kennan's views on military occupations, see his *Memoirs: 1925–1950* (Boston: 1967), pp. 371–72, 387, 438–39, 447–48.

our whole defensive position in the Far East [would be] definitely lost; that it could only result eventually in putting our defensive line back to the west coast of the continental United States."[50]

It is interesting to note, however, that neither the State Department, the Joint Chiefs, nor MacArthur intially favored using American forces to deny Taiwan to the new People's Republic of China. The Chiefs, citing "the current disparity between our military strength and our many global obligations," opposed military involvement on the grounds that "this might . . . lead to the necessity for relatively major effort there, thus making it impossible then to meet more important emergencies elsewhere."[51] MacArthur repeatedly made it clear that he did not favor the creation of American military bases on Taiwan; the important thing was to deny the island to potential adversaries, while retaining the use of such other more easily controlled strongpoints as Okinawa and the Philippines.[52] The State Department opposed military action on the grounds that overt attempts to detach Taiwan from China would risk offending Chinese nationalism and might undermine the Department's strategy of attempting to drive a wedge between the People's Republic and the USSR. As Acheson put it: "We are most anxious to avoid raising the spectre of an American-created irredentist issue just at the time we shall be seeking to exploit the genuinely Soviet-created irredentist issue in Manchuria and Sinkiang."[53]

The State Department's preferred solution, which the National Security Council and the President approved in February, 1949, was to deny the island to *both* the Chinese Communists and the Chinese Nationalists by discreetly promoting a Taiwan autonomy movement.[54] To this end, Acheson assigned Livingston Merchant, then Counselor at the United States Embassy in Nanjing, to contact authorities on Taiwan with a view toward discouraging any further influx of refugees from the mainland, encouraging Taiwanese participation in the government, and, upon receipt of assurances that action had been taken in these two areas, promising American economic aid. Acheson stressed the need for secrecy: "It is a cardinal point in our thinking that if the present policy is to have any hope of success in Formosa, we must carefully conceal our wish to separate the island from mainland control."[55] Merchant soon reported back that the Taiwanese autonomy movements were poorly organized and that even if an independent regime could be established, the United States would still run the risk of offending Chinese nationalism if it sent military forces to defend the island. Other reports indicated that Taiwan was already "packed with troops" loyal to Chiang Kai-shek. By May, Merchant was advising Acheson that the strategy of promoting Taiwan's autonomy had failed.[56]*

* In a Policy Planning Staff paper drafted early in July, 1949, but immediately canceled, Kennan argued that "Formosan separatism is the only concept which has sufficient grassroots appeal to resist communism." This could now be achieved only by persuading other East Asian powers to intervene in Taiwan, obviously an unlikely prospect, or through unilateral United States action to eject Chiang Kai-shek's forces from the island. "I personally feel that if the second course were to be adopted and to be carried through with sufficient resolution, speed, ruthlessness and self-assurance, the way Theodore Roosevelt

Acheson had anticipated the possibility that even with an independent Taiwan, the United States ultimately might find it necessary to send troops to defend the island. In a National Security Council meeting on March 1 he had urged the military not to exclude from its thinking "the possibility that it might later be called upon to employ modest military strength in Formosa in collaboration with other friendly forces."[57] Whether in response to this suggestion or not, the Joint Chiefs advised the Secretary of Defense that, while they did not favor overt military action with regard to Taiwan at that time, "there can be no categorical assurance, however, that other future circumstances, extending to war itself, might not make overt military action eventually advisable from the over-all standpoint of our national security."[58] Later that spring the Joint Staff Planners worked out a new emergency war plan specifying that, in case of war with the Soviet Union, provision would be made for "denial to the Soviets of the use of Formosa as a base for offensive operations."[59]* It is not clear to what extent the State Department was aware of this plan, which gained the final approval of the Joint Chiefs of Staff on December 8, 1949. Its general direction, though, was consistent with the position Acheson had taken in the National Security Council the previous March.

Meanwhile, the question of Taiwan had become embroiled in American domestic politics. Congressional supporters of Chiang Kai-shek had already demonstrated their power by forcing on the administration a continued program of limited military aid to the Nationalists; they also managed to provoke angry debates in August over the China White Paper and in September over W. Walton Butterworth's nomination to be Assistant Secretary of State for Far Eastern Affairs.[60] In October, Senator H. Alexander Smith, an influential Republican member of the Senate Foreign Relations Committee, traveled to Taiwan over the objections of the State Department;[61]† he returned

---

might have done it, it would not only be successful but would have an electrifying effect in this country and throughout the Far East." Kennan argued that if the President and the National Security Council were willing to act on this basis, "then my personal view is that we should take the plunge." If not, efforts should be made to prepare United States and world opinion for a Chinese Communist takeover of the island." [PPS/53, "United States Policy toward Formosa and the Pescadores," drafted by Kennan, July 6, 1949, but canceled the same day, *FR: 1949*, IX, 356–59. See also George F. Kennan, *Memoirs: 1950–1963* (Boston: 1972), p. 54.]

* The Joint Strategic Plans Committee had concluded in September, 1949, that "the future of Formosa is a critical factor, for should this strategic island come under active Communist control, and should its relations with the USSR be close enough to extend base rights or permit Soviet development in the area, a revision of our war plans would be required." [JSPC 877/72, September 14, 1949, Army Staff Records, P & O 1949–50, 381 TS, sec. 3, case 56, Modern Military Branch, National Archives.]

† Smith's diary and correspondence for 1949 provide detailed information about his decision to concentrate on the issue of Taiwan. There is strong evidence that the Moral Re-Armament movement played an important role in shaping Smith's views on this subject through the activities of John Roots, a member of Smith's staff, and H. Kenaston Twitchell, Smith's son-in-law. Roots and Twitchell, in turn, maintained close contacts

convinced that the United States should under no circumstances allow the island to fall into the hands of the People's Republic. Senator William F. Knowland, upon his return from a similar trip in December, called for the dispatch of a military mission to Taiwan, and during the first week in January, 1950, both Senator Robert A. Taft and former President Herbert Hoover endorsed the use of military force if necessary to deny the island to the Communists.[62]

These views found sympathy within the military establishment. MacArthur had continued to stress both the strategic importance of Taiwan and the ease of defending it; all that would be necessary, he argued, would be the dispatch of a military mission and the provision of limited military assistance.[63] By December, 1949, the Joint Chiefs had also come to the conclusion that "a modest, well-directed, and closely supervised program of military aid to the anti-communist government of Taiwan would be in the security interest of the United States."[64] But the State Department continued to resist efforts to deny Taiwan to Beijing by anything other than political or economic means. As one Department memorandum put it, any attempt to detach the island from mainland control either through the use of force or through some trusteeship arrangement on behalf of Taiwanese self-government "would outrage all Chinese elements and as a resort to naked expediency would destroy our standing with the smaller countries of the world."[65]

Pessimistic about the efficacy of political and economic measures, the Department began taking steps in December to prepare American and world opinion for a Communist takeover of the island, which it expected to occur sometime in 1950.[66]* And after an extensive series of discussions in the National Security Council during the last week in December, the Department was able to secure President Truman's endorsement of a statement that, while the United States could continue to attempt to deny Taiwan to the People's Republic by non-military means, it should at the same time recognize that such a policy might not succeed and "should make every effort to strengthen the overall U.S. position with respect to the Philippines, the Ryukyus, and Japan."[67] Truman made this policy public on January 5, 1950, in a statement

---

with high officials of the Chinese Nationalist government who were also active in Moral Re-Armament. [Details can be traced in the Smith Diary for April, 1949, all in the H. Alexander Smith Papers, Boxes 98 and 282, Seeley Mudd Library, Princeton University; see also Nancy Bernkopf Tucker, *Patterns in the Dust: Chinese-American Relations and the Recognition Controversy, 1949–1950* (New York: 1983), p. 256.]

* A Central Intelligence Agency estimate in October, 1949, had concluded that "failing U.S. military occupation and control, a non-communist regime on Taiwan probably will succumb to the Chinese communists by the end of 1950." [CIA ORE 76–49, October 19, 1949, quoted in NSC 48/1, December 23, 1949, U.S. Department of Defense, *United States-Vietnam Relations, 1945–67* (Washington: 1971), VIII, 245.] In an executive session of the Senate Foreign Relations Committee on January 13, 1950, Senator Smith asked Acheson: "Is it inevitable, then, that the island will fall to the Communists?" Acheson replied: "My own judgement is that it is." [U.S. Congress, Senate, Committee on Foreign Relations, *Historical Series: Reviews of the World Situation, 1949–1950* (Washington: 1974), p. 184.]

reaffirming the Cairo Declaration's commitment to return Taiwan to China*
and disavowing any intention of using American troops to defend the island
or to furnish military aid and advice.[68]

Needless to say, the administration's strategy of excluding Taiwan from
the American "defensive perimeter" was not popular with supporters of Chiang
Kai-shek. Senator Knowland warned Acheson that the Department was following "a fatal policy . . . which we would live to rue and regret."[69] "I cannot
get over the feeling," Senator Arthur H. Vandenberg snapped, in a sarcastic
reference to the Cairo Declaration, "that the final fate of six million people in
Formosa should be conclusively and forever settled by a mimeograph on the
porch of Shepherd's [sic] Hotel in Cairo on a Sunday afternoon."[70]† Senator
Smith noted in his diary: "We believed that Acheson misjudged the cause of
China's deterioration and defeat—that he did not understand that it is not a
civil war but a conquest by Russia and that the State Department has completely missed the significance of Formosa."[71] John Foster Dulles attacked the
whole idea of a "defensive perimeter" strategy in a public speech late in January: "If we renounce all goals beyond the reach of our military and economic
grasp, that means abandoning about 1,800,000,000 people. That, in turn, in-
vites the encirclement which Soviet Communism has long and openly planned
against us."[72]

In fact, the administration had not written off Taiwan *in the event of war
with the Soviet Union.* Acheson hinted at this in a press conference on January 5, when he was asked the significance of Truman's statement that day that
"the United States has no desire to obtain special rights or privileges or to establish military bases on Formosa at this time." The phrase "at this time,"
Acheson explained, "is a recognition of the fact that, in the unlikely and unhappy event that our forces might be attacked in the Far East, the United
States must be completely free to take whatever action in whatever area is
necessary for its own security."[73] General Omar Bradley, in off-the-record testimony before the Senate Foreign Relations Committee on January 25, indicated that the Joint Chiefs were fully aware of the dangers control of Taiwan
by a potential enemy would pose to the American position in the Pacific.[74]
The next day, the Joint Chiefs concluded that an emergency war plan providing for the denial of Taiwan to the Russians in case of war should remain
in effect through the middle of 1951.[75] It is significant also that General Mac-
Arthur, after a meeting with the Joint Chiefs in Tokyo early in February, told

---

* The Cairo Declaration, which promised to strip postwar Japan of its imperial posses-
sions, had been approved by Franklin D. Roosevelt, Winston Churchill, and Chiang Kai-
shek in the Egyptian capital on November 26, 1943.

† The Senator was poetically imprecise. In fact, the date was a Friday, the location
Roosevelt's villa at Mena House, and "Shepherd's Hotel" should be "Shepheard's." But
the establishment in question does appear to have had a porch. See Major Lyall Wilkes's
1946 complaint in the House of Commons that "we have sat on Shepheard's veranda too
long with the wrong kind of people." [Quoted in Wm. Roger Louis, *The British Empire
in the Middle East, 1945–1951* (Oxford: 1984), p. 240.]

them "that he had agreed completely with the Joint Chiefs of Staff point of view with respect to Formosa."[76]

But war plans, of course, could not be revealed; as a result the administration continued to project the image, as retired General William J. Donovan put it, of "an ineffectual angel beating in the void his luminous wings in vain."[77] Nor did Republican efforts to change administration policy let up. Senator Smith sent his son-in-law and an aide to Taiwan late in April, 1950; he then saw to it that their report, advocating a United States commitment to defend the island, gained wide circulation within Congress, the State Department, and the Pentagon.[78] Knowland, in a letter to Secretary of Defense Louis Johnson in May, argued that the situation had changed since Truman's January statement: the Chinese Communist regime was now aligned with and receiving military assistance from the Soviet Union; moreover it had seized American property. "Time is rapidly running out."[79] Meanwhile, Republicans had gained an advocate in the State Department with the appointment of Dulles as a special consultant with responsibility for the Japanese peace treaty. The future Secretary of State favored finding a formula to "neutralize" Taiwan; at a meeting with Republican senatorial leaders on May 23, it was agreed, as Smith put it, "that we would start no 'fireworks' until Dulles has a chance to move in on this with Acheson."[80]

Dulles already had such an effort well under way. On May 18, he had prepared a memorandum warning of dire consequences for the American position in the world "if our conduct indicates a continuing disposition to fall back and allow doubtful areas to fall under Soviet Communist control." This prospect could be avoided "if at some doubtful point we quickly take a dramatic and strong stand that shows our confidence and resolution. . . . Of all the doubtful areas where such a stand might be taken, Formosa has advantages superior to any other:"

> If the United States were to announce that it would neutralize Formosa, not permitting it either to be taken by the Communists or to be used as a base of military operations against the mainland, that is a decision which we could certainly maintain, short of open war by the Soviet Union. Everyone knows that that is the case. If we do not act, it will be everywhere interpreted that we are making another retreat because we do not dare risk war.[81]

Dulles submitted this document to Assistant Secretary of State for Far Eastern Affairs Dean Rusk, who was already leaning toward a revision of policy on Taiwan.[82] One week later, Rusk told Pentagon officials that he expected to be able to obtain a broadening of existing policy regarding military assistance to the island;[83] on May 30 he observed at a State Department meeting that world and domestic opinion were unhappy at the lack of forthright American action in East Asia, that Taiwan was a plausible place to "draw the line," and that the island was important politically if not strategically as an example of continuing Communist expansion.[84] That same day Rusk prepared for

Acheson a draft memorandum incorporating word for word Dulles's observations of May 18.[85]

Simultaneously, pressures were building within the Pentagon for a reconsideration of Taiwan policy. Retired Admiral Charles M. Cooke, then living on the island, repeatedly bombarded MacArthur and Admiral Forrest P. Sherman, Chief of Naval Operations, with warnings about a Soviet air buildup on the Chinese mainland: "If Formosa is lost to the Communists, which means to the Russians, which means further the setting up of a Russian jet plane air strength in Formosa, World War III sooner or later becomes inevitable."[86]* These views received powerful reinforcement on May 29, when MacArthur sent the Joint Chiefs a list of the reinforcements he would need to hold the "defensive perimeter" line if Taiwan should fall under the control of a hostile power. "The time has passed," he noted pointedly, "when this situation can be considered by the United States from a detached or an academic viewpoint":

> In the event of war between the United States and the USSR, Formosa's value to the Communists is the equivalent of an unsinkable aircraft carrier and submarine tender, ideally located to accomplish Soviet strategy as well as to checkmate the offensive capabilities of the central and southern positions of the FEC [Far Eastern Command] front line.[87]†

On June 9, Secretary of Defense Johnson asked the opinions of the Joint Chiefs on the question of whether "the United States should make every effort to keep the Communists out of Formosa even though this might entail holding Formosa with the aid of U.S. military forces."[88] And on June 14, MacArthur dispatched another lengthy memorandum emphasizing that "[u]nless the United States' political-military strategic position in the Far East is to be abandoned, it is obvious that the time must come in the foreseeable future when a line must be drawn beyond which Communist expansion will be stopped."[89]

As of June 25, though, no decision on a revision of policy had been made. The outbreak of fighting in Korea on that date obviously placed the Taiwan question in a dramatically different strategic context. General Bradley sug-

---

* Cooke claimed at one point to be working for the International News Service on Taiwan, at another to be affiliated with Commerce International China. He emphatically disclaimed any connection with the Chinese Nationalist government, but not before receiving a warning from Sherman on the impropriety of retired naval officers receiving emoluments from foreign governments. [Cooke to Sherman, April 14, 1950, Sherman to Cooke, May 29, 1950, Cooke to Sherman, undated but probably mid-June 1950, all in Forrest P. Sherman Papers, Folder 1, in Records of the Immediate Office of the Chief of Naval Operations, Operational Archives, Naval Historical Center, Washington.]

† General Bradley forwarded this message to Johnson with the suggestion that it was "of sufficient importance to be brought to the personal attention of the President." [Bradley to Johnson, May 31, 1950, Joint Chiefs of Staff Records, CJCS 901 China (31 May 50), Modern Military Records Branch, National Archives.]

gested to the Joint Chiefs of Staff that "if Korea falls, we may want to recommend even stronger action in the case of Formosa."[90] That night he read MacArthur's June 14 memorandum at a meeting with the President and his top advisers at Blair House. Acheson rejected MacArthur's suggestion that a military mission be sent to Taiwan, but he did recommend dispatching the Seventh Fleet to the Taiwan Strait to prevent either a Chinese Communist attack on the island or a Chinese Nationalist attack on the mainland.[91] Truman approved this action and announced it publicly on June 27. "It was all very wonderful and an answer to prayer," Senator Smith noted in his diary. "The saving of Formosa was clearly God guided."[92]

But the administration did not regard its action with respect to Taiwan as intervention on behalf of the Nationalists in the Chinese civil war. What it hoped to do instead was to forestall seizure of the island by hostile forces, while making no commitments as to its ultimate political disposition. American officials repeatedly emphasized the even-handedness of their action; the dispatch of the Seventh Fleet, they argued, had been aimed as much at containing Chiang Kai-shek's aspirations to return to the mainland as those of the Communists to invade Taiwan.[93]* The administration's rejection of Chiang's offer of 33,000 Nationalist troops for use in Korea reflected its concern not to associate itself too closely with his regime; so too did Truman's order to MacArthur in August to withdraw a public message to the Veterans of Foreign Wars which had condemned "the threadbare argument by those who advocate appeasement and defeatism in the Pacific that if we defend Formosa we alienate continental Asia."[94] The Chinese Nationalist government's conviction that it represented the only legal government in China "was not held by the rest of the world," Acheson reminded the American minister in Taipei: "Chi Govt wld therefore be well advised to appreciate realities of tenuous position it now occupies."[95]

As might be expected, efforts to maintain neutrality in the Chinese civil conflict and still deny Taiwan to the Communists proved difficult. As early as July 27, 1950, the Joint Chiefs had recommended that the United States continue to defend Taiwan regardless of what happened in Korea.[96] In August, the President approved the dispatch of a mission to survey Nationalist military needs; later that month, he authorized the allocation of over $14 million for military aid to the island.[97] Acheson and Dulles agreed in October on the desirability of working through the United Nations for the permanent neutralization of Taiwan. At that time, they took the view that such an arrangement would not allow use of the island as a base for military operations against the mainland;[98] but by November, following initial indications of Chinese Communist intervention in Korea, Acheson was refusing to rule out the use of Taiwan by United Nations forces for just this purpose.[99] Later that month, the

---

* The minutes of a Blair House meeting on June 26 record the President as commenting, with characteristic pungency, that "we were not going to give the Chinese [Nationalists] 'a nickel' for any purpose whatsoever. He said that all the money we had given them is now invested in United States real estate." [Philip C. Jessup notes, *FR: 1950*, VII, 180.]

State Department abandoned its plan for a U.N.-sanctioned neutralization, partly because the continued domestic political sensitivity of the issue remained a problem, but partly also because of the administration's failure to rally support for its policy on Taiwan from American allies.[100]

Great Britain was one such ally, and the Taiwan issue figured prominently in conversations held between President Truman, Prime Minister Clement Attlee, and their respective advisers in Washington during the first week in December. In response to a comment by British Ambassador Sir Oliver Franks questioning the wisdom of continuing to recognize Chiang Kai-shek, Acheson admitted that

> there was a lot of trouble wrapped up in this problem, and he did not know the answer. If one starts with the proposition that we want to deny Formosa to the mainland, there is no question that Chiang is a factor in this denial. He is on the spot. While we do not like the situation any better than the British do, it is dangerous to talk about the point Sir Oliver raised.

One might be able to render the American position consistent with the Cairo Declaration, Acheson noted, but "such arguments were not worthy of this discussion." The facts were that although the United States and its allies lacked the power to ensure that Korea remained both free and united, "we do not have to accept a communistic Formosa; we have the power to prevent that." Truman pointed out that the Cairo Declaration had been made at a time when Japan was the hostile power in the Pacific, not China or the Soviet Union. "When we thought that Formosa was not strategically important to us, we never considered that the Chinese Government would be one that would be very hostile to the United States. There is no question now that it is very hostile to us."[101]

Truman's observation reflects an underlying element of consistency in American policy on the Taiwan question: the fact that at no point during 1949 and 1950 was Washington prepared to acquiesce in control of the island by forces hostile to the United States *and* capable of taking military action against other links in the offshore island chain. The problem was to achieve this objective without getting further involved in the Chinese civil war. The United States was willing to install an autonomous regime on the island if that could be done without driving the Chinese Communists and the Russians together. But when it became apparent that autonomy was not feasible, Washington resigned itself to the prospect of control by the People's Republic as long as this did not involve a Soviet military presence as well. That possibility, too, had begun to appear increasingly unlikely by the spring of 1950; as a result, a revision of the administration's "hands-off" policy was well under way at the time the Korean War broke out.

Korea brought about the decision to "neutralize" Taiwan for military reasons, but with the hope that there might still remain some chance for a political *modus vivendi* with the Chinese Communists. Beijing's intervention in the Korean conflict destroyed that prospect;* hence, by the end of 1950, the Truman administration had found itself in precisely the position it had sought to avoid: yoked, as it were, for better or for worse, to Chiang Kai-shek.

# IV

Just as Taiwan represented an anomaly as an island strongpoint excluded from the original "defensive perimeter," so French Indochina, as a mainland area included within it, constituted another. Certainly there was little promising about the situation there, what with an unpopular colonial government waging an increasingly costly and ineffective war against a guerilla movement that was both communist and nationalist. Nevertheless, the United States had come, by 1950, to regard the defense of Indochina as an interest more vital than denial to the communists of either Taiwan or South Korea. As early as March, 1949, a Policy Planning Staff study had recommended that "we should . . . view the SEA [Southeast Asian] region as an integral part of that great crescent formed by the Indian Peninsula, Australia, and Japan."[102] NSC 48/1, a comprehensive review of East Asian policy submitted to the National Security Council in December, 1949, concluded that if Southeast Asia were to be swept by communism, "we shall have suffered a major political rout the repercussions of which will be felt throughout the rest of the world."[103]† And in April, 1950, the Joint Chiefs of Staff proclaimed that "the mainland states of Southeast Asia . . . are . . . of critical strategic importance to the United States."[104]

None of this meant, of course, that the United States was willing to endorse everything the French were doing in Indochina. "We will get nowhere by supporting the French as a colonial power against the Indochinese," Acheson told the Senate Foreign Relations Committee; "that is something which has very little future in it."[105]‡ Nor did Washington's policy extend to the point of being willing to promise American troops if Indochina was subjected to external attack.** But it did mean support for, and, by February, 1950, rec-

* Although the administration would make one additional highly secret attempt at such an arrangement early in 1951. See Chapter Six, below.

† "Isn't the importance of keeping the Chinese Communists out of the Southeast greater than holding a little island like Formosa," Senator Henry Cabot Lodge asked Ambassador Philip C. Jessup at an executive session of the Senate Foreign Relations Committee on March 29, 1950. Jessup's reply: "I think so." [*Reviews of the World Situation*, p. 279.]

‡ But there were limits to how far the French could be pushed. As Acheson put it, "the thing that we have to be careful about is that we do not press the French to the point where they say, 'All right, take over the damned country. We don't want it,' and put their soldiers on ships and send them back to France." [Executive session testimony, Senate Foreign Relations Committee, March 29, 1950, *Reviews of the World Situation*, p. 267.]

** "With regard to military assistance, the question is, what would be asked and what could we do. The French have a well-equipped and extremely good army on the border.

ognition of the Bao Dai government established by the French in an effort to encourage an anti-communist variety of nationalism in Indochina.[106] And it also meant approval by the President, on April 24, 1950, of a directive instructing the State and Defense Departments to "prepare as a matter of priority a program of all practicable measures designed to protect United States security interests in Indochina."[107]

American officials appear to have made an exception to their general rule of not regarding mainland areas as vital, in the case of Indochina, for several reasons: (1) the conviction that Ho Chi Minh was a more reliable instrument of the Kremlin than Mao Zedong; (2) the belief that the Soviet Union had designated Southeast Asia as a special target of opportunity; (3) concern over the importance of Southeast Asia as a source of food and raw materials; and (4) in an early version of what would come to be known as the "domino theory," fear of the strategic and psychological consequences for the rest of non-communist Asia if Indochina should fall to communism.

Ho Chi Minh's Moscow connections had been the object of concern in the State Department since 1947.[108] Reports from Americans on the scene in Indochina stressing the nationalist character of Ho's movement and the apparent absence of direct support from Moscow made little impression.[109] "Question whether Ho as much nationalist as Commie is irrelevant," Acheson cabled tersely—and with sweeping oversimplification—in May, 1949; "all Stalinists in colonial areas are nationalists. With achievement natl aims (i.e., independence) their objective necessarily becomes subordination state to Commie purposes."[110] Eight months later, following the Soviet Union's recognition of Ho's government, Acheson proclaimed that "the Soviet acknowledgment of this movement should remove any illusions as to the 'nationalist' character of Ho Chi Minh's aims and reveals Ho in his true colors as the mortal enemy of native independence in Indochina."[111] It is difficult to reconcile this position with Acheson's persistent optimism regarding prospects for nationalism in the People's Republic of China, although one possible explanation—admittedly speculative—is that reports from Indochina were subject to comment by French and West European specialists in the State Department who tended to be more preoccupied with the Soviet "menace" than were the China experts who normally reported directly to the Secretary of State.[112]

Related to concern about Ho's Moscow ties was the belief that the Russians regarded Southeast Asia as an especially promising area into which to attempt to project their influence. A State Department analysis in October, 1948, had warned that the Russians were using their legation in Bangkok as a center from which to direct communist movements in Southeast Asia previously coordinated through the Chinese Communists.[113] Soviet recognition of the Viet-

---

I doubt very much whether we would employ forces of the United States in that area. The problem would hardly be one, or is unlikely to be one, of mass assault on a thing, but [rather] of subversion." [Acheson executive session testimony, Senate Foreign Relations Committee, January 13, 1950, *Reviews of the World Situation*, p. 181.]

namese Communists in January, 1950, intensified this concern. As Charles Yost, Director of the Office of East European Affairs, put it, "Indo-China may now be the focal point of the most intensive and determined Communist pressure."[114]* An Army intelligence report in March predicted that "Communist military measures in Korea will be held in abeyance pending the outcome of their program in other areas, particularly Southeast Asia."[115] And in May, 1950, Edmund Gullion, the American chargé in Saigon, argued that the very indefiniteness of the United States commitment in Indochina had encouraged the Soviets:

> As Soviet power flows up to the margin, where it must be contained, key points are fewer and stand in bolder relief. Twilight zones in which we would not know what to do in case of attack (or what to propose to Congress) have either been eliminated by Soviet action or by decisions taken by American strategic planners. I fear that IC [Indochina] may still be in twilight zone and as long as it is it will remain temptation to Chinese Communists or Soviets.[116]

A third reason for considering Indochina more important than Taiwan or Korea had to do with the need to retain access to the food and strategic raw materials produced in the area, or at least to keep them out of the hands of the Russians. NSC 48/1 noted that neither Japan nor India could expect to be self-sufficient in food or cotton production without imports from Southeast Asia.[117]† A Joint Chiefs of Staff study in April, 1950, warned that Southeast Asia contained "major sources of certain strategic materials required for the completion of United States stock pile projects"; moreover, "Communist control of this area would alleviate considerably the food problem of China and would make available to the USSR important strategic materials." Soviet domination of Asia's war-making potential, the study concluded, might in the long run "become a decisive factor affecting the balance of power between the United States and the USSR."[118]

Finally, and most important, American officials were convinced that if Indochina fell to the communists, other countries vital to the American position in East Asia would follow suit. "The choice confronting the United States is to

---

* Yost speculated that the Soviet recognition of Ho suggested that a competition for influence in Indochina was developing between the Russians and the Chinese Communists which "bodes well for the creation of friction between the two and the possible eventual development of Titoism in China, [but] its immediate effects are likely to be unfortunate in that the revolutionary time-table in that area may be speeded up by the maneuvers of each of the two partners to forestall the other." [Yost to George W. Perkins, January 31, 1950, *FR: 1950*, VI, 710.]

† It should be noted that a major concern of U.S. officials during this period was to work out procedures whereby trade with mainland China could be maintained, as a means both of preventing China from becoming a Soviet satellite and of providing raw materials and markets for the reviving Japanese economy. See, on this point, Tucker, *Patterns in the Dust*, pp. 36–37; and Michael Schaller, *The American Occupation of Japan: The Origins of the Cold War in Asia* (New York: 1985), pp. 136–37.]

support the French in Indochina or face the extension of Communism over the remainder of the continental area of Southeast Asia and, possibly, further westward," a State Department working group noted in February, 1950; "we would then be obliged to make staggering investments in those areas and in that part of Southeast Asia remaining outside Communist domination or withdraw to a much-contracted Pacific line."[119] Livingston Merchant, writing in March, regarded it as a certainty "that the prestige of [the] psychological results of another Communist triumph in Asia, following on the heels of China, would be felt beyond the immediate area and could be expected adversely to affect our interests in India, Pakistan and even the Philippines."[120] The Joint Chiefs of Staff concluded in April that the loss of Indochina would mean the loss of other mainland states in Southeast Asia and a worsening of the internal security problems of the Philippines and Indonesia, which "would contribute to their probable eventual fall to the Communists"; this in turn would "result in virtually complete denial to the United States of the Pacific littoral of Asia."[121]

The onset of the Korean War reemphasized the strategic importance of Indochina, but it also imposed limits on what the United States could actually do to help the French there. The Truman administration did, on June 26, accelerate the provision of military assistance;[122] statements stressing the critical significance of the region continued to circulate within the government through the remainder of the year. The Joint Chiefs of Staff put the matter bluntly in November, following Chinese Communist intervention in Korea: "The United States should take action, as a matter of urgency, by all means practicable short of the actual employment of United States military forces, to deny Indochina to communism."[123]

But short of employing American troops, there appeared to be few feasible means of accomplishing that objective. There was little confidence in Washington regarding the ability of the French either to pacify Indochina by military means or to make the kinds of political accommodations that would swing the forces of nationalism there away from Ho Chi Minh.[124]* "The French, through their folly . . . have left us with the choice of following two ghastly courses of action," Charlton Ogburn, Jr., a Foreign Service officer with extensive experience in Southeast Asia, commented in August:

1. To wash our hands of the country and allow the Communists to overrun it.
2. To continue to pour treasure (and perhaps eventually lives) into

---

* One factor further eroding confidence in the French was a report in August, 1950, that they might seek to arrange a settlement of the Indochina question by working through the Chinese Communists. [See David Bruce to Acheson, August 12, 1950, *FR: 1950*, VI, 851–52; Acheson to Bruce, August 15, 1950, *ibid.*, pp. 854–56.] Confidence in Bao Dai, never high, had been shaken in October to the point that Acheson was willing to let him know "that US Govt does not regard him as indispensable to contd existence and growth in stability of legal Govt of Vietnam." [Acheson to U.S. legation, Saigon, October 30, 1950, *ibid.*, p. 913.]

a hopeless cause in which the French have already expended about a billion and a half dollars and about fifty thousand lives—and this at a cost of alienating vital segments of Asian public opinion.[125]

Three months later, John H. Ohly, Deputy Director of the Mutual Defense Assistance Program, warned Acheson: "We have reached a point where the United States, because of limitations in resources, can no longer simultaneously pursue all of its objectives in all parts of the world and must realistically face the fact that certain objectives, even though they may be extremely valuable and important ones, may have to be abandoned if others of even greater value and importance are to be attained."[126]

There was a fundamental difference, the Joint Strategic Survey Committee suggested that same month, between the strategic importance of Indochina in a global war with the Soviet Union and in a "cold war." War plans did not call for the retention of Indochina in the first eventuality, since the main enemy in such a conflict would be the Soviet Union and the main theater of action would probably be Western Europe. But in any situation short of global war, the loss of Indochina would imperil the security of the other Southeast Asian states, the Philippines, Indonesia, even India and Pakistan. Moreover, "this loss would have widespread political and psychological repercussions upon other non-communist states throughout the world." Even minor commitments of military forces, while possibly sufficient to defeat the Viet Minh, would probably lead "to a major involvement of the United States in that area similar to that in Korea or even to global war." Accordingly, there was little alternative to continuing the existing military aid program, even though the French had failed thus far "to provide adequate political and military leadership, to develop sound military plans, and to utilize properly their military resources."[127]

But what would the United States response be in the event of Chinese Communist aggression not part of a global war? The Joint Chiefs took the position that the United States "should not permit itself to become engaged in a general war with Communist China but should, in concert with the United Kingdom, support France and the Associated States by all means short of the actual employment of United States military forces." They also recognized, though, that the French might bring the Indochina question before the United Nations General Assembly under the "Uniting for Peace" resolution, in which case the United States would then probably be morally obligated to contribute its armed forces designated for service on behalf of the United Nations." Alarmed by this prospect, the Chiefs concluded that it was therefore "in the interests of the United States to take such action in Indochina as would forestall the need for the General Assembly to invoke the provisions of the resolution, 'Uniting for Peace.' "[128]*

* Ironically, the "Uniting for Peace" resolution had been an American proposal, designed to circumvent the Soviet veto in the Security Council. [See Dean Acheson, *Present at the Creation: My Years in the State Department* (New York: 1969), p. 450.]

By the end of 1950, then, the United States faced an apparently insoluble problem in Indochina. Administration officials were unanimous in their estimates of the region's strategic importance; nevertheless, the burdens of military commitment in Korea, a country once thought less vital than Indochina, meant that the United States had to continue to rely for the defense of the territory on the French, whose very ineptitude had made their colony vulnerable in the first place. It took longer than expected to validate it, but the reluctant conclusion of a 1951 National Security Council staff study proved, in the end, to be correct: "The United States cannot guarantee the denial of Southeast Asia to communism."[129]

# V

Korea, of course, represented the most striking departure from the original "defensive perimeter" concept. In contrast to Taiwan and Indochina, here was an area in which United States troops had been stationed. After deliberations in Washington lasting almost two years, these troops had been withdrawn in the spring of 1949, on the grounds that the defense of South Korea was not a vital strategic interest for the United States. Throughout this period, American officials harbored serious reservations about both the intentions and capabilities of the South Korean government. And yet, when that country was attacked on June 25, 1950, the Truman administration, with a rapidity that surprised itself as well as its adversaries, committed air, naval, and ground forces to repel the invasion. Five months later, Washington found itself in an undeclared war there with the People's Republic of China as well.

The initial decision to withdraw troops from southern Korea had been made in the fall of 1947, primarily for strategic reasons: it appeared unwise to retain some 45,000 men in that area at a time of increasingly severe manpower shortages and proliferating commitments in Europe. The United States had occupied the southern half of Korea at the end of World War II to forestall a Soviet takeover, but it had never expected to have to keep troops there indefinitely, nor did it consider it strategically sound to do so.[130] As the Joint War Plans Committee of the Joint Chiefs of Staff noted in June, 1947, existing forces in southern Korea would not be capable of repelling a Soviet attack if one should come; reinforcements from Japan would only weaken the security of that more vital and more defensible position, while in no way matching force levels the Russians had the capability to send in. "A withdrawal from Korea immediately after the outbreak of hostilities is indicated."[131] By September, the Joint Chiefs had concluded that "in the light of the present severe shortage of military manpower, the corps of two divisions . . . now maintained in south Korea, could well be used elsewhere."[132]

It is important to note, though, that Washington planners made a distinction between strategic interests in Korea, which they considered negligible, and the very different problem of interests in terms of credibility. "This is the one country within which we alone have for almost two years carried on ideological warfare in direct contact with our ideological opponents," the Joint Strategic Survey Committee noted in April, 1947, "so that to lose this battle would be gravely detrimental to United States prestige, and therefore security, throughout the world."[133] An analysis by the State-War-Navy Coordinating Committee concluded in August that "the U.S. cannot at this time withdraw from Korea under circumstances which would inevitably lead to Communist domination of the entire country."[134] General Wedemeyer, in his report to the President in September, argued that the withdrawal of American forces from southern Korea and the consequent occupation of the country by Soviet or northern Korean troops "would cost the United States an immense loss in moral prestige among the peoples of Asia."[135]

The compromise eventually reached was succinctly stated in the minutes of a meeting of State Department East Asian advisers held in Secretary Marshall's office on September 29, 1947:

> It was agreed that (a) ultimately the US position in Korea is untenable even with expenditure of considerable US money and effort; (b) the US, however, cannot "scuttle" and run from Korea without considerable loss of prestige and political standing in the Far East and in the world at large; (c) that it should be the effort of the Government through all proper means to effect a settlement of the Korean problem which would enable the US to withdraw from Korea as soon as possible with the minimum of bad effects.[136]

An agreement with the Russians looking toward unification of the country having proven impossible to achieve, the United States fell back on a policy of providing military and economic assistance to the anti-communist government of Syngman Rhee, established under United Nations auspices in 1948, while gradually withdrawing American troops. This policy did not mean the abandonment of South Korea to Soviet domination, though, as two National Security Council papers on the subject made clear: "The overthrow by Soviet-dominated forces of a regime established in south Korea under the aegis of the UN would . . . constitute a severe blow to the prestige and influence of the UN; in this respect the interests of the U.S. are parallel to, if not identical with, those of the UN."[137]

Just what the United States would do to defend South Korea in case of attack, however, remained unclear. A Central Intelligence Agency report warned in February, 1949, that "US troop withdrawal would probably result in a collapse of the US-supported Republic of Korea" and suggested that the continued presence of a moderate number of American forces in the area would discourage any invasion from the north while at the same time boosting morale in the south.[138] But MacArthur, the Joint Chiefs of Staff, and Secretary of Defense Johnson all advocated withdrawal, both because of the pressure of commitments elsewhere and because of the conviction that Korea would not provide favorable terrain upon which to fight if war should come.[139] Beneath the surface also was concern about the possibility that American troops might become involuntarily involved should Rhee make good on his frequent promises to "march north."[140]* The State Department, originally inclined to favor the retention of United States forces in Korea for a somewhat longer period than had been planned, acquiesced, and the last American troops were withdrawn at the end of June, 1949.[141] That same month, an Army study concluded that any "police action with U.N. sanction" in Korea including United States military units would "involve a militarily disproportionate expenditure of U.S. manpower, resources, and effort at a time when international relations in Europe are in precarious balance." Application of the Truman Doctrine to Korea "would require prodigious effort and vast expenditures far out of proportion to the benefits to be expected."[142]

Acheson's famous exclusion of South Korea from the American "defensive perimeter" was therefore, as he later claimed, consistent with existing policy. The Secretary of State elaborated on his thinking three days after the Press Club speech, in executive session testimony before the Senate Foreign Relations Committee:

> [T]he estimate that we have . . . is that South Korea could now take care of any trouble that was started by North Korea, but it could not take care of any invasion which was either started by the Chinese Communists or powerfully supported by them or by the Soviet Union.

Should such an event occur, Acheson added, the United States would not undertake to resist it independently by military force. "Of course, if under the [UN] Charter action were taken, we would take our part in that, but probably it would not be taken because they [the Russians] would veto it."[143] Although military and economic aid continued to flow to the South Korean government during the first half of 1950, there was in Washington no sense of urgency about the situation there comparable to the concerns that had developed over Taiwan and Indochina.[144] As late as June 19, John Foster Dulles was warning Syngman Rhee that the United States could help to resist aggression only "if the governments threatened were themselves taking active steps to create conditions within their countries which would prohibit [the] growth of communism."[145]

The decision to come to the aid of South Korea following the June 25 attack was by no means a foregone conclusion. MacArthur's initial impression was that the invasion was not an all-out effort, that the Russians were probably not behind it, and that the South Koreans would win.[146] Secretary of the Army Frank Pace and Secretary of Defense Johnson initially opposed the com-

---

* Rhee told Secretary of the Army Kenneth C. Royall in February, 1949, of his desire to reinforce the South Korean army and move into North Korea. "I told the President that, of course, no invasion of North Korea could in any event take place while the United States had combat troops in Korea, and that his suggestion was in my opinion tantamount to a request that we should have all American combat troops removed." [Royall memorandum of conversation with Rhee, February 8, 1949, *FR: 1949*, VII, 957.]

mitment of ground combat forces, and the Joint Chiefs expressed concern about the impact such a decision would have in weakening the defenses of Japan and reducing the number of troops available for deployment to Western Europe.[147] Dulles supported the use of air and naval forces in Korea but warned that the Russians and the Chinese could indefinitely supply the North Koreans and that "it was hazardous for us to challenge communist power on the mainland." Secretary Pace replied that "the Defense Department's disposition to send divisions into Korea was not because of *their* desire to do so, but because they thought it necessary to support the political policies of the government."[148]*

This was a perceptive comment, for in the end it was political and not strategic considerations that brought about American intervention in Korea. The blatant nature of the North Korean attack made resistance necessary, in the eyes of administration officials, not because South Korea was important in and of itself, but because any demonstration of aggression left unopposed would only encourage further aggressions elsewhere. "You may be sure," Charles Bohlen wrote to Kennan on June 26, "that all Europeans to say nothing of the Asiatics are watching to see what the United States will do."[149] Kennan himself believed that if the United States did not act, "there will scarcely be any theater of the east-west conflict which will not be adversely affected thereby, from our standpoint."[150] The fact that in attacking South Korea the North Koreans had directly challenged the United Nations made the argument even more compelling. Philip Jessup recalls Truman, at the Blair House meeting of June 25, repeating half to himself: "We can't let the UN down! We can't let the UN down!"[151]

The problem, once the inhibition about engaging in military operations on the mainland had been overcome, was to decide where to call a halt. "After all," Kennan noted in August, "when we start walking inland from the tip of Korea, we have about a 10,000 mile walk if we keep on going, and we are going to have to stop somewhere."[152] Kennan himself and other Soviet specialists in the State Department favored limiting United Nations action solely to the liberation of South Korea. Others in State, together with the Joint Chiefs of Staff, argued that the 38th parallel had neither political nor military significance, that the United Nations should seize the opportunity to unify Korea while carefully avoiding any expansion of the conflict into Soviet or Chinese territory. General MacArthur and his supporters pressed for yet a third alternative: expansion of the conflict through the elimination of "privileged sanctuaries" north of the Yalu, and the use of Chinese Nationalist troops.[153]

---

* "I had doubts as to the wisdom of engaging our land forces on the Continent of Asia as against any enemy that could be nourished from the vast reservoirs of the USSR. I expressed that doubt to the military as soon as I returned [from Japan] and before our decision was made." [Dulles to Walter Lippmann, July 13, 1950, John Foster Dulles Papers, Box 48, "Lippmann" folder, Seeley Mudd Library, Princeton University.] Publicly, though, Dulles endorsed the decision. [See his CBS radio interview, July 1, 1950, *Department of State Bulletin,* XXIII(July 10, 1950), 50.]

Kennan opposed crossing the parallel on the grounds that such a move would require the dispersal of United Nations forces while risking Soviet or Chinese intervention. "We must remember," he told a meeting at the State Department on July 21, "that what we were doing in Korea was, although for good political reasons, nevertheless an unsound thing, and that the further we were to advance up from the peninsula the more unsound it would become from a military standpoint."[154] A month later he reminded an off-the-record press conference that

> the Russians are terribly, terribly sensitive about places where foreign territory comes very close to their important centers. . . . I think you can see that if you put the shoe on the other foot and think how it would be with us if Soviet forces began to come within say seventeen miles of Southern California in fighting Mexico.[155]*

Kennan's friend and fellow Soviet specialist Bohlen also warned of the Russians' sensitivity about borders and suggested that they might not even wait for UN forces to reach the parallel before taking action, possibly in coordination with the Chinese.[156] The State Department's Policy Planning Staff and the Central Intelligence Agency both shared these concerns, pointing as well to the difficulty Washington would have in generating support among its allies for any decision to unify Korea by force.[157]

But there were strong countervailing pressures on the question of crossing the parallel within both the State and Defense Departments. John M. Allison, Director of the Office of Northeastern Asian Affairs at State, was particularly vehement on the subject. "I believe that the time has come when we must be bold and willing to take even more risks than we have already," he argued in a memorandum to Rusk on July 1.[158] Three weeks later he condemned the Policy Planning Staff's position as "a timid, half-hearted policy designed not to provoke the Soviets to war," adding:

> We should recognize that there is grave danger of conflict with the USSR and the Chinese Communists whatever we do from now on—but I fail to see what advantage we gain by a compromise with clear moral principles and a shirking of our duty to make clear once and for all that aggression does not pay. . . . That this may mean war on a global scale is true—the American people should be told and told why and what it will mean to them. When all the legal and moral right is on our side why should we hesitate?"[159]†

---

* Kennan's opposition to military operations north of the parallel did not extend to air and naval bombardment; indeed, during the first week of the conflict he suggested directing such actions against Chinese targets as well if Chinese Communist troops entered the fighting. [Kennan notes on meeting in Acheson's office, June 28, 1950, quoted in Kennan, *Memoirs: 1925-1950*, p. 487.]

† Allison's brief account of his position on the 38th parallel issue in his memoirs is, at best, misleading. [See John M. Allison, *Ambassador from the Prairie* (Boston: 1973), p. 153.]

Dulles also favored crossing the parallel on the grounds that it had no legal standing and that aggressors ought to be punished; unlike Allison, however, he was unwilling to carry military operations to the point of provoking the Russians.[160]

The Defense Department, reflecting the views of the Joint Chiefs of Staff, emphasized the military illogic of halting at the parallel and the difficulty of guaranteeing future South Korean security if that decision was made. It also advanced the interesting argument, later seconded by Allison, that a unified, non-communist Korea might induce Manchuria to gravitate away from China and that such a development in turn might cause the People's Republic to question its current alignment with the Russians.[161] Still other arguments stressed the unpopularity with both the South Koreans and the American public of any decision to stop at the parallel.[162] Would not public opinion be hard to satisfy if military operations halted at the 38th parallel, Kennan was asked at a press conference in August. "It is just one of those instances," he replied, "when the people here will have to think very hard about what it is they are after."[163]

On September 11, Truman approved a carefully worded compromise authorizing the invasion and occupation of North Korea *provided* Soviet or Chinese Communist intervention had neither taken place nor been threatened. Operations were in no circumstances to extend into Chinese or Russian territory, and only South Korean forces were to make the final approach to the Yalu. Should Soviet or Chinese intervention occur after the parallel had been crossed, efforts were to be made to stabilize the front at the most favorable possible position without risking escalation to general war.[164] This was, in effect, a kind of "floating perimeter" strategy, designed to allow the unification of Korea so long as enemy resistance remained manageable. As Rusk explained it later that month, "the thinking in Washington is that we should let the Soviet make the decision for us as much as possible so that United Nations forces would carry on until we get some indication of Soviet reaction to their northward movement."[165]*

As it turned out, it was the Chinese and not the Russians who determined the extent of the United Nations advance into North Korea. Confronted with Beijing's intervention late in November, MacArthur urged on Washington yet another strategic concept: a blockade of the mainland, the employment of Chinese Nationalist forces in Korea and elsewhere, the bombing of industrial

* Dulles objected to the amount of freedom this strategy left for the military to make political decisions, but Acheson assured him that "at the present time we had good coordination between our political objectives and the conduct of our military affairs in Korea. If we were lucky and neither the Russians nor the Chinese intervened in North Korea, General MacArthur could act consistently with our overall political plans." [Minutes, meeting of U.S. delegation to the United Nations, September 21, 1950, *FR: 1950*, VII, 745–46.] With equal prescience, Acheson later sought to reassure the Chinese about the march to the Yalu by calling attention to the U.S. record in the "brotherly development of border waters," citing the St. Lawrence and the Rio Grande. [*Department of State Bulletin*, XXIII(November 27, 1950), 855.]

facilities inside China and "privileged sanctuaries" along the Manchurian border, and, if necessary, the withdrawal of United Nations forces from Korea to more favorable terrain from which to carry on the struggle. MacArthur justified this expansion of the conflict on the grounds that the Chinese were already engaged in all-out war; the Russians, he maintained, would fight only in defense of their own interests, which did not necessarily parallel those of the Chinese. Failure to choose this course would mean United States involvement in "an indecisive campaign with the cost of holding a position in Korea becoming, in the long run, infinitely greater than were we to fight back along conventional lines."[166]

The administration rejected MacArthur's recommendation to widen the war, partly because it feared that an expanded Sino-American conflict would only serve Moscow's interests, partly because it could not count on support from allies, partly because it remained convinced, unlike MacArthur, that the decisive theater of action in the Cold War and in any future hot war as well would be Europe.[167] Accordingly, Washington reverted to the idea of attempting to stabilize a military line at or near the 38th parallel and, once this had been done, seeking an end to the fighting through negotiations. "Our purposes in Korea remain the same," Acheson assured Ernest Bevin, "namely, to resist aggression, to localize the hostilities, and to wind up the Korean problem on a satisfactory UN basis and in such a way as not to commit US forces in large numbers indefinitely in that operation."[168] It was MacArthur's inability to accommodate himself to this strategy that led to his removal from command in April of 1951.*

And yet the administration did not remain wholly unsympathetic to MacArthur's argument. Truman and his advisers did give serious consideration in November and December, 1950, to authorizing "hot pursuit" by fighter planes across the Yalu and the bombing of Manchurian airfields and supply depots.[169] And in May, 1951, one month after MacArthur's dismissal, Truman approved NSC 48/5, which provided:

> In order to be prepared for Chinese aggression outside Korea, to protect the security of UN and U.S. forces, and to provide for appropriate military action in the event that UN forces are forced to evacuate Korea, [the United States should] expedite the development of plans for the following courses of action, if such action should later be deemed necessary:
>
> (1) Imposing a blockade of the China coast by naval and air forces.

---

* MacArthur complained to Carlos P. Romulo on December 26, 1950: "This group of Europhiles just will not recognize that it is Asia which has been selected for the test of Communist power and that if all Asia falls Europe would not have a chance—either with or without American assistance. In their blind and stupid effort to undermine public confidence in me as something of a symbol of the need for balanced thinking and action, they do Europe the gravest disservice and sow the seeds of its possible ultimate destruction." [MacArthur Papers, Record Group 5, Box 1-A, File 5.]

(2) Military action against selected targets held by Communist China outside of Korea.

(3) Participation defensively or offensively of the Chinese Nationalist forces, and the necessary operational assistance to make them effective.[170]

As it happened, armistice talks began in July, and the administration never had to put these plans into operation. But the fact that they had been considered suggests that the administration and MacArthur were not so far apart at least in their conviction that the United States had no business attempting to fight with ground troops on the mainland of Asia, and in their determination to avoid in the future such costly departures from the original "defensive perimeter" idea.*

# VI

Ideally, a "defensive perimeter" strategy should seek to contain the expansive tendencies of potential adversaries without unnecessarily dispersing resources.[171] Such an approach assumes that because capabilities are finite, interests must be also; ends must be framed in such a way as to be consistent with means. Implicit also is the notion of selectivity, whether in the choice of terrain to be defended, instruments with which to carry out that defense, or allies to be enlisted in the effort. The overall objective is, or should be, to counter the other side's initiatives without unduly restricting one's own.

At first glance, American strategy in East Asia after World War II would appear to have met that standard. The primary interest involved was to ensure that that part of the world did not come under the domination of a single hostile power. But because United States capabilities lay more in the realm of technology than manpower, and because of competing obligations in Europe, it made sense to confine the American presence in Asia to islands capable of being defended by air and naval forces, thus avoiding operations against high-manpower but low-technology adversaries on the mainland. This was a realistic recognition both of global priorities and of regional asymmetries of power.

* Significantly, NSC 124/2, approved by Truman on June 25, 1952, provided that in the event of overt Chinese Communist aggression against Indochina, "The United States should take air and naval action in conjunction with at least France and the U.K. against all suitable military targets in China, avoiding insofar as practicable those targets in areas near the boundaries of the USSR in order not to increase the risk of direct Soviet involvement. In the event the concurrence of the United Kingdom and France to expanded military action against Communist China is not obtained, the United States should consider taking unilateral action." [NSC 124/2, "United States Objectives and Courses of Action With Respect to Southeast Asia," June 25, 1952, *FR: 1952–54*, XII, 132.]

As with most general concepts, though, application proved more difficult than articulation. It was all very well to relinquish commitments in mainland China, which was thought "lost" to the West for the foreseeable future, but the problems of Taiwan, Indochina, and Korea defied such easy solution. Taiwan had been excluded from the perimeter for reasons of international politics: Acheson's desire to avoid further involvement in the Chinese civil war and to exploit potential Sino-Soviet tensions. But domestic political pressures, together with concern over strategic implications should the island fall under Soviet control, quickly forced a reconsideration of that approach. Despite its mainland position, indigenous insurgency, and decaying colonial administration, Indochina was always included *within* the perimeter. South Korea was quite deliberately left out, only to be included abruptly as a consequence of the North Korean attack. Indecision regarding the new perimeter on the Korean peninsula in turn provoked intervention by the People's Republic of China, with the result that the "defensive perimeter" by the end of 1950 looked very different from the way it had at the beginning of that year.

These anomalies suggest that while both the immediate *strategy* of maintaining a "defensive perimeter" and the long-term *objective* of preserving a non-hostile Asia were capable of eliciting agreement in Washington, no such consensus existed as to how to get from one to the other. What, for example, was the threat to the balance of power: Soviet expansionism or international communism? Could the threat best be contained by encouraging resistance to it wherever it appeared, or by opposing it selectively with a view to promoting fragmentation? What allies might appropriately be enlisted in these efforts? And what priorities should be assigned to them, given responsibilities in other parts of the world? Nor was there always sufficient coordination of political, economic, and military planning, with the consequence that actions taken in one field were not always thought out in terms of their implications for others.

There was also a tendency to exaggerate the psychological dimensions of strategy: decisions to defend Taiwan, Indochina, and South Korea were based as much on considerations of "prestige" and "credibility" as on the importance of these territories in and of themselves.* Finally, the Truman administration may have erred in delineating its strategy too precisely. Governments should never be ambiguous with themselves in defining vital interests,

---

* "There may be times when the army and the nation fully understand the reasons for withdrawing to the interior, when confidence and hope may even be fortified as a result; but they are very rare. As a rule, the people and the army cannot even tell the difference between a planned retreat and a backward stumble; still less can they be certain if a plan is a wise one, based on anticipation of positive advantages, or whether it has simply been dictated by fear of the enemy. There will be public concern and resentment at the fate of abandoned areas; the army will possibly lose confidence not only in its leaders but in itself, and never-ending, rear guard actions will only tend to confirm its fears. *These consequences* of retreat should not be underrated." [Carl von Clausewitz, *On War* (first published in 1832), edited and translated by Peter Paret and Michael Howard (Princeton: 1976), p. 471. Emphases in original.]

but a certain amount of public ambiguity in such matters can, at times, contribute toward the deterrence of adversaries, both foreign and domestic.*

By 1951, the "defensive perimeter" concept was, to all intents and purposes, dead. Instead the Truman administration had backed into a strategy of resisting aggression wherever it occurred, but only at a corresponding level of violence. Almost immediately, frustrations over the costs of this approach led the administration to seek ways of achieving its objectives less expensively, but it never succeeded in implementing them. It would be left to Eisenhower and his advisers to devise a strategy that capitalized upon the advantages of ambiguity to achieve both deterrence and economy.† Two decades later, in reaction to an even more costly flirtation with "flexible response" in Asia, the Nixon administration would embark upon a strategy of encouraging Asian self-reliance while taking advantage of Sino-Soviet tensions to move toward a rapprochement with the People's Republic of China. It was an approach not too far removed from the original "defensive perimeter" concept as Acheson and his colleagues in the State Department had understood it. It was also—in a backhanded way—their ultimate vindication, for the long-delayed but now virtually complete withdrawal of American military power from the Asian mainland has produced, not a loss of American political and economic influence there, but on the whole a more successful reassertion of it than at any point since the end of World War II. Sometimes nations can, by losing, win.

---

* During the course of 1950, U.S. representatives in Taiwan, Indochina, and Korea all warned separately of the unfortunate consequences in their respective areas if Washington continued publicly to differentiate between regions of primary and secondary interest in East Asia. [John J. Muccio to Rusk, May 25, 1950, *FR: 1950*, VII, 88; Karl L. Rankin to Rusk, September 2, 1950, *ibid.*, VI, 481; Donald R. Heath to Rusk and Jessup, October 15, 1950, p. 896.]

† "There is a great attraction to this idea that we draw a line and say, 'If you cross this line, you get hit,'" Secretary of State Dulles admitted before the Senate Foreign Relations Committee in 1955. "Well, we found that it was almost impossible to draw a line in terms of concrete specific named places, and to say 'this is it' and nothing else is it. . . . [I]f you say 'nothing else is it,' then all you do is to let the enemy run around the lines that you have indicated. And even to say that 'this is it' is not easy." [Dulles executive session testimony, January 24, 1955, U.S. Congress, Senate Committee on Foreign Relations, *Historical Series: Eighty-Fourth Congress, First Session, 1955* (Washington: 1978), p. 85.]

# 5

# The Origins of Self-Deterrence:
# The United States and the Non-Use of
# Nuclear Weapons, 1945-1958

Within the vast hangar that houses the Air Force History Museum, outside Dayton, Ohio, there rests, like some gigantic stuffed pterodactyl, what must be one of the most imposing artifacts of the nuclear age: an entire, intact, B-36 bomber, with its six rear-mounted propellors, its four jet-booster engines, its extended cylindrical fuselage that was in fact little more than an unpressurized bomb-rack, its great drooping wings stretching almost the length of a football field, its miles of wiring, linking what was, in its day, the latest in vacuum-tube technology. Built and deployed during the late 1940's, the B-36 was capable of carrying a 10,000 pound bomb load 10,000 miles: it could, at least in theory, have taken off from bases in the United States, dropped its lethal cargo over Soviet targets, and then returned, all without refueling. Four hundred forty-six of these behemoths were eventually built, at a cost of more than a billion and a half dollars. Not one of them ever dropped a single bomb in combat.[1]

Once weapons are developed, it is often asserted, occasions will be found to use them. As with most truisms, this one is not always true; indeed, the nuclear era has made departures from it seem more the rule than the exception. Not only was the B-36 with its Volkswagen-sized thermonuclear weapons never used in anger: whole generations of intermediate- and intercontinental-range ballistic missiles have been built, deployed, and eventually dismantled

This paper was prepared for a seminar at the Institute of War and Peace Studies at Columbia University, organized by Robert Jervis and held in October, 1985. It has not been previously published.

without ever having left their launch sites. Russians and Americans have developed, begun to construct, but then by mutual consent abandoned full-scale anti-ballistic missile systems. And, most impressively, something like 70,000 nuclear weapons have been produced, not one of which has been used for military purposes since the ungainly and primitive Fat Man devastated Nagasaki more than four decades ago.*

The paradox of utility residing in non-use has become a central feature of the nuclear age. It rests upon two obvious facts of life: that nuclear weapons—even small ones—possess a destructive capacity sufficient to distort the relationship between ends and means that is the basis of strategy in the first place; and that the use of one or more such weapons by either of the superpowers would almost certainly bring swift and corresponding retaliation from the other. The security of nations now rests, as Robert Jervis has pointed out, not so much upon the exertions they themselves make, but on the restraint exhibited by their adversaries.[2]

Curiously, though, the tradition of nuclear restraint predated the capacity for nuclear retaliation: during the first four years of the Cold War, the United States enjoyed an absolute monopoly over nuclear weapons, and even after the Russians successfully tested their first atomic bomb in 1949, they lacked, for at least another half-decade, the means to deliver it against American territory in sufficient quantity and with sufficient surprise to forestall a devastating counter-response.

What deterred the United States from using nuclear weapons during the decade that separated Hiroshima from the development of a credible Soviet retaliatory capability? The precedent of combat use had already been established. There was no absence of occasions for such use, what with limited wars threatening the position of the United States and its allies in Korea, Indochina, and in the Taiwan Strait. Strategic doctrine prior to 1953 implicitly assumed resort to nuclear weapons if war came; after 1953 the assumption became explicit. We now know that during the year 1954, their use was recommended to the president on no less than five separate occasions.[3] And yet, at no point during the decade or more in which it could have used nuclear weapons with impunity did the United States actually do so. This essay inquires into the reasons for this restraint: it examines the process by which, even in the absence of a credible Soviet retaliatory capability, the United States established a tradition of not using the weapon it had been the first to use.

* A recent estimate places the total number of nuclear warheads in the arsenals of the United States and the Soviet Union as of 1985 at approximately 40,000. But the American arsenal alone in the mid-1960's contained some 30,000 warheads, and the Soviet arsenal came close to that figure during the 1970's; many of these warheads have since been retired. Nor does the current estimate of 40,000 include nuclear weapons in the arsenals of other countries. [Harold A. Feiveson, Richard H. Ullman, and Frank von Hippel, "Reducing U.S. and Soviet Nuclear Arsenals," *Bulletin of the Atomic Scientists*, XLI(August, 1985), 145–46.] Therefore, the figure of 70,000 weapons produced since 1945 seems, if anything, conservative.

# I

The date was October 5, 1945, just short of two months after American atomic bombs had ended World War II, but Harry S. Truman was sitting in the Oval Office worrying about the prospect of American military impotence. Demobilization, he told Budget Director Harold D. Smith, might be proceeding too fast: "There are some people in the world who do not seem to understand anything except the number of divisions you have." Smith found Truman's concern surprising: "Mr. President," he pointed out, "you have an atomic bomb up your sleeve." "Yes," Truman responded, "but I am not sure it can ever be used."[4]

Smith could perhaps be pardoned for feeling puzzled. After all, the United States had just spent some $2 billion to develop what was already being called the "absolute" weapon; it had demonstrated, in the most convincing way possible, that weapon's military effectiveness; there was no reason to believe that potential rivals would have their own bombs anytime soon, or that they would be able to prevail in an arms race with the United States once they did. Could it be so difficult, in these most favorable of circumstances, to think of uses for an atomic bomb?

Truman's instinct—for that is all it could have been at such an early date—was in fact prescient, because the very qualities that made the atomic bomb so impressive complicated consideration of what one might actually do with it. One could not, Bernard Brodie pointed out in 1946, come up with an explosive agent "several million times more potent on a pound-for-pound basis than the most powerful explosives previously known" without calling into question all previous thinking on the relationship between weaponry, strategy, and national policy.[5] The Truman administration was in something of the same position George Washington's had once been: correct or not, whatever it did would set precedents. But it was not at all clear that these would produce an appropriate alignment of military means with national needs.

*The "uniqueness" of nuclear weapons.* The first of the precedents Truman set was the most important: it was recognition of the fact that atomic weapons differed in character from all other weapons, and so could not be dealt with in purely military terms. "I don't think we ought to use this thing unless we absolutely have to," he commented in 1948, "this isn't a military weapon. . . . It is used to wipe out women and children and unarmed people. . . . So we have got to treat this differently from rifles and cannons and ordinary things like that."[6] Coming from the statesman who had authorized use of the bomb against Japanese cities, who repeatedly denied having second thoughts about that decision, who often said that he would not hesitate to use the bomb again if necessary, and who seemed occasionally even to gloat about what it could do—"Boy, we could blow a hole clean through the earth!"[7] he told David Lilienthal in 1949—Truman's insistence on distinguishing atomic weapons from all other forms of warfare might seem less than convincing.

But the President realized that Hiroshima and Nagasaki had made such a powerful impact on world opinion that those "first uses" were the last that would ever take place in so narrow a military context. One could never rule out resort to atomic weapons in the future, but any future decision to use them would carry profound moral and political as well as military implications: "When [people] think this is just another bomb, they are making a very serious mistake."[8]*

It was for this reason that Truman insisted on retaining total presidential authority over the atomic bomb. There was nothing inevitable about this: the Nagasaki weapon had been dropped, after all, without specific presidential authorization,[9] and the Army's initial proposals for postwar control would have left the military with effective custody over both stockpiles and production facilities. Concerned about such an arrangement, Truman had successfully supported creation of a civilian Atomic Energy Commission with full authority over the production and storage of atomic weapons.† As he explained to Secretary of Defense James Forrestal, he did not want to have "some dashing lieutenant colonel decide when would be the proper time to drop one."[10]‡

Truman was equally adamant in refusing to say categorically whether he would authorize the use of atomic weapons if war broke out. The first National Security Council study of this subject, undertaken at Forrestal's re-

---

* Truman added, significantly: "But I know the Russians would use it on us if they had it." [David E. Lilienthal Journal, February 14, 1949, quoted in *The Journals of David E. Lilienthal: The Atomic Energy Years, 1945–1950* (New York: 1964), p. 474.]

† The May-Johnson bill, originally drafted by the War Department in the summer of 1945, would have placed all nuclear facilities and raw materials in the hands of a nine-member commission made up of five civilians and four military representatives, all presidentially appointed, but with indefinite tenure. The McMahon bill, finally passed as the Atomic Energy Act of 1946, left custody of nuclear production facilities in the hands of a five-member fixed-term civilian commission, with no obligation to do anything other than consult with a Military Liaison Committee regarding military applications. For the history of legislation establishing the Atomic Energy Commission, see Richard G. Hewlett and Oscar E. Anderson, Jr., *A History of the United States Atomic Energy Commission: Volume I: The New World, 1939/1946* (University Park, Pennsylvania: 1962), pp. 408–530.

‡ Truman's Budget Director, James E. Webb, elaborated on administration reasoning in a memorandum to Truman in July, 1948: "Contrary to the opinion and attitudes of some military spokesmen, the atomic bomb is no ordinary piece of ordnance. It is destructive beyond anything known heretofore in military science. It has a symbolic value which is almost as important as an instrument of international influence as the bomb itself. The slowness of the Military Establishment to grasp these distinctions is a strong reason why custody of the stockpile should not be transferred to its hands." [Webb to Truman, July 22, 1948, Harry S. Truman Papers, PSF Box 200, "NSC: Atomic energy—budget," Harry S. Truman Library.]

quest in the summer of 1948, acknowledged that "in the event of hostilities, the National Military Establishment must be ready to utilize promptly and effectively all appropriate means available, including atomic weapons," but it emphasized that any decision actually to use them would involve political and moral issues only the President could resolve. Hence, there should be no decision in advance "either to use or not to use atomic weapons in any possible future conflict," or "as to the time and circumstances under which atomic weapons might or might not be employed."[11]

The President's insistence on full control was not without its price. It made it difficult for the military to train realistically for missions in which atomic weapons might be employed.[12] It greatly complicated the task of Pentagon strategists: lacking information about the number of bombs available or their physical characteristics, unsure as to whether use of the bomb would even be authorized, they found it impossible to formulate plausible contingency plans for war with the Soviet Union.[13] This planning vacuum may in turn have induced complacency among those responsible for producing the atomic bomb, because in the absence of detailed war plans setting out requirements for weapons, there was less incentive than there might have been to overcome production bottlenecks or to seek additional funding from an increasingly parsimonious administration.[14]

But Truman did succeed in establishing the precedent that any decision regarding the use of atomic weapons would have to be made at the top: this, in turn, served to emphasize the distinctive characteristics of those devices. In this way, Truman took the first step toward building what has turned out to be one of the most important principles of postwar international relations: the idea that nuclear weapons differ emphatically from all other weapons, and should be treated with corresponding respect.

*Deterrence, not compellence.* A second, though less clearly articulated, precedent involved how the bomb would be used in peacetime relations with the Soviet Union: it amounted to a choice in favor of deterrence over "compellence."* Prior to Hiroshima, those few Americans who knew about the bomb had anticipated that it would make a powerful impression on the Russians: their instinct had been to try to exploit that reaction in ways favorable to the United States. President Truman himself and his Secretary of State, James F. Byrnes, had expected the bomb to give them diplomatic leverage in dealing with Stalin: drawing upon their experience in domestic politics, they saw no reason why the Soviet dictator's awareness of this new weapon would not make him more cooperative on issues like Eastern Europe, just as political pressure at home might serve as a means of influencing—but without permanently alienating—a recalcitrant Congressman or party boss.[15] Others, like Secretary of War Henry L. Stimson, conceived of the bomb as an ultimate

---

* The term, of course, is Thomas C. Schelling's. [See his *Arms and Influence* (New Haven: 1966), pp. 69–78.]

instrument of reform: it might be used, Stimson thought, to induce nothing less than a transformation in the character of the Soviet system itself.[16]

The difficulty with these schemes was their vagueness on just *how* the bomb could be made to produce the desired results. As if to demonstrate that they had not been impressed, the Russians shifted to noticeably tougher negotiating positions in the weeks that followed Hiroshima: "atomic bombs," Stalin would later sniff, "are meant to frighten those with weak nerves."[17] Administration officials had worked out no strategy for applying pressure on the Russians beyond the simple fact of American possession; moreover they almost immediately found themselves distracted by pressures to place atomic weapons under some form of international control.[18] As a result, Truman and his advisers wound up giving more attention during the first year of the nuclear era to how they might unilaterally relinquish the atomic bomb than to how they might exploit it.

Administration thinking soon shifted from "compelling" more cooperative behavior on existing issues to "deterring" the Russians from future military action. The Red Army's capabilities at the time appeared awesome: one Pentagon estimate credited it with sufficient strength to overrun most of continental Europe, Turkey, Iran, Afghanistan, Manchuria, Korea, and North China.[19] But the Russians did not have the atomic bomb, and as long as that was the case, a State Department study concluded in November, 1945, "any war between the USA and the USSR would be far more costly to Russia than to the United States."[20] Two months later the Joint Chiefs of Staff noted that even "the threat of the use of the atomic bomb would be a great deterrent to any aggressor which might be considering embarking on an atomic war."[21] And by 1946, civilian strategists too had picked up the theme: hence Brodie's famous observation that the purpose of having a military establishment had now shifted from winning wars to averting them.[22]

How, though, did one make a deterrent work? "If we could just have Stalin and his boys see one of these things," Truman told David Lilienthal in 1948, "there wouldn't be any question about another war."[23] But when Winston Churchill proposed issuing a specific ultimatum—giving the Russians the choice of abandoning Berlin and East Germany or seeing their cities razed—administration officials refused to take the idea seriously: "You know better than I the practical infirmities in the suggestion," Ambassador Lewis Douglas wrote Under Secretary of State Robert Lovett.[24] Certainly explicit revelations about American atomic capabilities during this period would not have enhanced deterrence: there were only fifty atomic bombs in the American arsenal in mid-1948 and only thirty B-29 bombers equipped to carry them; the bombs themselves were primitive devices, requiring a specialized crew over two days to assemble; and because intelligence regarding the location of Soviet targets was sketchy at best, there could be no assurance that weapons dispatched would actually reach their targets.[25] Public opinion might also render the deterrent less than credible, as Secretary of State George C. Marshall observed late in 1948: "Until fairly recently I thought the Soviet leaders probably had felt the American people would never permit use of the bomb."[26]

What had changed Marshall's mind was the Truman administration's single deliberate attempt to exploit its atomic monopoly to deter Soviet military action prior to the Korean War: the quiet—but by no means secret—dispatch of B-29 bombers from American to British airbases at the height of the Berlin blockade crisis in the summer of 1948. We now know that not a single atomic bomb accompanied these bombers; indeed none of them had even been modified to carry atomic weapons.[27] Without access to Kremlin archives, it is impossible to say whether the deployment accomplished its objective, which was to keep the Russians from interfering with the Berlin airlift. But when the airlift proceeded without incident, it *appeared* that the bomber deployment had accomplished its purpose, and American officials drew the appropriate conclusions. "Soviet leaders must now realize," Marshall remarked with customary mildness, "that the use of this instrument would be possible and hence the deterrent influence now [is] perhaps greater than before."[28] Truman, as was his habit, was more blunt: if it had not been for the atomic bomb, "the Russians would have probably taken over Europe a long time ago."[29]

The Berlin B-29 deployment established two important points about how a deterrent might be made to work. First, it had not involved explicit threats—of the kind Churchill had recommended—that might have alarmed domestic opinion or upset allies. "The way to impress the Russian political mind," Dean Acheson had suggested a year earlier, "is to *understate* what we are doing,"[30] and the Berlin experience seemed to confirm the proposition. Second, it had emphasized the extent to which credibility could be made to compensate for capability: there had been no actual transfer of atomic bombs, nor could there easily have been, given the technical constraints of existing weaponry. But the deployment appeared to have had the desired effect, nonetheless. A National Security Council study completed in September, 1948, drew the appropriate conclusions: the Russians

> should in fact never be given the slightest reason to believe that the U.S. would even consider not to use atomic weapons against them if necessary. It might take no more than a suggestion of such consideration, perhaps magnified into a doubt, were it planted in the minds of responsible Soviet officials, to provoke exactly that Soviet aggression which it is fundamentally U.S. policy to avert.[31]

The whole affair had been handled "with great skill," British Foreign Secretary Ernest Bevin recalled two years later: "the Russians really believed that if they went too far they might be subjected to an attack."[32]

*War planning.* What if deterrence should fail the next time, though, and war should actually break out? There was little doubt that if a full-scale war with the Soviet Union did occur, atomic weapons would be used: all war plans formulated after the summer of 1948 assumed this, and indeed given the cuts in conventional military forces that had taken place since the end of World War II, there would have been no other choice.[33] Truman "prayed that he would never have to make such a decision," Secretary of Defense Forrestal recorded in his diary, "but . . . if it became necessary, no one need have a misgiving but that he would do so."[34] For John Foster Dulles, the matter was academic: "The American people would execute you if you did not use the bomb in the event of war."[35] But what would it be used against, and what would be the effects? These were not easy questions to answer, and the difficulty the administration had in dealing with them demonstrated the extent to which it still had not aligned national policy with the weapons now available to implement it.

The Truman administration had undertaken, during the summer of 1948, its first formal consideration of what American *political* objectives would be in the event of war with the Soviet Union. The resulting study, drafted largely by George F. Kennan and the State Department Policy Planning Staff, concluded that the experience of World War II would not apply: the United States could not expect to achieve the unconditional surrender of the Soviet government, or to impose its will upon the entire territory of the U.S.S.R. "We must recognize that whatever settlement we finally achieve must be a *political* settlement, *politically* negotiated."[36] The implications were clear: it would not be to the advantage of the United States to pursue a wartime strategy so indiscriminate in its effects as to destroy the Soviet Union totally, or to bring about the permanent alienation of its people.

And yet, the administration's own efforts to economize on military spending had forced reliance on a wartime strategy that would have been anything but discriminating: had war broken out in 1949, Pentagon plans called for the destruction over a thirty-day period of seventy Soviet urban targets with what was then virtually the entire American arsenal of some 133 atomic bombs.[37] "There are . . . grave policy issues involved which may have been overlooked," Budget Director Frank Pace warned Truman: For one thing, "[u]nless the United States itself were attacked, it is doubtful whether public opinion would support atomic warfare as a policy." It would also be important "that the concept of large-scale atomic attack, even if pointed to essentially industrial targets, be examined from the standpoint of a conscious national policy rather than solely as an aspect of a military plan." It was one thing, Pace noted, "to hold a substantial atomic stockpile in readiness for possible use, but a wholly different matter to base war strategy upon an uncritical acceptance of the idea of atomic warfare on what may amount to an unrestricted scale."[38]

Worried about some of the same problems, Secretary of Defense Forrestal late in 1948 had asked the Joint Chiefs of Staff to assess the effects of such an attack on the Soviet Union. The resulting report, drafted by an interservice committee headed by Air Force Lieutenant General Hubert R. Harmon, contained disturbing conclusions: An attack of the type proposed would kill some

2.7 million people and injure an additional four million. It would reduce Soviet industrial capacity by from 30 to 40 percent. But "the atomic offensive would not, per se, bring about capitulation, destroy the roots of Communism or critically weaken the power of the Soviet leadership to dominate the people." On the contrary, it would "for the majority of Soviet people . . . validate Soviet propaganda against foreign powers, stimulate resentment against the United States, unify these people and increase their will to fight." It would not seriously diminish the capacity of Soviet ground forces to advance into Western Europe, the Middle East, and the Far East. And, finally, "[a]tomic bombing would open the field and set the pattern for all adversaries to use any weapons of mass destruction and result in maximum retaliatory measures with Soviet capabilities."[39]

Perhaps not surprisingly, the Harmon committee report was not widely circulated within the government. Secretary of Defense Louis Johnson, who had succeeded Forrestal in March, 1949, saw to it that the President never actually received a copy.[40] But the study did reflect increasingly widespread concern that an air-atomic offensive might not in fact be the appropriate strategy if war came.* As Secretary of State Acheson acknowledged later that year, the military themselves now worried "that if the Red Army got started they would not be able to stop it, even with the bomb"; the effect was to make the Pentagon "not so unresponsive to the idea that our war preparations are designed to keep us out of war."[41]

For these reasons, the Soviet Union's successful test of its own atomic bomb in August, 1949, did less than one might have thought to shake American officials' faith in the weapon's wartime utility: that faith had never been robust to begin with. What the Soviet achievement did do was to pose the choices now available to the United States in stark terms: should it move away from reliance on atomic weapons toward a greater emphasis on conventional warfare capabilities, or should it build more such devices—and possibly a new generation of "super" or hydrogen bombs as well—in an effort to maintain indefinite nuclear superiority over the Russians?

It was George Kennan who made the case for the first alternative most clearly. The fact that the Soviet Union now had the bomb, he suggested, might well make it "impossible for us to retaliate with the atomic bomb [even] against a Russian attack with orthodox weapons." Since "neither total annihilation nor complete surrender of the enemy" was possible, Kennan's own view—as indeed it had been since 1947†—was that the United States

---

* Certainly this was the position of the Navy: locked in a desperate struggle with the Air Force over the defense budget, it used the arguments of the Harmon report—in sanitized form—to bolster its position in public Congressional hearings. [See, on this point, Paul Y. Hammond, "Super Carriers and B-36 Bombers: Appropriations, Strategy and Politics," in Harold Stein, ed., *American Civil-Military Decisions* (Birmingham, Alabama: 1963), pp. 516–27, 539–40.

† Kennan had warned, in January, 1947, of the danger that "unruly people elsewhere" might be tempted to seize "isolated and limited objectives" on the theory that, because

could deter wars most effectively by developing the capacity to fight them on a limited basis. Atomic weapons might well be irrelevant to that purpose: what were needed instead were small, highly trained mobile combat units—an early version of what would today be called a "Rapid Deployment Force"—capable of dealing quickly with limited war situations as they arose.[42] Even in a full-scale war, atomic weapons would be useful only as weapons of mass destruction: their very destructiveness would preclude their use in attaining any rational political objective. "Warfare," Kennan pointed out early in 1950, "should be a means to an end other than warfare," but atomic weapons "cannot really be reconciled with a political purpose directed to shaping, rather than destroying, the lives of the adversary."[43] Months earlier, even before news of the Soviet atomic test, he had concluded that "it would perhaps be best for this country, if it were decided that atomic bombs would never be used."[44]*

Advocates of the second position—that the United States had no choice now but to bolster its nuclear capabilities—found broader support within the administration. The Joint Chiefs of Staff, the Atomic Energy Commission, and the Department of State all argued for an increase in the production of atomic bombs, both as a deterrent and as a means of fighting future wars; President Truman approved their proposals in October, 1949.[45] The question of whether to build a hydrogen bomb was more controversial—the Atomic Energy Commission itself was divided on the issue—but in January, 1950, Truman authorized that option as well. It is important to note, though, that the hydrogen bomb decision was motivated less by the requirements of warfighting than by those of deterrence: war plans demonstrating a clear purpose for thermonuclear weapons had yet to be devised.[46] The choice was made on political grounds: deterrence could not be expected to work if the United States was perceived to be falling behind in *any* major category of weapons system, whether or not that system would be of any use in fighting a war.†

---

the United States possessed only the capacity to respond with atomic weapons, it would choose to do nothing at all. [Kennan speech to the National Defense Committee of the Chamber of Commerce of the United States, January 23, 1947, enclosed in Kennan to Dean Acheson, August 21, 1950, Dean Acheson Papers, Box 65, "Memoranda of conversations, August, 1950," Harry S. Truman Library. See also George F. Kennan, *Memoirs: 1925–1950* (Boston: 1967), pp. 310–12.]

* This position was similar to Kennan's advocacy, more than thirty years later, of a "no first use" strategy for the North Atlantic Treaty Organization. [See McGeorge Bundy, George F. Kennan, Robert S. McNamara and Gerard Smith, "Nuclear Weapons and the Atlantic Alliance," *Foreign Affairs*, LX (Spring, 1982), 753–68.]

† Truman's explanation of the hydrogen bomb decision to his staff is revealing: "The President said there actually was no decision to make on the H bomb. He said this really was a question that was settled in making up the budget for the Atomic Energy Commission last fall. . . . He went on to say that we had got to do it—make the bomb—though no one wants to use it. But, he said, we have got to have it if only for bargaining purposes with the Russians." [Eban A. Ayers Diary, February 4, 1950, Eban A. Ayers Papers, Box 27, Harry S. Truman Library.]

Insofar as war-fighting capabilities were concerned, the Truman administration actually moved, during the first half of 1950, to lessen its reliance on nuclear weapons. Kennan's arguments in favor of conventional force options had struck a responsive chord with Paul Nitze, who was shortly to succeed him as Policy Planning Staff Director: the Soviet atomic bomb, Nitze concluded in October, 1949, "might make conventional armaments and their possession by the Western European nations, as well as by ourselves, all the more important." Nitze agreed with Kennan that the Russians themselves were unlikely to start an all-out war. They might well, however, use their satellites as proxies to do their "dirty work": to embroil the West in a series of debilitating limited conflicts, no one of which would carry the risk of retaliation against the Soviet Union itself. To deal with this possibility, Nitze advocated a strengthening of American and West European conventional forces that went well beyond anything Kennan had envisaged:* it might even be necessary, he argued, to begin to shift economic priorities away from the production of consumer goods and to resort to a certain amount of "propaganda" to accomplish that objective.[47]

It was this line of reasoning that led to the drafting of NSC-68, the document Nitze considers in retrospect to have been his primary achievement in public life.[48] The conclusions of that lengthy and once-secret document are now familiar: it characterized the Soviet threat as world-wide in scope and called for a sharp increase in American defense expenditures to meet it; it demonstrated that the national economy could sustain such an increase without either crushing taxation or crippling inflation; it called for what one official acknowledged would be a "scare campaign" to shock the American people into supporting its recommendations.[49]

What is often not realized about NSC-68, though, is the conviction that pervaded it that nuclear weapons were not likely to be of much use in the kinds of wars the United States was most likely to confront. The threat now, it argued, was chiefly that of "piecemeal aggression," conducted on the assumption of "our unwillingness to engage in atomic war unless we are directly attacked." Excessive reliance on nuclear weapons would leave the United States, in such situations, with "no better choice than to capitulate or precipitate a global war." Because of their value as a deterrent, the United States could by no means abandon nuclear weapons: indeed "it would appear that we have no alternative but to increase our atomic capability as rapidly as other considerations make appropriate." Nor could it embrace Kennan's policy of "no first use," which would be interpreted "by the U.S.S.R. as an admission of great weakness and by our allies as a clear indication that we

---

* Kennan did acknowledge, in February, 1950, that lowering dependence on atomic weapons might well require "a state of semi-mobilization, involving some form of compulsory military service and drastic measures to reduce the exorbitant costs of national defense." [Kennan draft memorandum to Acheson (not sent), February 17, 1950, U.S. Department of State, *Foreign Relations of the United States* [hereafter *FR*]: *1950*, I, 165.]

intended to abandon them." But it did appear "imperative to increase as rapidly as possible our general air, ground and sea strength and that of our allies to a point where we are militarily not so heavily dependent on atomic weapons."[50]

"I think it is difficult to deduce any evidence," State Department Soviet expert Charles Bohlen wrote to Nitze in April, 1950, "that this monopoly on our part [has] influenced Soviet policy . . . or abated its aggressiveness."[51] This was, perhaps, an excessively gloomy epitaph for the four years in which the United States alone had possessed atomic weapons: indeed, Bohlen himself would subsequently acknowledge that American possession of the bomb may well have induced the caution the Russians exhibited during the Berlin blockade.[52] But the fact that it was so difficult to identify any specific benefits the United States had received from its monopoly, together with the fact that, by 1950, it was emphasizing a build-up of conventional forces once again, suggests that Truman may not have been far off the mark when he had suggested, at the beginning of the nuclear era, that it might be difficult to find uses for the atomic bomb.

# II

Prior to the North Korean invasion of South Korea in June, 1950, the Truman administration had thought about the military uses of atomic weapons only in the context of a general war with the Soviet Union. Although NSC-68 had warned that "piecemeal" aggression by Russian proxies was the more likely prospect, there had been little consideration of how the United States might respond to such challenges, and virtually none to the role the atomic bomb might play in such a response. Korea provided an effective "crash course" on the nature of "limited" wars, but it did little to clarify the uses of atomic weapons in fighting them. Indeed, one of the most remarkable aspects of the Truman administration's strategy in the Korean conflict is how inconspicuously the atomic bomb figured in it.

This is not what one might have expected. The entire "defensive perimeter" concept in East Asia had been built around the idea that American air and naval power, but not ground forces, would be the preferred instruments of containment. The use of atomic weapons would have been consistent with this "high technology-low manpower" response to aggression.[53] Korea was also the first instance since the end of World War II in which a nation possessing those weapons had actually engaged in combat: there was no reason to assume automatically that the bomb would not be used again, much as it had been in 1945. Even more striking is the fact that the United States and its allies came close to defeat more than once in Korea—particularly following Chinese intervention late in 1950—and that still Truman and his advisers never seriously considered using the most powerful weapon available to them.

There were several reasons for this self-imposed restraint. The first had to do with the simple matter of what to bomb. Atomic weapons had been developed as an extension of World War II strategic bombing campaigns. The prevailing assumption had been that they would be used, if war recurred, against important industrial and military targets inside the Soviet Union. Unexpected involvement in a limited war fought against adversaries not dependent on the technology strategic bombing had been designed to disrupt left military planners with no obvious targets whose destruction would ensure victory. "What would it be dropped on?" General Marshall wanted to know when Bernard Baruch proposed using the weapon in Korea.[54] The bomb might be helpful in breaking up enemy troop concentrations or artillery emplacements, Nitze suggested, but there was no reason to think that its use for that purpose would be "militarily decisive."[55]

Following China's intervention, the Joint Chiefs of Staff did raise with General MacArthur the possibility of using atomic bombs to repel the invading forces, but despite MacArthur's considerable interest in this option—he even speculated early in 1951 about the possibility of laying a belt of radioactive waste across the neck of North Korea—he at no point formally recommended that such weapons be employed.[56]* No further consideration of battlefield use appears to have taken place during the remainder of the Truman administration.

The possibility of bombing China itself did receive serious consideration—despite the fact that MacArthur's public advocacy of just this course of action had contributed to his removal from command in April, 1951—but these plans were to be implemented only if the Chinese committed aggression elsewhere in Asia, and they would probably *not* have involved the use of atomic weapons. "There are almost no appropriate atomic targets in China," a Policy Planning Staff study noted, and only "three or four in Manchuria."[57] By 1952 justifications for bombing or blockading China had expanded to include retaliation for the failure to reach an armistice agreement in Korea, or for the violation of one. But as General Omar Bradley explained to Winston Churchill and Anthony Eden, "it was not our intention to use these [atomic] bombs, since up to the present time no suitable targets were presented." The situation might change, but "so far this was entirely theoretical."[58]

* Rosemary Foot has argued that MacArthur did recommend use of the atomic bomb in Korea in December, 1950, even to the point of submitting a list of targets and requesting actual bombs. [*The Wrong War: American Policy and the Dimensions of the Korean Conflict, 1950–53* (Ithaca: 1985), pp. 114–15.] But both the official Army history of military operations in Korea and MacArthur's biographer deny that the General ever formally recommended the use of atomic weapons in Korea. [James F. Schnabel, *United States Army in the Korean War: Policy and Direction: The First Year* (Washington: 1972), p. 320n; D. Clayton James, *The Years of MacArthur: Triumph and Disaster, 1945–1964* (Boston: 1985), p. 579.] The accounts of Schnabel and James suggest that MacArthur, in the document cited by Foot, was simply responding to inquiries from the Joint Chiefs of Staff as to how such weapons *might* be used.

A second reason for Washington's reluctance to use atomic weapons in the Korean war involved the possibility of provoking some form of Soviet intervention. Attacks against the United States or its Western European allies were not the concern here: although intelligence estimates continued to credit the Russians with overwhelming conventional force superiority—and even with the ability to carry out one-way bombing missions against selected targets in the Western hemisphere—the possibility of general war was thought unlikely because the Soviet Union lacked the capacity to neutralize American retaliatory forces.[59] "[W]ould the Russians accept the risk of a global war if they believed they could not ward off a retaliatory atomic attack?" a Policy Planning Staff memorandum asked in August, 1951: "Can in fact a dictatorship which relies on the secret police to retain itself in power take the risk of having its elaborate apparatus destroyed at home?"[60] Basing its conclusion on Central Intelligence Agency estimates, the National Security Council concluded later that year that the "marked atomic superiority of the United States," together with "the uncertainty that must necessarily exist in the minds of the Soviet rulers whether, in the event of general war, strategic atomic attack on the Soviet Union could be avoided," made it unlikely that the Russians "would deliberately initiate or provoke war with the United States."[61]*

But what if the Soviet Union should intervene on behalf of the North Koreans and the Chinese? The State Department and the Central Intelligence Agency took quite seriously the Sino-Soviet Treaty of February, 1950, in which the Russians had promised to come to the assistance of the Chinese in case of attack.[62] Use of the atomic bomb in Korea would carry with it the "serious possibility" of provoking such intervention, Nitze argued in November, 1950; dropping it on Chinese or Manchurian targets "would almost certainly bring the Soviet Union into the war."[63] If that happened, it would be difficult to avoid a global conflict with the Russians, for as Acheson noted the following spring, American public opinion "would doubtless insist that the United States respond with all the means at its disposal including atomic weapons."[64] But that action, in turn, would mean the loss of Korea altogether, since contingency plans called for evacuating the peninsula in the event of general war with the Soviet Union.[65]

Given these gloomy alternatives, it is curious that the Truman administration appears never to have considered explicitly threatening the Soviet Union with atomic retaliation as a means of *deterring* its intervention on behalf of the North Koreans and the Chinese. After all, the B-29 deployment of 1948 seemed to have discouraged the Russians from interfering with the Berlin airlift; certainly American retaliatory capabilities had significantly

---

* The NSC report went on to note, though, that the Soviet Union might well attempt, "when local opportunities arise, to exploit by cold war tactics its geographic position and its preponderant ground and tactical air forces to obtain results advantageous to it." [NSC 114/2, "United States Programs for National Security," October 12, 1951, *FR: 1951*, I, 188.]

improved since that time.[66] The fact that the Russians had not invoked the Sino-Soviet Treaty when China entered the Korean War suggests that they treated their obligations under that document both flexibly and cautiously.[67] Had the United States been determined to use atomic weapons in Korea or China, the prospect of Soviet intervention, at least in retrospect, would not appear to have been great.

There was, however, a third and even more important inhibition against their use, and that had to do with the unique characteristics of the weapons themselves. Despite the fact that "the military results achieved by atomic bombardment may be identical to those attained by conventional weapons," John K. Emmerson of the State Department's Bureau of Far Eastern Affairs warned in November, 1950, "the effect on world opinion will be vastly different. The A-bomb has the status of a peculiar monster conceived by American cunning, and its use by us, in whatever situation, would be exploited to our serious detriment." The consequences, Emmerson argued, could include breaking apart the United Nations coalition then fighting in Korea and possibly the United Nations itself, a "revulsion of feeling" toward Americans throughout all of Asia where fears would be confirmed "that we reserve atomic weapons exclusively for Japanese and Chinese," a "disastrous" loss of confidence on the part of Western Europe, and irreparable damage to the "moral position" of the United States which the Russians would be well positioned to exploit in the event that they did wish to provoke a general war.[68]

That these were not merely speculative concerns became clear on November 30, 1950, when President Truman casually acknowledged, in answer to a reporter's question, that use of the atomic bomb in Korea had always been under "active consideration." Truman was careful to point out that he himself did not want to see the bomb used. "It is a terrible weapon, and it should not be used on innocent men, women, and children who have nothing whatever to do with this military aggression. That happens when it is used." But he quickly undermined whatever reassurance this last statement had conveyed by going on to observe—quite inexplicably, given his own past insistence on tight presidential control—that "the military commander in the field" would decide when the time had come to use the atomic bomb.[69]

The President had, in every sense of a word common to White House spokesmen of a subsequent generation, "misspoken."* By even inadvertently raising the possibility of using atomic weapons in Korea—and, even worse, by suggesting that it might be left to General MacArthur to decide on their use—Truman created an uproar among allies and neutrals that made painfully apparent what the diplomatic costs of such a decision would be.

"British opinion from top to bottom . . . is strongly opposed to any

---

* The White House quickly issued a clarifying statement pointing out that the President would still have to authorize any military use of the bomb, and that field commanders would be responsible only for its "tactical delivery." [White House press release, November 30, 1950, *Public Papers of the Presidents: Harry S. Truman, 1950* (Washington: 1965), p. 727n.]

action that would contribute to UN forces becoming entangled in war with [Communist] China," the American Embassy in London reported the day after Truman's press conference: "use of [the] bomb in Korea . . . would be likely [to] precipitate such an inextricable entanglement."[70] Prime Minister Attlee found Truman's statement so alarming that he immediately invited himself to Washington for consultations: "without moving a single man," he complained, "the Soviet Union had succeeded in embroiling the Democratic forces increasingly in the Far East. . . . We must remember what might happen in Europe."[71] The British Chiefs of Staff expanded on this argument in a discreet warning to MacArthur:

> in our view, if the atom bomb were used in Korea, it would not only be ineffective in holding up the Chinese advance, but it would make the situation more desperate by inevitably bringing the Soviet Air Force into the war. The atom bomb is our ultimate weapon and we must keep it in reserve as a deterrent or for use in the event of the Russians launching a third world war.[72]

Since, as Deputy Secretary of Defense Lovett put it, "Western Europe was our prime concern and we would rather see [the loss of Korea and even Japan] than lose in Western Europe"[73]—and since Truman himself had never intended a change of strategy in the first place—it was not difficult for Attlee and his colleagues to persuade the Americans of the need to take European considerations into account before any decision to use the bomb in Korea.*

Other reactions were more difficult to defuse. The fact that the only prior use of the bomb had been against Asians now came back to haunt the Truman administration as reports from the United Nations and from embassies overseas stressed the extent to which the weapon had come to be seen as a racist instrument. The impression was developing, Saudi Arabia's United Nations delegate told Eleanor Roosevelt, that the bomb was intended for use against "colored people."[74]† Indian Prime Minister Jawaharlal Nehru warned of the "wide-spread feeling in Asia that the atomic bomb is a weapon used only against Asiatics."[75] If Asia was to be kept "in step with the rest of the world in the stand against aggression," Attlee told French Prime Minister René

---

* Attlee himself believed that he had dissuaded the Truman administration from embarking on a limited war with China. [Report to the Cabinet, December 12, 1950, Cabinet Records, CM 85(50), CAB128/18, Public Record Office, London.] But, as Alan Bullock has pointed out, the impression within the Labour Party "that Attlee's visit to Washington was crucial in preventing the use of the A-bomb . . . is a myth." [*Ernest Bevin: Foreign Secretary, 1945–1951* (New York: 1983), p. 823.]

† Mrs. Roosevelt replied coolly that "war itself was [the] basic evil. Although she hoped it would not be necessary to use [the] A-bomb in Korea, choice of weapons would have to be decided in terms [of the] military situation at [the] particular time." [Warren Austin to Acheson, December 1, 1950, *FR: 1950*, VII, 1300.]

Pleven, "any action [regarding use of the bomb] must be thought of in relation to its effect on Asiatic opinion."[76]*

Truman's inadvertent remark had served, then, as a kind of trial balloon, revealing even before there had been any serious consideration of using the bomb in Korea what the overseas reaction would be. The results were anything but reassuring. As Emmerson had predicted, they included the potential of disarray among NATO allies, worried that the United States might be committing itself disproportionately in peripheral theaters while neglecting the defense of Western Europe. They included the probable alienation of newly independent nations in Asia and the Middle East at a time when Soviet influence was thought to be growing there. And perhaps most significantly— since the Truman administration had no plans actually to use the bomb for military purposes in Korea—they inhibited consideration of how the weapon might be used as a *political* instrument to bring an end to the fighting there.

Early in 1951, Stuart Symington, Chairman of the National Security Resources Board, sent a long memorandum to the President complaining that the Russians, taking advantage of the American determination to counter aggression without escalation, "can dictate not only how and where we fight— but when; and so far they have been allowed to dictate the choice of weapons." The one place in which this had not been allowed to happen was Berlin: there the Russians had been confronted with a line drawn "for all the world to see and understand." The Soviet Union knew that if it crossed that line, the result would be "war with the United States and all that such a war implies." Despite their overwhelming conventional force superiority, the Russians had not in fact done so; the reason, Symington argued, could only be their fear of "our atomic bomb stockpile plus our capability of delivery. . . . That same principle of policy we are now utilizing in Berlin could be extended throughout the world."[77]†

"[D]uring an era in which the naked power of aggression heeds only naked power," Symington explained in a supplementary report to the National Security Council, "the free nations do not in political discussion bring up their prime power advantage, the atomic bomb and the capacity to deliver it." If the United States were to make it clear "that any further Soviet aggression, in areas to be spelled out, would result in the atomic bombardment of Soviet Russia itself," this would not only deter Soviet expansionism and enhance American leadership in the world: it would

> [e]stablish moral justification for [the] use of United States' atom
> bombs in retaliation against Soviet aggression . . . [a]nd thus afford

---

* "It was necessary to bear in mind," Attlee added, "that the British and the French were more alive to Asiatic sentiment than were the Americans." [Minutes, Attlee-Pleven conversation, December 2, 1950, Foreign Office Records, F0371/83019/F1027/6G, Public Record Office, London.]

† Symington went on to warn, though, that with the Russians now rapidly increasing their own atomic stockpile, opportunities for implementing such a strategy would not exist much longer. [Symington to Truman, undated but January, 1951, *FR: 1951*, I, 24.]

the United States a measure of moral freedom it does not now have to use the atom bomb under circumstances other than retaliation out of what devastation might be left of this country after an initial Soviet atomic attack.[78]

Symington's idea of issuing an ultimatum to the Russians did not meet with wide approval. "My dear Stu," Truman wrote at the bottom of the memorandum Symington had sent him: "this is [as] big a lot of Top Secret malarky as I've ever read. Your time is wasted on such bunk as this."[79]* A study done several months later by the Joint Strategic Survey Committee and representatives from the State Department concluded that the "public definition of a 'stop-line' would be a grave mistake for, on the one hand, it would invite aggression up to the line and, on the other, would probably increase our overt commitments to go to war in given situations."[80]

But the Symington memorandum did reflect a widespread sense within the government that the United States had failed to devise strategies for deterring limited aggression at reasonable cost. When the British continued to press for clarification of the circumstances in which Washington proposed to use atomic weapons, there began to emerge a consensus that there might be a role for them in situations short of all-out war. Nitze pointed out in May, 1951, that the bomb might provide a means of "localizing" aggression: the weapon could be used, for example, to ward off a Soviet invasion of Yugoslavia without necessarily precipitating a global conflict.[81] The Joint Strategic Survey Committee–State Department study that had ruled out the idea of Symington's idea of an ultimatum nonetheless insisted that "the United States must retain its freedom of action to employ atomic weapons in . . . localized conflict[s] if the military situation dictates."[82]

It was natural for the British to worry about this issue, Acheson commented a few days later. "[T]hey are now the tail of the kite and they are concerned about where the kite is going." But the fact was that "we cannot imagine a real war without the use of the atomic bomb." And even if the Russians should intervene in Korea, "we would have to react with everything we had." "When talking of the atomic bomb," Lovett added, "we should not speak only of general war because we might . . . use the bomb without it being a general war." Acheson agreed. "[W]e would simply say," General Bradley suggested, "that we would use the bomb in a war against the U.S.S.R. and whether we would use it in other circumstances would depend on the situation existing at the time."[83]

The growing feasibility of tactical atomic weapons encouraged this line of thought. As the Chief of Special Projects of the Joint Congressional Committee on Atomic Energy wrote in the summer of 1951, these devices were likely to be as revolutionary in their effects as the Hiroshima bomb itself: they were "300 times more economical than conventional high explosives" and as such constituted "the natural armaments of numerically inferior but

---

* It is not clear whether the President ever actually conveyed this pungent reaction directly to Symington.

technologically superior nations. . . . Very probably we will want them . . . in the tens of thousands."[84] Bomb production rates were greatly accelerated during 1951 and 1952: as Lovett put it, "we must err, if we must, on the side of too much rather than too little."[85] This expansion in production, he stressed, was intended

> to afford the United States a greater advantage from this powerful weapon in any conflict with the Soviet Union *or any other active enemy of the United States.* We place no limit on the extent of the use of atomic or any other weapons, nor do we believe that the use of large numbers of atomic weapons against an enemy would have any adverse effect on neutrals or potential allies.[86]

Acheson accepted this argument, endorsing the desirability of having, by 1956, "a U.S. capability to deal repeated atomic blows at the USSR production potential together with a sufficient quantity of atomic weapons for battlefield use."[87]

Even so, this growing interest in the concept of using atomic weapons in limited wars brought about no reconsideration of the Truman administration's policy of refraining from their use in Korea.* The difficulties of finding appropriate targets, of avoiding Soviet intervention, and of unsettling allies all seemed as great as they had ever been. Moreover, armistice negotiations with the North Koreans and the Chinese Communists had been under way since the summer of 1951: any use of atomic weapons clearly would have ended them. By the time it became apparent that these negotiations were not going to produce quick results, the 1952 presidential campaign was under way, Truman himself had announced his intention not to run again, and a general attitude had developed of leaving controversial decisions for the next administration to make. "Our stockpile is now . . . regarded as frozen until and unless general war breaks out," Nitze commented in January, 1953. "We have not fully analyzed the balance between . . . using these weapons to increase . . . the capability of our conventional forces to deal with local situations as against the contra political and strategic considerations."[88]

The Truman administration's final review of national security policy, completed only a day before Eisenhower's inauguration, concluded that there

---

* Note, for example, the absence of any such recommendation in the Truman administration's final comprehensive reviews of national security policy, NSC 135/3, "Reappraisal of United States Objectives and Strategy for National Security," September 25, 1952, *FR: 1952–54,* II, 142–56; and NSC 141, "Reexamination of United States Programs for National Security," January 19, 1953, *ibid.,* pp. 209–22. In a belligerent 1952 diary entry signed "The C. in C.," Truman did pose the question to the Russians: "Now do you want an end to hostilities in Korea or do you want China and Siberia destroyed? You may have one or the other, whichever you want." [Truman Diary, May 18, 1952, Robert H. Ferrell, ed., *Off the Record: The Private Papers of Harry S. Truman* (New York: 1980), p. 251.] But the President used these diary entries largely as a means of blowing off steam; they were rarely if ever shown to anyone else, and certainly should not be taken as reflecting administration policy.

was a fundamental difference in the way in which the two superpowers were likely to use nuclear weapons. If the United States, but not the Soviet Union, should develop a credible thermonuclear capability during the next two years, "the free world would possess for the duration of this monopoly an enhanced deterrent to general war." But "[w]hether this margin of superiority would permit us, through the adoption of bolder initiatives, favorably to resolve a number of outstanding issues in the cold war is, however, problematical." If, though, the Soviet Union should also develop the hydrogen bomb,

> this would present an extremely grave threat to the United States, notwithstanding our own assumed thermonuclear capability. It would tend to impose greater caution on our cold war policies to the extent that these policies involve significant risks of general war.[89]

The implications were obvious: the Russians, because of the very nature of their system, faced fewer inhibitions than the United States in attempting to extract political advantages from the possession of nuclear weapons. Nitze himself posed the crucial question: would the United States ever "be willing to use the atomic threat or to follow through on it in the event of any Soviet move short of direct atomic attack on the United States?" Suspecting that the answer was no, he left the Policy Planning Staff much as he had entered it three years earlier at the time of the drafting of NSC-68, advocating action "to overcome our dependence on atomic weapons."[90]*

# III

As it happened, though, the incoming Eisenhower administration had a very different attitude toward the potential political uses of nuclear weapons. "Power," John Foster Dulles had insisted during the 1952 presidential campaign, "never achieves its maximum possibility as a deterrent of crime unless those of criminal instincts have reason to fear that [it] will actually be used against them." It was necessary "to make such power a deterrent of war instead of a mere means of waging war after we get into it."[91] Convinced that American nuclear superiority provided that kind of power, Dulles persuaded an initially skeptical Eisenhower to move well beyond the Truman administration's tentative and unpublicized plans to fight future wars with nuclear weapons toward a strategy of overtly threatening their use to achieve political objectives short of war.

Dulles's strategy appealed to Eisenhower on both military and economic

---

* Although, curiously, Nitze in this same memorandum expressed the view that "[i]f the use of atomic weapons could be limited to tactical uses, it is quite possible our very great superiority in numbers of weapons would be to our advantage. It is difficult to see, however, how a precise dividing line can be drawn, or lived up to, separating tactical from strategic uses." [Memorandum of January 12, 1953, *FR: 1952–54*, II, 204.]

grounds. From the military perspective, it promised to regain the initiative that had so obviously been lost in Korea: henceforth the United States would confront aggressors on terrain and with weapons of its own choice, not theirs. "[N]o foreign policy really deserves the name," the new Chief Executive argued, "if it is merely the reflex action from someone else's initiative."[92] From the economic perspective, reliance on nuclear deterrence promised solvency: if the nation had to continue conventional force expenditures on the scale the Korean conflict had required, Eisenhower told the National Security Council, there would be reason to wonder "whether national bankruptcy or national destruction would get us first."[93] NSC 162/2, the new administration's first comprehensive statement of national security policy, expressed the emphasis clearly:

> In specific situations where a warning appears desirable and feasible as an added deterrent, the United States should make clear to the USSR and Communist China . . . its intention to react with military force against any aggression by Soviet bloc armed forces. . . . In the event of hostilities, the United States will consider nuclear weapons to be as available for use as other munitions.[94]

Or, as Eisenhower publicly acknowledged: "atomic weapons have virtually achieved conventional status within our armed services."[95]

What did this mean, though, in practical terms? The Eisenhower administration had three distinct opportunities to apply this strategy during its first three years in office: in Korea, in Indochina, and in the Taiwan Strait. The results, as will become evident, were decidedly mixed:

*Korea.* Eisenhower and Dulles inherited, but were determined to end, the Korean war. The Truman administration had allowed armistice negotiations with the North Koreans and the Chinese Communists to drag on for a year and a half without results; meanwhile military operations—and American military casualties—had continued without letup. Eisenhower himself had traveled to Korea in December, 1952; upon his return, he met with General MacArthur, who had revived his earlier suggestion to end the Korean war through use of the atomic bomb against enemy military concentrations and "the sowing of fields of suitable radio-active materials . . . to close major lines of enemy supply and communication." The President-elect was noncommittal, noting only that "we have to make sure we're not offending the whole free world." But MacArthur was sure that Eisenhower had "agreed that I was right."[96]

Less than a month after taking office, the new Chief Executive suggested to the National Security Council "that we should consider the use of tactical atomic weapons" in Korea. Certainly "we could not go on the way we were [there] indefinitely." General Omar Bradley, Chairman of the Joint Chiefs of Staff and a veteran of the Truman administration's deliberations over this issue, advised caution, noting the difficulties such a move would create with allies. Secretary of State Dulles acknowledged the point, but insisted that it had been Soviet strategy all along to set "atomic weapons apart from all other weapons as being in a special category." The time had come to "try to break down this false distinction."⁹⁷* The following month, Eisenhower asked for information on the costs of assuming the offensive in Korea, on the assumption "that the use of atomic weapons in such a campaign should depend on military judgment as to the advantage of their use on military targets."⁹⁸

The outcome of these investigations was not particularly encouraging. Army Chief of Staff General J. Lawton Collins expressed himself as "very skeptical" about the military advantages: Chinese and North Korean forces were deeply entrenched along a 150-mile front, and recent bomb tests in Nevada had proven "that men can be very close to the explosion and not be hurt if they are well dug in." Paul Nitze, still serving as Director of the Policy Planning Staff, noted that if the weapons were not effective, their use might "depreciate the value of our stockpile." Certainly it would cause political difficulties with the allies. There was also the question of whether or not the Soviet Union might decide "to retaliate in kind." If that happened, Collins added, American harbor facilities at Pusan and Inchon would make better targets for atomic bombs than would the enemy.⁹⁹† Perhaps most discouragingly, a National Security Council staff study concluded that it could not predict what effect the use of atomic weapons would have on Communist forces in Korea, other than to demonstrate American determination.¹⁰⁰

Eisenhower's own thoughts on this question were ambivalent. On the one hand, he repeatedly questioned his military advisers' conclusion that atomic weapons would have little battlefield utility in Korea. "[W]e have got to consider the atomic bomb as simply another weapon in our arsenal," he told a still doubtful Bradley in May, 1953.¹⁰¹ But, on the other, he acknowledged that "we could not blind ourselves to the effects of such a move on our allies, which would be very serious since they feel they will be the battleground in an atomic war between the United States and the Soviet Union." Nor would the American people support a decision "to call off the armistice now and to go to war again in Korea." Moreover, the President acknowledged the possibility of Soviet retaliation, and not just against Pusan and Inchon: his "one great anxiety" was "the possibility of attacks by the Soviet Air Force on the almost defenseless population centers of Japan." There was, General Collins observed, "no clear answer to the President's anxiety."¹⁰²

But if Eisenhower was ambivalent regarding the actual use of atomic weapons in Korea, he was not at all reluctant to give the *impression* that such

* Eisenhower added that if the allies "objected to the use of atomic weapons we might well ask them to supply three or more divisions needed to drive the Communists back, in lieu of the use of atomic weapons." [Minutes, National Security Council meeting, February 11, 1953, *FR: 1952–54*, XV, 770.]

† Although General Bradley warned that if a renewed offensive produced heavy American casualties, "we may find that we will be forced to use every type of weapon that we have." [Minutes, meeting of State and Defense Department representatives, March 27, 1953, *FR: 1952–54*, XV, 818.]

weapons might be used to break the military stalemate there. Even before he took office, the State Department had suggested having the Central Intelligence Agency spread rumors about the possible use of atomic weapons in Korea and, if necessary, against China as well, if no armistice agreement was reached soon.[103]* What, if anything, the C.I.A. actually did—and to what extent Eisenhower was aware of it—is still not clear. But it quickly became apparent that idea appealed to him: as early as his return from Korea, in December, 1952, he had issued an ominously vague public statement noting that only deeds, not words, would impress the enemy there, and that these would have to be "executed under circumstances of our own choosing."[104] Dulles followed suit, announcing in May, 1953, that "the U.N. Command is not prepared indefinitely to continue bandying words about matters which have already been talked about for 2 years."[105] And later that month, while in New Delhi, the Secretary of State made a point of telling Indian Prime Minister Nehru that "if the armistice negotiations collapsed, the United States would probably make a stronger rather than a lesser military exertion, and that this might well extend the area of conflict." In his own memorandum of this conversation, Dulles noted: "I assumed this would be relayed."[106]†

The Korean armistice agreement, signed on July 27, 1953, made a decision as to whether or not to use atomic weapons there unnecessary. Given currently available sources, it is impossible to say how effective the administration's implied threats were in persuading Beijing and Pyongyang to accept the armistice, although it seems safe to say they could not easily have been disregarded.[107] For Eisenhower and Dulles, the conclusion was clear enough: "The principal reason we were able to obtain the armistice," the Secretary of State explained several months later,

> was because we were prepared for a much more intensive scale of warfare. . . . [W]e had already sent the means to the theater for delivering atomic weapons. This became known to the Chinese through their good intelligence sources and in fact we were not unwilling that they should find out.[108]‡

---

* Interestingly, this initiative appears to have originated with George F. Kennan, then serving as U.S. ambassador in Moscow, although it should be noted that Kennan did not specifically recommend, at this point, threatening to use atomic weapons. [Kennan to State Department, July 30 and August 19, 1952, *FR: 1952–54*, XV, 431–32, 484n.] The "Project Solarium" Task Force A, which Kennan chaired the following year, did recommend "[c]onsidering the question of announcing that the U.S. will feel free to use atomic weapons in case of local aggression in the future." [Task Force A summary, enclosed in James S. Lay to the National Security Council, July 22, 1953, *ibid.*, II, 402.]

† The following day, Nehru expressed concern that if hostilities became more intense in Korea, "it would be difficult to know what the end might be." "I made no comment," Dulles noted, "and allowed the topic to drop." [Dulles memorandum of conversation with Nehru, May 22, 1953, *FR: 1952–54*, XV, 1071.]

‡ The first transfer of atomic weapons to military control for deployment overseas took place in June, 1953. See, on this point, David Alan Rosenberg, "The Origins of Overkill:

Years later, when asked why the Chinese had accepted an armistice in Korea, Eisenhower replied succinctly: "Danger of an atomic war."[109]

The administration also relied heavily on the threat of atomic retaliation to deter violations of the armistice, once it had gone into effect. At its insistence, the sixteen nations that had fought under the United Nations flag in Korea declared on the day of the armistice that, in the event of renewed fighting, "in all probability, it would not be possible to confine hostilities within the frontiers of Korea."[110]* Eisenhower's comments on the subject were particularly vehement: if the Chinese Communists attacked again, he told the National Security Council in December, "we should certainly respond by hitting them hard and wherever it would hurt most, including Peiping itself. This . . . would mean all-out war against Communist China."[111] The United States would "hit them with everything we['ve] got," he informed Congressional leaders the following month.[112] And, several days later: "we should get tough right away quick and get into the business with both feet. . . . When you finally decide to resort to force you should plan no limits to its use."[113]

But did Eisenhower really believe this? If United States security interests dictated the use of atomic weapons, he assured the N.S.C. in October, 1953, he "would certainly decide to use them." But the President was speaking of general war. The Joint Chiefs of Staff, he told its new chairman, Admiral Arthur Radford, "should not . . . plan to make use of these weapons in minor affairs." There were places "where you would not be able to use these weapons because if you did it would look as though the U.S. were initiating global war." Moreover, "nothing would so upset the whole world as an announcement by the United States of a decision to use these weapons."[114] Not surprisingly, Radford found this guidance less than helpful. When, several days later, he pressed Eisenhower for clarification, the President commented that the bomb should be used if aggression was renewed in Korea, but wondered if this would not cause "a dangerous breach in allied solidarity." When asked whether the language of NSC 162/2, providing that "in the event of hostilities," nuclear weapons would be considered "to be available for use as other munitions," could be made more specific, Eisenhower replied, "[N]o, . . . we could not hope to do better than the presently agreed language on that point."[115]

Eisenhower's ambivalence reflected the fact that even though threats to use atomic weapons might have hastened the armistice, doubts still persisted as to whether their military effectiveness would outweigh the resulting dangers of escalation. Atomic bombs could prevent United Nations forces from being

---

Nuclear Weapons and American Strategy, 1945–1960," *International Security*, VII (Spring, 1983), p. 27.

* This so-called "Greater Sanctions" statement had originated during the Truman administration, but had not, at that time, been understood as implying the use of atomic weapons. [See, on this point, Foot, *The Wrong War*, pp. 154–55, 214–15.]

overrun, a National Security Council study pointed out that same month, but their use would expose those same forces "to possible atomic bombing by the Communists, if they were prepared to risk general war."[116] The Joint Chiefs of Staff insisted that if hostilities resumed in Korea, they would seek authorization to hit targets in Manchuria and China, together with "the immediate employment of nuclear weapons in sufficient quantity to insure success of the proposed operation."[117] But as another N.S.C. study pointed out, war with China would "almost certainly [result in] a split of the U.S.-led coalition," would make probable "military intervention by the USSR and a very high risk of global war," and would involve "[p]ossible use of a significant proportion of the U.S. atomic stockpile and employment of a major proportion of its atomic carriers."[118]

There were "grave disadvantages" in what the Joint Chiefs of Staff contemplated, Dulles told the National Security Council early in December. Not only would it mean fighting China and probably the Soviet Union as well; there would be "virtually no UN participants. . . . We would thus be isolated from our allies." There was the question of whether Japan would allow the United States to use bases there "if they concluded that such permission would expose them to direct Soviet attack." But, most important, such a conflict would divert United States forces away from Europe for the purpose of conducting a general war in Asia: the result would be that "most of the West European countries would immediately run for cover by seeking a neutrality pact with the USSR." Dulles did not entirely rule out use of the atomic bomb within Korea itself, or against troop concentrations "in or near the area of Korea." But he thought it "dangerous to provide the military with a decision now which might permit them to make a general war automatically in Asia in response to a Communist attack."[119]

The American people understood atomic weapons, Eisenhower commented early in 1954, "but we must be a little patient with our allies, who had not as yet grasped the import of atomic warfare." For this reason, the commander of American forces in Korea would be free to respond to any renewal of aggression there "with everything he had except the atomic weapon." Decisions on its use would have to be referred to Washington.[120] In the end, therefore, Eisenhower decided not to decide whether to use the atomic bomb in Korea, and events cooperated by not forcing the difficult choice upon him. As an intelligence estimate in March, 1954, noted, the Russians and the Chinese Communists now feared that attacks against Japan, Taiwan, the Philippines or South Korea "would almost certainly bring US actions against the Chinese mainland, possibly including attacks with nuclear weapons." Therefore, "[t]he Communists will probably not initiate new local aggressions in Asia with identifiable Soviet, Chinese Communist, or North Korean armed forces."[121]

No one can say with certainty what Eisenhower would have done if events had turned out differently in Korea. What is clear is that the President was more eager to *talk* about the possibility of using nuclear weapons there than he was actually to do so. It is significant that when a militantly aggressive

South Korean President Syngman Rhee visited the White House in July, 1954, Eisenhower took the occasion to deliver a stern lecture: Korea's fate, he said, was no different from that of other divided countries like Germany, Austria, and Indochina:

> We want to see your country unified, but I must tell you, Mr. President, that no one in this world will get America to go to war over these problems. . . . [L]et me tell you that if war comes, it will be horrible. Atomic war will destroy civilization. It will destroy our cities. There will be millions of people dead. War today is unthinkable with the weapons which we have at our command. If the Kremlin and Washington ever lock up in a war, the results are too horrible to contemplate. I can't even imagine them.[122]

A year earlier, after Rhee had almost torpedoed the armistice by unilaterally releasing North Korean and Chinese prisoners of war, Eisenhower had pointed out that the United States "can *do* all sorts of things to suggest to Rhee that we might very well be prepared to leave Korea, but the truth of the matter was, of course, that we couldn't actually leave."[123] Something like this may have been Eisenhower's strategy with regard to the use of nuclear weapons in Korea: it would have been no mean trick, after all, to talk loudly about doing things one had no desire to do, if through such talk one could obviate the necessity of having to do them.

*Indochina.* The Eisenhower administration's strategy of deterring aggression by threatening the use of nuclear weapons received its second test in Indochina, where French forces found themselves facing defeat early in 1954 at the hands of the Communist Viet Minh. "There is the risk that, as in Korea, Red China might send its own army into Indochina," Dulles had warned several months earlier. "The Chinese Communist regime should realize that such a second aggression could not occur without grave consequences which might not be confined to Indochina."[124] By March, it had become apparent that the French had blundered into a dangerous military situation by concentrating troops at the fortress of Dienbienphu, which the Viet Minh had now surrounded. The United States might have to take "fairly strong action" to help the French, Dulles told the Cabinet on March 26, but the risks involved "will be less if we take them now rather than waiting for several years."[125]

What action Washington should take, though, was not at all clear. There was "just no sense in even talking about United States forces replacing the French in Indochina," Eisenhower had told the National Security Council ("with great force," the minutes of the meeting record), in January, 1954:

> If we did so, the Vietnamese could be expected to transfer their hatred of the French to us. I can not tell you . . . how bitterly opposed I am to such a course of action. This war in Indochina would absorb our troops by the divisions![126]

That left the option, then, of either continuing to aid the French, in the hope that they could salvage the situation themselves, or of finding ways in which the United States could play a military role without committing ground forces.

Administration officials had discussed, off and on during the first months of 1954, the possibility of air strikes to take pressure off the French at Dienbienphu. Eisenhower told Dulles in March that he would not exclude the possibility of a single strike, "if it were almost certain this would produce decisive results."[127] Several days later, he mentioned the possibility of using carrier-based airplanes to bomb Viet Minh positions, although "of course, if we did, we'd have to deny it forever."[128] It was not until April that Pentagon strategists came up with a specific plan to use atomic weapons in Indochina: an "advance study group" had concluded, Admiral Radford informed Dulles, that three tactical atomic weapons, if properly employed, would be sufficient to "smash" the Viet Minh siege of Dienbienphu.[129]*

For State Department Counselor Douglas MacArthur II, through whom it had been conveyed, Radford's proposal raised "very serious questions affecting the whole position of US leadership in the world." It was not at all certain that the French would agree to the use of atomic weapons, but one could be very certain that they would leak the fact that the offer had been made. This would cause "a great hue and cry throughout the parliaments of the free world," especially within NATO. It would give the Russians—and other critics as well—the opportunity to charge "that we were testing out weapons on native peoples and were in fact preparing to act irresponsibly and drop weapons of mass destruction on the Soviet Union whenever we believed it was necessary to do so." Things would be different if the Chinese Communists overtly intervened in Indochina, but for the moment, MacArthur told Radford's emissary, the proposal would require careful consideration.[130]

At the time, though, the issue was not so much whether to use nuclear weapons as whether to get involved militarily at all. Two major impediments had presented themselves: Congressional leaders had emphatically insisted that no unilateral intervention in any form take place; the United States should go in only as part of an international effort in which the British and others would participate.[131] But the British, in turn, had manifested an extreme reluctance to get involved, not least because of fears that intervention would lead to the use of atomic weapons, and to all-out war. As Dulles cabled Eisenhower from Geneva at the end of April, "British seem to feel that we are disposed to accept present risks of a Chinese war and this, coupled also with their fear that we would start using atomic weapons, has badly frightened them."[132]†

* During a visit to France in March, 1954, Stuart Symington, by then a senator from Missouri, had raised with Defense Minister René Pleven the possibility of backing up French (and possibly Korean) troops in Indochina with United States carrier-based airplanes using tactical atomic weapons. Pleven's immediate reaction had been to point out the absence of suitable targets, and to suggest that it might be more useful for the Americans to assume responsibility for air defense against the Chinese. [Theodore C. Achilles to State Department, March 5, 1954, *FR: 1952–54*, XIII, 1096.]

† Eisenhower himself had noted, two days earlier, that the British "have a morbid ob-

The President was determined not to intervene alone. To do so, he told the National Security Council on April 29, "would mean a general war with China and perhaps with the USSR, which the United States would have to prosecute separated from its allies." It would amount "to an attempt to police the entire world. . . . We should be everywhere accused of imperialistic ambitions." It might almost be preferable, "[i]f our allies were going to fall away in any case, . . . to leap over the smaller obstacles and hit the biggest one with all the power we had. Otherwise, we seemed to be merely playing the enemy's game—getting ourselves involved in brushfire wars in Burma, Afghanistan, and God knows where."[133]

But if the French could be persuaded to "stay and fight," Eisenhower added, some form of intervention might be justified. Later that day, he suggested to his Assistant for National Security Affairs, Robert Cutler, that although it was unlikely that "new weapons" would be effective around Dienbienphu, "we might *consider* saying to the French that we had never yet given them any 'new weapons' and if they wanted some *now* for possible use, we might give them a few."* The President went on to note, though, that "the declarations which we had already made relevant to what we would do if China overtly intervened in Indo-China [were] the important deterrent to Chinese intervention, rather than whether or not we used the 'new weapon' in Vietnam." The most vital task, he emphasized, was to get a regional defense organization for Southeast Asia organized.[134]

The fall of Dienbienphu on May 7 made any immediate decision on the use of atomic weapons in Indochina unnecessary, but it did not end discussions about the possibility of some form of intervention there. Should such intervention take place, the Joint Chiefs of Staff pointed out later that month, they were still planning on the assumption that "[a]tomic weapons will be used whenever it is to our military advantage."[135] Once again, the Chiefs' narrowly military perspective evoked protests from the State Department. The only appropriate targets would be troop concentrations the size of those that had taken Dienbienphu, Policy Planning Staff Director Robert R. Bowie observed, and there had been only one other such operation during the past eight years. Moreover, "[t]he use of nuclear weapons would also cause an adverse Vietnamese reaction, which might inhibit the formation of indigenous armies, and seriously adverse reactions in Asian neutral nations."[136] Nor was there any

---

session that any positive move on the part of the free world may bring upon us World War III." [Eisenhower to Captain E. E. Hazlett, Jr., April 27, 1954, *FR: 1952–54*, XIII, 1428.]

* Later that summer, former French Foreign Minister Georges Bidault claimed that Dulles, at some point in April, had offered atomic weapons to the French for use in Indochina. Dulles remembered making no such offer, and expressed himself as "totally mystified" by Bidault's statement. The evidence suggests that no such offer was made. [See, on this point, Douglas Dillon to Dulles, August 9, 1954, *FR: 1952–54*, XIII, 1927–28; Dulles to Dillon, August 9, 1954, *ibid.*, p. 1928; and George C. Herring and Richard H. Immermann, "Eisenhower, Dulles and Dienbienphu: 'The Day We Didn't Go to War' Revisited," *Journal of American History*, LXXI(September, 1984), 357–58.]

way to be sure, the Central Intelligence Agency added, whether use of the bomb "would precipitate or deter Chinese Communist intervention."[137]

Frustration over the United States' apparent inability to project military power effectively in Indochina boiled over late in June, 1954, producing an anguished re-examination within the Eisenhower administration of the role nuclear weapons could have in deterring limited war. The Joint Chiefs of Staff set it off by pointing out that "[t]he engulfment of a large segment of the world and its people by the Soviet has been accomplished during the period in which the United States first held a monopoly and then a significant superiority in atomic weapons." Moscow's aggressiveness could only intensify once its own nuclear capabilities approximated those of the United States, a stage it would reach sometime between 1956 and 1959. The "obvious conclusion," the Chiefs remarked, was that if the West expected a just settlement of differences with the Soviet Union, it was going to have to agree on the need to press its demands "while the United States still holds atomic superiority." The alternative would be to allow "the lowest common denominator of the coalition to determine the level and scope of our actions in pursuit of our objectives."[138]*

Dulles acknowledged, in reply, that "[t]here was much to be said for . . . these JCS views, but nevertheless, none of our allies would go along with these views except Rhee, Chiang [Kai-shek], and possibly the Greeks and the Turks." Eisenhower added a bit plaintively that "perhaps Franco would join us." The British failure to take a tough stand on Indochina demonstrated, the Secretary of State continued, that "[t]he tide is clearly running against us in the channel of this tough policy. If we are to continue to pursue it we shall lose many of our allies, and this itself compels a reappraisal of our basic policy." Eisenhower responded sharply: "if this were indeed the situation, we should perhaps come back to the very grave question: Should the United States now get ready to fight the Soviet Union?" He had brought this point up more than once, the President pointed out, and he had "never done so facetiously."[139]

But after the Geneva Conference had concluded—having produced a cease-fire in Indochina and a divided Vietnam—the President was prepared to take a more philosophical view. "It was frustrating," he acknowledged on August 5, "not to have plans to use nuclear weapons generally accepted." But "to attempt to educate public opinion now on the weapons that might have to be used in war might produce very great strain on our alliances." Dulles agreed,

---

* Dulles had expressed similar frustrations in a conversation with Eisenhower the previous month: there were great disadvantages, he argued, "in a situation where we were obviously subject to UK veto, which in turn was in Asian matters largely subject to Indian veto, which in turn was largely subject to Chinese Communist veto. Thereby a chain was forged which tended to make us impotent, and to encourage Chinese Communist aggression to a point where the whole position in the Pacific would be endangered and the risk of general war increased." [Dulles notes, conversation with Eisenhower, May 11, 1954, *FR: 1952–54*, XIII, 1533.]

noting ruefully that "talk of atomic attack tended to create 'peace-at-any-price' people. . . . The Russians are smarter on this question because they never talk about using atomic weapons." The trouble with retaliation, Eisenhower added, was that "[i]n many cases aggression consists of subversion or civil war in a country rather than an overt attack on that country. In such cases it is difficult for us to know whom to retaliate against." Still, "it would be fatal to our national security to have relatively immobile U.S. forces stationed all around the globe. . . . If people don't want to be free and won't fight for freedom . . . there is not much we can do."[140]*

*Taiwan Strait.* Sometimes, though, allies could be all too willing to fight. That had been the case with Syngman Rhee in Korea, and the Eisenhower administration confronted a similar situation in its relations with Chiang Kai-shek. The Chinese Nationalists had established themselves on Taiwan in 1949, but without relinquishing control of several small islands just off the China coast. Eisenhower and Dulles had stated publicly—primarily for domestic political reasons—that the United States would not oppose attempts by Chiang to re-take the mainland.[141] In fact, however, they regarded his prospects for accomplishing this as quite remote, and soon found themselves worrying that Nationalists' determination to hold onto the offshore islands might lead to fighting with the People's Republic of China which could, in turn, involve the United States.[142]†

These concerns intensified when the Communists began shelling the island of Quemoy on September 3, 1954. Determined not to yield further territory to the People's Republic, and yet convinced of Chiang's error in seeking to hold military positions not critical to the defense of Taiwan, the Eisenhower administration found itself once again, as in Korea, attempting simultaneously to deter action by an adversary and to minimize the risk of American involvement at the hands of an ally.

Nuclear weapons, it was assumed, would be considered for use against the Chinese Communists if they attacked Taiwan itself. "Their fleet of junks "might make a good target for an atomic bomb," Eisenhower had observed a month before the shelling of Quemoy began.[143] Dulles, too, regarded the area off the China coast as a good place "actively to show Communist China . . .

* "This is indeed a strange and puzzling situation," Assistant Secretary of State Robert D. Murphy commented that same month. "With what is this nation left to defend itself if the instrumentalities brought forward out of our technical inventiveness are themselves allowed to become the object of brooding misgivings and indecision?" [Speech to Air Force Association, Omaha, Nebraska, August 20, 1954, *Department of State Bulletin*, XXXI(August 30, 1954), 291.]

† Dulles told the National Security Council in October, 1954, that "the Generalissimo's chances of getting back on the mainland were growing dimmer every day. . . . [I]f the people of Formosa had complete freedom of choice they would vote to be an independent state." [Minutes, National Security Council meeting of October 6, 1954, *FR: 1952–54*, XIV, 700.]

that we are 'willing and able' to make the aggressor suffer at places and by means of our choosing, i.e., where our air and sea power are preponderant."[144]* But when it came to the question of defending the offshore islands, the Secretary of State was much more hesitant. The islands were "not demonstrably essential" to the security of Taiwan, he argued; moreover, any American decision to defend them "would alienate world opinion and gravely strain our alliances . . . because it would probably lead to our initiating the use of atomic weapons."[145] Eisenhower agreed: war with China, he told the National Security Council, would be real war; he was "firmly opposed to any holding back like we did in Korea." But the offshore islands "were only important psychologically."[146]

Psychological effects could not be disregarded, though. There was reason to think, Dulles warned, that the Geneva compromise on Indochina had given "the Chinese Communists their head. . . . A powerful case can be made that unless we stop them, a Chinese Nationalist retreat from the islands would have disastrous consequences in Korea, Japan, Formosa and the Philippines." But to go to war with China over the offshore islands would mean that "outside of Rhee and Chiang, the rest of the world would condemn us, as well as a substantial part of the U.S. people." It was all, Dulles thought, a "horrible dilemma."[147]†

By November of 1954, the prospect of war in the Taiwan Strait—together, no doubt, with the experiences of Korea and Indochina—had forced the Secretary of State into a fundamental reconsideration of the whole strategy of nuclear deterrence. It was all very well to threaten escalation as had been done in Korea, he reminded the National Security Council, "but one thing leads to another, and . . . as General MacArthur had so emphatically stated, victory is the only proper objective in war."[148] What would "victory" mean, though? "[T]otal war would be an incalculable disaster," he wrote later that month, underlining his own words for emphasis. *Both* communist aggression *and* nuclear war had to be avoided; this required not only firmness but prudence as well:

> The U.S. . . . should (1) forego actions which would generally be regarded as provocative, and (2) be prepared, if hostilities occur, to

---

* Dulles acknowledged "that the broad policy of showing strength at places and by means of our choosing lends itself to confusion on the part of those who are close only to bits of the picture and who do not see the whole sweep of our policy from Korea to Indochina. I suspect that those at Moscow or Peiping who see the picture as a whole and who read our policy speeches carefully, do not suffer from such confusion." [Dulles to John M. Allison, August 20, 1954, *FR: 1952–54*, XIV, 546.]

† "You can talk all you want of the bad effect on Asia if the United States does not fight to defend these offshore islands," Dulles told the National Security Council in October, 1954, "but you say nothing about the bad effect on Europe if we do undertake to fight to hold these islands. . . . [W]e would be in this fight in Asia completely alone. Europe could be written off in such a contingency." [Minutes, NSC meeting, October 6, 1954, *FR: 1952–54*, XIV, 699.]

meet them, where feasible, in a manner and on a scale which will not inevitably broaden them into total nuclear war. . . . [S]uch policies are necessary to assure the support of our allies against aggression and to avoid risks which do not promise commensurate strategic or political gains. These conclusions have an obvious bearing on basic military strategy and on our policy toward Communist China.[149]

It was a remarkable conclusion for Dulles, who more than anyone else had originated the idea of "massive retaliation." But that strategy had never meant "that any local war would automatically be turned into a general war with atomic bombs being dropped all over the map," he explained in a public address that same month. "The important thing was "that we and our allies should have the means and the will to assure that a potential aggressor would lose from his aggression more than he could win."[150]

How, though, was one to contain aggression, prevent escalation, and still meet Eisenhower's strictures about avoiding costly conventional military obligations? Dulles's answer, at least in the Taiwan Strait crisis, was ambiguity. Discussions had already been under way, at the time the Communists began shelling the offshore islands, for some kind of defense treaty between the United States and Taiwan.[151] By proceeding with the treaty, but at the same time leaving unclear whether it covered the offshore islands, the administration could achieve two objectives: It could discourage Chiang from using the islands as a base from which to attempt an invasion of the mainland; but it could also simultaneously deter the Communists from attacking Chiang's positions there. The treaty should make it clear, Dulles insisted, that "we are not going to defend our partner while our partner attacks."[152] But it would also not be a bad idea to "fuzz up" the text sufficiently "to maintain doubt in the minds of the Communists as to how the U.S. would react to an attack on the offshore islands."[153]*

The Mutual Defense Treaty between the United States and the Republic of China, signed on December 2, 1954, committed Washington to oppose an armed attack on Taiwan, the Pescadores, and "such other territories as may be determined by mutual agreement."[154] Its purpose, as Assistant Secretary of State Walter Robertson explained to Chiang Kai-shek's foreign minister,

> was to formalize the understanding that without mutual consent, the Chinese Government would not take any offensive action which might provoke retaliation by the Communists leading to invocation of the Treaty. At the same time the U.S. did not want to encourage the Communist Chinese to think they could seize additional territories without serious risk.[155]

* "Let's keep the Reds guessing [about the offshore islands]," Dulles told Eisenhower's Press Secretary, James C. Hagerty, "and not make any clearcut statement about them." [Hagerty Diary, December 2, 1954, *FR: 1952–54*, XIV, 982.]

To reinforce the message, the administration then secured—although not without considerable debate—a Congressional resolution authorizing the President to take whatever action he deemed necessary in defense of this treaty, including "the securing and protection of such related positions and territories . . . as he judges to be required or appropriate. . . ."[156]*

As if in direct response, the Chinese Communists overran the Tachen Islands, where the Nationalists had maintained a small defensive force, in January, 1955. They then began a military buildup opposite Quemoy and Matsu, to such a point that Eisenhower and Dulles felt obliged to remove some of the ambiguity that had been written into the Taiwan Defense Treaty and its accompanying Congressional resolution. "[D]oubt as to our intentions was having a bad effect on our prestige in the area," the Secretary of State told the President; "it was in many quarters assumed that we would defend the [offshore] islands, and our failure to do so indicated that we were running away when actual danger appeared."[157] The difficulty with deterrence, Eisenhower wrote Churchill that same month, was that the Russians and Chinese knew "that we, in our democracies . . . by instinct and training abhor the thought of mass destruction . . . that would necessarily involve helpless people." This left them "a great area of fruitful opportunity . . . lying between the excitation of a global war on the one hand and passive acceptance of the status quo on the other." But, Eisenhower went on to point out, "there can be local deterrents as well as global deterrents."[158]

It was with this idea in mind that the President began an effort in March, 1955, to convince the Chinese Communists that nuclear weapons *might* be used against them if they attempted to invade Quemoy or Matsu. When Dulles commented on March 6 that defense of the two islands "would require the use of atomic missiles," Eisenhower "thoroughly agreed with this" and suggested that the Secretary of State include in a forthcoming speech a paragraph "indicating that we would use atomic weapons as interchangeable with conventional weapons," although not "weapons of mass destruction."[159]† Dulles did warn the National Security Council on March 10 that "urgent steps" needed to be taken "to create a better public climate for the use of atomic weapons by the United States if we found it necessary to intervene in the defense of Formosa."

---

* The point of the Congressional resolution, Hagerty noted in his diary, was to let the Chinese Communists "know that we mean business . . . and [to make them] think twice about starting any nonsense." [Hagerty Diary, January 22, 1955, Robert H. Ferrell, ed., *The Diary of James C. Hagerty: Eisenhower in Mid-Course, 1954–1955* (Bloomington: 1983), p. 172.]

† The next day, the two men again discussed, as Dulles recorded, "the importance of education with reference to the distinction between atomic missiles for tactical purposes and the big bomb with huge radioactive fall-outs." [Dulles memorandum of conversation with Eisenhower, March 7, 1955, John Foster Dulles Papers, White House Memoranda, Box 3, "Meetings with the President 1955 (7)."] Dulles also assured Senator Walter George, on the same day, that "the missiles we had in mind had practically no radioactive fall-out and were entirely local in effect." [Dulles memorandum of conversation with George, March 7, 1955, *FR: 1955–57*, II, 337.]

Military advisers had convinced him that these would be "the only effective weapons which the United States could use against a variety of mainland targets," and yet "[w]e might wake up one day and discover that we were inhibited in the use of these weapons by a negative public opinion." It was, therefore, of "vital importance" to "educate our own and world opinion as to the necessity for the use of tactical atomic weapons."[160] But it was left to Eisenhower himself to make the point most vividly in public: as long as they were used against strictly military targets, he told a press conference on March 16, he could see no reason why atomic weapons should not be employed "just exactly as you would use a bullet or anything else."[161] As he subsequently noted in his memoirs, "I hoped this answer would have some effect in persuading the Chinese Communists of the strength of our determination."[162]

It is clear now, though, that this was more a declaratory than an actual policy. In an Oval Office discussion on March 11, Dulles had warned of the need to avoid military involvement of any kind on Quemoy and Matsu until treaties establishing the Western European Union had been ratified.* Eisenhower had agreed that the use of atomic weapons there would have a "bad impact," and then had gone to rule out their employment except as a last resort. The United States "should do every practical thing that could be done" to help the Chinese Nationalists defend themselves, but "if it was necessary for the U.S. to intervene, it should do so with conventional weapons." The time might come when atomic weapons would have to be used, "but that should come only at the end, and we would have to advise our allies first. . . . we [can] not afford to be isolated from our allies in the world." The objective, therefore, should be "to delay [a Chinese Communist] attack in strength on Quemoy and Matsu, without thereby provoking [such an] attack."[163]

The Central Intelligence Agency confirmed the political risks of using nuclear weapons in a National Intelligence Estimate issued on March 16. If the United States were to attack the Chinese mainland with such devices, it predicted, "the predominant world reaction would be one of shock. These reactions would be particularly adverse if these weapons were used to defend the offshore islands or destroy military concentrations prior to an all-out Chiese Communist attempt to take the offshore islands." Certain European and Asian allies might tolerate resort to nuclear weapons to ward off an attack on Taiwan itself, but even in that case "the general reaction of non-Communist Asians would be emotional and would be extremely critical of the US. In the case of Japan, the Government would probably attempt to steer a more neutral course."[164]

* In a separate meeting on the same day, Dulles had told Eisenhower that "it would, I thought, be extremely important to avoid, if possible, any U.S. hostilities, particularly involving atomic missiles, while the WEU [Western European Union] situation was still unsettled. After that was buttoned up he [Eisenhower] could have more freedom of action in Asia." [Dulles notes, conversation with Eisenhower, March 11, 1955, *FR: 1955–57*, II, 355.]

Secretary of State Dulles saw still other difficulties. Might not Chiang Kai-shek himself have the feeling "that an atomic attack on the mainland as a beginning would be a poor way to gain the support of the Chinese people for his cause?" he asked his top subordinates on March 28. Moreover, "we cannot splurge our limited supply of atomic weapons without serious danger to the entire international balance of power; and therefore any use which is made of them must be very carefully planned and thought out." That had not been done in this situation: "we are drifting in very dangerous waters without an adequately prepared chart."[165]

Nor was it at all clear that the effects of atomic weapons, if used to defend Quemoy and Matsu, could be confined to the kinds of military targets Eisenhower had talked about at his March 16 press conference. Central Intelligence Agency Director Allen Dulles warned the White House early in April that it might be difficult to use such devices against military emplacements on the mainland without subjecting Quemoy itself to dangerous fallout; furthermore, "if the winds were wrong, the fallout would endanger the city of Amoy with its several hundred thousand civilian residents." It would be possible, Eisenhower himself observed several days later, to slow a Chinese Communist attack on the islands by using atomic weapons, "but I do not think that it would be wise, unless we are forced to do it, to atomize the Mainland opposite them. And even if we did, they could just wait for a while and start the attack over again."[166]

"I would personally be very happy," the President wrote Churchill on March 29, "both as a political leader and as an ex-soldier who may have a bit of competence in the strategic field, to see Chiang, *voluntarily* and in accordance with what he believed to be his own interests, withdraw from Quemoy and the Matsus."[167] The possibility of persuading the Generalissimo to scale down his military presence on the offshore islands was extensively discussed within the administration;[168] as an inducement, Secretary of State Dulles even suggested stationing, "with public knowledge," United States troops possessing "atomic capabilities" on Taiwan. Eisenhower questioned the idea of publicizing such a measure, but apparently not the idea itself.[169] Whether the offer to place atomic weapons on Taiwan was actually conveyed to Chiang when Admiral Radford and Assistant Secretary of State Robertson visited the island in mid-April is not clear from currently available documents.* What is clear is that the Chinese Nationalist leader firmly rejected any redistribution of forces away from Quemoy and Matsu, and that the President's representatives informed Chiang with equal firmness that he would henceforth be on his own in defending them.

The United States would not participate in the defense of Quemoy and

---

* Radford and Robertson apparently did take with them the document in which Dulles had made this proposal, but the subject is not mentioned in Eisenhower's brief written instructions to them [Hoover to Robertson and Radford, April 22, 1955, *FR: 1955–57*, II, 501–2], nor is it referred to in the reports Robertson and Radford sent back of their discussions with Chiang Kai-shek and his advisers. [*Ibid.*, pp. 509–17, 521, 523–25, 528.]

Matsu, Robertson explained, because such an operation would very likely require the use of nuclear weapons. That decision, in turn, would mean war, in which case Eisenhower believed it "essential" to retain the "full support [of] US public opinion and world opinion." The United States would need bases for operations against the Soviet Union which might be denied it "unless [the] countries concerned supported our position." Although such support would probably be forthcoming for the defense of Taiwan proper, it could not, in the President's view, "be marshalled in support of war in defense [of the] offshore islands." Moreover, as Radford pointed out, if nuclear weapons were used,

> President Eisenhower would have to consider [the] feeling generated throughout the world and in China too, particularly if many civilians were killed. He [Radford] was sure [Chiang Kai-shek] could well appreciate [the] terrible responsibilities of President Eisenhower in this regard.*

Robertson admitted that the President had, earlier in the year, planned to assist the Chinese Nationalists if Quemoy and Matsu were attacked. But there was now strong opposition to such a course of action: "Therefore . . . President Eisenhower could not now use US forces in defense of these islands without [a] large loss [of] public support at home and abroad."[170]

But if Eisenhower had changed his position, so too, at almost the same moment, had the Premier of the People's Republic of China, Zhou Enlai. Reports from the Bandung Conference of Asian and African nations late in April indicated that Zhou had suggested a cease-fire in the Taiwan Strait;† subsequently, he stressed that the Chinese Communists hoped to "liberate" Taiwan by peaceful means. Dulles found this a "significant" response, indicating that the Chinese might now be willing to accept the principle, already established in Germany, Korea, and Vietnam, of seeking the reunification of divided countries only by peaceful means.[171] There followed a series of contacts with the Chinese through intermediaries, and then, in Geneva, direct bilateral discussions with representatives of the People's Republic that had the effect of at least defusing—if not resolving—the Taiwan Strait crisis. "We were using the time thus gained," Dulles explained to Eisenhower in August, "to try to build

---

* The President was reluctant, Dulles told several senators in a private conversation two days later, "to see a wholesale use of atomic weapons against the densely populated mainland where land bursts would be required which would have a fall-out which might involve heavy casualties. This might alienate Asian opinion and ruin Chiang Kai-shek's hopes of ultimate welcome back to the mainland." [Dulles memorandum of conversation with Senators Hickenlooper, Knowland and Smith, April 27, 1955, *FR: 1955–57*, II, 526.]

† Dulles, not uncharacteristically, was willing to take a certain amount of credit for what had happened at Bandung. "I said that we had worked very hard to produce the . . . result and that our friends had pitched in and done a job which had led Chou to follow a pacific rather than a belligerent course." [Dulles memorandum, conversation with Senators Hickenlooper, Knowland and Smith, April 27, 1955, *FR: 1955–57*, II, 527.]

up a world opinion which would compel the Chinese Communists to accept the status quo and not seek to change it by force."[172]

What precise effect threats to use nuclear weapons had in persuading the Chinese to seek a cease-fire is no clearer with regard to the Taiwan Strait crisis than it is for Korea. Certainly Eisenhower and Dulles had difficulty convincing themselves, as well as the American people and their allies, that Quemoy and Matsu—a "bunch of rocks," as the Secretary of State had at one point referred to them[173]—were worth such drastic means of defense. And yet, Dulles, at least, believed that the Chinese had got the message:

"Why do we not make our position clear on Matsu and Quemoy?" a reporter asked the Secretary of State in January, 1956.

"I think it is clear," Dulles replied.

"It is not clear to me, sir."

"It is not clear to you because you, like me, cannot read the minds of the Chinese Communists. But to them I think it is quite clear."[174]

# IV

The main subject of the Secretary of State's press conference that day was a smug and self-congratulatory interview he had given to James Shepley, just published in *Life* magazine. In it, Dulles had acknowledged that although no one could "prove mathematically" that deterrence had worked in the Korean, Indochinese, and Taiwan Strait crises, "I think it is a pretty fair inference that it has." He had then gone on, imprudently, to generalize:

> You have to take risks for peace, just as you must take chances in war. Some say that we were brought to the verge of war. Of course we were brought to the verge of war. The ability to get to the verge without getting into the war is the necessary art. If you try to run away from it, if you are scared to go to the brink, you are lost. We've had to look it square in the face—on the question of enlarging the Korean war, on the question of getting into the Indochina war, on the question of Formosa. We walked to the brink and we looked it in the face. We took strong action.[175]

Combined with his earlier public pronouncements about "massive retaliation," Dulles's "brinksmanship" interview reinforced his image as a dangerously trigger-happy warrior-statesman, eager to use nuclear weapons at the slightest provocation. In fact, though, this image was not quite fair: the archives reveal that the Secretary of State repeatedly urged caution with respect to the use of nuclear weapons in these three situations, primarily because of the effect their use would have on allies. It was the President himself who seemed prepared, more often than Dulles, to "go to the brink."

The records are full of statements by Eisenhower about the need to erase the distinction between nuclear and conventional weapons: with global commitments necessarily sustained by limited resources, he argued time and time again, the United States had no choice but to be prepared to use nuclear weapons wherever its interests came under attack. If it lacked the resolve to do this, he would snap, then it might be better to take on the Russians in an all-out war right away, while the United States could still count on winning it.[176]

But what Eisenhower said was one thing; what he actually did was something else again. Although he never explicitly ruled out the employment of nuclear weapons in Korea, Indochina, and in the Taiwan Strait, the President did manage in each case to find alternatives to their use. In Korea and in the Taiwan Strait, he simply deferred action until the other side backed down. Ho Chi Minh was not as cooperative, but Eisenhower carefully insisted upon Congressional and allied approval before he would authorize intervention in Indochina. When these conditions were not met—and it is difficult to believe that he ever thought they would be—Eisenhower was in a position to diffuse responsibility for a thinly disguised defeat at the hands of the Viet Minh. In none of these instances did he demonstrate any overwhelming eagerness to use nuclear weapons; indeed one gets the impression, despite his rhetoric, that he was looking for excuses not to.

Eisenhower's only real departure from Truman's strategy on the use of nuclear weapons in limited wars was, therefore, one of appearances: he was prepared conspicuously to consider—and thereby to appear to threaten—such use, while his predecessor never was.[177] But both Eisenhower and Truman in fact shared the view, when confronted with specific situations in which the weapons might be employed, that the costs of using them would very likely outweigh the prospective benefits. They did so for a combination of military, political and moral reasons:

*Military:* Because of the absence of appropriate targets, there could be no assurance, whether in Korea, Indochina, or the Taiwan Strait, that the use of nuclear weapons would produce decisive military results. Their ineffectual use, moreover, might compromise the over-all deterrent: if the bomb was seen to have no dramatic effect upon the North Koreans, the Chinese Communists, or the Viet Minh, then how could it be expected to impress the Russians, or to reassure endangered allies? Better not to use it at all, and thus preserve the credibility of a vague and therefore ominous threat, than by using it to remove uncertainties and thus risk the contempt that familiarity breeds.*

*Political:* Nuclear weapons were, after all, only one of several instruments of

* The argument here—made most clearly by Paul Nitze [see footnotes 55 and 99], but also in NSC 147 "Analysis of Possible Courses of Action in Korea," April 2, 1953, [*FR: 1952–54*, XV, 845]—curiously parallels that of the atomic scientists who rejected a publicly announced test of the atomic bomb prior to Hiroshima on the grounds that if the test was not successful, the credibility of future uses of the bomb would be called into question. [See Peter Wyden, *Day One: Before Hiroshima and After* (New York: 1984), pp. 150–51.]

containment; both the Truman and the Eisenhower administrations attached at least equal importance, in maintaining the global balance of power, to the creation and preservation of alliances. And yet, the Western European members of NATO made it clear in the most emphatic terms that the use of nuclear weapons in Korea, Indochina, and in the Taiwan Strait would provoke such opposition within their own countries as to call the stability of the alliance into question. The Japanese, in more subtle ways, conveyed similar impressions. Since the beginning of the Cold War, Washington officials had regarded the defense of Western Europe and Japan as critical to the security of the United States: if the use of nuclear weapons to defend peripheral interests was to have the effect of deranging vital interests, then one would clearly have to think twice before using them.*

*Moral:* Any nation that is the first to make use of a new and terrible weapon is likely to bear—both in the eyes of its own citizens and those of the rest of the world as well—a particular moral responsibility, even if, as seems probable in the case of nuclear weapons, other nations would sooner or later have found opportunities to develop and use them. The fact that the first American bombs had killed Asians compounded the problem by introducing the suspicion—justified or not—of racism. Whatever one felt about the morality of nuclear weapons, one could hardly deny the clearly devastating effect their use once again against Asians would have on the American position in that part of the world. "You boys must be crazy," Eisenhower told his advisers at the time of Dienbienphu: "We can't use those awful things against Asians for the second time in less than ten years. My God."[178]†

Self-deterrence, based upon military, political, and moral considerations, was thus clearly a potent force, but what about Soviet deterrence? The possibility of nuclear retaliation by the Russians, though never entirely absent from the calculations of Truman and Eisenhower administration officials, did not figure as prominently in their thinking as one might have expected. It was hardly mentioned in connection with the Indochina and Taiwan Strait crises. There was some concern, in Korea, that the Russians might use nuclear weapons against American port facilities or troop concentrations there, or even against bases in Japan. Certainly the prospect of Soviet intervention on behalf of China—whether nuclear or non-nuclear—was a significant deterrent to ex-

---

* Although, as Under Secretary of State Walter Bedell Smith argued with respect to the use of atomic weapons in Korea, "[t]he reaction of our allies and the effect on the neutrals would also depend on the achievement of success in a short period of time. Much would be forgiven us if we were quickly successful and ended the war." [Minutes, NSC meeting, May 13, 1953, *FR: 1952–54*, XV, 1015.]

† "[O]ur whole. international security structure [is] in jeopardy," Dulles warned Eisenhower late in 1955. "The basic thesis [is] local defensive strength with the backing up of United States atomic striking power. However, that striking power [is] apt to be immobilized by moral repugnance." [Dulles memorandum of conversation with Eisenhower, December 26, 1955, Dulles Papers, White House memoranda, Box 3, "Meetings with the President, 1955 (1)."]

panding the fighting in that direction. But any use of Soviet nuclear weapons against American forces would have meant all-out war, and the simple fact was that the Russians—still far behind in the production of such weapons and the means of delivering them, still lacking the capacity to neutralize overwhelming American retaliatory capabilities—were in no way prepared for such a conflict. Before worrying too much about what the Russians could do to the United States, Eisenhower told his military planners in 1953, they should consider what the United States could do to the Russians: "They must be scared as hell."[179]

That situation would not last indefinitely, though. By the end of 1954, the President was acknowledging that "for the first time . . . the United States . . . was no longer immune from attack."[180]* A year later he recommended to his advisers the virtues of "withdraw[ing] into a quiet room and contemplat[ing] . . . the real nature of a future thermonuclear war. . . . The destruction might be such that we might have ultimately to go back to bows and arrows."[181] Soviet long-range missile capabilities were being taken seriously by 1956: the Russians might have an operational ICBM in another five years, the National Security Council estimated;[182] and a special presidential commission concluded at the end of that year that American casualties in an all-out war with the Russians would approximate fifty million.[183] Just a single attack would produce twenty-five million killed, with another sixty million needing hospitalization, Eisenhower noted in 1957: "When you begin to think of things like that, you know there must not be war."[184]

The implications did not bode well for a strategy of threatening the use of nuclear weapons in situations short of total war. The United States could not altogether abandon that option, the National Security Council had concluded as early as December, 1954, but the ability "to apply force selectively and flexibly" was becoming more important:

> As the fear of nuclear war grows, the United States and its allies must never allow themselves to get into the position where they must choose between (a) not responding to local aggression and (b) applying force in a way which our own people and our allies would consider entails undue risk of nuclear devastation.[185]

By the time of his 1956 "brinksmanship" interview, Dulles was privately acknowledging "throughout the world, a growing, and not unreasonable, fear that nuclear weapons are expanding at such a pace as to endanger human life on this planet." If that trend continued, "repugnance to the use of nuclear weapons could grow to a point which would depreciate our value as an ally, undermine confidence in our 'collective defense' concepts, and make questionable the reliability of our allies and the availability to SAC of our foreign bases."

---

* Until recently, Eisenhower told a press conference the following month, "the oceans had seemed to us such wonderful protective areas that we could well afford the . . . unpreparedness that had been our history from the Revolutionary War down to the Korean War. We can no longer afford it." [Press conference, January 12, 1955, *Public Papers of the Presidents: Dwight D. Eisenhower, 1955* (Washington: 1960), p. 59.]

The only solution, Secretary of State thought, would be to turn all nuclear weapons over to a strengthened and veto-proof United Nations: that would relieve the United States of its "present vulnerable position of having sole responsibility within the free world for determining the use of such weapons, "a responsibility which is not governed by any clearly enunciated principles reflecting 'decent respect for the opinions of mankind.' "[186]

Eisenhower was by no means prepared to go that far. He told General Maxwell Taylor in May, 1956, that "planning should go ahead on the basis of the use of tactical atomic weapons against military targets in any small war in which the United States might be involved."[187] But he acknowledged before a press conference the following February that the likelihood of any nation using nuclear weapons in an attack "grows less, I think, every year. . . . [A]ny such operation today is just another way of committing suicide." Nor would the United States respond defensively with nuclear weapons in all situations: "a picture of the great Strategic Air Command charging all over the world for little police troubles . . . would be entirely wrong."[188] The opinions of others, too, had to be taken into account: "the new thermonuclear weapons are tremendously powerful," the President observed in August of 1958; "however, they are not, in many ways, as powerful as is world opinion today in obliging the United States to follow certain lines of policy."[189]*

If there had been any doubt about the accuracy of this last observation, the second Taiwan Strait crisis, which broke out that same month when the Chinese Communists resumed shelling the offshore islands from which Chiang Kai-shek had never withdrawn, quickly confirmed it. Should it become necessary to use nuclear weapons to ward off an invasion, Dulles warned, "there would be strong popular revulsion against the US in most of the world. It would be particularly intense in Asia and particularly harmful to us in Japan." Nor could there be any assurance that operations could be kept limited: "the risk of a more extensive use of nuclear weapons, and even a risk of general war, would have to be accepted."[190]

The possible use of nuclear weapons was indeed "the heart of the matter," a worried Eisenhower commented. It was not only that, Dulles replied, it was the central component in the administration's whole strategy: "I thought we had acknowledged the risk of the political and psychological dangers of the use of these weapons when we included them in our arsenal."[191] It would be an "unpleasant prospect" to have to use nuclear weapons in the defense of Quemoy and Matsu, the Secretary of State wrote British Prime Minister Harold Macmillan immediately after his conversation with the President. But it was one "we must face up to because our entire military establishment assumes more and more that the use of nuclear weapons will become normal in the event of hostilities."[192]

Apparently concerned that his Secretary of State might be losing sight of

---

* This observation was made in the context of pressures for a nuclear test ban, but it clearly reflected Eisenhower's broader concerns as well.

the distinction between declaratory and actual policy, Eisenhower resorted to a tactic he had used with Dulles several times in the past: he had his secretary, Ann Whitman, forward without comment "a very private message" from one of the President's personal correspondents, in this case Abbott M. Washburn, Deputy Director of the United States Information Agency. Washburn had insisted that if Washington used nuclear weapons to defend Quemoy and Matsu, it "could lose the respect of mankind for all time." Civilian casualties would be enormous, and there would be the possibility as well of nuclear retaliation. "There is no such thing as a limited atomic war."[193]*

Soviet Premier Nikita Khrushchev took the occasion to make the same point in a message to Eisenhower several days later. "Those who harbor plans of an atomic attack on the People's Republic of China should not forget," he warned,

> that the other side too has atomic and hydrogen weapons and the appropriate means to deliver them. If the People's Republic of China falls victim to such an attack, the aggressor will at once get rebuff by the same means. . . . To touch off a war against People's China means to doom to certain death sons of the American people and to spark off the conflagration of a world war.[194]

It would be stretching a point to argue that Khrushchev's threat—the first overt attempt by the Russians to deter the use of nuclear weapons by the Americans in a limited war situation—significantly influenced Eisenhower's position: he had shown little sympathy for pursuing the nuclear option in any event. But he did acknowledge, in his memoirs, that improved Soviet retaliatory capabilities had created a situation that had not been present in the Taiwan Strait crisis of 1954–55: "I did not doubt our total superiority, but any large-scale conflict stimulated here was now less likely to remain limited to a conventional use of military power."[195]

Once again, Eisenhower was fortunate enough to avoid having to resolve the painful dilemmas reliance on nuclear deterrence had created: the Chinese Communists continued to shell the offshore islands, but made no attempt to invade them or to interfere with United States operations to resupply Chinese Nationalist garrisons there. But the 1958 crisis did reveal the extent to which threats to use nuclear weapons in situations where something less than national survival was at stake had become counter-productive: Eisenhower pointedly reminded Dulles that "as much as two-thirds of the world, and 50% of US, opinion opposes the course which we have been following."[196] The crisis also demonstrated, more clearly than any of the others that took place during his administration, the extent to which Eisenhower was prepared to

---

* It was "not adequate simply to say that we will stand on Quemoy and Matsu," Eisenhower told Secretary of Defense Neil McElroy the following day: "We must move beyond that." [Goodpaster notes, Eisenhower conversation with Neil McElroy, September 11, 1958, Eisenhower Papers, Whitman DDE Diary, Box 22, "Staff Notes—September, 1958."]

restrain his own subordinates when he believed they had accepted too literally the logic of his own strategy.

# V

History, it is useful to remind ourselves, did not necessarily have to happen in the way that it did. There was nothing foreordained about the fact that no sooner had they been developed than nuclear weapons would be used, twice, within three days of one another, but then not again for at least the next four decades. This outcome was all the more remarkable for the fact that the United States retained an absolute monopoly over those weapons for four years after Hiroshima, and an effective monopoly—because Soviet retaliatory capabilities were so primitive—for another half-decade. During those years Washington confronted a series of actual and potential military conflicts in which American vital interests appeared to be endangered. And yet, even then, no use of nuclear weapons took place. When one steps back from an awareness of what *actually* happened to consider what *might* have happened—when one shifts from the factual to the counterfactual—one cannot help but be impressed by how easily things might have gone the other way.

There is, of course, no way to know with certainty what the world today would be like if Presidents Truman and Eisenhower had accepted the recommendations they received to use nuclear weapons in Korea, Indochina, and the Taiwan Strait. But it does seem likely that their employment in those situations—whether the weapons produced the desired results or not—would have diminished the profound sense of awe with which the world today still regards these particular instruments of war. If familiarity breeds contempt, then it is probably also true that remoteness induces respect. Resort to what had come to be thought of as the absolute weapon to achieve less than absolute political or military objectives could only have had a cheapening effect: the result could well have been more frequent use, but less effective deterrence.

For the Russians, it made sense from the beginning not to initiate the use of nuclear weapons because the prospect of American retaliation was always present. For the Americans, the issue was not that simple: They enjoyed at least a decade in which nuclear weapons could have been used without any realistic possibility of Soviet retaliation. What deterred the Americans—and caused them to embrace in practice the principle of "no first use"—was the simple dilemma of disproportion: how does one actually use means that are clearly incommensurate with the ends one has in view?[197] The fact that Americans worried about this sort of thing—not all other countries in similar circumstances would have—may well account for the fact that our experience of nuclear war is still as providentially limited as it is.

# 6

# Dividing Adversaries:
# The United States and
# International Communism, 1945-1958

IT IS NOT a good idea, as a rule, to revise one's view of the past on the basis of seeing a single document. One runs the risk of committing what the historian David Hackett Fischer has called the "fallacy of the lonely fact," best illustrated by his story of a scientist who had published "an astounding and improbable generalization about the behavior of rats." When asked for the records upon which his conclusions were based, the scientist triumphantly produced a notebook from his desk. "Here they are," he said. And pointing to a cage in the corner, he added: "there's the rat."[1]

But there are times when seeing a single document can produce more useful results. It can illuminate, with abrupt clarity, a pattern of events hitherto obscure. It can break through the encrustations of interpretation imposed by historians, who had the luxury of knowing what was going to happen next, to reveal the very different perspectives of people living at the time who lacked that luxury. It can provide a healthy corrective to the historian's too-easily made, if usually unconscious, assumption that his own point of view must necessarily be more sophisticated than those about whom he writes.

The need for such correction became clear to me one afternoon in 1979 while reviewing some recently declassified documents at the Eisenhower Li-

Portions of this essay were prepared as a paper, "American Policy and Perspectives: The Sino-Soviet 'Wedge' Strategy, 1949–1955," for a conference on "Sino-American Relations, 1945–1955," sponsored by Peking University and the Committee on Scholarly Communication with the People's Republic of China, and held in Beijing in October, 1986. It has not been previously published.

brary. The previous year I had published a short history of Russian-American relations in which I had criticized President Eisenhower and his advisers for making no effort "to exploit growing Sino-Soviet antagonism to the advantage of the United States."[2] But before me, now, lay the transcript of a briefing John Foster Dulles had given to the President, British Prime Minister Winston Churchill, and French Foreign Minister Georges Bidault at the Mid-Ocean Club on Bermuda on December 7, 1953. In it, the Secretary of State had acknowledged the existence of a strained relationship between the Soviet Union and the People's Republic of China, had proclaimed Mao Zedong to be "an outstanding Communist leader in his own right" who would not willingly submit to dictation from Moscow, and had suggested that this situation "may eventually give us an opportunity for promoting division between the Soviet Union and Communist China in our own common interest." Dulles had then gone on to deliver the following startling recommendation:

[T]he best hope for intensifying the strain and difficulties between Communist China and Russia would be to keep the Chinese under maximum pressure rather than by relieving such pressure. . . . [P]ressure and strain would compel them to make more demands on the USSR which the latter would be unable to meet and the strain would consequently increase. . . . [T]his was the course to be followed rather than to seek to divide the Chinese and the Soviets by a sort of competition with Russia as to who would treat China best.[3]

This was, indeed, enough to break the somnolence of an archival reading room on a quiet afternoon. Here was Dulles, the very symbol of the American tendency to see communism as monolithic, not only acknowledging the existence of Sino-Soviet differences as early as 1953, but advocating a sophisticated strategy for exploiting them. Even more remarkable is the fact that when the Sino-Soviet alliance did begin to break up some five years later, it did so in very much the way Dulles had anticipated: because the Russians refused to satisfy Chinese demands for military and economic assistance at a time when the United States was exerting maximum pressure against the People's Republic.[4] I could only conclude that Dulles's own strategy—and that of the administration he served—had been more sophisticated than I and most other historians had suspected.[5]

But there was more to the matter than this. The revelation that Dulles had sought to encourage a Sino-Soviet split made me wonder how his strategy related to other—and better known—efforts on the part of the United States to promote fissiparous tendencies within the international communist movement at earlier stages in the Cold War. These broader speculations, in turn, produced an arresting—if still provisional—conclusion: that despite what they said in public, American policy-makers at no point during the postwar era actually believed in the existence of an international communist monolith. A single document can take a historian quite a long way.

# I

The spectre of an enemy with a coordinated plan—and with concealed means of implementing it—has always worried Americans, perhaps because their own approach to foreign affairs has so often lacked precisely those qualities of purposeful direction. Certainly the fear of an international communist movement, controlled from Moscow and aimed at subverting capitalism throughout the world, had resided uneasily in the minds of Washington officials since the earliest days of the Bolshevik Revolution.[6] Abolition of the Comintern in 1943 had, to some extent, moderated that concern, but when it became apparent in the months following the end of World War II that the Soviet Union was still determined to dominate communists beyond its borders, anxieties about a renewed crusade for world revolution—and about the possible inability of the United States to deal with it—began to surface once again.

As early as June, 1945, the State Department was warning President Truman of the dangers inherent in a revival of international communist militancy, even within the United States itself: the Comintern, it pointed out, had been "a tool or weapon such as no other country possessed, and the Soviet Union never hesitated to use it when the occasion demanded."[7] The President's Chief-of-Staff, Admiral William D. Leahy, noted that same month that communism was a religion people were willing to die for, and that wherever such a phenomenon existed, "the United States must of necessity be concerned and be ready to defend itself against the onslaught of such a religion."[8] Nor were such sentiments confined to Americans. To suggest that because it had now become a powerful national state the Soviet Union had "abandoned interest in Communism abroad or in Marxist-Leninism at home," Sir Archibald Clark-Kerr warned the British Foreign Office from Moscow late in 1945, "would be as idle as to suggest that Pope Julius II [had] abandoned Catholicism for Vatican Imperialism."[9]

But if religion had the potential for crusading zeal, it also carried within it the seeds of heresy. What is remarkable about American policy toward international communism in the early days of the Cold War is how quickly the possibility of encouraging heretical growths came to be seen, and acted upon. The objective of separating communism from its source of inspiration and central point of control—the Soviet Union—became with surprising speed a consistent, if not always obvious, element of United States strategy in the Cold War.

The central assumption behind this strategy was that the interests of communists outside the Soviet Union—and of left-wing non-communist movements as well—would not always coincide with those of the Kremlin. As early as January, 1945, the Research and Analysis Branch of the Office of Strategic Services had pointed out that although the Russians would seek to use foreign communist parties to promote their own objectives, they would soon realize "that these parties cannot maintain indefinitely a sufficient popular follow-ing to make them useful as Soviet instruments unless each of them puts for-ward . . . a domestic leftist program for its own country." Such a program might well come into conflict with the security requirements of the Soviet state, since "the makers of Soviet foreign policy must know that the form of Soviet expansionism that is most likely to arouse powerful opposition abroad is the promotion of leftism as a means of strengthening Soviet influence or establishing Russian predominance."[10]

It followed that although the growth of left-wing movements might well be inevitable in the wake of fascism's defeat, domination of these movements by the Soviet Union was not. "It is definitely in the interest of the United States," State Department Soviet expert Charles E. Bohlen asserted early in 1946, "to see that the present left movement throughout the world, which we should recognize and even support, develops in the direction of democratic as against totalitarian systems." Washington should make it clear "that governments based squarely on the principles of the preservation of civil and political lib-erties, no matter how far to the left they may be, will have the support and encouragement of the United States." Such a policy would undermine Soviet charges "that the Western democracies are in effect the supporters of reaction and that the only progressive force in the world is the Soviet Union and the Communist party."[11]*

Bohlen's fellow Soviet specialist George F. Kennan came to much the same conclusion, but by a different route. For Kennan, it was not the triumph of the left that was inevitable, but rather the decline of empires. Paraphrasing Edward Gibbon, he reminded his Foreign Service colleagues late in 1946 that "nothing in human affairs is more difficult to hold in obedience than distant provinces."[12] Ideology would be of little use in that regard because it reflected more than it determined social and political action: "the Soviet ideology of today flows with iron logic and with irresistable force from the inner neces-sities of Soviet power."[13] Far from being a reliable means by which to expand and maintain Soviet imperial authority, communism might indeed prove to be the Kremlin's most vulnerable point of weakness.

Kennan developed this argument in a speech delivered at the University of Virginia early in 1947. "The emotional carrying power of international communism," he suggested, "is greatest in the areas where it has never been tried. . . . Those children who are listening for the first time to the entranc-ing notes of the Pied Piper and have never seeen the mysterious land toward which those notes entice, are the ones least able to resist them." But in coun-tries "where the communists have been forced into the unpleasant and dis-

* Robert Hooker, of the State Department's Division of European Affairs, subsequently credited Bohlen with having originated the strategy of working with the non-communist left to contain the Russians. "Only the NCL can oppose Soviet expansion without laying itself open to the charge of serving reactionary interests. Only the NCL can command the broad basis of popular support that is necessary successfully to resist Soviet expan-sion." [Hooker memorandum, September 20, 1946, Department of State Records, 711.61/9-2046, Box 3428, Diplomatic Branch, National Archives.]

turbing position of having to put their ideas into practice, nowhere today do they command the hopes and enthusiasms of the majority of the people." It was not a matter of familiarity breeding contempt—the power of the Kremlin was too great not to be respected. "But familiarity has indeed bred disillusionment; and those who live under the yoke of communism know full well that however elevated its ideological aims, however progressive certain of its concepts of human society, it is animated by a political will as despotic and intolerant as any that history can recall."

Perhaps the Russians were not as hypocritical as some might think when they denied their ability to control international communism beyond their borders:

> I sometimes think they have created something more powerful than themselves: a force which they do not dare let get out of their hands because they fear that it might be turned against them, that they have sown their dragon's teeth and now they find themselves, willy-nilly, for better or for worse, the masters and the servants of the weird and terrifying warriors who have grown up in their pasture.

Indeed, the United States might even find it advantageous for a communist government to come to power somewhere beyond the reach of Soviet military and secret police authority:

> A communist regime in power in some such country which either failed to meet its responsibilities and discredited itself in the eyes of the people or which turned on its masters, repudiated the Kremlin's authority, and bit the hand which had reared it, might be more favorable to the interests of this country and of world peace in the long run than an unscrupulous opposition party spewing slander from the safe vantage point of irresponsibility and undermining the prestige of this country in the eyes of the world.

Certainly the United States should not openly oppose communist governments that came to power by democratic means; "otherwise, we are apt not only to put ourselves in the wrong with world opinion but we may well have the effect of rallying people in the respective countries even more firmly around our communist adversaries."[14]*

These anticipations of fragmentation within the international communist

---

* The Russians had "no desire to see any country move in the direction of a modified form of socialism except under the guidance of persons who recognize Moscow's authority," Kennan had noted several months earlier. "[T]here is nothing that the Russians fear and detest more than a rival in the use of the slogans of social progress." Even if there were to be a socialist revolution within the United States itself, "unless it were to be led by people who accept the authority of Moscow, the only reaction of the men in the Kremlin would be to stamp it a form of fascism and to oppose it even more violently than they now oppose the purposes of the present government of the United States." [Kennan to Admiral Harry Hill, October 7, 1946, George F. Kennan Papers, Box 28, Seeley Mudd Library, Princeton University.] See also, for a further expression of these arguments, Kennan's lecture at the National War College, May 6, 1947, *ibid.*, Box 17.

movement by no means reflected a majority viewpoint in Washington during the early years of the Cold War. The steadiness of Soviet ideological objectives—especially when compared with those of the United States—continued to impress American observers.[15] Moreover, there existed a tendency for those who were *not* specialists on the Soviet Union to attach greater importance to ideological explanations of that country's behavior than those who were.[16*] Certainly the Truman administration's use of alarmist rhetoric in securing aid to Greece and Turkey and in justifying its domestic "loyalty" program did nothing to lessen the tendency to explain Soviet behavior in ideological terms.[17†] And Stalin himself seemed to confirm these explanations when he authorized resuscitation of the Comintern—this time in the guise of the Cominform—in September, 1947.[18]

What is striking, though, is the extent to which skepticism about the unity of international communism continued to carry weight within the Truman administration, even in these unpromising circumstances. That skepticism had already provided the basis, by the middle of 1947, for a multi-faceted strategy aimed at driving a wedge between Moscow and its ideological allies throughout the world: as Kennan himself put it, "we should see to it that no action of this Government in the field of foreign affairs is taken without attention to the effect it might have upon this situation within the international communist movement."[19]

# II

As implemented between 1947 and 1950, the "wedge" strategy took several forms. There was, first of all, an attempt to make it clear that policies aimed at containing the Soviet Union did not imply opposition to communism everywhere. A second manifestation of the strategy involved the use of Marshall Plan aid to strain the relationship between Moscow and its satellites. Yugoslavia's break with the Kremlin in 1948 provided the opportunity for a third major initiative, aimed at encouraging "Titoist" tendencies elsewhere in Eastern Europe. And, finally, the Truman administration sought to promote the spread of "Titoism" in Asia as well by leaving open the possibility of cooperation in

---

* The reports of Ambassador Jefferson Caffery from Paris, for example, were consistently more alarmist regarding international communism than those from the American Embassy in Moscow. [See Caffery to Byrnes, August 23, 1946, Department of State Records, 711.61/8–2346, Box 3428; and Caffery to Marshall, January 28 and February 19, 1947, U.S. Department of State, *Foreign Relations of the United States* [hereafter *FR*]: *1947* III, 689–92.] These reports may well have contributed, in turn, to the Department's tendency to attribute Ho Chi Minh's behavior to his communist connections at a time when it was not doing the same for Mao Zedong. [See pp. 90–91, above.]

† "One cannot help suspecting," an official in the British Foreign Office noted, "that the anti-communist drive is being stimulated by the Administration in order to put pressure upon Congress." [F. B. A. Rundall minute, March 31, 1947, Foreign Office Records, FO 371/61054/AN1216, Public Records Office. London.]

some form with the newly created People's Republic of China.

*Anti-Sovietism versus anti-communism.* The need to clarify this distinction grew out of President Truman's speech to Congress in March, 1947, asking for aid to Greece and Turkey. In an effort to prod skeptical legislators into approving his proposals, the Chief Executive had described the world as divided between two "alternative ways of life"—one based upon "the will of the majority," the other upon "the will of a minority forcibly imposed upon the majority."[20] Even though Truman had carefully avoided using the term "communism" in this context—the struggle, as he portrayed it, was between "democracy" and "totalitarianism"—the sharply ideological tone of the address left a widespread impression that the "doctrine" that bore his name required opposition to communism throughout the world.*

Both for reasons of costs and as a point of principle this was not what the administration had intended. At a time when heroic efforts had been required to pry $400 million for Greece and Turkey from a parsimonious Congress, the possibility of a global campaign against communism seemed wildly improbable. "If I thought for a moment that the precedent of Greece and Turkey obliged us to try to do the same thing in China," Kennan told students at the National War College in May, "I would throw up my hands and say we had better have a whole new approach to the affairs of the world.[21]† One of the first recommendations of the new State Department Policy Planning Staff, which Kennan now headed, was that steps be taken to remove the impression "that the Truman Doctrine is a blank check to give economic and military aid to any area in the world where the communists show signs of being successful."[22]

But the potential costs of an anti-communist crusade were not the only concern: it was also necessary, as one of the drafters of the Truman Doctrine speech later insisted, to show the world "that we have something positive and attractive to offer, and not just anti-communism."[23] For Bohlen, who had

---

* "It . . . gives promise to the world that whenever factions in any country are threatened with communism, it will be our policy to give them money and other support." [Joseph E. Davies Diary, March 12, 1947, Joseph E. Davies Papers, Box 25, Library of Congress.] Presidential assistant Eban Ayres later pointed out that an effort had been made in the speech "to avoid direct reference to communism or communists but rather to use the term 'totalitarianism.'" [Ayres Diary, May 22, 1947, Eban A. Ayres Papers, Box 26, Harry S. Truman Library.]

† A report from the British Embassy in Washington noted that the Truman Doctrine speech, in Kennan's view, "should have been confined to the specific question of rendering economic assistance [to Greece and Turkey] without raising broader implications as was eventually done. . . . [H]e felt that it was unnecessary and perhaps even dangerous to over-dramatize the situation. . . . Mr. Kennan does not believe that, as distinct from fostering political instability in such areas, the Kremlin is desirous of promoting the actual attainment of power by the Communist parties in Western [European] countries beyond the shadow of Russian bayonets." [John Balfour to Ernest Bevin, May 15, 1947, Foreign Office Records, FO 371/61047/AN1795.]

emphasized the need to retain the support of the non-communist left, the point was particularly important. It would be a mistake, he argued, to brand "as a Communist anyone who used the language of Marx and Lenin since there is much in Marxism . . . which in no sense reflects a belief in Communist theory or involvement in modern day Communist organization."[24] When, in the summer of 1947, the Argentine government proposed organization of an anti-communist pact in the Western Hemisphere, Bohlen urged rejection of the proposal on the grounds that "while we were fully aware of the problem of Communism, . . . our policy did not include the prospect of entering into anti-Communist agreements with other governments—a move which smacked all too strongly of Fascist policy."[25]*

If rigid anti-communism risked alienating the non-communist left, though, total inaction raised the even more dangerous possibility that communists in some countries might align themselves with other disaffected elements and by such means gain power. The question of how the United States would deal with such a situation posed agonizing difficulties. "If we were to try to make war on the Russians in protest over the activities of Italian communists," Kennan noted in December, 1947, "it would appear . . . as an act of unprovoked action against Russia. . . . [T]he moral basis of our war effort would be polluted and shattered from the start." But the alternative would be "the use of American forces to fight irregular bands of armed civilians in Italy. . . . Certainly that is not what we want." The only way out of the dilemma was to strengthen "the natural forces of resistance within the respective countries which the communists are attacking and that has been, in essence, the basis of our policy."[26]

What Kennan had in mind here, of course, was the European Recovery Program, the chief goal of which had been, from its proclamation by Secretary of State George C. Marshall several months earlier, to create positive alternatives to communism without generating sympathy for that ideology by opposing it directly. There might not be much that the United States could do about rolling back Soviet influence in the Russian-occupied areas of Eastern and Central Europe, Kennan had admitted in May, 1947, but where communist parties existed "beyond the shadow of the power of the Red Army" the situation was very different: "Here we have the weakest and most vulnerable points in the Kremlin armor." Because these communists lacked—as yet—"the

---

* Kennan agreed that such a pact "could not fail to evoke shades of Ribbentrop's Anti-Comintern Pact." [Kennan to Robert Lovett, August 11, 1947, Policy Planning Staff Records, Box 33, "Chronological—1947," Department of State Records, Diplomatic Branch, National Archives.] The United States was not in a position "where it must accept as friends everyone who is anti-Communist," George Butler, the Policy Planning Staff's Latin American specialist, noted in September; "we should choose our friends among those nations and peoples who are in accord with our fundamental principles and institutions. Communism very probably is the most serious threat today, but many anti-Communist elements are only a little less opposed to what we stand for." [Butler to Kennan, September 10, 1947, Policy Planning Staff Records, Box 8, "Communism 1947—51."]

supports of the totalitarian state," their fate might still be influenced "by the electorates of those countries[,] or by the governments there in power, or by the actions of other free governments such as our own."[27]

The Marshall Plan was designed to exploit precisely that vulnerability. It was to be directed, the Policy Planning Staff emphasized, "not to the combatting of communism as such but to the restoration of the economic health and vigor of European society":[28] if that could be achieved, then there would be little to fear from communism. It proceeded by indirection: the use of economic assistance to achieve a political objective would not only produce the quickest possible result by the most efficacious means; it would also avoid generating the resistance—in the form of charges that the United States was interfering in the political affairs of other countries—that a direct assault on communism in Western Europe almost certainly would have.[29]

It is significant that when the staff of the newly organized National Security Council did in fact propose, early in 1948, "a world-wide counter-offensive" aimed at "Soviet-directed world communism,"[30] the State Department quickly rejected it. The way to handle communism was not to seek its suppression, Assistant Secretary of State Willard Thorp argued: "We must avoid any appearance of behaving like a 'police state.' "[31] George H. Butler, the Policy Planning Staff's Latin American specialist, insisted that:

> Instead of basing our fight . . . on anti-Communism alone, we might better place the emphasis on support of those free countries which are similar to our own in institutions and systems of government and of other non-Communist countries which do not indulge in the police-state type of repression of individual rights and civil liberties. If the survival and progress of these countries can be achieved, Soviet-directed world communism will meet defeat.[32]

President Truman himself seemed to endorse this viewpoint in a carefully drafted speech early in June, 1948, in which he argued that to attempt to outlaw or suppress communism was to miss the point: "Communism succeeds only when there is weakness, or misery, or despair. It cannot succeed in a strong and healthy society." The answer was not repression, but "more and better democracy."[33]

Indiscriminate anti-communism, therefore, was not the Truman administration's preferred strategy: it would cost too much, it would run the risk of associating the United States with unsavory elements on the right, and it would fail to deal with what Washington regarded as the real causes of political and economic instability in non-communist Europe.

*Straining relations between Moscow and its satellites.* But what about communist Europe? Although skeptical about what the United States could do to reduce the Soviet Union's influence in those parts of Central and Eastern Europe where communist governments were already in power, Kennan had not totally given up on this possibility in the spring of 1947: for this reason he had proposed extending Marshall Plan aid, not just to the non-communist states of Western Europe, but to the East Europeans and the Russians as well.

The motives behind this offer were hardly altruistic: "it would be essential," Kennan wrote, "that this be done in such a form that the Russian satellite countries would either exclude themselves by unwillingness to accept the proposed conditions or agree to abandon the exclusive orientation of their economies."[34] Either way, the West would win: if, on the one hand, the Russians turned down the offer, they would not only take onto themselves the responsibility for dividing Europe; they would also create frustration and bitterness within their own satellites, where the prospect of such aid was certain to arouse keen expectations. If, on the other hand, Moscow allowed the aid to flow, the effect would be far greater influence for the West in Eastern Europe, and a corresponding loss of control there for the Kremlin.[35]

Kennan's proposal caused no little nervousness in Washington: "there was no chance of Russia's *not* joining in this effort," a worried Secretary of the Navy James Forrestal told the Cabinet in June.[36] But British Foreign Secretary Ernest Bevin, a man with long experience in dealing with European communists, thought otherwise: "I feel that it is the quickest way to break down the iron curtain . . . Russia cannot hold its satellites against the attraction of fundamental help toward economic revival in Europe."[37] And when the Russians in fact rejected participation, both for themselves and for their disappointed satellites, Kennan felt vindicated. "Strain placed on communist movement by effort to draw up plan for European rehabilitation," he wrote in rough notes drafted in July, 1947: "Communist parties in West[ern Europe] forced to show their hand. Russians smoked out in relations with satellite countries. . . . Events of past weeks the greatest blow to European Communism since termination of hostilities."[38]

When Stalin authorized creation of the Cominform early in the fall of 1947, Kennan interpreted the decision as a defensive measure brought on by strains that had already accumulated between Moscow and the East European communist parties. The Russians were worried that these parties might "escape from their real control into a series of national-liberal movements with which they would eventually have to come into conflict." Accordingly, he predicted, the Soviet Union would move to tighten its authority over existing satellites, even if this meant alienating communists and other left-wing movements in Western Europe. "All this indicates that they must have a sense of serious weaknesses and dangers within the communist movement. . . . We should be able to capitalize effectively on this situation."[39]*

---

* F. B. A. Rundall, of the British Foreign Office, noted that creation of the Cominform had been seen in the United States "primarily as a counter-move to the Marshall Plan," and worried that "as it is thought to be dictated by Russian weakness rather than strength" the effect might be "to confirm the fairly prevalent view that Communism is on the run and thus . . . decrease the sense of urgency for American economic aid." [Rundall minute, October 21, 1947, Foreign Office Records, FO 371/61056/AN3582.]

"I have a certain theory relating to Russian history," Kennan told a group of industrial leaders in an extemporaneous talk in January, 1948, "which is that the Czars' regime actually perished of indigestion [from] the Western minorities in Europe which it had been foolish enough to bite off." The Soviet government's success during the first years of its existence might well have resulted from the fact "that [it] had lost those same border territories and had only Russians to deal with." Now, though, Russians were moving into these areas again, and "I don't think their problem of political control throughout eastern-central Europe has been, by any means, solved. I think the main tests of that are still to come, and it is going to become more difficult, rather than less, with the passage of time."[40]

The February, 1948, coup in Czechoslovakia, which Kennan had anticipated,[41]* provided an all-too-vivid confirmation of the argument that the Russians were in fact worried about their position in Eastern Europe, and felt the need to try to strengthen it. The effect was to discredit the Soviet Union even further in the eyes of the West European left; it also hastened final Congressional passage of the European Recovery Program and stimulated the beginnings of discussions that would lead, a year later, to the creation of the North Atlantic Treaty Organization.[42] The Czech coup provided painfully little evidence, at least on the surface, that the Soviet "empire" in Eastern Europe was about to crumble, but Kennan expected further developments: "If pressure is kept on [the] Soviet Union and satellite states," he told a Canadian diplomat in Tokyo early in March, "within six months [a] spectacular retreat of Soviet and communist influence in Europe can be expected."[43]

Once again, Kennan proved to be a good prophet, although in a way not even he had anticipated. Yugoslavia had been, until the spring of 1948, one of the most reliable of Moscow's Eastern European satellites. "This Government is . . . tied hand and foot to the Kremlin," the British ambassador had reported from Belgrade as late as June 18, 1948. "The bird . . . is trussed for the pot and can be roasted or boiled as and when convenient. . . ."[44]† But on the same day, the American Embassy there was reporting that Soviet-Yugoslav disagreements over the Danube constituted the "first direct and irrevocable challenge [of] any satellite to [the] supreme authority [of the] Communist overlords in [the] Kremlin."[45] And by the end of the month, it had become clear, as a Policy Planning Staff memorandum largely drafted by Kennan put it, that "[f]or the first time in history we may now have

---

* Kennan expresses doubt in his memoirs as to whether Marshall understood his warnings about Czechoslovakia or brought them to the attention of the President and the Pentagon. [George F. Kennan, *Memoirs: 1925–1950* (Boston: 1967), p. 403.] In fact, though, Marshall himself conveyed this warning, using language very similar to Kennan's, directly to the President and the Cabinet on November 7, 1947. [*FR: 1947*, I, 770n.]

† Although Sir Charles Peake's dispatch did go on to point out that "Tito is a very vain man and it is just conceivable that he might be driven beyond his limit." [Foreign Office Records, FO 371/72630/R7301.]

within the international community a communist state . . . independent of Moscow."[46]

*Encouraging Titoism in Eastern Europe.* Yugoslavia's break with the Kremlin confirmed, as little else could have, the potential for disarray within the international communist movement, and the Truman administration moved quickly to capitalize on what had happened. "A new factor of fundamental and profound significance has been introduced into the world communist movement by the demonstration that the Kremlin can be successfully defied by one of its own minions," Kennan pointed out:

> By this act, the aura of mystical omnipotence and infallibility which has surrounded the Kremlin power has been broken. The possibility of defection from Moscow, which has hitherto been unthinkable for foreign communist leaders, will from now on be present in one form or another in the mind of every one of them.[47]*

Another State Department official compared what had happened to "the Trotsky fall from grace" and rated it as "probably the most important single development since the conclusion of hostilities as far as internal Soviet and Communist internal affairs are concerned."[48]

But it was not at all clear just how the United States could exploit this situation. Too rapid an embrace of Tito, Kennan pointed out, could only arouse "feelings of disgust and revulsion" throughout the international communist movement and among his own followers: the effect could be to undermine his position and bring Yugoslavia "back into the fold." On the other hand, a policy of coldness or ridicule toward Tito would give the Russians the excuse to argue "that foreign communists have no alternative but to stay with Moscow; that desertion only places them at the mercy of the wolves of capitalism."[49] The compromise eventually reached was to maintain a policy of public coolness toward Yugoslavia—an approach that not only avoided discrediting Tito, but that also minimized the possibility of upsetting an American public and Congress not yet accustomed to differentiating between varieties of communism—while quietly moving toward the provision of economic and, if necessary, military assistance to sustain his regime in power.[50] The Yugoslav dictator might indeed be a "son-of-a-bitch," Secretary of State

---

* "[W]hat really caused the difficulty," Kennan told students at the National War College in October, 1948, "was the Politburo in Moscow because they were not content with the direct line of authority to Tito. . . . The Politburo tried to infiltrate its own people at lower levels [in Yugoslavia] almost out of force of habit. It had never tried to rule any other way anywhere, and it assumed that was the way it ought to be done. [It] assumed it was the natural right of the Kremlin to control Tito, and . . . that is, I believe, what really got his goat . . . and caused the split that came." [Kennan National War College lecture, "The Soviet Internal System," October 14, 1948, Kennan Papers, Box 17.]

Dean Acheson told a group of business executives in September, 1949, but he had the decided merit of being "our son-of-a-bitch."[51]*

With regard to the rest of Eastern Europe, the Truman administration had high hopes that the Titoist heresy might spread. The President himself in November, 1948, endorsed a National Security Council paper calling for efforts to bring about "the gradual retraction of undue Russian power and influence from the present perimeter areas around traditional Russian boundaries and the emergence of the satellite countries as entities independent of the USSR."[52] Kennan told the Policy Planning Staff the following April that the relationship between Moscow and its satellites was "the most vulnerable point of attack," and that "everything possible should be done to increase the suspicion between the Kremlin and its agents abroad."[53] And by December, 1949, a full-scale National Security Council review of policy toward Eastern Europe, initiated by the Policy Planning Staff, had concluded that "the time is now ripe . . . to consider whether we cannot do more to cause the elimination or at least a reduction of predominant Soviet influence in the satellite states of Eastern Europe."[54]

The specific efforts the United States made to undermine Soviet authority elsewhere in Eastern Europe ranged from the highly conspicuous to the highly secret. In the United Nations, the Truman administration mounted a vigorous campaign against human rights abuses in Rumania, Bulgaria, and Hungary, using as its legal justification the provisions of peace treaties signed with those nations in 1947. "[O]ur best traditions and our present interests require . . . stimulating resistance to Sovietization [in the] countries [of] this area," career diplomat Foy Kohler argued from Moscow early in 1949; the "fighting spirit" of the East Europeans "will surely wither away unless kept exercised."[55] Simultaneously, the administration sought the cooperation of European allies and neutrals in restricting trade with the Soviet Union and Eastern Europe: the intent here was to strain Moscow's relations with its satellites by forcing them to look to the Russians for industrial equipment the U.S.S.R. was in no position to supply.[56]†

At the same time, but less conspicuously, the administration maintained ties with a bewildering variety of East European exile groups, all of them united only by their determination somehow to challenge Soviet hegemony in that part of the world.[57] It also lent its endorsement—and, through the Cen-

---

* The formulation was an infectious one. British Foreign Secretary Ernest Bevin told Acheson on the same day that "although [Tito] was a scoundrel, [he] was our scoundrel." [Acheson memorandum, conversation with Bevin, September 14, 1949, *FR: 1949*, V, 956; see also Alan Bullock, *Ernest Bevin: Foreign Secretary* (New York: 1983) pp. 719–20.]

† There is some reason to think that the United States may have deliberately allowed blueprints for theoretically plausible but practically unworkable industrial equipment to fall into the hands of the Russians. [See a memorandum prepared by the Economic Section of the U.S. Embassy in Moscow, October 1, 1949, enclosed in Alan Kirk to Acheson, October 1, 1949, *FR: 1949*, V, 147.]

tral Intelligence Agency, discreet financial support—to an ostensibly private organization, the National Committee for Free Europe, which provided financial aid and employment opportunities for East European émigrés, and through its subsidiary, Radio Free Europe, the means to broadcast anti-Soviet propaganda to their homelands. The Committee, Kennan wrote Acheson, had been designed "to become one of the principal instrumentalities for accomplishing a number of our most important policy objectives."[58]

There were also, we now know, covert operations aimed at creating centers of anti-Soviet resistance within Eastern Europe itself. The most elaborate of these involved Albania, a small but at that time staunchly reliable Soviet satellite that appeared vulnerable to such activities because of the defection of Yugoslavia. Between 1949 and 1952, the Central Intelligence Agency, in collaboration with the British Secret Intelligence Service (MI6), infiltrated agents and even paramilitary forces into that country in the hope of overthrowing the government of Enver Hoxha; these efforts came to naught, in part because the British spy, Kim Philby, leaked information about them to the Russians.[59] A similar result awaited a second major CIA enterprise—an effort during 1951–52 to reconstitute the anti-communist World War II Home Army inside Poland—which in retrospect appears from the beginning to have been orchestrated by Soviet and Polish security forces for the purpose of exposing the anti-Soviet underground and embarrassing the West.[60]*

American efforts to encourage the spread of Titoism elsewhere in Eastern Europe were not successful: it would not be until the early 1960's that another Communist country in that region—Rumania—would proclaim and succeed in maintaining a foreign policy relatively free from dictation by the Kremlin.[61] The treason of Philby and others may have contributed this failure, but that is hardly the whole story. For one thing, Titoism itself had developed in Yugoslavia quite independently of anything the United States had done; it is not at all clear that it was ever within Washington's power to affect, in any substantial way, the relationship between Moscow and its East European satellites in the first place. Certainly the very uniqueness of Tito's position as a communist leader with genuine national support made it unlikely that his example would spread: "Except for Yugoslavia," Kennan pointed out in 1948, "the satellite governments are the slaves, not the partners, of Russia. The area of self-determination in their policies is not large."[62]

But there were also self-imposed constraints on American policy in Eastern Europe. The United States had extended diplomatic recognition to most of the Soviet satellite governments there, and could not now openly seek to undermine them without appearing to practice, as Kennan put it, "precisely that sort of interference in the internal affairs of other countries which [the Rus-

---

* Kennan is on record as arguing, in August, 1949, that "some covert operations should be applied at the appropriate time. . . . [I]f we wanted to cause difficulties among the communist leaders in Poland this probably could be done immediately by effective covert operations." [Minutes, Under Secretary of State Staff Meeting, August 31, 1949, Executive Secretariat Files, Box 13, Department of State Records.]

sians] like to practice themselves. They would love to get us in this position."[63] There was also the danger of provoking a Soviet military response. The circumstance most likely to bring this about, Kennan argued, would be "an abrupt weakening of [the Russians'] power in Eastern Europe, which in their view might leave no choice other than military action."[64] Moscow was not likely to respond to Tito's defection by going to war, CIA analysts concluded in the fall of 1948, but it might well prefer war to the prospect of losing Eastern Europe altogether.[65]

Despite this disappointing immediate outcome, though, there were more hopeful long-term lessons that American officials could draw from the Tito experience: first, that nationalism could serve as an antidote to communism; second, that the creation of a Soviet "empire" was as likely to cause difficulties as advantages for the Russians; and third, that as a result not all communists everywhere need be considered enemies of the United States. "The Russians fear Titoism above everything else," Walter Bedell Smith told the Policy Planning Staff in March, 1949, upon his return from having spent three years as Ambassador to the Soviet Union. "[T]he United States does not fear communism if it is not controlled by Moscow and not committed to aggression."[66]

*Encouraging Titoism in China.* "I can't say to you today whether Titoism is going to spread in Europe," Kennan admitted to students at the Naval War College in October, 1948. But he added: "I am almost certain that it is going to spread in Asia."[67] Kennan's confidence on this point—a confidence shared by many of his colleagues in the State Department—reflected a set of assumptions about East Asia that had grown out of the experience of World War II and the events that had followed there.

The first of these was that, whatever else happened, no external power was likely to dominate China. Franklin D. Roosevelt's insistence on treating that country as one of the postwar "Four Policemen" had reflected this assumption: highly sensitive to the rising power of nationalism in Asia, concerned as well to limit the expansion of Soviet influence there, the President believed that the long-term interests of the United States would better be served by encouraging China's emergence as an independent force than as a satellite of either Moscow or Washington.[68] Even after accumulating evidence of Chiang Kai-shek's ineptitude had made it painfully clear that Nationalist China was unlikely to play the ambitious role Roosevelt had assigned it, the expectation remained that no outside force—American or Russian—would find it easy to control the course of events in postwar China.[69]

The second assumption, closely linked to the first, was that communism in China was an indigenous rather than an imported phenomenon. Those few Americans who had studied the history of the Chinese Communist Party were aware of how little assistance—and how much bad advice—it had received from its Soviet counterpart prior to 1945; most Americans who made contact with Mao Zedong and his associates during the war had come away im-

pressed by their competence, their incorruptibility, and their apparent independence from Moscow.[70] To be sure, these characteristics did not make the
Chinese Communists pro-American; Washington's continuing recognition of
Chiang Kai-shek ensured that relations with the Communists would not be
easy, as General George C. Marshall found out during his long but unsuccessful attempt to resolve their differences with the Chinese Nationalists.[71] It is
also the case that the developing Cold War in Europe caused American officials to begin to worry about the extent of Russian influence within the
Chinese Communist Party.[72] But there still was no automatic tendency in
Washington to assume that Chinese Communists would be docile puppets of
the Kremlin, especially once they confronted the task of defending Chinese
national—not just party—interests.[73]*

The third assumption, growing out of the experience of both the war and
the Marshall mission, was that the ability of the United States to affect events
on the mainland of Asia was severely limited. This proposition made it easier
than it might otherwise have been for the Truman administration to accept
the argument that a victory for communism in China would pose no overwhelming threat to American interests, both because the task of ruling that
country would, it was thought, absorb the communists' energies for years to
come, but also because Mao and his colleagues were unlikely to defer blindly
to Moscow's wishes.[74] Kennan summed up the prevailing view succinctly for
Marshall in November, 1947: there was "no convincing evidence . . . that,
even should the Chinese National Government collapse, the communists could
in the foreseeable future assume effective authority over all China and at the
same time remain seriously susceptible to Soviet guidance or control in international affairs. Thus while a collapse of the National Government would be
deplorable, it probably would not be a catastrophe for American interests in
China."[75]

For these reasons, then, the idea was already in place, even before Tito's
break with the Kremlin in the summer of 1948, that the potential existed for
an independent Chinese communist movement at some indefinite point in the
future. But the effect of what happened in Yugoslavia, together with increasing indications that the Communist seizure of power in China was itself not
far off, was to transform the prospect of "Chinese Titoism" from a theoretical
possibility into an immediate probability; that development in turn caused
American officials to begin to think about what the United States might do to
bring such a thing about.[76] These discussions centered—as had earlier consideration of how to split Moscow from its satellites—in Kennan's Policy
Planning Staff.

* "[T]here is a good chance," Kennan told students at the National War College in May,
1947, "that if you let the Russians alone in China they will come a cropper on that problem just as everybody else has for hundreds of years. . . . If they [the Chinese Com-
munists] were to become a majority, if they were [to] come to control, let's say, a large
portion of the territory of China, I am not sure their relations with Moscow would be
much different than those of Chiang today." [Transcript, Kennan question and answer
session, National War College, May 6, 1947, Kennan Papers, Box 17.]

The dominant influence there on East Asian affairs was John Paton Davies, a career Foreign Service officer with long experience in China whom Kennan had come to know during their brief period of service together in Moscow in 1945–46. As early as 1943, Davies had warned that too close an American alignment with Chiang Kai-shek might push the Chinese Communists into the arms of the Russians;[77] by the end of 1947, as a newly appointed member of the Policy Planning Staff, he was calling for careful studies of communism in East Asia based on the premise that that phenomenon could not be understood simply "by applying mechanistically the European pattern to the Far Eastern scene."[78] The first of such studies, completed in September, 1948, concluded that if events in Yugoslavia were any guide, "Moscow faces a considerable task in seeking to bring the Chinese Communists under its complete control, if for no other reason than that Mao Tse-tung has been entrenched in power for nearly ten times the length of time that Tito has."[79]*

The Truman administration found this reasoning persuasive. Early in March, 1949, the President authorized a policy of seeking, "while scrupulously avoiding the appearance of intervention . . . to exploit through political and economic means any rifts between the Chinese Communists and the USSR and between the Stalinist and other elements in China both within and outside of the communist structure."[80] Two strategies were considered for accomplishing this: either to treat the People's Republic of China as an international pariah, isolating it from contact with the non-communist world in the hope of encouraging the overthrow or collapse of the communist government there; or to provide economic inducements to the Chinese Communists—in the form of carefully regulated trade with Japan and the Western world—to maintain their independence from Moscow, with the implied threat that such trade would be terminated if they failed to do so. The administration endorsed the latter alternative, on the grounds that a policy of isolating China would not only reinforce that country's dependence on the Russians, but would also retard economic recovery in Japan.[81]

It has been correctly pointed out[82] that there were contradictions in this approach. For one thing, the Truman administration proposed to maintain diplomatic relations with the Chinese Nationalist government "until the situation is further clarified." It also left open the possibility of providing "military and political" support to anti-communist groups operating on the mainland if it appeared "that such support would mean the overthrow of, or at least successful resistance to, the Communists."[83] The administration was also working secretly at this time to deny the island of Taiwan to *both* the Nationalists and the Communists by encouraging the creation of an independent government there, a policy that would have improved relations with

---

* Even if Mao was "fearfully loyal," the document continued, "Moscow still cannot be satisfied with the situation. China is too big, too populous. Even Mao and his colleagues cannot be permitted eventually to acquire all of it—the temptation might be too great for them, especially as they would have, in part, risen to power on the heady wine of nationalism. The Kremlin prefers, where possible, not to take chances in such matters." [PPS/39, United States Policy Toward China," September 7, 1948, *FR: 1948*, VIII, 148.]

neither of them had it become known.[84] But it is clear, nonetheless, that the State Department, with the approval of the President himself, had by the spring of 1949 come to rely upon the long-term possibility of a Sino-Soviet rift as the best hope for minimizing the damage to American interests that was sure to follow the final Chinese Communist consolidation of power.[85]

This strategy rested, Kennan pointed out several months later, not on the facile assertion that events in China would replicate precisely those that had taken place in Yugoslavia, but rather upon the remarkable capability of the Soviet system eventually to alienate even its most sympathetic admirers: "The Russians can be as mean and exacting in their friendships as they can in their enmities. They have a hard time being anything else." Because the Chinese Communists, like their Yugoslav counterparts, had come to power on their own and did not depend upon the Russians to remain in that position, they could be expected—as had the Yugoslavs—to resist Moscow's constricting embrace. That resistance, in turn, would pose problems for the Kremlin, because a communist state that defied its authority would be "a more horrible prospect in Moscow's eyes than the [most] incorrigible capitalist government. . . . Russian Communism may some day be destroyed by its own children in the form of the rebellious Communist parties of other countries. I can think of no development in which there would be a greater logic and justice."[86]*

# III

The Truman administration encountered relatively little difficulty, prior to 1950, in justifying its strategy of driving a "wedge" between the Soviet Union and European communists. Bipartisan cooperation still largely insulated diplomacy in that part of the world from domestic political interference; "McCarthyism," which would later impose severe constraints on East Asian policy, had not yet taken hold. But another reason why there was so little opposition to the "wedge" strategy in Europe was that its successes—or at least some of its successes—were so quickly apparent. The Marshall Plan did, as intended, force communist parties in France, Italy, and other parts of Western Europe to choose between continued fidelity to Moscow and the prospect of gaining political power at home; the result, since most of them remained loyal, was a significant diminution of their popular influence. At the same time, Tito's heresy showed that states that had already become communist could break with the Kremlin and get away with it, thereby confirming

---

* "I'm not predicting a repetition in China of what happened in Yugoslavia," Kennan commented the following month. "I'm only saying that I think the Russians are very alive to the fact that you can get a lot of people, ideologically, on your side and still the logic of power compulsions can cause them to challenge your physical authority at some stage along the way." [Kennan comment, State Department China Round Table discussions, October 6, 1949, Harry S. Truman Papers, PSF, Box 174, "Subject File: Foreign Affairs: China: Record of Round Table Discussions," Harry S. Truman Library.]

the administration's assumption that not all communists need be Soviet puppets.

China, though, was another matter. Here Washington had to base its policy upon an *anticipation* of events rather than—as in the case of Yugoslavia—upon what had already happened. Administration officials were confident that differences between the Russians and the Chinese Communists would eventually arise. President Truman himself in the spring of 1949 cited an unimpeachable authority on the difficulty of adapting communist theory to Chinese reality: "Joe Stalin says that the people of North China will never be Communists and he's about right, at that." But it was not at all clear how long it would take for these differences to emerge. Nothing could be done, the President admitted, "until things kind of settle down." Eventually, the "dragon" would "turn over and after that perhaps some advances can be made out of it."[87] Dean Acheson had had the same point in mind several months earlier when he characterized American China policy—to his subsequent regret—as one of "waiting for the dust to settle."[88]

Implicit in these counsels of patience was a reliance on long-term historical forces. Nationalism was the most important of these, Acheson told the Senate Foreign Relations Committee in October: "if we put ourselves sympathetically on the side of . . . nationalism, which is the dominant spiritual force in that area, we have put ourselves on the side of the thing which more than anything else can oppose communism."[89] It was important, the Secretary of State added several months later, to exploit the leverage to be derived from associating American interests with irreversible trends: "We think we have a great force operating with us, and instead of fighting that force if what you do is roll with it, you get the advantage of the gravitation of the earth or the turning of the earth, whatever it is that is behind that force." It was inevitable that the Chinese Communists would come into conflict with the Russians, "because the very basic objectives of Moscow are hostile to the very basic objectives of China."[90]

The administration's major public initiatives on China during this period—the "White Paper" of August, 1949, the January 1950, announcement that the United States would not seek to defend the Chinese Nationalists on Taiwan, and Acheson's National Press Club speech several days later—all can be understood as efforts to "buy" the time necessary for these long-term Sino-Soviet differences to emerge. It would be a major error, Acheson warned in the Press Club speech, to do anything for short-term reasons that would "deflect to ourselves the righteous anger, and the wrath, and the hatred of the Chinese people [toward the Russians] which must develop."[91]* At the same

---

* Acheson's main intention, the British Ambassador in Washington reported to the Foreign Office, "was to . . . impress on the minds of both Chinese and Americans that the United States is desirous of following its earlier benevolent line of 'hands off China.' If the Chinese can be convinced of this the Secretary of State clearly hopes that their xenophobic tendencies can be channeled against Soviet Russia." [Sir Oliver Franks to Foreign Office, January 16, 1950, Foreign Office Records, FO 371/83013/F1022/5.]

time, Acheson had the State Department carefully looking for signs that Sino-Soviet antagonism had already emerged, even to the point of planting rumors to this effect with favored columnists.[92]

But this insulation of long-term interests from short-term preoccupations proved difficult to sustain. One problem was that there were few, if any, indications that "Titoism" was actually taking hold in China. If anything, the tendency—especially after Mao's "lean to one side speech" at the end of June, 1949, appeared to lie in the opposite direction; the conclusion of a Sino-Soviet Treaty of Friendship in February, 1950, only reinforced the prevailing impression. This initial alignment of the new Chinese government with the Soviet Union was by no means unexpected: Acheson had predicted, as early as March, 1949, that the Communists would "go out of their way to show their sympathetic attitude of cooperation with the Russians."[93] Nor did these events cause the State Department to give up its "wedge" strategy.[94]* But the absence of any immediate evidence that such a strategy seemed likely to work with respect to China shifted the burden of proof against that approach much more than had been the case in the Yugoslav situation, where quick results had been there for all to see.

Further complicating the situation was the fact that, whatever their long-term attitude toward the Russians, the Chinese Communists could be expected for some time to manifest considerable hostility toward the United States. Once again, American officials understood this prospect clearly enough, viewing it as an unpleasant but unavoidable price to be paid for the administration's reluctant—but Congressionally mandated—continuation of military and economic assistance to Chiang Kai-shek. "I think we should recognize," Acheson had told the Senate Foreign Relations Committee early in 1949, "that the initial period [of Communist rule in China] will be a period unfavorable to us."[95] But the new Chinese government seemed particularly determined to prove the Secretary of State correct: the bitterness it felt obliged to demonstrate toward the United States in public—whatever its actual intentions—also made it difficult for the administration to sustain its policy of waiting for long-term Sino-Soviet differences to emerge.[96]

Yet another complication was the growing tendency, inside the United States, to perceive foreign policy issues in ideological terms. Historians still debate the reasons for this: some would argue that the tendency grew out of the partisan instincts of a Republican Party unexpectedly humiliated at the polls in 1948; others that it stemmed from the rhetorical excesses of a Truman administration determined to frighten the country into supporting containment in Europe.[97] But for whatever the reason, there had developed in the

---

* "It is regrettable but not surprising," the as yet undiscovered Soviet spy Guy Burgess noted from his post in the British Foreign Office in March, 1950, "that U.S. public opinion and even official comment was reluctant fully to face up to the possible implications of the Sino-Soviet Treaty, so particularly serious if you have no policy." [Burgess minute, March 11, 1950, attached to Franks to Foreign Office, March 6, 1950, Foreign Office Records, FO 371/83013/F1022/10.]

country by 1949, to a degree not present previously, a tendency to see ideology more as a cause than as a reflection of the behavior of nations. It is significant that newly appointed Secretary of Defense Louis Johnson saw fit, in June of that year, to raise with the National Security Council the question of whether "a major objective of United States policy" was not "to contain communism in order to reduce its threat to our security," and to ask whether the administration's policies toward Asia had been framed with that principle sufficiently in mind.[98]

Requirements of military strategy also made it hard to sustain a strategy of waiting for Sino-Soviet differences to emerge. Concerned about the costs of keeping ground forces in East Asia, the Truman administration had moved, during 1948 and 1949, to liquidate major responsibilities on the mainland in favor of reliance on air and naval power to hold such offshore island positions as Japan, Okinawa, and the Philippines. Precisely because it wanted to avoid driving the Chinese Communists into the arms of the Russians, the State Department—not without difficulty—had prevented Taiwan from being included within this "defensive perimeter," despite its incontestable status as an offshore island. But this attempt to subordinate geography to geopolitics made little military sense, as critics of the administration's policy argued with increasing emphasis during the first half of 1950: a Taiwan under hostile control, they pointed out, would imperil both the Philippines to the south and Okinawa to the north. There was, thus, significant pressure growing both within and outside the administration to include Taiwan within the "defensive perimeter," whatever the additional burdens this might impose upon the Sino-Soviet "wedge" strategy.[99]

All of these short-term considerations—the absence of overt Sino-Soviet antagonism, the persistence of Chinese Communist hostility toward the United States, the increasingly ideological orientation of American foreign policy, and the military anomaly of not defending Taiwan—worked against the Truman administration's long-term goal of waiting for Sino-Soviet differences to emerge. But they did not, in themselves, cause a reversal of that strategy. The two principal objectives of the United States in the Far East, Acheson told Thomas E. Dewey in April 1950, were still to sign a Japanese peace treaty and "to drive a wedge between Peiking [sic] and Moscow."[100]

What did cause these short-term considerations to override long-term interests was a wholly unanticipated event: the North Korean invasion of South Korea at the end of June, 1950. Although developments on the Korean peninsula had had little to do with the evolution of the American "wedge" strategy prior to that moment, the outbreak of fighting there affected implementation of that strategy in several decisive ways:

First, and most significantly, the fighting in Korea produced an immediate revision of policy with respect to Taiwan, as the Truman administration ordered the Seventh Fleet into the Taiwan Strait to prevent either Chinese Communist attacks on the island or Chinese Nationalist attacks on the mainland. Even at this point, the administration did not see itself as intervening on behalf of Chiang Kai-shek: its intention, as American officials said at the time, was to "neutralize" the area while military operations on the Korean peninsula were under way. The consistency with which Truman and his advisers rejected General Douglas MacArthur's repeated recommendations to allow Chinese Nationalist forces to fight in Korea supports the thesis that the administration still hoped to avoid taking sides in the Chinese civil war.[101] It is clear in retrospect, though, that the Taiwan Strait decision produced the impression in Beijing that the United States *was* taking sides, and that the result was to undermine whatever inclination yet remained in that capital to leave the door open for eventual cooperation with the United States.[102]*

Second, the outbreak of the Korean War reinforced the growing tendency within the United States to see ideology rather than national interests as determining the behavior of communist states. As Ambassador George V. Allen explained to Yugoslav Foreign Minister Edvard Kardelj early in July, "many people in [the] US regarded Communism, like Fascism and other dictatorships by one group or class, as synonymous with aggression."[103] There was an emotional groundswell of public opinion in the United States, the British Embassy in Washington reported the following month, that "leads people to want to bash anything that can be labelled Red or Russian. . . . This feeling . . . makes it easier to talk of 'No more Munichs with China' or not letting another acre of ground go to the Reds than it is to see the varying shades of Red in the [communist] areas of the world. . . ."[104]†

Third, Korea demonstrated as clearly as any event in recent memory the problem of psychological vulnerabilities in international relations. As early as 1947, the Truman administration had decided that defense of the peninsula was not among the vital interests of the United States.[105] But the events of June 25, 1950—and, in particular, the dramatic way in which they occurred—gave Korea a symbolic importance that completely and almost instantly overrode coolly rational distinctions between vital and peripheral interests. What Korea showed was that even regions not deemed vital could become vital if threatened by hostile military force. Whether that force emanated from states acting in unison with the Soviet Union or not became largely an academic question: the issue at stake now, in the eyes of most Washington officials, was the credibility of American commitments to resist aggression, from whatever source.[106] That viewpoint, too, weakened efforts to distinguish between varieties of communism.

---

* Kennan, interestingly, anticipated this development. He told Acheson in August, 1950, that "our policy toward the rival Chinese regimes is one almost sure . . . to strengthen Peiping-Moscow solidarity rather than weaken it." [Kennan to Acheson, August 21, 1950, *FR: 1950*, VII, 624.]

† "They [the State Department] appear up to now to have judged Chinese intentions without much regard to what the Chinese are likely to be thinking themselves. . . . Since the principal danger of an extension of the conflict in the Far East is the tension between the United States and China, we should rather like to ride the Americans off this if we can." [M. E. Dening to B. A. B. Burrows, August 24, 1950, Foreign Office Records, FO 371/83296/FC1023/6.]

It is important to recognize that the outbreak of the Korean War did not completely discredit the strategy of seeking to promote Sino-Soviet differences. Those differences might actually intensify, State Department intelligence specialists speculated, if the fighting in Korea had the effect of denying Taiwan to the Chinese Communists, or of bringing about a strengthened American military position in East Asia.[107] There was also some expectation that a reunification of Korea brought about by a successful United Nations attack across the 38th parallel might cause the Chinese to question their alignment with the Russians.[108] Acheson's public statements continued to stress the threat the Soviet Union posed to Chinese sovereignty.* And as late as November 27, 1950, just as full-scale Chinese intervention in the Korean conflict was getting under way, Deputy Assistant Secretary of State Livingston Merchant could still argue, in a top secret memorandum, that "our objective, of course, is to destroy the basis for a durable alliance between the Soviet Union and China."[109]

But most American officials had long since relegated this prospect to the distant—and therefore not immediately policy-relevant—future. For the moment, Charles Bohlen told a meeting of British and French diplomats in August, it could be assumed that on questions of general foreign policy the Chinese would follow the Soviet line. Rifts might eventually appear between the Russians and the Chinese, but "we could not afford to predicate our policy on the expectation of Communist China splitting away from the Soviet world." Such a split, if it should occur, would not in any event be the result of Western efforts: "kindness from the West will not tempt them [the Chinese] to break away from the Soviet world. If a break should come, it may be expected to come from within."[110] A colloquy between Senator J. William Fulbright and Representative Walter Judd at a Congressional hearing the following month reflected the extent to which optimism about the "wedge" strategy had waned:

FULBRIGHT:  I think the only hope for an ultimate solution is that they [the Chinese] break away from the Russians.
JUDD:  Boy, you are leaning on a weak reed.
FULBRIGHT:  I admit it is not very favorable at the moment.[111]

Chinese intervention in the Korean conflict late in November, 1950, made prospects for encouraging a Sino-Soviet split even bleaker, as Prime Minister Attlee discovered during his hurried trip to Washington early in December. The United States was making a mistake, Attlee suggested, by treating China

---

* "[A] great cloud from the north, Russian penetration, is operating, and it is quite obvious that the plan is to absorb those northern areas of China under Soviet domination. . . . Why they [the Chinese] should want to further their own dismemberment and destruction by getting at cross purposes with all the free nations of the world who are inherently their friends and have always been friends of the Chinese against this imperialism coming down from the Soviet Union I cannot see." [CBS television interview with Acheson, September 10, 1950, *Department of State Bulletin*, XXIII (September 18, 1950), 463.]

in such a way as to leave the Soviet Union as its only friend. The Chinese were "hard-shelled Marxists-Leninists" but they were probably not "Soviet imperialists." There was still "a chance of Titoism."

Acheson replied that few of the President's advisers would disagree with that appraisal: indeed, he himself had probably been more "bloodied" than anyone else in trying to make this case. "The question was not whether this was a correct analysis but whether it was possible to act on it."

> Perhaps in ten or fifteen years we might see a change in the Chinese attitude but we do not have that time available. . . . If in taking a chance on the long future of China we affect the security of the United States at once, this is a bad bargain. . . . All that the Prime Minister had said was correct if we had time but we can't buy our way into this poker game; the cost of coming in is too high.

It was also the case, Acheson argued, that the American people would never accept a policy of standing up to Soviet aggression in Europe while accommodating Chinese aggression in Asia. "The public mind was not delicate enough to understand such opposing attitudes and even if it were that difference would be wrong." If Americans "accepted the proposition that because an aggression is a very large one we can submit to it," then they would have changed their attitudes "very deeply" and would have little choice but to "adjust ourselves to power and aggression everywhere."[112] Truman agreed: the Chinese, he told Attlee, "are satellites of Russia and will be satellites so long as the present Peiping regime is in power. . . . The Chinese people do, of course, have national feelings. The Russians cannot dominate them forever, but that is a long-range view and does not help us just now."[113]*

Even so, the administration believed strongly enough in the possibility of exploiting eventual Sino-Soviet differences that early in 1951 it took the extreme risk—given the domestic political climate that existed at that time—of authorizing highly secret State Department contacts with Chinese believed to represent the views of at least some elements within the government in Beijing. Precisely what the administration had in mind remains unclear, but it appears to have hoped for a cease-fire with Chinese and North Korean forces—probably arranged independently of the Russians—in exchange for an eventual cessation in American support for Chiang Kai-shek, recognition of the People's Republic of China, and admission of that country to the United Nations. "We are actuated," Charles Burton Marshall of the Policy Planning Staff told his still-unnamed Chinese negotiating partner, "by the hope that something may occur to bring China to its senses so that it will cease to serve the inter-

---

* Truman added in a separate meeting with Attlee on December 7 that he was not "in any mood for an unnecessary surrender to give in to China which is actually the Russian government. He hoped that time would bring them [the Chinese] to realize that their friends are not in Siberia but in London and Washington." [Minutes, Truman-Attlee meeting, December 7, 1950, *FR: 1950,* VII, 1456.]

ests of [a] conspiracy that is aimed against Chinese independence just as much as ours."[114]

But there were obvious difficulties with such an approach. The State Department was pressing, at just this moment, for public United Nations condemnation of the People's Republic as an aggressor: that effort created a less than favorable climate for secret attempts to appeal to the government in Beijing.[115]* Nor was the Department certain that it wanted to negotiate with Mao Zedong: much attention was also being given, at this time, to promoting the emergence of a "third force" on the mainland—opposed to both Mao and Chiang Kai-shek—which could seize power in Beijing and then make peace.[116] Nor had much thought been given to how such a settlement with China could be justified inside the United States. When a State Department representative cautiously broached with House Majority Leader John McCormack the possibility of a negotiated cease-fire in Korea in return for American recognition of the People's Republic, the reaction was explosive:

> His response was that it would be a calamity. He . . . would rather see us pull out of Korea than to be guilty of such an act of "appeasement." . . . He said that such a move would completely destroy all of the Democratic support for the Administration.[117]

By June, 1951, Marshall was forced to report that his secret contacts with the Chinese had produced no results, that the Beijing government was "thoroughly locked into collaboration with Moscow," that the "third force" option had turned out to consist "mostly of petty politicking among inconsequential people," and that Chiang Kai-shek's reputation on the mainland was "much better now than many of us have tended to think." Formosa, Marshall concluded, "constitutes our main tangible asset in respect to the China problem."[118]

With the onset of cease-fire negotiations in Korea in July—arranged through the Russians—the administration's efforts to use the Korean conflict to split the Sino-Soviet alliance became academic in any event. Even if that had not happened, it is difficult to see how the approach to the People's Republic could have succeeded, given the intensity of domestic opposition within the United States to the granting of any concession whatever to the Chinese Communists. It is an indication of the depth of Congressional sentiment on this point that in September, 1951, in what proved to be an unsuccessful effort to gain senatorial approval of Philip C. Jessup's nomination to the United States delegation to the United Nations, Acheson was forced to deny "persis-

---

* "It is important to realise," the British Embassy in Washington reported, "that in pursuing their present policy the Administration, and in particular Mr. Acheson, are not actuated mainly by the desire to appease the China lobby but are acting on what they believe to be a vital moral principle, the neglect of which led to the destruction of the League of Nations and by indirect but nonetheless definite stages to the outbreak of the second World War." [Weekly Political Summary, January 27, 1951, Foreign Office Records, FO 371/90903/AU1013/6.]

tent but baseless reports" that the State Department had *ever* considered recognizing the People's Republic of China, or its admission to the United Nations.[119]

To be sure, the long-term strategic objective of somehow breaking up the Sino-Soviet alliance still persisted. On May 17, 1951, President Truman had approved NSC 48/5, which listed as the first of several "current objectives" of United States policy in Asia to "detach China as an effective ally of the USSR and support the development of an independent China which has renounced aggression." This would be done both by "stimulat[ing] differences between the Peiping and Moscow regimes" and by "creat[ing] cleavages within the Peiping regime itself by every practicable means."[120] Assistant Secretary of State Dean Rusk's public condemnation of the People's Republic, the following day, as "a colonial Russian government—a Slavic Manchukuo in a larger scale" was intended to be yet another attempt to discredit the Russians in the eyes of the Chinese: as Acheson assured Truman several days later, "Mr. Rusk had not suggested or in any way made any change in policy, but had merely repeated what had been said by both the President and me many times in the past."[121]*

Unfortunately, the image of a "Slavic Manchukuo" resonated more with Americans than it did with the Chinese: in the wake of several months of deadly combat in Korea, and with the domestic political situation inside the United States in an uproar over the alleged "loss" of China, the firing of General MacArthur, and charges of treason in high places, few in the United States were prepared to acknowledge any redeeming features at all in either the Chinese people or their government; fewer still were prepared to defend the administration's continued—but increasingly muted—belief in the principle, as John Paton Davies had expressed it, "that when one is confronted with two enemies it is often profitable to play them off against one another."[122]

There were, in retrospect, several reasons for the Truman administration's difficulties in implementing the "wedge" strategy. First, it required the pursuit of objectives that promised no immediate benefits. With a domestic climate of opinion increasingly disinclined to differentiate between adversaries, with a People's Republic of China determined to demonstrate its solidarity with the Soviet Union, and with the eruption of a wholly unforeseen but desperate military struggle on the Korean peninsula, the argument that one should wait for long-term historical forces to manifest themselves was not easy to sell. It was a strategy that demanded the luxury of time; but that commodity, for an unpopular administration beset with crises both at home and abroad, was in decidedly short supply. A Sino-Soviet split had seemed

* The Department explained to the American Embassy in London that although the speech "contained no modification nor change in policy," it had been "slanted in part for use in psychological warfare within China which may in part explain distortion achieved by certain extracts lifted out of context." [Telegram of May 22, 1951, *FR: 1951*, VII, 1673n.]

"a real possibility" prior to the outbreak of the Korean War, Acheson admitted to Winston Churchill early in 1952. But Chinese intervention "had made this hope seem very distant and impossible of attainment at the present. I did not think that *over any period of time with which we could now be concerned* it was possible to create a divergence between the two communists [sic] groups."[123]

Second, the President and his advisers never made a clear choice between the two obvious methods of implementing the "wedge" strategy: the "Chinese Tito" option, which would have involved seeking to wean Mao Zedong's government away from its alignment with the Russians without trying to replace it; and the "third force" option, which would have required treating Mao's regime as a Soviet puppet while building a non-communist "nationalist" opposition on the mainland capable of overthrowing it. The decision, admittedly, would not have been a simple one. The "Chinese Tito" alternative had the advantage of not depending upon the dubious prospect of creating a mainland opposition movement, but it involved the disadvantage of being willing to deal openly with a communist government, an equally dubious prospect given the American domestic political situation at the time. The "third force" option would have been easier to justify domestically—although only marginally, since it would surely have encountered the wrath of the powerful Nationalist Chinese lobby in Washington—but the task of creating such an opposition movement out of the disorganized and mutually antagonistic array of Chinese exile and resistance groups that remained beyond the control of either Mao or Chiang Kai-shek would have been a daunting prospect. The path of least resistance was to leave options open rather than to choose between them, but that course then left the administration vulnerable to the possibility that the simultaneous pursuit of two such obviously contradictory options might undercut them both.

Explicit alignment with the Chinese Nationalists on Taiwan was, of course, yet another alternative, but Truman administration officials regarded it as one that would preclude altogether the goal of detaching the Chinese Communists from the Russians. Accordingly, they limited their objectives there to keeping the island out of the hands of any regime associated with the Soviet Union, while avoiding any direct commitment to defend the Chinese Nationalists.[124] There was, the State Department admitted late in 1951, "no *presently* achievable solution for the disposition of Formosa which will satisfy United States policy objectives."[125]

What is surprising, then, is not that the "wedge" strategy was difficult to explain, or unpopular with those who did comprehend it, or vague in its anticipated benefits, but rather that Truman and his advisers had sufficient faith in the triumph of long-term over short-term considerations to cause them to stick with it as persistently as they did.

# IV

John Foster Dulles, too, believed in the importance of long-term historical forces: like Kennan and other architects of the Truman administration's "wedge" strategy, he saw such forces as antithetical to the ability of the Soviet Union, over time, to maintain influence over its satellites. The "great weakness in the present brand of communism," he had written in 1949, "is insistence upon absolute conformity to a pattern made in Russia. That does not work in areas where the economic and social problems are different from those in Russia and where there are deep-seated national and cultural loyalties."[126] Asia was certainly one such place: "It is not necessary to reconquer China by subsidizing a vast military operation. Communism will disintegrate in China, and the Chinese themselves will take care of that, because of its inability to solve the problems of China."[127] There was no immediate possibility of breaking up the Sino-Soviet alliance, Dulles acknowledged after Chinese intervention in the Korean War late in 1950, but in the long run "our best defense lies in exploiting potential jealousies, rivalries, and disaffections within the present area of Soviet communist control so as to divert them from external adventures to the problem of attempting to consolidate an already overextended position."[128]

The new Secretary of State differed from his predecessor, though, in that he was able to devise a viable domestic political rationale for pursuing such a strategy, something the Truman administration had never quite managed. That rationale was, of course, the concept of "liberation," which Dulles made a central theme of the 1952 Republican presidential campaign. Dulles had not been the first to endorse the idea: the objective of "liberating" Soviet satellites from Moscow's control had been implicit in Kennan's thinking about "containment" from the beginning, and had long since been quietly endorsed by Truman himself.[129]* Nor did Dulles question the Truman administration's determination to proceed in this direction by peaceful means, even if his public rhetoric did not always make this point as clearly as it might have.[130]

But Dulles did insist—as Truman and Acheson had not—that the United States could most effectively strain the relationship between the Soviet Union and the rest of the communist world by applying maximum pressure on it, not by trying to conciliate disaffected communists in the hope of persuading them to break with Moscow.[131] "My own feeling," he wrote Chester Bowles in March, 1952, "is that the best way to get a separation between the Soviet Union and Communist China is to keep pressure on Communist China and make its way difficult so long as it is in partnership with Soviet Russia." Tito

---

* A British report of a conversation in February, 1952, with Truman's last CIA Director, Walter Bedell Smith, quotes him as arguing "very vehemently on the need to advance and meet the Russians on their own ground. By waiting passively we would, in his view, be ultimately and entirely outclassed." [William Elliott memorandum, conversation with Smith, February 7, 1952, Foreign Office Records, FO 371/100825/NS1023/1.]

had not broken with Stalin "because we were nice to Tito. On the contrary, we were very rough on Tito." If China could win American favors while remaining aligned with the Kremlin, "then there is little reason for her to change."[132] The Yugoslav precedent, Dulles reminded presidential candidate Dwight Eisenhower several months later, "showed a possibility that other countries, such as Czechoslovakia, Poland and China, might in due course peacefully resume effective control of their affairs."[133]*

Not the least advantage of a strategy that would seek to divide the Soviet Union from its satellites by applying pressure rather than attempting conciliation was that it would avoid the problem of differentiating between adversaries that had caused such domestic political difficulties for the Truman administration. One could condemn "communism" in general, one could even take the rhetorical position of rejecting "containment" in favor of "rolling back" communist influence in the world, without worrying about driving the Soviet Union and its allies into closer alignment with each other: differences within the communist bloc were already so great that pressure would intensify rather than minimize them. Specific opportunities could not be publicized, Dulles acknowledged, without running the risk of destroying them. "But believe me, they exist, and if availed of, can transform the world, not overnight, but within a reasonable period."[134]

Dulles came to this position from a long-standing belief—similar to Kennan's—in the vulnerability of empires. "Dictatorships usually present a formidable exterior," he had reminded readers of his book, *War or Peace,* published just prior to the outbreak of the Korean War. "They seem, on the outside, to be hard, glittering, and irresistible." But within, "they are full of rottenness."[135] In his first radio-television address as Secretary of State, Dulles pointed out that the "Russian Communists" had "swallowed" something like 800 million people, "but you know there is such a thing as indigestion. People don't always get stronger by eating more."[136]† Several days later, Presidential assistant Robert Cutler placed before the newly constituted Eisenhower National Security Council the central question Dulles's arguments had raised: "Do existing policies sufficiently weigh or consider the vulnerabilities of the Kremlin regime (such as the ingestive results of swallowing such large areas and populations so rapidly), or the psychological aspects related thereto?"[137]

The idea of applying "pressure" against communist vulnerabilities while

---

* Dulles added that "while Yugoslavia was not symbolic of what Americans like as a form of government, and while we would wish it different, it was symbolic of the possibility of breaking up the Soviet empire without war, and that was a symbol which I did not think the free world should want to see struck down." [Dulles to Eisenhower, June 25, 1952, John Foster Dulles Papers, Box 57, "Bebler" folder, Seeley Mudd Library, Princeton University.]

† Kennan had made a similar argument the month before in an off-the-record address at the National War College: "We often forget that there is such a thing as an overextension of the battle line in the political field as well as in the military, and that there may be times when there can be advantages as well as disadvantages in luring your adversary into the assumption of responsibilities and commitments far afield." [National War College lecture transcript, December 18, 1952, Kennan Papers, Box 18.]

at the same time reaping the domestic advantages of such an approach is apparent in several of the early initiatives of the Eisenhower administration. It lay behind the decision, early in 1953, to withdraw the Seventh Fleet from the Taiwan Strait, thus—in theory, at least—freeing Chiang Kai-shek to attack the mainland.[138] It motivated administration support for a Congressional resolution expressing solidarity with the "captive nations" of Eastern Europe and East Asia: the intent here, Dulles explained, was to "allay the fears of some enslaved peoples that the United States is abandoning them to their fate" and, as a result, to cause "a little indigestion" behind the Iron Curtain.[139] The strategy of "pressure" also bolstered the administration's determination not to repatriate Chinese Communist and North Korean prisoners-of-war, even if this delayed concluding an armistice in Korea: knowing that they could expect political asylum in any future conflict, Dulles insisted, "soldiers in these armies who want freedom will be more apt to desert and surrender, . . . the Red armies [will] become less dependable and there is far less risk that the Communists will be tempted to use these armies for aggression."[140]

But it was the death of Joseph Stalin on March 5, 1953, that provided the new administration with its most promising—if unexpectedly early—opportunity to exploit vulnerabilities within the Soviet bloc. Dulles informed American embassies overseas the following day that they should seek "to sow doubt, confusion, uncertainty about [the] new regime not only among both Soviet and satellite elites and masses, but among local Communist parties outside [the] Soviet Union."[141] Several days later, he predicted in a National Security Council meeting that "the Communist leaders in the satellites would experience far greater difficulty today in subordinating the impulse of nationalism in their respective countries to the relatively unknown individual who had taken Stalin's place." What the United States needed to do "was to play up this nationalism and discontent for all it was worth, to seize every opportunity by this device to break down the monolithic Soviet control over the satellite states."[142] Moscow's power was already overextended, Dulles pointed out in another National Security Council meeting two weeks later: "If we keep our pressures on, psychological and otherwise, we may either force a collapse of the Kremlin regime or else transform the Soviet orbit from a union of satellites dedicated to aggression, into a coalition for defense only." The dictator's death clearly marked "the end of an era. There is no real replacement for Stalin the demi-god."[143]

But the Secretary of State also emphasized the need for caution. Too gleeful a reaction on the part of the West might drive Russian nationalism into a position of sympathy for the new regime. "The Soviet was now involved in a family funeral," Dulles noted on March 12, and it might be best to wait "until the corpse was buried and the mourners gone off to their homes to read the will, before we begin our campaign to create discord in the family." Moreover, American allies might react negatively if there were too overt an attempt too quickly "to carry the offensive direct to the Soviet Union."[144] With these strictures in mind, Eisenhower several months later approved employing a variety of "political, economic, propaganda and paramilitary operations, including controls on East-West trade, . . . to delay the consolidation of Soviet bloc power," but with the qualification that these efforts to strain Moscow's relations with other communist countries were to be employed "without taking undue risks."[145]

The administration's restraint was evident in June, 1953, when a series of anti-communist riots suddenly broke out in East Berlin and spread through East Germany before being suppressed by the Russians. The Central Intelligence Agency appears to have rejected suggestions that it distribute weapons to the rioters,[146] and Secretary of State Dulles went out of his way to make it clear publicly that encouraging internal difficulties within the Soviet bloc "does not mean an armed revolt which would precipitate a massacre."[147] The United States hoped for free elections in Eastern Europe, Eisenhower told a press conference at the beginning of July, but there was no thought of "taking any physical action of any kind that could be classed as intervention."[148] Later that month, when the possibility of reviving covert efforts to detach Albania from the Soviet bloc came up in a National Security Council meeting, the President cautioned that Albania would be "a very difficult case because of the question of who gets it and who gets hurt."[149] Increasing Soviet military capabilities imposed limits, as well, on how far the United States should go: even before the Russians had tested their first thermonuclear device in August, 1953, Eisenhower told his Assistant for National Security Affairs, Robert Cutler, he had had doubts "about how much we should poke at the animal through the bars of the cage."[150]

The Eisenhower administration's first comprehensive review of national strategy, NSC 162/2, completed at the end of October, 1953, reinforced the prevailing mood of caution with respect to the Soviet Union's European satellites.* Unrest in East Germany and elsewhere in Eastern Europe had made clear the Russians' failure "fully to subjugate these peoples or to destroy their desire for freedom." As a result, the Kremlin was in no position to count on the loyalty of satellite armed forces; the situation moreover had clearly "placed internal and psychological strains upon the Soviet leadership." But these events had in no appreciable way reduced Moscow's ability to dominate Eastern Europe through the use of its own armed forces, and that situation did not appear likely to change soon: "The detachment of any major European satellite from the Soviet bloc does not now appear feasible except by Soviet acquiescence or by war."[151]†

---

* NSC 162/2, in turn, had been very much influenced in this respect by conclusions reached during a major review of national security policy, "Operation Solarium," carried out during the summer of 1953. [See, on this point, *FR: 1952–54*, II, 463–64, 491.]

† Policy Planning Staff Director Robert Bowie had pressed for the inclusion in this policy statement of language specifying that the United States would not "initiate aggressive actions involving force against Soviet bloc territory," but Dulles rejected this as long as it was understood that the National Security Council would have to approve any such operation. [Bowie to Dulles, October 28, 1953, *FR: 1952–54*, II, 566–67; Minutes, NSC meeting, October 29, 1953, *ibid.*, p. 569.]

China presented more promising opportunities. Even before Stalin's demise had been confirmed, Eisenhower was speculating that although that event might not make a great deal of difference in Eastern Europe, "one specific area of the world where Stalin's death could make a very great difference was Communist China."[152] Charles Bohlen, soon to become ambassador to the Soviet Union, agreed, pointing out that "in spite of some pretense of originality in the field of Communist theory, Mao has been willing to acknowledge Stalin as the master." It was "highly doubtful" that he would accord such a position to whatever new leadership emerged in the Soviet Union, especially if the United States could make a point, in its propaganda, of contrasting the 'bloody little butcher' Malenkov to the 'formidable Stalin.'" It was one thing for Mao to "play second fiddle to Stalin, but quite another to accept the supremacy of Malenkov."[153]

With these opportunities in mind, the National Security Council staff completed its first major review of American policy toward the People's Republic a month after Stalin's death. The evolution of a friendly, independent, and non-communist China would never occur, it maintained, without detachment of that country from "the Soviet orbit." That event could take place, in turn, either through the Beijing government's defection from Moscow, or through its overthrow. Both options presented advantages and disadvantages for the United States, but there was no immediate need to choose between them because "a policy of increasing pressure on Communist China . . . promotes both courses; it does not render the eventual detachment of China from the Soviet orbit impossible by way of either course."

Eventually a choice might have to be made, but in the absence of any evidence that Mao's government actually *wanted* to break with Moscow, "the question of providing an 'avenue of escape' from the Soviet relationship is academic . . . especially when its provision would severely handicap, if not nullify, the accomplishment of other important U.S. objectives." China's alienation from Russia would come about, moreover, only partly as the result of American actions: "Soviet dealings with the Chinese Communist regime may in the end prove more decisive in determining whether a change in the *status quo* occurs in China." American policy should therefore be confined to "demonstrating to the Chinese that the pro-Soviet posture of the Peiping regime does not pay off but in fact causes them increasing hardships and sacrifices." Such an approach would provide no immediate "avenue of escape," but it would, over time, "stimulate a desire for an avenue of escape." When that happened, Washington could re-examine its options.[154]*

* The study went on to note the possibility that, even with the application of pressure, the Chinese Communist government might not break with the Russians. "In such a case, nothing less than complete obliteration of the regime would satisfy U.S. objectives." It was also conceivable that a Chinese regime that had broken from Moscow might remain hostile to the United States, and "as a purely Asian power . . . might attract far more Asian support than it does now." [National Security Council Staff Study, "Basic U.S. Objectives Toward Communist China," April 6, 1953, *FR: 1952–54*, XIV, 177.]

Eisenhower had mixed feelings about this strategy of "pressure." There was an inconsistency involved in maintaining diplomatic relations with the Soviet Union but not with Communist China, he reminded a group of legislators in May, 1953: it was unfortunate that "ever since President Wilson's time, recognition [had] meant approval of a government."[155] The following month, he successfully opposed Congressional efforts to bar American financial support for the United Nations if that organization admitted the People's Republic to membership, on the grounds that "it is not wise to tie our own hands irrevocably about affairs in advance. . . . [J]ust think back to 1945, when Germany was our deadly enemy; who could then have foreseen that in only a few years it would become a friendly associate?"[156] But the President also assured Congressional leaders that "so long as Red China was constituted on its present basis, under its present leaders, and so obviously serving the ends of Soviet Russia . . . I would *never* be a party to its recognition and its acceptance in the United Nations."[157]

Eisenhower saw the possibility, as well, of using trade as an inducement to wean the Chinese away from the Russians. Restrictions on trade had been useful in forcing Beijing to seek an armistice in Korea,[158] but if the long-term objective was to "weaken the Sino-Soviet alliance," he told the National Security Council in November, 1953, then "trade might be a very useful tool in accomplishing this purpose." It could also provide a solution to Japan's economic difficulties:

If . . . we could get the Japanese to send harmless manufactured goods, such as crockery, knives and forks, and wholly non-strategic materials, and sell them to China, this would serve the dual purpose of relieving Communist China's dependence on the USSR and Japan's dependence upon our own Treasury.

When Secretary of Defense Charles E. Wilson confessed puzzlement as to "how you could love the Chinese Communists and fight them at the same time," Eisenhower acknowledged "the great difficulty [posed by] the public relations aspect of . . . trading with the Chinese Communists." Demagogues were sure to "raise a hue and cry about building up the economies of nations who would use their resources to kill our soldiers." Still, the President said, he "shuddered to contemplate the hard and fixed rules which this Government was setting up to guide its policy on trade with the Communist powers."[159]*

Nevertheless, on November 6, 1953, Eisenhower approved NSC 166/1, which proclaimed it to be United States policy to "reduce the relative power

---

* Eisenhower raised the question again in the National Security Council several months later, noting that "the trouble was that so many members of Congress want to crucify anyone who argues in favor of permitting any kind of trade between the free nations and Communist China." But the President "could discern no other effective means of weakening the tie between these two nations [China and the Soviet Union]." [Minutes, NSC meeting, April 13, 1954, *FR: 1952–54*, XIV, 409.]

position of Communist China" by "developing the political, economic and military strength of non-communist Asian countries, by "weakening or at least retarding the growth of Chinese Communist power in China," and by "impairing Sino-Soviet relations." This lengthy document provided the most specific prediction yet of how hostility between Moscow and Beijing might arise:

> As the inevitable differences in interest, viewpoint, or timing of actions develop between the Russians and the Chinese; as the Chinese tend to become importunate in their demands for Russian assistance or support; or as the role of the Chinese as viceregents for international communism in the Far East becomes too independent and self reliant—there will be strong temptation for the Russians to attempt to move in the direction of greater disciplinary control over the Chinese Communists. If the time ever comes when the Russians feel impelled to contest with the Chinese Communist leaders for primacy in the domestic apparatus of control of the Chinese regime, the alliance will be critically endangered. For . . . the Chinese Communist leaders are Chinese as well as Communists.

It was unlikely that the West could, solely by applying pressure on the Sino-Soviet relationship, bring about its demise. But attempting to wean the Chinese away from the Russians was an even more improbable possibility: the experiences of 1949, "when the Western powers, including the United States, had obviously reconciled themselves to the defeat of the Nationalists and the supremacy of the Communists in China, and were making gestures of accommodation, [have] already given some indication of the limited efficacy of appeasement as a weapon against the continuation of the alliance."[160]

Given the existence of domestic political constraints that militated against trade or the establishment of diplomatic relations with the People's Republic, given the intensity of Congressional support for Chiang Kai-shek, the Eisenhower administration in fact had little choice but to opt for a strategy of "pressure" over "appeasement" as the most feasible way to strain the relationship between Moscow and Beijing. This amounted to saying, as one frustrated State Department analyst noted, "that the Chinese Nationalist Government in Formosa represents a key instrument for detaching China from the Soviet Union." It was an argument that "a few years hence will be read with puzzlement," because the Chinese on the mainland who eventually "throw the Russians out will have no intention of recognizing or submitting to the authority of the regime in Formosa," a regime that, in time, "will become much more of an embarrassment to us than anything else."[161] Eisenhower and Dulles would not have disagreed with that long-term view, but their problem in the fall of 1953 was one of adapting it to immediate realities. From that perspective, the illogic of alignment with the Chinese Nationalists could become quite logical indeed.

"One might ask what was our purpose in aiding Chiang," Dulles acknowledged in his briefing for Eisenhower, Churchill, and Bidault at Bermuda in December, 1953. Answering his own question, the Secretary of State went on to explain that "this aid helped to hold the island which would probably fall without it to the Communists, [thereby causing] a serious breach in the off-shore island chain anchored on the Korean and Indo-Chinese peninsulas and running through Japan, Formosa and the Philippines." But there was a second consideration as well, which was that in case of war "the threat from Formosa would tend to concentrate a large measure of Communist strength opposite Formosa." Even without actual fighting going on, Chiang Kai-shek's forces were tying down some 400,000 Chinese Communist troops on the mainland opposite them, because "the Communists were unwilling to expose their seacoast. This was another of the measures we liked to pursue on the theory of exerting maximum strain causing the Chinese Communists to demand more from Russia and thereby placing additional stress on Russian-Chinese relations."[162]

But what was to happen *after* a Sino-Soviet split had taken place? Army Chief of Staff General Matthew B. Ridgway raised the issue in August, 1954, in connection with a National Security Council review of policy toward China: "If then we accept the objective of splitting Red China and the USSR, the statesmanlike approach would seem to be to bring Red China to a realization that its long-range benefits would derive from friendliness with America . . . [and] that these benefits could reasonably be expected *in time,* if Red China would mend its ways."[163] Ridgway's implication that an eventual *rapprochement* between the United States and the People's Republic might be possible provoked a wrathful outburst from the Chairman of the Joint Chiefs of Staff, Admiral Arthur Radford, who expressed great skepticism about "any policy based on trying to split Communist China and the Soviet Union. We had been trying to do precisely this ever since 1950, and with very scant success." The Sino-Soviet "tie-up," Radford thought, "was something religious in nature, and he doubted the possibility of breaking it."

Eisenhower's response was revealing. He agreed with Radford that there was no immediate prospect, "short of some great cataclysm," of breaking China away from the Soviet Union and from communism. But "history did seem to indicate that when two dictatorships become too large and powerful, jealousies between them spring up. Then, and only then, is there a chance to split them apart." It might take a quarter of a century, Secretary of State Dulles added, but China and Russia would eventually become adversaries "because of the pressure of basic historical forces and because the religious fervor of Communism would have died down." The problem was whether Washington "could play this thing for 25 years. Could we afford to wait that long for a split between these two enemies?"

For Vice President Richard Nixon, a man who would subsequently play a role of some importance in bringing about a Sino-American *rapprochement,* the option of a more conciliatory policy toward the People's Republic was, for the foreseeable future, "wholly academic." Ultimately, "we would have to face the final decision whether to adopt a hard or a soft policy toward Communist China," but no policy of accommodation would work "over the period of the next 25 or 50 years." The immediate choice, however, need not be between war and appeasement:

> There was an area of action in between . . . which we should explore, on the basis that in the long run Soviet Russia and Communist China can and must be split apart. If we follow [a policy of accommodation], Communist Chinese power would sweep over Asia. Coexistence in that sense we certainly reject. This, however, did not mean that we must go to war with Communist China. In fact, a tough coexistence policy may be in the long run the best method of driving a wedge between China and Russia.

As he saw it, Secretary of Defense Wilson noted, "the Vice President was attempting to make a distinction between cohabitation and coexistence." The President, "amidst laughter . . . said he thought Secretary Wilson had something there."[164]

Whether one characterizes their strategy as one of "coexistence," "cohabitation," or "confrontation," Eisenhower and his advisers had clearly resolved, by the end of 1954, to continue the Truman administration's efforts to break up the international communist "monolith." They sought to accomplish this, though, not by encouraging defections, as Truman and Acheson had attempted to do with China between 1949 and 1951, but rather by applying pressures that would increase the dependence of communist states upon one another, and thus speed up the long-term tendencies toward fragmentation that they believed existed within all imperial structures. To borrow from the terminology of a not unrelated area of contemporaneous concern, fusion, not fission, was to be the method of choice.

Like the Truman-Acheson approach, the Eisenhower strategy associated American interests with what were believed to be irreversible historical forces. But by avoiding any possible appearance of "appeasement," it also minimized domestic political opposition of the kind that had bedeviled the previous administration's China policy. In a curious anticipation of what would happen in Nixon's own administration two decades later, a public posture of hardline anti-communism created greater opportunities for exploiting differences within the communist world than did less rigid ideological stances.

# V

Having a strategy, though, provides no guarantee that one will actually use it: the transition from theory to practice is no more easy to accomplish in the realm of national security affairs than it is in most others. It is not always possible to distinguish what is done in the name of "strategy" from initiatives taken—or not taken—for reasons of inertia, expediency, or pique. Because all of these things would influence the Eisenhower administration's policy toward international communism to one degree or another during its remaining years in office, determining to what extent "strategy" lay behind it is not a simple matter.

*Quemoy and Matsu.* The best case for a linkage between the "wedge through pressure" strategy and actual policy can be made with respect to the People's Republic of China. Here the dominant issue was the fate of Quemoy and Matsu, the two small islands just off the coast of China that had remained under Nationalist control after 1949, but also under the perpetual threat of Chinese Communist attack. Eisenhower's handling of the Quemoy-Matsu crises of 1954–55 and 1958—his public support for Chiang Kai-shek's determination to hold the islands, even to the point of appearing to threaten the use of nuclear weapons to defend them—has been generally understood as a response to domestic political imperatives in the United States: the continuing influence of the Chinese Nationalists in the Congress and with public opinion, together with a corresponding reluctance to sanction any form of *rapprochement* with the People's Republic.[165]

But newly released documents make it clear that the President and his Secretary of State did not view their tough line on Quemoy and Matsu simply as a way to placate domestic constituencies; it was intended, as well, to undermine the relationship between Moscow and Beijing. Dulles in September, 1954, raised the possibility of taking the issue to the United Nations Security Council, where the Russians would be confronted with the option of either supporting the Chinese, which would impair Moscow's worldwide "peace offensive," or not doing so, an omission that would "put a serious strain on Soviet-ChiCom relations."[166] Eisenhower sought to weaken the relationship in another way: by projecting the impression that war with China would mean war with Russia itself. He would not allow "Russia to help China fight us without getting involved," he told the National Security Council; he would "want to go to the head of the snake."[167]* If the Russians refused to honor their treaty commitments to help the Chinese, "the Soviet empire would quickly fall to pieces."[168] "Our attitude with respect to the offshore islands," Eisenhower commented in December, seemed to him "perfectly OK."[169]

Dulles became more explicit early in 1955. The long-term objective of

---

* Dulles, at least in his dealings with the Chinese Nationalists, was more cautious: the United States would welcome the collapse of the Communist regime, he acknowledged, "but it is important not to move prematurely. We must await a propitious moment for action when such action would not be likely to provoke war with the Soviet Union. The U.S. would have to accept war if the Soviet Union starts hostilities, but the U.S. must not incite it." [McConaughy memorandum, Dulles conversation with Chinese Nationalist Foreign Minister George Yeh and Ambassador Wellington Koo, November 2, 1954, *FR: 1952–54*, XIV, 846.]

American policy in East Asia, he told British Ambassador Sir Roger Makins in February, was to bring about "sufficient independence between Peiping and Moscow as to create the beginning of a balance of power relationship." That goal required the United States "to put its power into the scales," at least until such time as Japan had regained the strength it had lost as a result of World War II. It also required the defense of Taiwan, because if morale there should collapse, "a lot of things would break quickly. The result would be serious in Japan, the Philippines, and possibly through South East Asia."[170]

Such exertions of American power on behalf of Beijing's adversaries would not, Dulles believed, drive the People's Republic into a closer relationship with the Russians, for the simple reason that Moscow would not be able to afford the costs of linking its own priorities to those of Mao Zedong. "Undoubtedly the Soviet Union was overextended," he explained to Chinese Nationalist Foreign Minister George Yeh:

> The Soviet Union was trying to match U.S. military power with an industrial base only one-third or one-fourth that of the U.S. Communist China was undoubtedly pressing the Soviet Union hard for more military and industrial assistance. Through the Chinese Communists, the North Korean and Viet Minh regimes were making large demands. The military requirements in the European satellite countries were heavy. The economy of the European satellite countries had been squeezed. The satellite peoples were squirming under the demands made of them. They were restive. The whole Communist domain was overextended. . . . The Communist regimes are bound to crack. The leaders will fall out among themselves, or the people will rise up, or both, or the excesses of the regime will eventually cause all the non-Communist world to agree that the Communist dictators must be driven out as enemies of mankind.

It was important, therefore, "to keep the Communist regimes under economic and other pressures . . . which will lead to disintegration." Dulles could not guarantee "that every act of the American Government would be consistent with this theory of pressures, but . . . that would be the general approach and he himself was convinced of the soundness of it."[171]*

The Secretary of State's confidence on this point no doubt reflected indications that had already begun to surface of Moscow's uneasiness about the intentions of its Chinese "ally." After meeting Soviet Foreign Minister Vyacheslav Molotov in Berlin the previous winter, Dulles had reported that

---

* "We must have faith that the dissolution of this evil system is gradually taking place even when there is no surface evidence," the Secretary of State added. He then quoted St. Paul: " 'Faith is the substance of things hoped for, the evidence of things not seen.' We must know in our hearts that Communism contains the seeds of its own destruction. External pressures hasten the destructive process." [McConaughy notes, Dulles conversation with Yeh, February 10, 1955, *FR: 1955–57*, II, 258.]

the Russians seemed "worried over the possibility of new aggression by the Chinese Communists."[172]* Ambassador Bohlen reported from Moscow shortly after the onset of the Quemoy-Matsu crisis that the Soviet Union was probably not prepared "to run [a] serious risk of involvement in [a] major war over Chinese claims to Formosa."[173] The Central Intelligence Agency, Director Allen Dulles assured the National Security Council, was inclined to take recent Soviet expressions of support for the Chinese Communists "with a grain of salt."[174]† And Eisenhower himself expressed repeated doubts about the extent to which the Russians and the Chinese were in agreement on the Quemoy-Matsu question: "I have a feeling that the Chinese Communists are acting on their own on this," he told Press Secretary James C. Hagerty early in 1955, "and that is considerably disturbing to the Russians."[175]

The President and his advisers did not wholly exclude the possibility of a more conciliatory approach to the People's Republic during this period. The Secretary of State had been careful, before the Taiwan Strait crisis broke, not to rule out the Beijing government's *eventual* admission to the United Nations.[176]‡ When the Commerce Department late in 1954 challenged Dulles's assertion that "the best prospect of disrupting the Sino-Soviet alliance is through maximizing the dependence of Communist China on the USSR,"[177] Eisenhower admitted that "under present conditions, no change of our attitude was possible, [but] . . . if the Chinese Communists met certain quite obvious requirements, then the situation might be different."[178] And when Premier Zhou Enlai abruptly defused the Quemoy-Matsu crisis by offering at the Bandung Conference in April, 1955, to enter into negotiations with the United States, the administration after some hesitation accepted the proposal, thus setting in motion what was to be a long series of Sino-American am-

---

* Molotov had warned Dulles that American policy toward China was "bankrupt" because it "merely forced China closer to [the] Soviet Union which was not to US advantage." [Dulles to Eisenhower, January 30, 1954, *FR: 1952–54*, XIV, 354.] But since Dulles considered it *advantageous* to force the Chinese into a position of dependency on the Russians, it is unlikely that Molotov's warning caused him to lose much sleep. For reasons best known to himself, the Soviet Foreign Minister also made a point of reminding Under Secretary of State Walter Bedell Smith in May that "China is always going to be China, she is never going to be European." [Smith to State Department, May 23, 1954, *ibid.*, p. 431.]

† One reason for the Agency's position, Director Dulles explained with an uncharacteristic lack of foresight, was that the assurances had been delivered by Khrushchev, "rather a brash fellow who for some reason is permitted a lot of latitude by Malenkov. Accordingly, this rather extreme statement by Khrushchev . . . was not as significant as what Malenkov might say on the same subject." [Minutes, NSC meeting, October 6, 1954, *FR: 1952–54*, XIV, 690.]

‡ Dulles had actually called for the admission of the People's Republic to the United Nations in his book, *War or Peace*, which had been published just prior to the outbreak of the Korean War. Since that time, he acknowledged, there had been "a very marked change in the situation." [Press conference, July 8, 1954, *Department of State Bulletin*, XXXI(July 19, 1954), 88.]

bassadorial-level talks with the Chinese on a narrow range of outstanding issues.[179]

But the administration was not prepared, in 1955 or at any point thereafter, to resume the Truman administration's attempts to wean the Chinese away from the Russians through conciliation. Too friendly an approach to the People's Republic risked unsettling allies and alienating domestic constituencies at a time when the support of neither could be assumed. Any immediate consideration of diplomatic recognition or of Chinese admission to the United Nations would create "a whirlpool in the free world," Dulles warned the National Security Council in December, 1954; this moved NSC assistant Robert Cutler to remind those present that it would create an "equally dangerous whirlpool" in the United States as well.[180]* The administration "had no intention of supporting Red China's entry into the UN," Dulles assured a delighted Chiang Kai-shek the following March. "I said I did not know how I could possibly add anything to my firmness in this regard. The President [Chiang] laughingly agreed."[181]

Throughout the remainder of his term as Secretary of State, Dulles would persistently rebuff suggestions from Beijing that the ambassadorial-level talks be extended to cover the Taiwan issue, or the possibility of normalizing relations with the mainland.[182] "There are some who suggest that, if we assist the Chinese Communists to wax strong, then they will eventually break with Soviet Russia," he told an audience in San Francisco in June, 1957. "No doubt there are basic power rivalries between Russia and China in Asia." But it was important to remember that both countries—whether allies or not— shared an ideology antithetical to the interests of the United States. The Axis powers might well have fallen to quarreling among themselves if they had won the Second World War, "but no one suggested that we should tolerate and even assist an Axis victory because in the end they would quarrel over the booty—of which we would be a part."[183]

When the second Quemoy-Matsu crisis suddenly erupted in August, 1958, both Eisenhower and Dulles initially interpreted it as a joint Sino-Soviet probe intended to test Western resolve.[184] But by November, after the Chinese had once again backed down, the President was wondering—apparently on the basis of intelligence reports†—whether "the Soviets were not really be-

---

* Three years later Eisenhower acknowledged, in a letter to Henry Wallace, that the strategy of "creating divisive rather than unifying influences between China and the Soviets is obviously a correct one. The problem is to discover ways of doing this without weakening our own ties with numerous Allies—particularly in the Far East." [Eisenhower to Wallace, June 8, 1957, Dwight D. Eisenhower Papers, Ann Whitman File, DDE Diary, Box 14, "June 57 Misc (2)," Dwight D. Eisenhower Library.]

† Intelligence reports were showing Sino-Soviet disagreements, CIA Director Allen Dulles reported to the Senate Foreign Relations Committee early in 1959, over Chinese belligerence during the Quemoy-Matsu crisis the previous autumn, as well as Mao's "Great Leap Forward," relations with Yugoslavia, Soviet shipments of industrial equipment to China, and Moscow's reluctance to supply Beijing with nuclear weapons. There was also an emerging personal dislike between Khrushchev and Mao Zedong. "[Mao] has never liked

coming concerned about Communist China as a possible threat to them in the future."[185] Several days later, Eisenhower discussed with Dulles "at some length"

> our policy of holding firm until changes would occur within the Sino-Soviet bloc. He felt these were inevitable but realized that the policy we were following might not be popular. There were some who wanted to give in; others who wanted to attack. The policy that required patience was rarely popular.[186]

Dulles himself, in his final appearance before the Senate Foreign Relations Committee early in 1959, acknowledged that "you could very well have a struggle between . . . Mao Tse-tung and Khrushchev as to who would be the ideological leader of International Communism." But their common ideological threat would remain the same: there was "no early prospect of a division there which would be helpful to the West."[187]

It is not yet possible, given currently available documentation, to say to what extent the strategy of stimulating Sino-Soviet differences through the application of "pressure" caused the administration to reject conciliatory overtures from Beijing and to continue its hard line after 1955. Certainly domestic political constraints, as well as the requirements of dealing with the Chinese Nationalists and other anti-communist allies in Asia, would have provided ample reasons for such an approach, even in the absence of a "wedge" strategy. But it is now at least demonstrable that the idea of promoting Sino-Soviet differences by forcing the Chinese into a position of dependence on the Russians had been a major influence on the administration's behavior during its first two and a half years in office; given the infrequency with which administrations alter existing stategies in mid-stream,[188] it seems a plausible assumption that the "wedge through pressure" strategy—however distant its payoff might be—continued to shape the thinking of Eisenhower and his advisers through the end of their term.[189]

*Eastern Europe.* The administration's policies with regard to Eastern Europe can also be understood in terms of a "wedge through pressure" strategy, although here it proceeded with less purposefulness and greater circumspection than was the case with China. Despite the unrest that had taken place in East Germany in 1953, there seemed little reason to expect any imminent spread of "Titoist" tendencies among the Soviet Union's European satellites. National Intelligence Estimates during the spring and summer of 1954 detected less potential for independent action among them than in China,[190] and several months later Allen Dulles reported to the National Security Council that there

---

cocktail parties like Khrushchev. He is much more of a philosopher, and he likes to retire and study." [Dulles executive session testimony, January 26, 1959, U.S. Congress, Senate, Committee on Foreign Relations, *Historical Series: Eighty-Sixth Congress, First Session, 1959* (Washington: 1982), pp. 103, 117–18.]

was "little chance of Soviet control [in Eastern Europe] being shaken by internal revolt in the next few years."[191]

There was also the suspicion within the administration that the Russians would risk war to retain control of Eastern Europe, an assumption that seemed less plausible with respect to China. "[I]t would be extremely dangerous," State Department Soviet specialists warned the White House in March, 1954, "to assume that the USSR, because of internal difficulties or trouble in the satellites, is so weakened that it will not under any circumstances resort to war." Such a response could be expected "against any action on the part of the United States or its allies which it considered to be a sufficiently serious threat to its own position."[192] There should be "long-range plans for a rollback in the satellites," Secretary of State Dulles told the National Security Council the following August, but "these plans would have to be very long-range indeed."[193] "[H]ow far are you going?" an impatient Eisenhower demanded, in response to a press conference question about "liberation" in Eastern Europe some months later. "You are certainly not going to declare war, are you?"[194]

One thing the United States could do was to support the continued independence of Tito's Yugoslavia, in the hope that it might yet provide a model for what could happen elsewhere in that part of the world. "It was "extremely unlikely," Dulles told Eisenhower in August, 1955, "that Yugoslavia would ever again go under the yoke of Moscow leadership." Tito's ambition was "to make himself the leader of a group of Communist states and attract them away from Moscow"; his "Bukharin brand of Communism" accepted the possibility "that you would have Communism on a national basis and that Communist countries need not necessarily be under the iron discipline of the Soviet Communist Party as the leader of the world proletariat." This, Dulles argued, was an ambition "we could afford quietly to countenance."[195] A year later, Eisenhower went out of his way to emphasize publicly that Tito's first visit to Moscow since his defection did not mean the reconstitution of unity within the international communist movement: "I should think that in the central headquarters of communism they would be thinking very seriously about what their satellite governments think . . . of Marshal Tito. . . . [T]hey might be tempted at other places to emulate him."[196]*

That prospect had become more than just a hypothetical possibility in 1956 as rumors had begun to circulate of Nikita Khruschev's de-Stalinization campaign inside the Soviet Union. Administration officials initially tended to downplay the importance of this development in their public comments,[197]

---

* What had passed between Khrushchev and Tito was not completely clear, Dulles told Eisenhower the following October, but "I went on to say it seemed to me that in the main our policy of backing Tito was paying off in terms of an increasing desire on the part of the satellites for independence from Moscow." [Dulles memorandum, conversation with Eisenhower, October 11, 1956, John Foster Dulles Papers, White House Memoranda, Box 4, "Meetings with the President, August-December, 1956 (4)," Dwight D. Eisenhower Library.]

but in mid-April an abrupt shift in position took place. Allen Dulles openly suggested that dissatisfaction within the Soviet Union itself had prompted the attack on Stalin.[198] Eisenhower pointed out that "any time a policy is winning and the people are completely satisfied with it, you don't change. You change policies that markedly, you destroy old idols as they have been busy doing, only when you think a great change is necessary."[199] And Secretary of State Dulles, noting the Kremlin's professed desire for a reconciliation with Tito, pointedly drew from this a conclusion that could not have been welcome in Moscow: "If the Soviet Communists now say that it is all right to have communism on a national basis, that offers a great prospect to the Poles, the Czechs, and so fourth, who would much rather have their own national brand of communism than be run by Moscow."[200]

It is not precisely clear, from the available documentation, what prompted this change in administration rhetoric, but one very likely explanation is that the Central Intelligence Agency had, by April, procured the text of Krushchev's secret speech to the 20th Soviet Party Congress, delivered two months earlier. By early June, on the prompting of Allen Dulles but no doubt with the approval of his brother and the President as well, the decision had been made to leak the text of the speech to the *New York Times*, where it appeared on June 4.[201] It was, John Foster Dulles commented, "the most damning indictment of despotism ever made by a despot";[202] its publication, he explained to Eisenhower, had left the Russians with the choice "of either allowing liberal forces to grow and obtain recognition, or else revert[ing] to [a] Stalinist type of repression, in which case they would lose the ground they had been trying to gain with the free nations as having become more civilized and more liberal."[203]*

The Russians soon made it clear that, confronted with this choice, they would opt for repression over reform. Within weeks of the publication of Khrushchev's speech, unrest had broken out in Poland, for which Dulles quickly claimed credit. Soviet difficulties in Eastern Europe had been "touched off by our publication of the Khrushchev secret speech," he told the Senate Foreign Relations Committee. "Khrushchev is on the ropes and, if we can keep the pressure up . . . there is going to occur a very great disintegration within the apparatus of the international Communist organization."[204] The administration had at no point actually promised "liberation," Dulles reminded Eisenhower in September, but it had, through the Voice of America and by

---

* Eisenhower raised the question with Dulles of whether he should be speaking publicly about these matters. The Secretary of State responded that it was "very important from the standpoint of the Mutual Security legislation [then before the Congress] to portray our past policies as successful and to have some reason such as their success for continuing these policies. Furthermore, all that I said and did in this matter was very carefully weighed not only in the Department of State but also with Mr. Allen Dulles. The President indicated his complete understanding and approval of what I had done." [Dulles memorandum of conversation with Eisenhower, July 13, 1956, Dulles Papers (Eisenhower Library), White House memoranda, Box 4, "Meetings with the President, January–July, 1956 (1)."]

other means, "done much to revive the influences which are inherent in freedom, . . . thereby contribut[ing] toward creating strains and stresses within
the captive world."[205]

It is tempting to see what followed—a leadership crisis in Poland in October, the spread of unrest into Hungary that same month, and the Soviet
Union's brutal suppression of what had become an all-out revolution in the
latter country early in November—as an intended consequence of the Eisenhower administration's efforts to strain the relationship between Moscow and
its satellites. But there is reason to think that what happened in Eastern
Europe in the fall of 1956 went well beyond what the President and his advisers had been hoping to accomplish.* A direct revolt against Soviet power
in Eastern Europe, they believed, could not succeed without United States and
NATO military assistance, the provision of which would almost certainly
have led to war.† "The Russians were scared and furious," Eisenhower
pointed out at the height of the Hungarian crisis, "and nothing is more dangerous than a dictatorship in that frame of mind."[206] Annihilating Hungary,
"should it become the scene of a bitter conflict, is no way to help her."[207]

Nor did the administration seize this opportunity to activate the corps of
East European refugees and émigrés the Central Intelligence Agency had
been training for several years, with a view to exploiting unrest in that part
of the world.‡ The precise objectives of this project, code-named "Red Sox/
Red Cap," remain unclear, but Allen Dulles's refusal to authorize its use in
October and November of 1956—a decision that provoked intense opposition
and even extreme psychological distress among some of his subordinates in
the Agency—suggests how cautious the administration's commitment to "liberation" actually was.[208]

Eisenhower and his advisers did, however, clearly see events in Eastern
Europe as confirming what they had suspected all along: that Moscow's means

---

* Subsequent investigations cleared Radio Liberty and Radio Free Europe—both CIA-
supported organizations—of having called directly for an uprising against the Russians,
although broadcasts to Hungary during the rebellion there did repeat, without comment,
local broadcasts implying that outside assistance might be provided. [See John Ranelagh,
*The Agency: The Rise and Decline of the CIA* (New York: 1986), pp. 308–9.]

† Dulles had warned the National Security Council two years earlier that even if the
United States should succeed in splitting the Soviet Union from its satellites, "we would
still have to face the terrible problem and threat of an unimpaired nuclear capability in
the USSR itself." [Minutes, NSC meeting, December 21, 1954, *FR: 1952–54*, II, 834.]

‡ NSC 5412, approved by Eisenhower in March, 1954, had authorized the Central Intelligence Agency "in accordance with established policies and to the extent practicable in
areas dominated or threatened by International Communism, [to] develop underground
resistance and facilitate covert and guerilla operations and ensure availability of those
forces in the event of war, including whether practicable provisions of a base upon which
the military may expand these forces in time of war with active theaters of operation as
well as provision for stay-behind assets and escape and evasion facilities." [NSC 5412,
"Covert Operations," March 15, 1954, Eisenhower Papers, White House Office Files: Office
of the Special Assistant for National Security Affairs, Box 7, "NSC 5412/2."]

of control there were tenuous, and that the *judicious* application of pressure—even so simple a matter as publishing Khrushchev's own colorful prose—could deny the Russians many of the benefits of the empire they had created. Moscow had "lost a satellite and gained a conquered province," Allen Dulles told a meeting of legislative leaders on November 9: "the myth of [the] sweet reasonableness of communism has been destroyed . . . and the Soviets now realize that satellite armies are not at all trustworthy."[209] Secretary of State Dulles argued before a similar meeting several weeks later that "our policy should continue to be the encouragement of an evolutionary process leading toward national Communism as a first step prior to a complete departure from international Communism."[210] "[A]s far as encouraging this growing independence of Moscow," Eisenhower explained at a press conference the following April, "we believe in that." But the satellites were not going to have complete freedom all at once: "we try to help each step as far as we can," so as not to leave the satellites with the belief that they "are completely and absolutely dependent on Moscow for [their] livelihood and no place else."[211]

*Other applications.* Did the "wedge through pressure" strategy affect the implementation of policy in areas apart from China and Eastern Europe? Once again, available documentation permits no conclusive answer, but there is some basis for selective speculation. However cautious the Eisenhower administration may have been about using the Central Intelligence Agency against Soviet satellites, the fact remains that covert action was one of its preferred methods of operation. The Agency's techniques offered the advantages of discretion, deniability, and, not least, economy; its director, Allen Dulles, had succeeded—as his brother, the Secretary of State, had not—in insulating his subordinates from the ravages of McCarthyism, thus preserving a capacity for flexible and imaginative approaches to the task of dealing with international communism.[212] The administration's first formal guidelines on covert action, issued in March, 1954, had encouraged efforts to:

> a. Create and exploit troublesome problems for International Communism, impair relations between the USSR and Communist China and between them and their satellites, complicate control within the USSR, Communist China and their satellites, and retard the growth of the military and economic potential of the Soviet bloc.
>
> b. Discredit the prestige and ideology of International Communism, and reduce the strength of its parties and other elements.[213]

In the light of such instructions, it seems not implausible to suggest that some of the Agency's major activities during the Eisenhower administration—the staging of successful coups in Iran and Guatemala and an unsuccessful one in Indonesia, plans to overthrow Fidel Castro's government in Cuba, behind-the-scenes support for left-wing student groups and publications, and close coordination with both American and Western European labor movements[214]—

may have had as a common objective the separation of international communism from potential supporters through the application of pressures against them.

"Wedge through pressure" tactics may also help to explain certain aspects of Eisenhower's Middle East policy. The best way to deal with Egypt's increasingly pro-Soviet orientation, the President speculated in his diary in March, 1956, might be to leave that country "with no ally in sight except Soviet Russia." At that point, "she would very quickly get tired of that prospect and would join us in the search for a just and decent peace in that region."[215] When Senator Fulbright subsequently brought up the prospect of letting the Russians take over previous American commitments to build the Aswan dam, Dulles acknowledged that they might indeed "find that they had a white elephant on their hands," both because of the complexity of the project, and because the burdens it would impose on the Egyptian economy would make them unpopular in that country. "[Y]ou have to balance what might seem to be an immediate gain to the Soviet Union as against what I think might very well prove to be, in the end, a boomerang."[216]

Many would argue that with President Gamel Abdel Nasser's seizure of the Suez Canal late in July, the decision to withdraw from the Aswan project had "boomeranged" on Dulles instead, but the Secretary of State remained optimistic. Admitting that there was now a "close partnership" between the Egyptians and the Russians, he nonetheless told Eisenhower

> that I did not believe that any such partnership was durable. I pointed out that where countries were physically adjacent to the Soviet Union and where Soviet troops were there to sustain a pro-Soviet government, the people had little recourse. However, that was not the case where a country was not adjacent to the Soviet Union and where Soviet military power was not available to support the government. The President recalled, in this connection, Guatemala.[217]

Would it be tolerable, a reporter asked Eisenhower in August, 1957, to have in the Middle East a regime subject to communist control which could cut off oil supplies to the West, as the Egyptians had done at the height of the Suez crisis the previous November? The United States did not approve of communism under any circumstances, the President replied, but there were distinctions to be kept in mind: "international communism and subordination to the views of Moscow are one thing. Independent communism is something else. And . . . there are all degrees of its application."[218]

As the outcome of both the Suez crisis and certain of the CIA's covert operations suggest, efforts to drive "wedges" between adversaries by applying pressures on them did not always work out as planned. Nor is it possible to determine conclusively—given the present inaccessibility of Soviet, East European, and Chinese sources—to what extent the existence of that strategy contributed, if at all, to the breakdown of international communist solidarity that had begun to be apparent by the time Eisenhower left office. All one can say now is that the *intention* of promoting fragmentation existed within Eisenhower's administration, as it had within Truman's as well; and that what subsequently happened to the communist world corresponded, more than is usually the case in matters of policy and strategy, to the objectives Washington had sought.

# VI

The long-term perspective that informed the Truman and Eisenhower "wedge" strategy has proven to be remarkably accurate: the Russians have indeed had difficulty sustaining their authority beyond the immediate reach of their own military power, not just in Egypt, as Dulles suggested, but in Asia, Africa, and much of the rest of the Middle East as well. Even in those regions where Soviet military control does prevail, as in Eastern Europe and Afghanistan, loyalty to Soviet interests obviously does not. The ideological bond that many Americans feared would unite all communists under Moscow's leadership after World War II has proven instead to be—as Kennan suggested it might four decades ago—a source of divisiveness and bitter contention. If the Cold War ever was an ideological competition—and many people thought it was, for many years—then the West has long since won it.

The architects of the "wedge" strategy based their confidence in the ultimate fragmentation of international communism upon predictions drawn from historical experience: that, in the long run, nationalism would be durable, but empires would not; that those who aspired to global or even regional hegemony would sooner or later defeat themselves because the further they extended their authority, the greater the forces of resistance they would provoke. "[T]he dream of world domination by one power or of world conformity is an impossible dream," Eisenhower told the United Nations General Assembly in August, 1958.[219] A week later, in an extemporaneous press conference comment, he looked forward to the day when

> even the Soviets begin to learn that it is not to their benefit to go in and try to buy, bribe and subvert generally people that are themselves trying to lead their own lives; because, finally, what all history shows, [is] that when any dictatorship goes too far in its control, . . . whether it be the Roman Empire or Genghis Khan's or Napoleon's or anyone else's, just the very size of the thing begins to defeat them.[220]

The phrasing may have been faulty, but the lesson for the future drawn from the experience of the past clearly was not: the quarter-century that has passed since Eisenhower left office has indeed provided little basis upon which to encourage aspirants to global hegemony, whether in Moscow, Washington, or anywhere else.

The problem with such long-term perspectives is that they are not of much help in dealing with short-term problems. The tangible benefits, for the West, of fragmentation within the communist world would not become fully apparent until well after Truman and Eisenhower had left office: they began to show up in Moscow's growing interest in détente and in controlling the proliferation of nuclear weapons during the 1960s, in the failure of the Russians and the Chinese to agree on coordinated action against American military operations in Vietnam, and, most significantly, in the long-delayed *rapprochement* between the United States and the People's Republic of China that began when Richard Nixon stepped off Air Force One in Beijing in 1972—seven years earlier than his most optimistic prediction for such an event in 1954.[221]

Even if anticipated, such distant "payoffs" would have been of little use to Truman and Acheson as they grappled with the China lobby, or the Korean War, or General MacArthur, or Senator McCarthy; or to Eisenhower and Dulles as they wrestled with crises in French Indochina, or Quemoy and Matsu, or Hungary, or Suez. No doubt this problem of how to relate long-term considerations to short-term preoccupations helps to account for the less-than-arduous efforts both administrations made to explain the "wedge" strategy in public, or to try to build a domestic base of support for improving relations with communist states not under Moscow's control. At a time when support for foreign and military policies could by no means automatically be assumed, it was more convenient to retain the image of a coordinated, conspiratorial, and highly competent adversary than to reveal what was known—and what was anticipated—of adversary weaknesses. The result was such a confusion of interests and threats that the United States would come to be seen in the 1960's—and, to some extent, would come to see itself—as a nation that had taken on imperial characteristics of its own in the process of attempting to resist the imperial aspirations of others.[222]

But what happened in Vietnam should not obscure the perceptiveness of the long-range strategy the Truman and Eisenhower administrations worked out for dealing with the problem of international communism. Correspondence between intentions and consequences is a sufficiently unusual phenomenon—whatever the field of endeavor, and however long it takes—that when one finds a strategy that really did, whether by direction or indirection, achieve its objectives, then the historian may, perhaps, permit himself a certain grudging respect for the cleverness of its architects, and at the same time a moderate degree of awe over the comparative rarity of their achievement.

# 7

# Learning to Live with Transparency: The Emergence of a Reconnaissance Satellite Regime

ESPIONAGE, the philosopher Michael Walzer has suggested, might—under certain circumstances—promote rather than hinder communication among nations.* The idea seems improbable at first glance, given the efforts great powers have always made to guard themselves against the loss of state secrets. Certainly the history of the Cold War would not appear to contain very many instances in which Washington and Moscow welcomed each other's attempts to ferret out such information. But if one effect of espionage were to be to reduce the danger of surprise attack, then, in theory at least, states should derive mutual benefits from tolerating a certain amount of it. And, in practice, something like this has happened in relations between the United States

This essay was prepared for the Stanford University project on "U.S.–Soviet Efforts to Cooperate in Security Matters: Achievements, Failures, Prospects," organized by Alexander Dallin, Philip Farley, and Alexander George. I am particularly indebted to Philip Farley for valuable suggestions on an earlier version of this essay.

* "Another form of great power communication, this one . . . undervalued, is espionage, which makes for a sharing of information about new weapons systems and recent troop deployments and so, perhaps, reduces the risks such things involve." [Michael Walzer, "The Reform of the International System," Øyvind Østerud, ed., *Studies of War and Peace* (Oslo: 1986), p. 236.] For one possible confirmation of Walzer's theory, see Christopher Andrew's recent account of Anglo-Italian relations during the Italian-Ethiopian War (1935–36) and the Spanish Civil War (1936–39), when both countries were intercepting each other's military and diplomatic cable traffic. [*Her Majesty's Secret Service: The Making of the British Intelligence Community* (New York: 1986), pp. 401–3.]

and the Soviet Union during the past quarter-century, albeit discreetly and without explicit agreements governing the procedures involved. The fact that Americans and Russians have actually *cooperated* in spying upon one another was in itself, for many years, one of the better kept secrets of the Cold War; the fact that they have come to regard such activities as consistent with the principles of international law is certainly one of that conflict's least expected developments.

Reconnaissance satellites are no longer a secret, although both governments remain cautious about formally acknowledging their existence.* The critical role these instruments have played in the verification of arms control agreements is now generally understood;[1] the threat that anti-satellite weaponry might pose to them is now openly discussed.[2] But what has not received attention, until recently,[3] is the question of how the Soviet Union and the United States came to tolerate, and even to rely upon, the collection of sensitive intelligence about each other from these devices in the first place. Their decision to do so represents the clearest example in postwar Soviet-American relations of *tacit* cooperation on matters of mutual interest. It was also an implicit acknowledgment that certain forms of espionage can not only facilitate communication: they can also serve the cause of peace.

# I

There was, to be sure, little in the history of great power rivalries to suggest that nations might willingly allow potential adversaries to reconnoiter their territories.† Observation balloons had been used, but also fired upon, as early

---

* The first official—if inadvertent—acknowledgment of the benefits of satellite photography came in what was supposed to have been an off-the-record comment by Lyndon Johnson in March, 1967. [*New York Times*, March 17, 1967.] There was also an oblique reference to the use of satellites for the verification of arms control agreements in Secretary of State William P. Rogers's letter of June 10, 1972, formally transmitting the Anti-Ballistic Missile Treaty to President Nixon prior to submission to the Senate. [*Weekly Compilation of Presidential Documents*, VIII (June 19, 1972), 103.] No further public reference to the role of reconnaissance satellites would come until Jimmy Carter described them, in October, 1978, as "an important stabilizing factor in world affairs in the monitoring of arms control agreements." [*Public Papers of the Presidents: Jimmy Carter, 1978* (Washington: 1979), p. 1686.] The first published photograph from a reconnaissance satellite appeared in *Jane's Defence Weekly* in 1984 as the result of a security breach for which former Navy employee Samuel Loring Morison was sentenced to two years in prison. [*New York Times*, December 5, 1985.] It is reproduced in David Hafemeister, Joseph J. Romm, and Kosta Tsipis, "The Verification of Compliance with Arms-Control Agreements," *Scientific American*, CCLII (March, 1985), 38.

† One possible exception to this generalization would be the custom, prior to World War I, of allowing foreign officers to attend military maneuvers, but even that access tended to be cut off in periods of crisis. [See, on this point, Ernest R. May, ed., *Knowing One's Enemies: Intelligence Assessment Before the Two World Wars* (Princeton: 1984), especially pp. 42–44, 179–80.]

as the Wars of the French Revolution.[4] Military reconnaissance conducted from aircraft came into its own during World War I, but so too did countermeasures: the first true fighter aircraft were developed for the purpose of shooting down observation planes.[5] World War II provided few instances in which belligerents perceived it to be to their advantage for their adversaries to conduct successful overhead reconnaissance,* nor were such flights left unopposed during the Korean War.[6] And, of course, the most famous reconnaissance aircraft of all time, the U-2, entered the public's consciousness only as a result of being shot down over the Soviet Union in May, 1960; still another U-2 would be destroyed at the height of the Cuban Missile Crisis two years later.[7]

The U-2 program grew out of a series of efforts Washington had made since the onset of the Cold War to compensate for one of that conflict's most obvious asymmetries: the disparity between an almost totally closed Soviet Union, given to making available virtually no accurate information about its military capabilities, and the almost totally open United States, where details about new technologies appeared regularly in newspapers and periodicals,[8] and in which the location of sensitive military installations could be pinpointed from the detailed road-maps available—in those days, free—at corner service stations.

That disparity had stimulated, during the first postwar decade, several ingenious but not always effective attempts by the United States to penetrate Soviet secrecy: they included the use of defectors, émigrés, and—more rarely—actual spies; the careful analysis of World War II and even tsarist-era maps; eavesdropping in the form of intercepted cable and radio communications; the use of radar to track early Soviet missile experiments; regular monitoring of the upper atmosphere to detect Soviet nuclear tests; the launching of balloons equipped with cameras designed to float across Soviet territory for subsequent recovery; and regular reconnaissance flights along Soviet and East European borders and on several occasions deep into Soviet territory itself.[9] None of these efforts—with the exception of those directed toward the monitoring of nuclear tests—had produced much useful information. There were "shortcomings of a serious nature" in the accuracy of intelligence estimates regarding the Soviet Union, CIA Director Allen Dulles admitted to the National Security Council early in the Eisenhower administration: "We must remain highly critical of our intelligence effort . . . but we must not be defeatist in the face of the difficulties of securing adequate information."[10]

As if in response to Dulles's injunction, Eisenhower in the months that followed authorized two separate but related initiatives—one covert, the other

---

* The exception here would be instances in which specific measures were undertaken to deceive enemy observers. For examples, see R. V. Jones, *The Wizard War: British Scientific Intelligence, 1939–1945* (New York: 1978), pp. 405–12; and Stephen E. Ambrose, *Ike's Spies: Eisenhower and the Espionage Establishment* (Garden City, New York: 1981), pp. 83–86.

conspicuously overt—aimed at improving the collection of intelligence about the Soviet Union. Early in 1954, he established a Technological Capabilities Panel, headed by James R. Killian, president of the Massachusetts Institute of Technology, to investigate ways of reducing the danger of surprise attack. Placing its faith in rapidly developing remote-sensing technology, the Killian Committee advised immediate construction of a high-altitude photoreconnaissance aircraft (which turned out to be the U-2), and, as a longer-term measure, investigation of the potential of reconnaissance satellites. Eisenhower accepted these recommendations, thus committing his and subsequent administrations to reliance on overhead reconnaissance as the primary method of breaching Soviet secrecy.[11]*

But the President authorized an overt approach to this problem as well: one that sought to legitimize these new reconnaissance techniques through diplomatic means. The world first learned of Eisenhower's "Open Skies" inspection plan when he suggested it to the Russians—in what appeared to be a spontaneous gesture—at the Geneva four-power summit conference in July, 1955.[12] We now know that a working group headed by presidential assistant Nelson Rockefeller had originated this plan, which would have involved an exchange of information on military facilities and the unrestricted right of aerial photoreconnaissance over both Soviet and American territory; Eisenhower had approved it, and indeed had insisted on presenting it over the objections of a skeptical John Foster Dulles.[13] What is interesting about this sequence of events is that Rockefeller's working group apparently knew nothing of what the Killian Committee had recommended regarding the U-2.[14]† Only the President and a few trusted top advisers were aware that the United States would soon have the capacity to institute its own wholly unilateral "open skies" plan.

The question arises, then, as to why Eisenhower undertook the Geneva initiative at all. Surely he must have expected the Soviets to reject it, given the disproportionate benefits it would have provided to the United States.‡ Surely Eisenhower was aware that the U-2 and satellite reconnaissance programs could proceed—at least for a while—without the Russians' permission, since it would take them time to develop effective countermeasures. That situ-

---

* The theoretical possibility of reconnaissance satellites had been the subject of speculation within the U.S. government since at least 1945. [See, on this point, Paul B. Stares, *The Militarization of Space: U.S. Policy, 1945–84* (Ithaca: 1985), pp. 23–33.]

† Rockefeller was presumably aware of the potential benefits of satellite reconnaissance. [See his memorandum of May 17, 1955, included in NSC 5520, "U.S. Scientific Satellite Program," May 20, 1955, Dwight D. Eisenhower Papers, White House NSC Assistant, NSC Series, Policy Paper Subseries, Box 16, Dwight D. Eisenhower Library.]

‡ Admiral Arthur Radford, Chairman of the Joint Chiefs of Staff, candidly acknowledged that "it would be to the advantage of the U.S. to make such an agreement, since the Soviets already have most of the information they could obtain through such a privilege, whereas we have little or none." [Quoted in W. W. Rostow, *Open Skies: Eisenhower's Proposal of July 21, 1955* (Austin: 1982), p. 53.]

ation would not last indefinitely, though, and it is this prospect of counter-measures that makes one wonder whether Eisenhower's "open skies" plan might not have been a far-sighted attempt to build a climate of legitimacy for overhead reconnaissance, in anticipation of the day when the Russians would develop the capability to act against it.

As is often the case with the elusive Eisenhower, his intentions in this matter are not easy to pin down. But there is no question that his World War II experience had thoroughly sensitized him—as few other political leaders at the time could have been—to the potential military significance of overhead reconnaissance.[15] We know as well that he worried about how the Soviets might respond to unilateral American reconnaissance efforts: in May, 1956, for example, he warned of the need "to be wise and careful in what we do" because he wanted "to give the Soviets every chance to move in peaceful directions and to put our relations on a better basis."[16]* But the underlying motive of the "Open Skies" plan appears most clearly—if obliquely—in a comment Eisenhower made to a group of advisers shortly after the launching of *Sputnik* in October 1957: the Russians, he argued, "have in fact done us a good turn, unintentionally, in establishing the concept of freedom of inter-national space."[17]†

# I I

Unfortunately, the U-2 incident of May, 1960, confirmed a somewhat different proposition: that the Soviet Union, once it had the capacity to do so, would shoot down whatever flew over its territory. Russian secretiveness had long been a matter of state policy, one that not even collaboration in the wartime anti-Hitler coalition had in any significant way breached.[18] This attitude continued after the war, with the Soviet government refusing—almost alone among independent states at that time—to participate in international civil aviation agreements providing for the right of "innocent passage" through sovereign airspace.[19] And although it acknowledged in principle the need for verification in monitoring arms-control agreements, the U.S.S.R. insisted on

* Eisenhower's comment took place in the context of a discussion concerning a Soviet protest over what had probably been a RB-47 reconnaissance flight in the Arctic. (The document in question, cited in the notes, is partially sanitized.) The first U-2 overflight of the Soviet Union took place on July 4, 1956. [Michael Beschloss, *Mayday: Eisenhower, Khrushchev and the U-2 Affair* (New York: 1986), pp. 121–22.]

† A RAND Corporation report had speculated about the legality of satellite reconnais-sance as early as 1950, and in May, 1955, NSC 5520, which dealt with future satellite pro-grams, had stressed the importance of establishing a legal precedent for satellite over-flights. [See Walter McDougall, *The Heavens and the Earth: A Political History of the Space Age* (New York: 1985), pp. 108–10, 120–21; and NSC 5520, May 20, 1955, p. 3.]

defining the concept in the narrowest possible way with a view to minimizing opportunities for espionage;[20] as a result, the immediate postwar years saw no progress made toward the international control of atomic energy, or toward mutually agreed-upon reductions in conventional forces. Moscow also protested, loudly and frequently, the various unilateral efforts the United States had made prior to Eisenhower's "Open Skies" proposal to carry out overhead reconnaissance, and had, on occasion, taken more active countermeasures as well.*

Even so, the Russians' initial response to "Open Skies" was not entirely negative. In a shift from their earlier position that disarmament should *precede* the establishment of verification procedures, they themselves had put forward in May, 1955, a proposal that would have had the United Nations set up "control posts at large ports, at railway junctions, on main motor highways and in aerodromes" for the purpose of ensuring "that no dangerous concentration of military land forces or of air or naval forces takes place."[21] And even though Party Chairman Nikita Khrushchev dismissed "Open Skies" at Geneva as "nothing more than a bald espionage plot,"[22] there is reason to think that the Russians saw both advantages and disadvantages in Eisenhower's proposal, and did not immediately rule out the possibility of accepting it.[23]

In the end, though, the Soviet Union did reject the plan, ostensibly on grounds that aerial inspection alone would not prevent the concealment of military forces, that the "Open Skies" plan made no provision for reconnaissance over the territories of countries other than the United States and the U.S.S.R., and that the proposal did not provide for arms reduction.[24] The real reason was probably closer to the concerns Khrushchev had expressed, as the official history of Soviet foreign policy retrospectively acknowledges: "All [the plan] had in mind was espionage . . . and in this respect it was of immense interest to those who were contemplating war and working on military plans."[25]

As Eisenhower had anticipated, the launching of *Sputnik* in October, 1957, presented difficulties for Soviet legal experts who had earlier asserted the inviolability of sovereign airspace: one of them ingeniously—but unconvincingly—took the position that *Sputnik* did not actually fly *over* other countries' territories, but rather that those territories rotated *beneath* it.[26] As the prospect of American reconnaissance satellites became more immediate, however, the Russians found it necessary to reassert the principle of vertical sovereignty, without at the same time calling into question the right of their own satellites to overfly the United States. They did this by attempting to distinguish between "innocent" passage and espionage: it was permissible for

---

* The U-2 was by no means the first U.S. reconnaissance plane to be shot down by the Russians. [See, on this point, James Bamford, *The Puzzle Palace: A Report on America's Most Secret Agency* (New York), pp. 181–82.] For Russian protests over earlier balloon and U-2 reconnaissance, see Stephen E. Ambrose, *Eisenhower: The President* (New York: 1984), pp. 309–10, 341, 563.

satellites to pass overhead, but not if they were to be used for purposes of reconnaissance.[27]*

However difficult this principle might have been to enforce, it did carry disturbing implications for the U.S. reconnaissance satellite program. The Americans were already some years ahead of the Soviet Union in developing such systems; clearly they stood to benefit from them far more than did the Russians, who had the advantage of monitoring a society in which little was kept secret in the first place. With these considerations in mind, Eisenhower early in 1958 authorized the beginning of research on an American anti-satellite system, designed to deter Moscow from interfering with the reconnaissance satellites Washington expected soon to launch. He did so, though, with considerable misgivings, lest such a program compromise the possibility—implicit in the "Open Skies" plan—of eventually persuading the Russians that reconnaissance could provide mutual benefits; it was for this reason that Eisenhower and his advisers strongly resisted pressures actually to deploy anti-satellite weaponry.[28]†

Convinced of the value of satellite reconnaissance—the Central Intelligence Agency's "Discoverer" system had returned the first satellite photographs of the Soviet Union in August, 1960, only three months after the U-2 had been shot down[29]—the Kennedy administration quickly embraced Eisenhower's goal of seeking to legitimize this new and impressive form of reconnaisance. It did so, though, by means that were at once more energetic and more imaginative than anything its predecessor had contemplated.

First, the White House imposed a strict news blackout on information concerning the development and launching of reconnaissance satellites. There had been no effort to conceal American programs in this area prior to 1961: the Eisenhower administration had prided itself on the openness of the American space program—successes and failures alike—and since the latter had outnumbered the former during the late 1950's, the Air Force had not been at all reluctant to publicize the success of its SAMOS reconnaissance satellite

* Khrushchev did suggest, in an off-hand remark at the abortive Paris summit that followed the U-2 incident in May, 1960, that the Russians objected only to reconnaissance from airplanes, not satellites. [Dwight D. Eisenhower, *The White House Years: Waging Peace, 1957–1960* (Garden City, New York: 1965), p. 556; George B. Kistiakowsky, *A Scientist at the White House: The Private Diary of President Eisenhower's Special Assistant for Science and Technology* (Cambridge, Massachusetts: 1976), p. 334.] But this was not the consistent Soviet position at the time. For an overall summary of attempts by Soviet and East European scholars to wrestle with the legal implications of earth satellites, see C. Wilfred Jenks, *Space Law* (New York: 1965), pp. 133–47.

† NSC 5814/1, approved by Eisenhower on August 18, 1958, pointed out that "[r]econnaissance satellites are of critical importance to U.S. national security." They would have "a high potential use as a means of implementing the 'open skies' proposal or policing a system of international armaments control." There was, as a consequence, an urgent need to seek "a political framework which will place the uses of U.S. reconnaissance satellites in a political and psychological context most favorable to the United States." [NSC 5814/1, "Preliminary U.S. Policy on Outer Space," August 18, 1958, Eisenhower Papers, White House NSC Assistant, NSC Series, Policy Papers Subseries, Box 25.]

in late 1960 and early 1961.[30]* This all changed shortly after President John F. Kennedy took office: henceforth "Discoverer" and SAMOS launches received only minimal publicity, if any at all. The purpose of this news black-out was not to deny information about launches to the Russians, whose own tracking systems were fully capable of monitoring them. Instead it appears to have been an attempt to avoid provoking Moscow into categorical public condemnations of overhead reconnaissance;† there may also have been the assumption that the Russians would have less of an incentive to develop their own anti-satellite system if the success of American reconnaissance satellites was kept quiet.[31]

Second, and somewhat contradictorily, the Kennedy administration under-took to let the Russians know—although very discreetly—something of the intelligence collection capabilities of reconnaissance satellites. It did this in the form of a carefully worded speech by Deputy Secretary of Defense Ros-well Gilpatric in October, 1961, in which Gilpatric acknowledged that "the Iron Curtain is not so impenetrable as to force us to accept at face value . . . Kremlin boasts" about Soviet missile capabilities.[32] Made at the height of the Berlin crisis, this decision to reveal what the United States knew about the absence of a "missile gap" had the obvious purposes of precluding any fur-ther attempts by Khrushchev to extract political advantages from weapons he did not possess, while at the same time reassuring the American public and allies overseas. An indirect effect, however, could only have been to confirm for the Russians the value of the intelligence the Washington was now re-ceiving from reconnaissance satellites.[33]

Third, the Defense Department late in 1962 unilaterally "reoriented"—in effect, cancelling—the major American anti-satellite system then under devel-opment. This was the Air Force's satellite interception (SAINT) program, an effort that had been under way since 1958 to devise methods of locating and "inspecting" Soviet satellites in orbit; once that capability had been per-fected, it had been assumed, actual destruction of the satellite would be a simple matter.[34] Anti-satellite development did not entirely end with the phas-ing-out of SAINT: both the Army and the Air Force were allowed to continue work on "direct ascent" systems, which would work by firing rockets from the ground directly at satellites. The capabilities of these systems were se-verely limited, though: there were never any more than two launch sites, and only a handful of missiles were actually produced. The pattern of the early 1960's was one, then, of refraining from developing the full-scale anti-satellite systems that could have been put in place by that time.[35]‡

* The Central Intelligence Agency had been more discreet about its "Discoverer" series, but the first successful recovery of a "Discoverer" film capsule in August, 1960, had been fully publicized in the press. [See Eisenhower, *Waging Peace*, p. 688.]

† Philip J. Farley to the author, May 27, 1986. Former Secretary of Defense Robert S. McNamara, who played the major role in cutting off information about reconnaissance satellite launches, has confirmed to me in a private conversation that his intention was to avoid the kind of public challenge the U-2 incident had presented to the Russians.

‡ Stares points out that SAINT was cancelled primarily for technical and financial rea-

Finally, the United States began a diplomatic offensive in the United Nations aimed at establishing international legal precedents for satellite reconnaissance. The United Nations General Assembly had created a Committee on the Peaceful Uses of Outer Space in 1958, but because of procedural objections raised by the Soviet Union the new organization had remained inactive until 1961. By the end of the year, though, it had become clear that the Russians had decided to use the committee as a forum in which to press their case against satellite reconnaissance, and in June of 1962 they introduced a resolution that would have declared "the use of artificial satellites for the collection of intelligence information in the territory of foreign states . . . incompatible with the objectives of mankind in its conquest of outer space."[36] Washington had anticipated this initiative, and responded to it by stressing the difficulty of separating peaceful from military uses of space, the potential scientific value of observations made from satellites, and, very quietly, the possibility that satellites could be useful in monitoring arms control agreements.[37]*

These U.N. discussions got nowhere, though, with the Soviet delegate still insisting that satellite reconnaissance was inconsistent with international law, that "the object to which such illegal surveillance is directed constitutes a secret guarded by a Sovereign State," and that "regardless of the means by which such an operation is carried out, it is in all cases an intrusion into something guarded by a Sovereign State in conformity with its sovereign perogative."[38] By the summer of 1963, it appeared that the campaign to get the Russians to accept the legitimacy of overhead reconnaissance—begun with Eisenhower's "Open Skies" proposal and continued on several different fronts by Kennedy—had flatly failed.

# III

But then a surprising series of events took place. They began in July, 1963, with a newspaper report that Khrushchev—in the characteristically improbable setting of a picnic along the banks of the Dnieper—had half-seriously offered to show Belgian Foreign Minister Paul Henri Spaak a selection of Soviet reconnaissance satellite photographs.[39] The following month, Moscow abruptly dropped previous objections to the use of photography from weather satellites. Then in September, in the United Nations Committee on the Peace-

sons, and argues that the decision to do so was not intended as a signal to the Russians. He does acknowledge, though, that the Kennedy administration did deliberately constrain itself from full-scale anti-satellite weapons development, in an effort to avoid jeopardizing satellite reconnaissance legitimacy. [Stares, *The Militarization of Space*, pp. 81–82, 239–40.]

* One part of this campaign was a full set of briefings for American allies on the capabilities of reconnaissance satellites. [See, on this point, Stares, *The Militarization of Space*, p. 69.]

ful Uses of Outer Space, the Russians expressed a willingness to modify their earlier insistence on the illegality of reconnaissance from satellites. And in October, 1963, the Soviet Union proposed—without requiring as a precondition the banning of reconnaissance satellites—a United Nations resolution prohibiting the placement of nuclear weapons or other weapons of mass destruction in outer space. The Americans quickly agreed, and the General Assembly approved the resolution unanimously that same month. Two months later, the General Assembly endorsed as well—also by a unanimous vote—a "Declaration of Legal Principles Governing the Activities of States in the Exploration and Use of Outer Space" which made no mention at all of reconnaissance satellites.[40]

The reasons for this sudden shift in the Soviet position can only be surmised, but there are several possibilities. One is simply that the Americans had made it clear, by this time, that they did not propose to negotiate away the right to send satellites over the Soviet Union for reconnaissance purposes; they had also shown that they would develop the means to deter attacks on such satellites if necessary. In this sense, the Soviet Union confronted a *fait accompli*, and had little choice but to accept it.

But the Russians had also now developed their own reconnaissance satellites and had presumably come to recognize the value of the intelligence derived from them. The first Soviet reconnaissance satellite went into orbit in April, 1962, and others soon followed.[41] There is no way to know how good the photographs from these Soviet satellites were, except to point out that they were apparently good enough for Khrushchev to be boasting about them by the following summer.[42] It had previously been assumed that reconnaissance satellites would benefit the United States more than the Soviet Union, and that the Russians would find it preferable to call for banning them rather than to tolerate them. But it may well be that their first actual satellite photographs were of greater use to the Russians than they themselves had expected. Certainly the Cuban missile crisis, which occurred between the first Soviet reconnaissance satellite launch and Moscow's change of heart on the legality of such reconnaissance, could well have illustrated the value of intelligence collected in this way; it is worth noting also that Sino-Soviet relations had seriously deteriorated by this time and that a capacity to monitor Chinese military developments might not have been unwelcome in Moscow.[43]

It is also possible that the Russians had now come to recognize the value reconnaissance satellites could have in stabilizing the arms race. Soviet spokesmen as early as 1960 had informally acknowledged the possibility of such an effect;[44] by 1963, U-2 overflights had played a demonstrably vital role, first in alerting the United States to the Soviet missile buildup in Cuba, and then in monitoring Soviet compliance with the Kennedy-Khrushchev agreement that ended the crisis.[45] And, of course, the Limited Nuclear Test Ban Treaty, signed in August, had just established the precedent of maintaining arms control agreements by non-intrusive means of inspection.[46]

It has also been suggested—although there is no way to prove it—that the realization had now begun to dawn in the Kremlin that its policy of secrecy regarding military capabilities had backfired: the result had been an American proclivity for "worst case analysis" that had produced military buildups larger than otherwise would have been the case. The very fact that the one successful breach of Soviet secrecy prior to the advent of satellites—the U-2 program—had led Eisenhower to *reject* demands to close the non-existent "missile gap" only confirmed the point. As Deputy Defense Secretary Gilpatric suggested in 1962: "The Soviets are forced to work very had to keep up with what *they know* we are doing in order to keep up with what *we think* they are doing."[47]

The over-all improvement in Soviet-American relations that followed the Cuban missile crisis should also be taken into account in explaining the Soviet decision to tolerate satellite reconnaissance. For had the Russians not developed some sense of mutual interest in stabilizing the arms race—a sense that had been noticeably absent during the years of Khrushchev's "strategic deception" between 1957 and 1962—then it is hard to see how very much progress could have been made toward the mutual toleration of satellite reconnaissance.

Was there any direct connection between the Kennedy administration's efforts to legitimize satellite reconnaissance and the tacit Soviet agreement to do so? One possibility is that the Americans' unilateral decision to phase out the SAINT satellite interception system, and to exhibit restraint in developing other anti-satellite programs, may have induced the Russians to respond by not pushing their anti-reconnaissance campaign.[48] Whether or not the cancellation of SAINT was intended as a gesture to the Russians,[49] it is undeniable that the United States did refrain from pressing ahead with the development of full-scale anti-satellite systems during the late 1950's and early 1960's, and that one reason for this was Washington's determination to do nothing to interfere with the possibility of legitimizing satellite reconnaissance.[50] But whether the Russians were sophisticated enough to recognize this restraint— particularly in view of the fact that a limited anti-satellite program did continue through the mid-1960's—is highly questionable. Certainly their commitment to maintaining a tacitly agreed-upon satellite reconnaissance regime would not prevent them from initiating their own considerably more ambitious and, in its effects, highly destabilizing anti-satellite program in the mid-1970's.[51]

There may be another sense, though, in which unilateral American restraint did contribute to the Soviet decision to tolerate such reconnaissance. The most obvious change that the Kennedy administration had made from its predecessor's policy on reconnaissance satellites had been to minimize publicity about their existence. This may well have been an important consideration in making these satellites more tolerable to the Russians: they had reason to expect, not least from the quiet way in which the October, 1961, Gilpatric speech had been handled, that although the United States would take maximum possible intelligence advantage of its reconnaissance satellite capabilities, it would not trumpet the fact, thereby embarrassing the Soviet Union.

Certainly Kennedy's sensitivity to the importance of not humiliating Khrushchev is acknowledged to have played an important role in the successful resolution of the Cuban missile crisis;[52] there is no reason to think that such an approach might not have had an equally beneficial effect with regard to satellite reconnaissance as well.


# I V


The reconnaissance satellite regime tacitly agreed upon in 1963 has been in existence now for a quarter of a century. This record of durability suggests the extent to which both Moscow and Washington have found it advantageous to tolerate this new "non-intrusive" form of espionage, but both governments have been reticent about revealing just what these advantages are, or how they are brought to fruition. Nevertheless, enough information has filtered into the public domain to make possible certain basic generalizations about both the capabilities of reconnaissance satellites and—to a lesser extent—their political purposes. *

The capabilities of reconnaissance satellites fall into four general categories:

*Photoreconnaissance.* Taking photographs from outer space was the original purpose of reconnaissance satellites, and it remains their most important function. Quite early in its history space photography attained a remarkable capacity to distinguish even minute features on the face of the earth: today's satellites are said to be able to detect objects as small as ten centimeters. Infrared and ultraviolet spectra are employed, in addition to visible light, with the resulting photographs returned either through capsules ejected from the satellite or, more frequently now, direct transmissions. Orbits are usually low, and most reconnaissance satellites are now maneuverable.[53]

*Early warning.* Satellites have also been used since the early 1970's to detect missile launchings and surreptitious nuclear tests. Their capacity to do this

---

* Reconnaissance satellite launchings are generally announced—although without specifying their function—and their orbital parameters are provided. With the voluntary cooperation of both the United States and the Soviet Union, the United Nations Secretary General began maintaining a public registry of all objects launched into space in March, 1962. This procedure became mandatory with the coming into force of the United Nations Convention on Registration of Objects Launched into Outer Space in September, 1976. [Jenks, *Space Law*, pp. 221–24; J. E. S. Fawcett, *Outer Space: New Challenges to Law and Policy* (Oxford: 1984), pp. 27–28, 154–59.] For an indication of what can be learned about satellite missions from a careful analysis of orbital parameters, see G. E. Perry, "Identification of Military Components Within the Soviet Space Programme," in Bhupendra Jasani, ed., *Outer Space—A New Dimension of the Arms Race* (London: 1982), pp. 135–54. An excellent introduction to the military uses of satellites in general is Ashton B. Carter, "Satellites and Anti-Satellites: The Limits of the Possible," *International Security*, X (Spring, 1986), especially pp. 46–72.

takes advantage of the same infrared detecting capacity used in low-orbiting photoreconnaissance satellites, but early warning satellites are generally placed in geosynchronous orbit some 22,000 miles above the earth so that their coverage of targeted areas is broad and constant.[54]

*Radar reconnaissance.* These satellites rely upon the development of side-looking synthetic-aperture radar, which makes it possible, not only to penetrate cloud cover over land targets, but to measure wave-heights and other ocean conditions. They are of obvious value in monitoring the movement of surface vessels, and they may have some potential in the future to track submerged submarines.[55]

*"Ferret" or electronic surveillance satellites.* This function of satellites is the one about which least is known, but presumably it includes the ability to eavesdrop on military and civilian telecommunications, as well as to analyze radar signals and to monitor the telemetry from missile tests.[56]

Determining the *political* functions of reconnaissance satellites is not as easy as describing their physical functions: here one is forced to rely upon a small number of official disclosures—both intentional and inadvertent—and upon a very large amount of well-informed speculation. Such an analysis suggests the following:

*Guarding against surprises.* The most important political function reconnaissance satellites have served has been to increase the confidence each superpower feels that it will be able to detect preparations by its rival to launch a surprise attack. Early warning satellites double the time that would otherwise be available to respond to an ICBM launch; photoreconnaissance and radar satellites can easily track movements of conventional forces; and "ferret" satellites have the capability to intercept communications that might reveal adversary intentions. This array of warning systems also provides useful safeguards in the case of false alarms, as recent experience has indicated.[57] There remains, of course, no guarantee that one super-power cannot achieve surprise in using force against the other or against its allies. But reconnaissance satellites do greatly reduce the chances of that happening.

*Assessing adversary forces.* Reconnaissance satellites have also been valuable in providing a means by which each super-power can evaluate the configuration of the other's military arsenal, and hence make more informed decisions than had been possible prior to their development about its own military priorities. Obviously, as a relatively "open" society seeking to learn the secrets of one largely "closed," the United States has benefited more from this use of satellite intelligence than has the Soviet Union: its very first reconnaissance satellites torpedoed Khrushchev's strategy of seeking political benefits from non-existent rockets,[58] and ever since the Russians have found it much more difficult than it had been during the first decade and a half of the Cold War to obscure the size and nature of their military establishment. But the Americans have managed to maintain some secrets of their own,* and presumably Moscow has found it convenient to be able to check what appears in the open literature against what its own reconnaissance systems reveal about military research, development and deployment in this country and among its allies.

*Monitoring compliance with arms control agreements.* This is the only function of reconnaissance satellites that Washington and Moscow have explicitly—if euphemistically—agreed to endorse. Both the Strategic Arms Limitation Interim Agreement and the Treaty on the Limitation of Anti-Ballistic Missile Systems, signed in Moscow in May, 1972, provide for "assurance of compliance . . . [by] national technical means of verification . . . in a manner consistent with generally recognized principles of international law." The SALT I "package" further provided that no interference with "national technical means" would take place, and that neither side would seek to impede such means of verification through "deliberate concealment measures."[59] The SALT II agreement of 1979, which the United States never ratified, carried these arrangements even farther by providing for the deliberate incorporation into aircraft and cruise missile design of "functionally related observable differences" and "externally observable design features"—external characteristics *intended* to be visible from satellites as a means of ensuring compliance with the agreement.[60]

*Keeping track of third party crises.* One by-product of the long postwar Soviet-American rivalry has been that all of the actual fighting that has gone on since 1945 has taken the form of limited regional conflicts involving third parties. At times—as in Korea, Vietnam and Afghanistan—these conflicts have drawn in one of the super-powers as a belligerent; more often, though, Moscow and Washington have been content to watch these confrontations nervously from the sidelines. Reconnaissance satellites, of course, greatly enhance their ability to do this. Careful reconstruction of satellite orbital paths has demonstrated a tendency on the part of both the Russians and Americans to increase coverage of those parts of the world where regional conflicts are taking place: the pattern can be clearly seen in crises as diverse as the 1969 Sino-Soviet border clash, the 1971 India-Pakistan War, the 1973 Arab-Israeli War, the 1974 Cyprus crisis, and the 1982 Falklands War.[61] There have even been instances of super-powers *sharing* satellite reconnaissance information about third parties: the clearest example is the warning conveyed from Mos-

---

* The U-2 is perhaps the best example of a secretly developed American military system that the Russians probably would have detected if they had had reconnaissance satellites functioning at that time. "Stealth" bomber development might have been another, had the Carter administration not chosen, for reasons that must certainly have puzzled the Russians, to reveal the fact that it was under way. [See, on this latter point, Elizabeth Drew, *Portrait of an Election: The 1980 Presidential Campaign* (New York: 1981), pp. 267–68.]

cow to Washington in 1977 that the South Africans appeared to be about to test a nuclear weapon in the Kalihari desert.[62]

*Evaluating an adversary's resource base.* The launching of the American Earth Resources Technology Satellite (since renamed Landsat) in July, 1972, immediately demonstrated the ability of even low-resolution satellite photography to detect, and distinguish between, specific varieties of minerals and vegetation on the earth's surface.[63] Although the Landsat program was public from its inception, its techniques of using false-color and infrared photography to bring out contrasts in geological features and even patterns of agricultural cultivation have no doubt been available to intelligence analysts as well, probably at higher levels of resolution.* Such information makes possible calculations of harvest yields; it may also provide at least a basis for estimating certain mineral resource reserves as well. Information of this type obviously could be useful in estimating the future performance of the Soviet economy.

It is doubtful that this short list exhausts the benefits, actual and potential, that reconnaissance satellites provide to the Soviet Union and the United States. But it should at least provide a partial explanation of why a mutually tolerated reconnaissance satellite regime has survived as long as it has, and with so few attempts at interference from either side.

# V

Consideration of how one might in fact interfere with the operation of reconnaissance satellites has been going on, in both the United States and the Soviet Union, for as long as the satellites themselves have been in place,[64] but it is only within the past decade that the two superpowers have made serious efforts actually to develop means of doing this. The relatively low priority given research on anti-satellite weapons until the mid-1970's provides striking evidence of the benefits both sides saw in preserving the satellite reconnaissance regime; but what has happened since then does create the possibility that that regime may not remain sacrosanct in the future.

The United States developed the first operational system for destroying orbiting satellites—a system that relied upon the use of Thor missiles armed with nuclear warheads—and maintained it from 1964 through 1975. But Project 437, as it was known, was intended primarily as protection against an anticipated threat from Soviet orbital bombardment weapons that never materialized. It never had anything more than a limited capability against re-

* Landsat operates at 30 meters resolution. A new French satellite, launched in 1986, provides similar photographs, but at 10 meters resolution. [D. D. Edwards, "Making Remote Sense Out of Space Commercialization," *Science News*, CXXVIII(December 21 and 28, 1985), 393.]

connaissance and other kinds of satellites; its nuclear warhead would have endangered American satellites as much as whatever Soviet target at which it might have been aimed; and after 1967 the Outer Space Treaty, which banned altogether the placement of nuclear weapons beyond the earth's atmosphere, appeared to remove the threat of orbital bombardment that Project 437 had been intended to counter. By 1970, the program's operational readiness had been cut back to such an extent that it would have taken thirty days to launch a single missile.[65]

Soviet anti-satellite weapon development began—a good deal more purposefully—in 1968, and involved the actual launching of "killer" satellites, capable of intercepting and destroying target satellites in low earth orbit. These tests were suspended from 1971 until early 1976, but they have since continued periodically.[66]* Moscow's motives for beginning to develop true "killer" satellites just as a much more primitive American anti-satellite system was being phased out remain unclear. It has been suggested that the Soviets had acquiesced all along only in the use of satellites to verify arms control agreements, not to gather military intelligence; but their tacit acceptance of the reconnaissance satellite regime dates from 1963, long before arms control agreements specifically dependent upon satellite verification had been concluded. The more plausible explanation is that the Russians saw the need to have a capability in *wartime* to destroy American satellites whose functioning they were willing to tolerate as long as war did not occur.[67]

American officials did not regard the first series of Soviet anti-satellite tests as a significant threat: they went ahead with the phase-out of Project 437 even after the Soviet experiments had taken place, and despite some puzzlement over Moscow's intentions did not respond by initiating an updated American program. The general atmosphere of détente during the early 1970's no doubt contributed to Washington's relaxed attitude, as did the fact that Moscow refrained from further anti-satellite testing after 1971 and that provisions for "national technical means of verification" in the 1972 SALT I agreements appeared to constitute a binding—if inexplicit—obligation on Russians' part not to impede satellite reconnaissance when used as an instrument of arms control.[68]

But when the second series of Soviet anti-satellite tests began in 1976, the political climate was much less auspicious. Détente had begun to crumble, both as the result of domestic pressures within the United States and growing signs of Soviet interventionism in Africa.[69] Rumors of Soviet experiments with directed-energy weapons had begun to surface, and in an ambiguous series of incidents late in 1975, the infrared sensors on three American satellites had been blinded by what may—or may not—have been laser beams

---

* Raymond Garthoff has suggested that a significant opportunity was lost during the SALT I negotiations to trade off the American operational anti-satellite capability for a complete ban on anti-ballistic missile systems, in which the Soviets were leading at that time. [*Détente and Confrontation: American-Soviet Relations from Nixon to Reagan* (Washington: 1985), pp. 189–90.] This argument may exaggerate the extent to which Project 437 can be considered a workable anti-satellite system, though.

directed from Soviet territory.[70] Concern about levels of Soviet military expenditure had begun to grow as well, as had disputes about the adequacy of American intelligence in assessing Moscow's intentions.[71] It was within this context that the Ford administration, just before leaving office in January, 1977, directed the Defense Department to begin development of a new American anti-satellite weapon system.[72]

Just as the Soviet anti-satellite program had constituted a significant advance in sophistication over the primitive Project 437, so now the new American development effort produced a system that exceeded the capabilities of its Soviet counterpart. Relying on the use of a small but highly accurate rocket launched from an F-15 fighter, the system works by directly ramming the target satellite. It does not require, as does the Soviet "killer" satellite, time-consuming orbital rendezvous maneuvers; moreover its reliability, at least in the limited tests conducted so far, appears to exceed that of the Soviet anti-satellite system.[73] And, of course, since the surprise announcement of President Reagan's Strategic Defense Initiative in March, 1983, research has been proceeding on a much wider variety of systems—including laser and particle beam weapons—that if developed could destroy enemy satellites as well as the enemy missiles that are the officially announced targets of a space-based defensive capability.[74]

Meanwhile, efforts to negotiate agreements that would safeguard the right of satellite reconnaissance have come to naught. The Carter administration coupled its pursuit of a new anti-satellite system with an offer to the Russians to begin discussions on how such weapons might be prohibited altogether, and in June, 1978, talks on this subject began in Helsinki, followed by two further sets of talks that took place in Bern and in Vienna in 1979. But because of the difficulty of specifying in advance just what kinds of activities might threaten reconnaissance satellites, neither government found it a simple matter to formulate a negotiating position, or to address the problem of how an anti-satellite treaty might be verified. Asymmetries in capabilities on both sides also created difficulties: the Americans, noting that the Russians already had an operational anti-satellite system but that they did not, resisted any ban on research and testing; the Russians, pointing to the well-advertised satellite interception and retrieval potential of the soon-to-be-launched American space shuttle, countered with demands for guarantees against its use as an anti-satellite weapon.

Further discussions might have narrowed these differences, but the increasingly acrimonious debate over SALT II inside the United States froze all progress on arms control for the remainder of 1979; the Soviet invasion of Afghanistan at the end of that year ensured that none would take place during what was left of Carter's term. The Russians now took the initiative, proposing a draft space weapons treaty in the United Nations in 1981, but the Reagan administration quickly decided not to follow Carter's example of simultaneous negotiations and anti-satellite weapons development, but rather to concentrate upon the latter altogether.[75]

Does the development of anti-satellite weaponry, together with the failure of negotiations on their control, mean that the reconnaissance satellite regime is now at risk? It clearly does, in the sense that the *capability* to destroy satellites on short notice with reasonable accuracy now exists on both sides, and can be expected to improve. But whether capability produces *intention* is another matter entirely. One characteristic of the nuclear age has been precisely the distinction between these two things: the *capability* for mutual destruction has been present for at least three of the four decades during which nuclear weapons have existed; but the *intention* to commit such destruction has been mercifully absent.

There is little reason to think that this distinction between capabilities and intentions will not apply to the satellite reconnaissance regime in the future, much as it has to the nuclear arms competition in the past. For it is precisely the connection between the two—the value of satellites in providing some measure of protection against surprise nuclear attack—that would cause any actual employment of anti-satellite weapons against reconnaissance satellites to be regarded as an act almost as provocative as a full-scale missile launch would be. The existence of anti-satellite weapons, therefore, may have no greater effect upon the security of satellites in peacetime than the proliferation of highly accurate missiles armed with nuclear warheads has had on the likelihood of nuclear weapons actually being used.

# VI

The quiet evolution of a reconnaissance satellite regime that both Washington and Moscow could find reasons to want to perpetuate was at least as important an example of Soviet-American cooperation to lower the risk of war as the highly publicized Limited Test Ban Treaty of 1963 or the Strategic Arms Limitation Agreements of 1972. Cooperation on reconnaissance was all the more remarkable for the way in which it came about: in this case, the superpowers identified mutual interests and evolved procedures for enhancing them without resort to the formal negotiations that are generally thought necessary to accomplish such results. This fact raises interesting questions about the respective advantages of tacit as opposed to explicit agreements as a means of managing super-power rivalries.[76]

Tacit cooperation has the advantage of minimizing the extent to which prestige on either side is engaged. It would have been considerably more difficult for the Russians to have accepted American reconnaissance satellite overflights had the existence of such satellites had been given the publicity accorded other elements of the United States space program. Certainly one senses that at least some of the Soviet Union's current vociferous objections to the American Strategic Defense Initiative grow out of the highly public manner in which that program has been pursued, and the implications of Soviet technological inferiority that are so explicitly drawn from it.[77] The American reconnaissance satellite program was handled in a very different way in the early 1960's, and that may account in part for the ease with which the Russians accepted its legitimacy.

The absence of publicity also makes it possible for governments to act quickly, without the requirement for intensive consultation within the bureaucracy and among affected constituencies that is normally required for initiatives taken openly. It is illustrative to contrast the speed with which Eisenhower and his immediate advisers put together the "Open Skies" proposal in 1955, or with which the Kennedy administration was able to develop a combination of initiatives in 1961–62 intended to persuade the Russians to accept the legitimacy of satellite reconnaissance, with the length of time it has taken both the United States and Soviet governments to resolve internal disagreements prior to presenting positions on the control of strategic arms publicly since negotiations on that subject began in 1969.*

Finally, tacit cooperation tends to lift delicate issues in Soviet-American relations out of the arena of political debate inside the United States. It is interesting to contemplate what the Kennedy administration's domestic opposition might have made of the fact that Soviet reconnaissance satellites were overflying the United States after 1962, had that information become widely known. Recent intrusions of domestic political considerations into foreign policy—the Jackson-Vanik Amendment of 1972 linking the extension of credits and "most-favored nation" trade privileges to the relaxation of Soviet restrictions on emigration, the manner in which the term "détente" became unacceptable during the 1976 presidential campaign, and the 1979 controversy over a suddenly discovered Soviet "combat brigade" in Cuba are only the most prominent examples—provide little assurance that mutual interests in Soviet-American relations will always override the narrow partisan interests of American political leaders.[78] The fact that cooperation in reconnaissance has proceeded on a tacit basis has made it possible to avoid these difficulties as well.

But the tacit pursuit of mutual interests is not without its disadvantages. First, one is never quite sure what is included within a tacit agreement and what is not. The fact that research on anti-satellite weapons has proceeded alongside reliance on satellite reconnaissance illustrates the point; nor is there any clear understanding between the super-powers as to the kinds of actions that would constitute abrogation of the informal reconnaissance regime.[79] If one believes—and there is some reason to do so—that deterrence is best achieved through ambiguity,[80] then the very vagueness of the super-power "understanding" on reconnaissance satellites could be an asset. But this does nothing to lessen the danger of misperception or accident: it is all too easy

---

* The SALT I negotiations took three years, from 1969 to 1972; SALT II negotiations required seven years, from 1972 to 1979. For the Reagan administration's difficulties in formulating a position on strategic arms control, see Strobe Talbott, *Deadly Gambits: The Reagan Administration and the Stalemate in Nuclear Arms Control* (New York: 1984).

for casual, thoughtless, or even unintended behavior on one side to appear purposeful, calculated, and sinister to the other.[81]

Second, tacit cooperation requires that each side continue to value it, regardless of the changes of leadership or of circumstance that may take place. Formal treaties provide protection—admittedly imperfect—against future uncertainties; informal arrangements like the satellite reconnaissance regime do not. There is nothing to prevent leaders in either Washington or Moscow from simply abandoning, at any point, their practice of tolerating each other's remotely conducted espionage, should they choose to do so.

Third, the very secrecy upon which these programs depend narrows the range of those who are knowledgeable about them, whether within government or outside of it. This makes it difficult to conduct informed public discussion about such important issues as the verification of arms control agreements, a fact that became painfully apparent during the 1979 debate over the ratification of SALT II.[82] Secrecy can also raise questions about the appropriate uses of such publicly financed programs as the space shuttle, as the recent controversy over that vehicle's classified military missions has shown.[83]

But whatever its advantages and disadvantages, the emergence of a tacitly agreed-upon satellite reconnaissance regime does illustrate that nations need not always confine themselves to traditional forms of negotiation to achieve meaningful cooperation on areas of mutual interest. It also suggests the extent to which long-term systemic interests—the interests both sides share in avoiding nuclear war and in preserving the international system as it has evolved since 1945—can, at times, override the immediate national interests of the two nations whose rivalry has defined that system during the four decades it has been in existence.

# 8

# The Long Peace:
# Elements of Stability in the
# Postwar International System

I SHOULD like to begin this essay with a fable. Once upon a time, there was a great war that involved the slaughter of millions upon millions of people. When, after years of fighting, one side finally prevailed over the other and the war ended, everyone said that it must go down in history as the last great war ever fought. To that end, the victorious nations sent all of their wisest men to a great peace conference, where they were given the task of drawing up a settlement that would be so carefully designed, so unquestionably fair to all concerned, that it would eliminate war as a phenomenon of human existence. Unfortunately, that settlement lasted only twenty years.

There followed yet another great war involving the slaughter of millions upon millions of people. When, after years of fighting, one side finally prevailed over the other and the war ended, everyone said that it must go down in history as the last great war ever fought. To everyone's horror, though, the victors in that conflict immediately fell to quarreling among themselves, with the result that no peace conference ever took place. Within a few years each of the major victors had come to regard each other, and not their former enemies, as the principal threat to their survival; each sought to ensure that sur-

This essay was presented at the Nobel Institute Symposium on "The Study of War and Peace," Noresund, Norway, June, 1985, and was summarized at the International Congress of Historical Sciences, Stuttgart, West Germany, August, 1985. It has appeared, in a slightly different form, in *International Security*, X(Spring, 1986), 99–142; and in Øyvind Osterud, ed., *Studies of War and Peace* (Oslo: 1986), pp. 125–60. I am grateful as well to Stanley Hoffmann, Robert Jervis, and Uwe Nerlich for providing opportunities to discuss this paper before seminars conducted by them, and to Pierre Hassner, Kjell Goldmann, Harold Molineu, and Joseph S. Nye, Jr., for helpful suggestions.

vival by developing weapons capable, at least in theory, of ending the survival of everyone on earth. Paradoxically, that arrangement lasted twice as long as the first one, and as the fable ended showed no signs of coming apart anytime soon.

It is, of course, just a fable, and as a general rule one ought not to take fables too seriously. There are times, though, when fables can illuminate reality more sharply than conventional forms of explanation are able to do, and this may well be one of them. For it is the case that the post-World War II system of international relations, which nobody designed or even thought could last for very long, which was based not upon the dictates of morality and justice but rather upon an arbitrary and strikingly artificial division of the world into spheres of influence, and which incorporated within it some of the most bitter and persistent antagonisms short of war in modern history, has now survived twice as long as the far more carefully designed World War I settlement, has approximately equaled in longevity the great 19th-century international systems of Metternich and Bismarck, and unlike those earlier systems after four decades of existence shows no perceptible signs of disintegration. It is, or ought to be, enough to make one think.

To be sure, the term "peace" is not the first that comes to mind when one recalls the history of the Cold War. That period, after all, has seen the greatest accumulation of armaments the world has ever known, a whole series of protracted and devastating limited wars, an abundance of revolutionary, ethnic, religious, and civil violence, as well as some of the deepest and most intractable ideological rivalries in human experience. Nor have those more ancient scourges—famine, disease, poverty, injustice—by any means disappeared from the face of the earth. Is it not stretching things a bit, one might well ask, to take the moral and spiritual desert in which the nations of the world conduct their affairs, and call it "peace"?

It is, of course, but that is just the point. Given all the conceivable reasons for having had a major war in the past four decades—reasons that in any other age would have provided ample justification for such a war—it seems worthy of comment that there has not in fact been one; that despite the unjust and wholly artificial character of the post-World War II settlement, it has now persisted for the better part of half a century. That may not be grounds for celebration, but it is at least grounds for investigation: for trying to comprehend how this great power peace has managed to survive for so long in the face of so much provocation, and for thinking about what might be done to perpetuate that situation. For, after all, we could do worse.

# I

Anyone attempting to understand why there has been no third world war confronts a problem not unlike that of Sherlock Holmes and the dog that did not bark in the night: how does one account for something that did not happen? How does one explain why the great conflict between the United States and the Soviet Union, which by all past standards of historical experience should have developed by now, has not in fact done so? The question involves certain methodological difficulties, to be sure: it is always easier to account for what did happen than for what did not. But there is also a curious bias among students of international relations that reinforces this tendency: "For every thousand pages published on the causes of wars," Geoffrey Blainey has commented, "there is less than one page directly on the causes of peace."[1] Even the discipline of "peace studies" suffers from this disproportion: it has given far more attention to the question of what we must do to avoid the apocalypse than it has to the equally interesting question of why, given all the opportunities, it has not happened so far.

It might be easier to deal with this question if the work that has been done on the causes of war had produced something approximating a consensus on why wars develop: we could then apply that analysis to the post-1945 period and see what has been different about it. But, in fact, these studies are not much help. Historians, political scientists, economists, sociologists, statisticians, even meteorologists, have wrestled for years with the question of what causes wars, and yet the most recent review of that literature concludes that "our understanding of war remains at an elementary level. No widely accepted theory of the causes of war exists and little agreement has emerged on the methodology through which these causes might be discovered."[2]

Nor has the comparative work that has been done on international systems shed much more light on the matter. The difficulty here is that our actual experience is limited to the operations of a single system—the balance of power system—operating either within the "multipolar" configuration that characterized international politics until World War II, or the "bipolar" configuration that has characterized them since.* Alternative systems remain abstract conceptualizations in the minds of theorists, and are of little use in advancing our knowledge of how wars in the real world do or do not occur.[3]

But "systems theory" itself is something else again: here one can find a useful point of departure for thinking about the nature of international relations since 1945. An "international system" exists, political scientists tell us, when two conditions are met: first, interconnections exist between units within the system, so that changes in some parts of it produce changes in

---

* One can, of course, question whether the postwar international system constitutes true "bipolarity." Peter H. Beckman, for example, provides an elaborate set of indices demonstrating the asymmetrical nature of American and Soviet power after 1945 in his *World Politics in the Twentieth Century* (Englewood Cliffs, New Jersey: 1984), pp. 207–9, 235–37, 282–85. But such retrospective judgments neglect the perceptions of policymakers *at the time,* who clearly saw their world as bipolar and frequently commented on the phenomenon. See, for example, David S. McLellan, *Dean Acheson: The State Department Years* (New York: 1976), p. 116; and, for Soviet "two camp" theory, William Taubman, *Stalin's America Policy: From Entente to Détente to Cold War* (New York: 1982), pp. 176–78.

other parts as well; and, second, the collective behavior of the system as a whole differs from the expectations and priorities of the individual units that make it up.[4] Certainly demonstrating the "interconnectedness" of post-World War II international relations is not difficult: one of their most prominent characteristics has been the tendency of major powers to assume that little if anything can happen in the world without in some way enhancing or detracting from their own immediate interests.[5]* Nor has the collective behavior of nations corresponded to their individual expectations: the very fact that the interim arrangements of 1945 have remained largely intact for four decades would have astonished—and quite possibly appalled—the statesmen who cobbled them together in the hectic months that followed the surrender of Germany and Japan.[6]†

A particularly valuable feature of systems theory is that it provides criteria for differentiating between stable and unstable political configurations: this can help to account for the fact that some international systems outlast others. Karl Deutsch and J. David Singer have defined "stability" as "the probability that the system retains all of its essential characteristics; that no single nation becomes dominant; that most of its members continue to survive; and that large-scale war does not occur." It is characteristic of such a system, Deutsch and Singer add, that it has the capacity for self-regulation: the ability to counteract stimuli that would otherwise threaten its survival, much as the automatic pilot on an airplane or the governor on a steam engine would do. "Self-regulating" systems are very different from what they call "self-aggravating" systems, situations that get out of control, like forest fires, drug addiction, runaway inflation, nuclear fission, and of course, although they themselves do not cite the example, all-out war.[7] Self-regulating mechanisms are most likely to function, in turn, when there exists some fundamental agreement among major states within the system on the objectives they are seeking to uphold by participating in it, when the structure of the system reflects the way in which power is distributed among its respective members, and when agreed-upon procedures exist for resolving differences among them.[8]

---

* Robert Jervis points out that "almost by definition a great power is more tightly connected to larger numbers of other states than is a small power. . . . Growing conflict or growing cooperation between Argentina and Chile would not affect Pakistan, but it would affect America and American policy toward those states. . . ." [Robert Jervis, "Systems Theories and Diplomatic History," in Paul Gordon Lauren, ed., *Diplomacy: New Approaches in History, Theory, and Policy* (New York: 1979), p. 215.]

† "A future war with the Soviet Union," retiring career diplomat Joseph C. Grew commented in May, 1945, "is as certain as anything in this world." [Memorandum of May 19, 1945, quoted in Joseph C. Grew, *Turbulent Era: A Diplomatic Record of Forty Years, 1904–1945* (Boston: 1952), II, 1446.] A. W. DePorte has observed that "[t]here is, after all, something to be explained—about perceptions as well as events—when so much that has been written has dismissed the new state system as no system at all but an unstable transition to something else." [*Europe Between the Super-Powers: The Enduring Balance* (New Haven: 1979), p. 167.]

Does the post-World War II international system fit these criteria for "stability"? Certainly its most basic characteristic—bipolarity—remains intact, in that the gap between the world's two greatest military powers and their nearest rivals is not substantially different from what it was four decades ago.[9] At the same time, neither the Soviet Union nor the United States nor anyone else has been able wholly to dominate that system; the nations most active within it in 1945 are for the most part still active today. And of course the most convincing argument for "stability" is that, so far at least, World War III has not occurred. On the surface, then, the concept of a "stable" international system makes sense as a way of understanding the experience through which we have lived these past forty years.

But what have been the self-regulating mechanisms? How has an environment been created in which they are able to function? In what way do those mechanisms—and the environment in which they function—resemble or differ from the configuration of other international systems, both stable and unstable, in modern history? What circumstances exist that might impair their operation, transforming self-regulation into self-aggravation? These are questions that have not received the attention they deserve from students of the history and politics of the postwar era. What follows is a series of speculations—it can hardly be more than that, given present knowledge—upon these issues, the importance of which hardly needs to be stressed.

I should like to emphasize, though, that this essay's concentration on the way the world is and has been is not intended to excuse or to justify our current predicament. Nor is it meant to preclude the possibility of moving ultimately toward something better. We can all conceive of international systems that combine stability with greater justice and less risk than the present one does, and we ought to continue to think about these things. But short of war, which no one wants, change in international relations tends to be gradual and evolutionary. It does not happen overnight. That means that alternative systems, if they ever develop, probably will not be total rejections of the existing system, but rather variations proceeding from it. All the more reason, then, to try to understand the system we have, to try to distinguish its stabilizing from its destabilizing characteristics, and to try to reinforce the former as a basis from which we might, in time and with luck, do better.

# II

Any such investigation should begin by distinguishing the structure of the international system in question from the behavior of the nations that make it up.[10] The reason for this is simple: behavior alone will not ensure stability if the structural prerequisites for it are absent, but structure can under certain circumstances impose stability even when its behavioral prerequisites are unpromising.* One need only compare the settlement of 1945 with its precedessor of 1919 to see the point.

If the intentions of statesmen alone had governed, the Paris Peace Conference of 1919 would have ushered in an era of stability in world politics comparable to that brought about in Europe by the Congress of Vienna almost a century earlier. Certainly the diplomats at Paris had that earlier precedent very much in mind;[11] conscious of what victory had cost, they approached their task wondering whether war had not altogether lost its usefulness as a means of resolving disputes among nations.[12]† Few if any peace negotiators have been able to draw upon such an impressive array of technical expertise as was available in 1919.[13] Moreover, the most influential of them, Woodrow Wilson, had determined to go beyond the practices and procedures of the "old diplomacy" to construct a settlement that would integrate power with morality. "Tell me what's right and I'll fight for it," Wilson is said to have demanded of his advisers,[14] and at least as far as the idea of self-determination was concerned, the Versailles settlement did come about as close as any in modern history to incorporating within itself the principles of justice.[15]

Unfortunately, in so doing, it neglected the realities of power. It broke up the old Austro-Hungarian Empire, a move that reflected accurately enough the aspirations of the nationalities involved, but that failed to provide the successor states of Poland, Czechoslovakia, Austria, and Hungary with the military or economic means necessary to sustain their new-found sovereignty.[16] Even more shortsightedly, there was no effort to accommodate the interests of two nations whose population and industrial strength were certain to guarantee them a major influence over postwar European developments—Germany and Soviet Russia. It should have been no surprise, therefore, that when the Versailles system finally broke down in 1939, it did so largely as the result of a deal cut at the expense of the East Europeans between these two countries whose power had been ignored, twenty years earlier, in the interests of justice.[17]‡

Nobody, in contrast, would picture the post-World War II settlement as a triumph of justice. That settlement arbitrarily divided sovereign nations like Germany, Austria, and Korea, not because anyone thought it was right to do

---

* "[S]tructure designates a set of constraining conditions. . . . [It] acts as a selector, but it cannot be seen, examined, and observed at work. . . . Because structures select by rewarding some behaviors and punishing others, outcomes cannot be inferred from intentions and behaviors." [Kenneth Waltz, *Theory of International Politics* (Reading, Massachusetts: 1979), pp. 73–74.]

† "Mr Evelyn Waugh's view, that what began as a crusade turned into a tug of war between indistinguishable teams of sweaty louts, is idiosyncratic. Most of us [in World War II] did not feel like that. But it is evident that by the end of the First World War a large number of intelligent people did; and ten years later their doubts had become general." [Michael Howard, *Studies in War and Peace* (New York: 1970), p. 99.]

‡ "[T]he victors at Versailles . . . failed . . . because, as if lulled by their own rhetoric, they continued to assert morality while they neglected armaments." [Geoffrey Blainey, *The Causes of War* (London: 1963), p. 163.]

so, but because neither the United States nor the Soviet Union could agree on whose occupation forces would withdraw first.[18] It did nothing to prevent the incorporation of several of the countries whose independence the 1919 settlement had recognized—and, in the case of Poland, whose independence Great Britain had gone to war in 1939 to protect—into a Soviet sphere of influence, where they remain to this day.[19] It witnessed, in response to this, the creation of an American sphere of influence in Western Europe, the Mediterranean and the Pacific, which although different from its Soviet counterpart in the important fact that the nations lying within it for the most part voluntarily associated themselves with the United States,[20] nonetheless required, however willingly, some sacrifice of national independence as well.

What resulted was the first true polarization of power in modern history. The world had had limited experience with bipolar systems in ancient times, it is true: certainly Thucydides' account of the rivalry between Athens and Sparta carries an eerie resonance for us today; nor could statesmen of the Cold War era forget what they had once learned, as schoolboys, of the antagonism between Rome and Carthage.[21] But these had been regional, not global conflicts: not until 1945 could one plausibly speak of a *world* divided into two competing spheres of influence, or of the *super-powers* that controlled them. The international situation had been reduced, Hans Morgenthau wrote in 1948, "to the primitive spectacle of two giants eyeing each other with watchful suspicion. . . . Thus contain or be contained, conquer or be conquered, destroy or be destroyed, become the watchwords of the new diplomacy."[22]

Now, bipolarity may seem to many today—as it did forty years ago—an awkward and dangerous way to organize world politics.[23] Simple geometric logic would suggest that a system resting upon three or more points of support would be more stable than one resting upon two. But politics is not geometry: the passage of time and the accumulation of experience has made clear certain structural elements of stability in the bipolar system of international relations that were not present in the multipolar systems that preceded it:

(1) The postwar bipolar system realistically reflected the facts of where military power resided at the end of World War II\*—and where it still does today, for that matter. In this sense, it differed markedly from the settlement of 1919, which made so little effort to accommodate the interests of Germany and Soviet Russia. It is true that in other categories of power—notably the economic—states have since arisen capable of challenging or even surpassing

---

\* "[W]hat *was* dominant in their consciousness," Michael Howard has written of the immediate post-World War II generation of statesmen, "was the impotence, almost one might say the irrelevance, of ethical aspirations in international politics in the absence of that factor to which so little attention had been devoted by their more eminent predecessors, to which indeed so many of them had been instinctively hostile—military power." [*The Causes of Wars*, 2nd edition (Cambridge, Massachusetts: 1984), p. 55.]

the Soviet Union and the United States in the production of certain specific commodities. But as the *political* position of nations like West Germany, Brazil, Japan, South Korea, Taiwan, and Hong Kong suggests, the ability to make video recorders, motorcycles, even automobiles and steel efficiently has yet to translate into anything approaching the capacity of Washington or Moscow to shape events in the world as a whole.

(2) The post-1945 bipolar structure was a simple one that did not require sophisticated leadership to maintain it. The great multipolar systems of the 19th century collapsed in large part because of their intricacy: they required a Metternich or a Bismarck to hold them together, and when statesmen of that calibre were no longer available, they tended to come apart.[24] Neither the Soviet nor the American political system has been geared toward identifying statesmen of comparable prowess and entrusting them with responsibility; demonstrated skill in the conduct of foreign policy has hardly been a major prerequisite for leadership in either country. And yet, a bipolar structure of international relations—because of the inescapably high stakes involved for its two major actors—tends, regardless of the personalities involved, to induce in them a sense of caution and restraint, and to discourage irresponsibility. "It is not," Kenneth Waltz notes, "that one entertains the utopian hope that all future American and Russian rules will combine in their persons . . . nearly perfect virtues, but rather that the pressures of a bipolar world strongly encourage them to act internationally in ways better than their characters may lead one to expect."[25]

(3) Because of its relatively simple structure, alliances in this bipolar system have tended to be more stable than they had been in the 19th century and in the 1919–39 period. It is striking to consider that the North Atlantic Treaty Organization has now equaled in longevity the most durable of the pre-World War I alliances, that between Germany and Austria-Hungary; it has lasted almost twice as long as the Franco-Russian alliance, and certainly much longer than any of the tenuous alignments of the interwar period. Its principal rival, the Warsaw Treaty Organization, has been in existence for almost as long. The reason for this is simple: alliances, in the end, are the product of insecurity;[26] so long as the Soviet Union and the United States each remain for the other and for their respective clients the major source of danger in the world, neither super-power encounters very much difficulty in maintaining the coalitions it controls. In a multipolar system, sources of insecurity can vary in much more complicated ways; hence it is not surprising to find alliances shifting to accommodate these variations.[27]

(4) At the same time, though, and probably because of the overall stability of the basic alliance systems, defections from both the American and Soviet coalitions—China, Cuba, Vietnam, Iran, and Nicaragua, in the case of the Americans; Yugoslavia, Albania, Egypt, Somalia, and China again in the case of the Russians—have been tolerated without the major disruptions that might have attended such changes in a more delicately balanced multipolar system. The fact that a state the size of China was able to reverse its alignment

twice during the Cold War without any more dramatic effect upon the position of the super-powers says something about the stability bipolarity brings; compare this record with the impact, prior to 1914, of such apparently minor episodes as Austria's annexation of Bosnia and Herzegovina, or the question of who was to control Morocco. It is a curious consequence of bipolarity that although alliances are more durable than in a multipolar system, defections are at the same time more tolerable.[28]

In short, without anyone's having designed it, and without any attempt whatever to consider the requirements of justice, the nations of the postwar era lucked into a system of international relations that, because it has been based upon realities of power, has served the cause of order—if not justice—better than one might have expected.

# III

But if the structure of bipolarity in itself encouraged stability, so too did certain inherent characteristics of the bilateral Soviet-American relationship. It used to be fashionable to point out, in the days before the Cold War began, that despite periodic outbreaks of tension between them Russians and Americans had never actually gone to war with one another; the same claim could not be made for the history of either country's relations with Great Britain, Germany, Italy, Austria-Hungary, Japan, or (if the Americans' undeclared naval war of 1798–1800 is counted) France. This record was thought to be all the more remarkable in view of the fact that, in ideological terms, Russian and American systems of government could hardly have been more different. Soviet-American friendship would not evolve easily, historian Foster Rhea Dulles noted in the wake of the first meeting between Roosevelt and Stalin in 1943, but the fact that "its roots were so deep in the past, and that it had developed through the years out of common interests transcending all other points of difference, marked the effort toward a new rapprochement as conforming not only to the immediate but also to the long-term interests of the two nations."[29]

The onset of the Cold War made this argument seem less than convincing. To assert that relations between Russia had once been good, students of the subject now suggested, was to confuse harmony with inactivity: given the infrequency of contacts between Russia and the United States in the 19th century, their tradition of "friendship" had been decidedly unremarkable. Once contacts became more frequent, as they had by the beginning of the 20th century, conflicts quickly followed, even before Western statesmen had begun to worry about the impact of the Bolshevism, or the imminence of the international proletarian revolution.[30] But even after this breakdown in cordiality—and regardless of whether that cordiality had been real or imagined—Dulles's point remained valid: there still had been no Russian-American war, despite the fact that Russians and Americans had at one time or another fought virtually every other major power. This raises the question of whether there are not structural elements in the Russian-American relationship itself that contribute to stability, quite apart from the policies actually followed by Russian and American governments.

It has long been an assumption of classical liberalism that the more extensive the contacts that take place between nations, the greater are the chances for peace. Economic interdependence, it has been argued, makes war unlikely because nations who have come to rely upon one another for vital commodities cannot afford it. Cultural exchange, it has been suggested, causes peoples to become more sensitive to each other's concerns, and hence reduces the likelihood of misunderstandings. "People to people" contacts, it has been assumed, make it possible for nations to "know" one another better; the danger of war between them is, as a result, correspondingly reduced.[31]*

These are pleasant things to believe, but there is remarkably little historical evidence to validate them. As Kenneth Waltz has pointed out, "the fiercest civil wars and the bloodiest international ones are fought within arenas populated by highly similar people whose affairs are closely knit."[32] Consider, as examples, the costliest military conflicts of the past century and a half, using the statistics conveniently available now through the University of Michigan "Correlates of War" project: of the ten bloodiest interstate wars, every one of them grew out of conflicts between countries that either directly adjoined one another, or were involved actively in trade with one another.[33] Certainly economic interdependence did little to prevent Germany, France, Britain, Russia, and Austria-Hungary from going to war in 1914; nor did the fact that the United States was Japan's largest trading partner deter that country from attacking Pearl Harbor in 1941. Since 1945, there have been more civil wars than interstate wars;† that fact alone should be sufficient to call into question the proposition that interdependence necessarily breeds peace.

---

* Geoffrey Blainey labels this idea "Manchesterism" and satirizes it wickedly: "If those gifted early prophets of the Manchester creed could have seen Chamberlain—during the Czech crisis of September 1938—board the aircraft that was to fly him to Bavaria to meet Hitler at short notice they would have hailed aviation as the latest messenger of peace. If they had known that he met Hitler without even his own German interpreter they would perhaps have wondered whether the conversation was in Esperanto or Volapuk. It seemed that every postage stamp, bilingual dictionary, railway timetable and trade fair, every peace congress, Olympic race, tourist brochure and international telegram that had ever existed, was gloriously justified when Mr Chamberlain said from the window of number 10 Downing Street on 30 September 1938: 'I believe it is peace for our time.' In retrospect the outbreak of war a year later seems to mark the failure and the end of the policy of appeasement, but the policy survived. The first British air raids over Germany dropped leaflets." [*The Causes of War*, p. 28.]

† The "Correlates of War" project identifies 44 civil wars as having been fought between 1945 and 1980; this compares with 30 interstate and 12 "extra-systemic" wars during the same period. [Melvin Small and J. David Singer, *Resort to Arms: International and Civil Wars, 1816–1980* (Beverly Hills, California: 1982), pp. 92–95, 98–99, 229–32.]

The Russian-American relationship, to a remarkable degree for two nations so extensively involved with the rest of the world, has been one of mutual *in*dependence. The simple fact that they occupy opposite sides of the earth has had something to do with this: geographical remoteness from one another has provided little opportunity for the emergence of irredentist grievances comparable in importance to historic disputes over, say, Alsace-Lorraine, or the Polish Corridor, or the West Bank, the Gaza Strip and Jerusalem. In the few areas where Soviet and American forces—or their proxies—have come into direct contact, they have erected artificial barriers like the Korean demilitarized zone, or the Berlin Wall, perhaps in unconscious recognition of an American poet's rather chilly precept that "good fences make good neighbors."

Nor have the two nations been economically dependent upon one another in any critical way. Certainly the United States requires nothing in the form of imports from the Soviet Union that it cannot obtain elsewhere. The situation is different for the Russians, to be sure, but even though the Soviet Union imports large quantities of food from the United States—and would like to import advanced technology as well—it is far from being wholly dependent upon these items, as the failure of recent attempts to change Soviet behavior by denying them has shown. The relative invulnerability of Russians and Americans to one another in the economic sphere may be frustrating to their respective policy-makers, but it is probably fortunate, from the standpoint of international stability, that the two most powerful nations in the world are also its two most self-sufficient.*

But what about the argument that expanded international communication promotes peace? Is not the failure of Russians and Americans to understand one another better a potential source of instability in their relationship? Obviously it can be if misunderstandings occur at the level of national leadership: the most serious Soviet-American confrontation of the postwar era, the Cuban missile crisis, is generally regarded as having arisen from what appear in retrospect to have been quite remarkable misperceptions of each side's intentions by the other.[34] But "people to people" contacts are another matter. The history of international relations is replete with examples of familiarity breeding contempt as well as friendship: there are too many nations whose people have known each other all too well and have, as a result, taken an intense dislike to one another—French and Germans, Russians and Poles, Japanese and Chinese, Greeks and Turks, Arabs and Israelis—to lend very much credence to the invariably pacifying effects of "people to people" contacts.[35]†

* Soviet exports and imports as a percentage of gross national product ranged between 4 and 7% between 1955 and 1975; for the United States the comparable figures were 7–14%. This compares with figures of 33–52% for Great Britain, France, Germany, and Italy in the four years immediately preceeding World War I, and figures of 19–41% for the same nations plus Japan for the period 1949–76. [Waltz, *Theory of International Politics*, pp. 141, 212.]

† It is worth noting, in this connection, the striking tendency of American diplomats who

Moreover, foreign policy in the United States depends only to a limited extent upon mass perceptions; in the Soviet Union, it depends upon them hardly at all.[36] There is little reason to think that opportunities for travel, academic and cultural exchanges, and even "sister city" contacts have any consistently destabilizing effect on relations between the United States and the Soviet Union; but there is little evidence of their consistently stabilizing effect either.

It may well be, then, that the extent to which the Soviet Union and the United States have been independent of one another rather than interdependent—the fact that there have been so few points of economic leverage available to each, the fact that two such dissimilar people have had so few opportunities for interaction—has in itself constituted a structural support for stability in relations between the two countries, whatever their respective governments have actually done.

# I V

Structure can affect diplomacy from another angle, though: that has to do with the domestic roots of foreign policy. It was Karl Marx who first called attention to the effect of social and economic forces upon political behavior; John A. Hobson and V. I. Lenin subsequently derived from this the proposition that capitalism causes both imperialism and war. Meanwhile, Joseph Schumpeter was working out an alternative theory that placed the origins of international conflict in the "atavistic" insecurities of aristocracies, bureaucracies, and individual leaders.[37] Historians of both Marxist and non-Marxist persuasions have stressed the importance of domestic structural influences in bringing about World War I;[38] and there has been increasing scholarly interest as well in the role of such factors in interwar diplomacy.[39] But to what extent can one argue that domestic structures have shaped the behavior of the Soviet Union and the United States toward each other since 1945? What has been the effect of such influences upon the stability of the post-World War II international system?

The literature on the relationship between domestic structures and diplomacy in the United States is both vast and diffuse: certainly there is no clear consensus on how internal influences determine behavior toward the world at large.[40] There has been, though, a persistent effort to link the structure of the American economy to foreign policy, most conspicuously through the asser-

---

have spent time inside the Soviet Union to become Russophobes. Comparable tendencies seem strikingly absent among China specialists in the Foreign Service. Compare, for the contrast, Hugh DeSantis, *The Diplomacy of Silence: The American Foreign Service, the Soviet Union, and the Cold War, 1933–1947* (Chicago: 1980); and E. J. Kahn, Jr., *The China Hands: America's Foreign Service Officers and What Befell Them* (New York: 1975). Whether Soviet diplomats who serve in the United States develop "Americophobic" tendencies is difficult to say, given currently available information.

tion that capitalism requires an aggressive search for raw materials, markets, and investment opportunities overseas in order to survive. The theory itself pre-dates the Cold War, having been suggested by Charles A. Beard during the 1920's and 1930's, but it was left to William Appleman Williams to work out the most influential characterization of what he called "open door" expansionism in his classic work, *The Tragedy of American Diplomacy*, first published in 1959.[41] More recently—and in a much more sophisticated way—the linkage between domestic economic structure and foreign policy has taken the form of studies demonstrating the effects of "corporatism": the *cooperation* of business, labor, and government to shape a congenial external environment.[42]

Both the "open door" and "corporatist" models have been criticized, with some justification, for their tendency toward reductionism: the explanation of complex phenomena in terms of single causes.[43] But for the purposes of this analysis, these criticisms are beside the point. What is important here is that these most frequently advanced arguments linking the structure of American capitalism with American foreign policy do not assume, from that linkage, the inevitability of war. One of the great advantages of the "open door," Williams has pointed out, was precisely the fact that it *avoided* military confrontations: it was a way to "extend the American system throughout the world without the embarrassment and inefficiency of traditional colonialism"; *"it was conceived and designed to win the victories without the wars."*[44] Similarly, "corporatist" historiography stresses the stabilizing rather than the destabilizing effects of American intervention in Europe after World Wars I and II; here, if anything, attempts to replicate domestic structure overseas are seen as reinforcing rather than undermining existing international systems.[45] Neither the "open door" nor the "corporatist" paradigm, therefore, offers evidence sufficient to confirm the old Leninist assertion that a society committed to capitalism is necessarily precluded from participation in a stable world order.

There have been, of course, Schumpeterian as well as Leninist explanations of how domestic influences affect American foreign policy. C. Wright Mills some three decades ago stressed the interlocking relationship of businessmen, politicians, and military officers whose "power elite" had imposed a form of "naked and arbitrary power" upon the world;[46] subsequent analysts, no doubt encouraged by Dwight D. Eisenhower's perhaps inadvertent endorsement of the term,[47] transformed Mills's argument into a full-blown theory of a "military-industrial complex" whose interests necessarily precluded any significant relaxation of world tensions.[48] There were, to be sure, certain difficulties with this model: it did not plausibly explain the Truman administration's low military budgets of the 1945–50 period, nor did it deal easily with the dramatic shift from defense to welfare expenditures presided over by Richard Nixon during the early 1970's.[49] It neglected evidence that a "military-industrial complex" existed inside the Soviet Union as well.[50] But even if one overlooked these problems, it was not clear how the existence of such a "military-industrial complex" necessarily made war anymore likely, given the opportunities deterrence offered to develop and deploy a profusion of military hardware without the risks war would pose to one's ability to continue doing precisely this.

More recently, attention has been given to the problems created by the structure of American domestic politics in attempting to formulate coherent policies for dealing with the Soviet Union. There is, of course, nothing new about this: the constitutionally mandated division of authority over foreign affairs has always made policy formulation in the United States a less than orderly process. But there is reason to think that the problem is getting worse, partly because of the increasing number of government departments, Congressional committees, and interest groups who have a stake in foreign policy decisions, partly because of an increasingly protracted presidential selection process that has eroded an already imperfect tradition of keeping electoral politics apart from world politics.[51] Even here, though, the effect of such disarray on the long-term Soviet-American relationship has not been as great as might have been expected: what is impressive, when one considers all of the domestically motivated mutations American foreign policy has gone through during the past four decades, is how consistent its fundamental objectives in dealing with the Soviet Union have nonetheless remained.[52]

But what about domestic structural constraints inside the Soviet Union? Here, of course, there is much less hard information with which to work; generalizations, as a result, are not as firmly grounded or as richly developed as they are with regard to the United States. One point seems clear enough, though: in attempting to understand the effect of internal influences on Soviet foreign policy, American analysts have found Schumpeter a more reliable guide than Lenin; they have stressed the extent to which the structural requirements of legitimizing internal political authority have affected behavior toward the outside world. It was George F. Kennan who most convincingly suggested this approach with his portrayals, in 1946 and 1947, of a Soviet leadership at once so insecure and so unimaginative that it felt obliged to cultivate external enemies in order to maintain itself in power. Without at least the image of outside adversaries, he argued, "there would be no justification for that tremendous crushing bureaucracy of party, police and army which now lives off the labor and idealism of [the] Russian people."[53] Whatever the validity of this theory—and however limited Kennan himself considered its application to be*—this characterization of a Kremlin leadership condemned by its own nervous ineptitude to perpetual distrust nonetheless remains the most influential explanation in the West of how domestic structure influences Soviet foreign policy.[54]

But this theory, too, did not assume the inevitability of war. Institutional-

---

* Kennan has emphasized that his recommendations advanced at that time applied only to the Stalin regime. [See his *Memoirs: 1925–1950* (Boston: 1967), pp. 364–67.] But he does still see the role of institutionalized suspicion in Soviet society as making relations with the outside world unnecessarily difficult. [See, for example, George F. Kennan, "Letter to a Russian," *New Yorker*, LX (Septembr 24, 1984), 55–73.]

ized suspicion in the U.S.S.R. resulted from weakness, not strength, Kennan argued; as a consequence, the Kremlin was most unlikely actually to initiate military action.[55] With rare exceptions,* American officials ever since have accepted this distinction between the likelihood of hostility and the probability of war: indeed, the whole theory of deterrence has been based upon the assumption that paranoia and prudence can co-exist.[56] By this logic, then, the domestic structures of the Soviet state, however geared they may have been to picturing the rest of the world in the worst possible light, have not been seen as likely in and of themselves to produce a war.

One should not make too much of these attempts to attribute to domestic constraints the foreign policy of either the United States or the Soviet Union. International relations, like life itself, are a good deal more complicated than these various models would tend to suggest. But it is significant that these efforts to link internal structure to external behavior reveal no obvious proclivity on either side to risk war; that despite their striking differences, Soviet and American domestic structures appear to have posed no greater impediment to the maintenance of a stable international system than has bipolarity itself or the bilateral characteristics of the Soviet-American relationship.

## V

Stability in international systems is only partly a function of structure, though; it depends as well upon the conscious behavior of the nations that make them up. Even if the World War II settlement had corresponded to the distribution of power in the world, even if the Russian-American relationship had been one of minimal interdependence, even if domestic constraints had not created difficulties, stability in the postwar era still might not have resulted if there had been, among either of the dominant powers in the system, the same willingness to risk war that has existed at other times in the past.

Students of the causes of war have pointed out that war is rarely something that develops from the workings of impersonal social or economic forces, or from the direct effects of arms races, or even by accident. It requires deliberate decisions on the part of national leaders; more than that, it requires calculations that the gains to be derived from war will outweigh the possible costs. "Recurring optimism," Geoffrey Blainey has written, "is a vital prelude to war. Anything which increases that optimism is a cause of war. Anything which dampens that optimism is a cause of peace."[57] Admittedly,

---

* The most conspicuous exception would appear to be the authors of NSC-68, the comprehensive reassessment of national security policy drafted early in 1950, who argued that when Soviet *capabilities* reached the point of being able to win a war, Soviet *intentions* would automatically be to provoke one. [See NSC 68, "United States Objectives and Programs for National Security," April 14, 1950, U.S. Department of State, *Foreign Relations of the United States* [hereafter *FR*]: *1950*, I, especially pp. 251–52, 266–67.]

those calculations are often in error: as Kennan, in his capacity as a historian, has pointed out, whatever conceivable gains the statesmen of 1914 might have had in mind in risking war, they could not have come anywhere close to approximating the costs the ensuing four-year struggle would actually entail.[58] But it seems hard to deny that it is from such calculations, whether accurately carried out, as Bismarck seemed able to do in his wars against Denmark, Austria, and France in the mid-19th century, or inaccurately carried out, as was the case in 1914, that wars tend to develop. They are not something that just happens, like earthquakes, locust plagues, or (some might argue) the selection of presidential candidates in the United States.

For whatever reason, it has to be acknowledged that statesmen of the post-1945 super-powers have, compared to their precedessors, been exceedingly cautious in risking war with one another.[59] In order to see this point, one need only run down the list of crises in Soviet-American relations since the end of World War II: Iran, 1946; Greece, 1947; Berlin and Czechoslovakia, 1948; Korea, 1950; the East Berlin riots, 1953; the Hungarian uprising, 1956; Berlin again, 1958–59; the U-2 incident, 1960; Berlin again, 1961; the Cuban missile crisis, 1962; Czechoslovakia again, 1968; the Yom Kippur war, 1973; Afghanistan, 1979; Poland, 1981; the Korean airliner incident, 1983—one need only run down this list to see how many occasions there have been in relations between Washington and Moscow that in almost any other age, and among almost any other antagonists, would sooner or later have produced war.

That they have not cannot be chalked up to the invariably pacific temperament of the nations involved: the United States participated in eight international wars involving a thousand or more battlefield deaths between 1815 and 1980; Russia participated in nineteen.[60] Nor can this restraint be attributed to any unusual qualities of leadership on either side: the vision and competency of postwar Soviet and American statesmen does not appear to have differed greatly from that of their precedessors. Nor does weariness growing out of participation in two world wars fully explain this unwillingness to resort to arms in their dealings with one another: during the postwar era both nations have employed force against third parties—in the case of the United States in Korea and Vietnam; in the case of the Soviet Union in Afghanistan—for protracted periods of time, and at great cost.

It seems inescapable that what has really made the difference in inducing this unaccustomed caution has been the workings of the nuclear deterrent.[61]*

---

* It is interesting to speculate as to whether Soviet-American bipolarity would have developed if nuclear weapons had never been invented. My own view—obviously unverifiable—is that it would have, because bipolarity resulted from the way in which World War II had been fought; the condition was already evident at the time of Hiroshima and Nagasaki. Whether bipolarity would have lasted as long as it has in the absence of nuclear weapons is another matter entirely, though: it seems at least plausible that these weapons have perpetuated bipolarity beyond what one might have expected its normal lifetime to be by minimizing super-power risk-taking while at the same time maintaining an apparently insurmountable power gradient between the super-powers and any potential military rivals.

Consider, for a moment, what the effect of this mechanism would be on a statesman from either super-power who might be contemplating war. In the past, the horrors and costs of wars could be forgotten with the passage of time. Generations like the one of 1914 had little sense of what the Napoleonic Wars—or even the American Civil War—had revealed about the brutality, expense, and duration of military conflict. But the existence of nuclear weapons—and, more to the point, the fact that we have direct evidence of what they can do when used against human beings[62]—has given this generation a painfully vivid awareness of the realities of war that no previous generation has had. It is difficult, given this awareness, to generate the optimism that historical experience tells us prepares the way for war; pessimism, it appears, is a permanent accompaniment to our thinking about war, and that, as Blainey reminds us, is a cause of peace.

That same pessimism has provided the super-powers with powerful inducements to control crises resulting from the risk-taking of third parties. It is worth recalling that World War I grew out of the unsuccessful management of a situation neither created nor desired by any of the major actors in the international system. There were simply no mechanisms to put a lid on escalation: to force each nation to balance the short-term temptation to exploit opportunities against the long-term danger that things might get out of hand.[63] The nuclear deterrent provides that mechanism today, and as a result the United States and the Soviet Union have successfully managed a whole series of crises—most notably in the Middle East—that grew out of the actions of neither but that could have involved them both.

None of this is to say, of course, that war cannot occur: if the study of history reveals anything at all it is that one ought to expect, sooner or later, the unexpected. Nor is it to say that the nuclear deterrent could not function equally well with half, or a fourth, or even an eighth of the nuclear weapons now in the arsenals of the super-powers. Nor is it intended to deprecate the importance of refraining from steps that might destabilize the existing stalemate, whether through the search for technological breakthroughs that might provide a decisive edge over the other side, or through so mechanical a duplication of what the other side has that one fails to take into account one's own probably quite different security requirements, or through strategies that rely upon the first use of nuclear weapons in the interest of achieving economy, forgetting the far more fundamental systemic interest in maintaining the tradition, dating back four decades now, of never actually employing these weapons for military purposes.

I am suggesting, though, that the development of nuclear weapons has had, on balance, a stabilizing effect on the postwar international system. They have served to discourage the process of escalation that has, in other eras, too casually led to war. They have had a sobering effect upon a whole range of statesmen of varying degrees of responsibility and capability. They have forced national leaders, every day, to confront the reality of what war is really like, indeed to confront the prospect of their own mortality, and that, for those who seek ways to avoid war, is no bad thing.

# VI

But although nuclear deterrence is the most important behavioral mechanism that has sustained the post-World War II international system, it is by no means the only one. Indeed, the very technology that has made it possible to deliver nuclear weapons anywhere on the face of the earth has functioned also to lower greatly the danger of surprise attack, thereby supplementing the self-regulating features of deterrence with the assurance that comes from knowing a great deal more than in the past about adversary capabilities. I refer here to what might be called the "reconnaissance revolution," a development that may well rival in importance the "nuclear revolution" that preceded it, but one that rarely gets the attention it deserves.

The point was made earlier that nations tend to start wars on the basis of calculated assessments that they have the power to prevail. But it was suggested as well that they have often been wrong about this: they either have failed to anticipate the nature and the costs of war itself, or they have misjudged the intentions and capabilities of the adversary they have chosen to confront.[64]* Certainly the latter is what happened to Napoleon III in choosing to risk war with Prussia in 1870, to the Russians in provoking the Japanese in 1904, to the Germans in World War I when they brought about American entry by resuming unrestricted submarine warfare, to the Japanese in World War II by attacking Pearl Harbor, to Adolf Hitler in that same conflict when he managed within six months to declare war on *both* the Soviet Union and the United States, and, most recently, to General Galtieri and the Argentine junta in deciding to take on Mrs. Thatcher.

Now, it would be foolish to argue that Americans and Russians have become anymore skillful than they ever were at discerning the other's *intentions:* clearly the United States invasion of Grenada surprised Moscow as much as the Soviet invasion of Afghanistan surprised Washington. The capacity of each nation to behave in ways that seem perfectly logical to it but quite unfathomable to the other remains about what it has been throughout the entire Cold War. But both sides are able—and indeed have been able for at least two decades—to evaluate each other's *capabilities* to a degree that is totally unprecedented in the history of relations between great powers.

What has made this possible, of course, has been the development of the reconnaissance satellite, a device that if rumors are correct allows the reading of automobile license plates or newspaper headlines from a hundred or more miles out in space, together with the equally important custom that has evolved among the super-powers of allowing these objects to pass unhindered over their territories.[65] The effect has been to give each side a far more ac-

* Geoffrey Blainey, citing an idea first proposed by the sociologist Georg Simmel, has suggested that in the past war was the only means by which nations could gain an exact knowledge of each other's capabilities. [Blainey, *The Causes of War*, p. 118.]

curate view of the other's military capabilities—and, to some degree, economic capabilities as well—than could have been provided by an entire phalanx of the best spies in the long history of espionage. The resulting intelligence does not rule out altogether the possibility of surprise attack, but it does render it far less likely, at least as far as the super-powers are concerned. And that is no small matter, if one considers the number of wars in history—from the Trojan War down through Pearl Harbor—in the origins of which deception played a major role.[66]

The "reconnaissance revolution" also corrects, at least to an extent, the asymmetry imposed upon Soviet-American relations by the two countries' sharply different forms of political and social organization. Throughout most of the early Cold War years the Soviet Union enjoyed all the advantages of a closed society in concealing its capabilities from the West; the United States and its allies, in turn, found it difficult to keep anything secret for very long.[67] That problem still exists, but the ability now to see both visually and electronically into almost every part of the Soviet Union helps to compensate for it. And, of course, virtually none of the limited progress the two countries have made in the field of arms control would have been possible had Americans and Russians not tacitly agreed to the use of reconnaissance satellites and other surveillance techniques to monitor compliance;[68] clearly any future progress in that field will depend heavily upon these devices as well.

There is no little irony in the fact that these instruments, which have contributed so significantly toward stabilizing the postwar international system, grew directly out of research on the intercontinental ballistic missile and the U-2 spy plane.[69] Technological innovation is not always a destabilizing force in the Soviet-American relationship. There have been—as in this case—and there could be again instances in which the advance of technology, far from increasing the danger of war, could actually lessen it. It all depends upon the uses to which the technology is put, and that, admittedly, is not an easy thing to foresee.

# VII

If technology has had the potential either to stabilize or destabilize the international system, the same cannot as easily be said of ideology. One cannot help but be impressed, when one looks at the long history of national liberation movements, or revolutions against established social orders, or racial and religious conflict, by the continuing capacity of ideas to move nations, or groups within nations, to fight one another.[70] It is only by reference to a violent and ultimately self-destructive ideological impulse that one can account for the remarkable career of Adolf Hitler, with all of its chaotic consequences for the post-World War I international system.[71] Since 1945, the ideology of self-determination has not only induced colonies to embroil colonial masters in protracted and costly warfare; it has also led factions within newly independent states forcibly to seek their own separate political existence.* Ideologically motivated social revolution, too, has been a prominent feature of the postwar international scene, what with major upheavals in nations as diverse as China, Cuba, Vietnam, Cambodia, and Nicaragua. But the most surprising evidence of the continuing influence of ideology has come in the area of religion, where conflicts between Hindus and Muslims, Arabs and Israelis, Iranians and Iraqis, and even Catholics and Protestants in Northern Ireland provide little reason to think that ideas—even ideas once considered to have little relevance other than for historians—will not continue to have a major disruptive potential for international order.[72]

The relationship between the Soviet Union and the United States has not been free from ideological rivalries; it could be argued, in fact, that these are among the most ideological nations on the face of the earth.[73] Certainly their respective ideologies could hardly have been more antithetical, given the self-proclaimed intention of one to overthrow the other.[74] And yet, since their emergence as super-powers, both nations have demonstrated an impressive capacity to subordinate antagonistic ideological interests to a common goal of preserving international order. The reasons for this are worth examining.

If there were ever a moment at which the priorities of order overcame those of ideology, it would appear to be the point at which Soviet leaders decided that war would no longer advance the cause of revolution. That clearly had not been Lenin's position: international conflict, for him, was good or evil according to whether it accelerated or retarded the demise of capitalism.[75]† Stalin's attitude on this issue was more ambivalent: he encouraged talk of an "inevitable conflict" between the "two camps" of communism and capitalism in the years immediately following World War II, but he also appears shortly before his death to have anticipated the concept of "peaceful coexistence."[76]‡ It was left to Georgii Malenkov to admit pub-

---

* One thinks, in this connection, of the successful struggles of the Vietnamese and the Algerians against the French and of Portugal's African colonies against that country, but also of equally successful separatist movements within India and later Pakistan, and of the unsuccessful Biafran rebellion against Nigeria.

† It is fashionable now among Soviet scholars, as was noted in Chapter One, to minimize the ideological component of Moscow's foreign policy; indeed Lenin himself is now seen as the original architect of "peaceful coexistence," a leader for whom the idea of exporting revolution can hardly have been more alien. A representative example is G. A. Trofimenko, "Uroki mirnogo sosushestvovaniia," *Voprosy istorii*, Number 11(November, 1983), pp. 6–7. It seems not out of place to wonder how the great revolutionary would have received such perfunctory dismissals of the Comintern and all that it implied; certainly most Western students have treated more seriously than this the revolutionary implications of the Bolshevik Revolution. [See, for example, Seweryn Bialer, *The Soviet Paradox: External Expansion, Internal Decline* (New York: 1986), pp. 177–80.]

‡ It is possible, of course, that Stalin followed both policies intentionally as a means both of intimidating and inducing complacency in the West.

licly, shortly after Stalin's death, that a nuclear war would mean "the destruction of world civilization"; Nikita Khrushchev subsequently refined this idea (which he had initially condemned) into the proposition that the interests of world revolution, as well as those of the Soviet state, would be better served by working within the existing international order than by trying to overthrow it.[77]

The reasons for this shift of position are not difficult to surmise. First, bipolarity—the defining characteristic of the postwar international system—implied unquestioned recognition of the Soviet Union as a great power. It was "no small thing," Khrushchev later acknowledged in his memoirs, "that we have lived to see the day when the Soviet Union is considered, in terms of its economic and military might, one of the two most powerful countries in the world."[78] Second, the international situation in the 1950's and early 1960's seemed favorable, especially because of the decline of colonialism and the rise of newly independent nations likely to be suspicious of the West, to the expansion of Soviet influence in the world.[79] But third, and most important, the proliferation of nuclear capabilities on both sides had confirmed Malenkov's conclusion that in any future war between the great powers there would be no victors at all, whether capitalist or communist. "[T]he atomic bomb," Soviet leaders reminded their more militant Chinese comrades in 1963, "does not observe the class principle."[80]

The effect was to transform a state which, if ideology alone had governed, should have sought a complete restructuring of the existing international system, into one for whom that system now seemed to have definite benefits, within which it now sought to function, and for whom the goal of overthrowing capitalism had been postponed to some vague and indefinite point in the future.* Without this moderation of ideological objectives, it is difficult to see how the stability that has characterized great power relations since the end of World War II could have been possible.

Ideological considerations have traditionally played a less prominent role in shaping American foreign policy, but they have had their influence nonetheless. Certainly the Wilsonian commitment to self-determination, revived and ardently embraced during World War II, did a great deal to alienate Americans from their Soviet allies at the end of that conflict. Nor had their military exertions moderated Americans' long-standing aversion to collectivism—of which the Soviet variety of communism appeared to be the most

---

* "[P]layers' goals may undergo very little change, but postponing their attainment to the indefinite future fundamentally transforms the meaning of . . . myth by revising its implications for social action. Exactly because myths are dramatic stories, changing their time-frame affects their character profoundly. Those who see only the permanence of professed goals, but who neglect structural changes—the incorporation of common experiences into the myths of both sides, shifts in the image of the opponent ('there are reasonable people also in the other camp'), and modifications in the myths' periodization—overlook the great effects that may result from such contextual changes." [Friedrich V. Kratochwil, *International Order and Foreign Policy: A Theoretical Sketch of Post-War International Politics* (Boulder, Colorado: 1978), p. 117.]

extreme example.[81] But there had also developed, during the war, an emphatic hostility toward "totalitarianism" in general: governments that relied upon force to sustain themselves in power, it was thought, could hardly be counted on to refrain from the use of force in the world at large. Demands for the "unconditional surrender" of Germany and Japan reflected this ideological position: there could be no compromise with regimes for whom arbitrary rule was a way of life.[82]

What is interesting is that although the "totalitarian" model came as easily to be applied to the Soviet Union as it had been to Germany and Japan,[83] the absolutist call for "unconditional surrender" was not. To be sure, the United States and the U.S.S.R. were not at war. But levels of tension were about as high as they can get short of war during the late 1940's, and we now know that planning for the *contingency* of war was well under way in Washington—as it presumably was in Moscow as well.[84] Nevertheless, the first of these plans to be approved by President Truman, late in 1948, bluntly stated that, if war came, there would be no "predetermined requirement for unconditional surrender."[85]* NSC-68 a comprehensive review of national security policy undertaken two years later, elaborated on the point: "our over-all objectives . . . do not include unconditional surrender, the subjugation of the Russian peoples or a Russia shorn of its economic potential." The ultimate goal, rather, was to convince the Soviet government of the impossibility of achieving its self-proclaimed ideological objectives; the immediate goal was to "induce the Soviet Union to accommodate itself, with or without the conscious abandonment of its [ideological] design, to coexistence on tolerable terms with the non-Soviet world."[86]

It is no easy matter to explain why Americans did not commit themselves to the eradication of Soviet "totalitarianism" with the same single-minded determination they had earlier applied to German and Japanese "totalitarianism." One reason, of course, would have been the daunting prospect of attempting to occupy a country the size of the Soviet Union, when compared with the more manageable adversaries of World War II.[87] Another was the fact that, despite the hostility that had developed since 1945, American officials did not regard their Russian counterparts as irredeemable: the very purpose of "containment" had been to change the *psychology* of the Soviet leadership; but not as had been the case with Germany and Japan, the leadership itself.[88]

---

* In an earlier version of this document, Kennan had explained that "we could not hope to achieve any total assertion of our will on Russian territory, as we have endeavored to do in Germany and Japan. We must recognize that whatever settlement we finally achieve must be a *political* settlement, *politically* negotiated." [NSC 20/1, "U.S. Objectives with Respect to Russia," August 18, 1948, in Thomas H. Etzold and John Lewis Gaddis, eds., *Containment: Documents on American Policy and Strategy, 1945–1950* (New York: 1978), p. 193.] George H. Quester has made the point that "containment" itself reflected, by its very nature, a repudiation of "unconditional surrender." ["The Impact of the Strategic Balances on Containment," in Terry L. Deibel and John Lewis Gaddis, eds., *Containment: Concept and Policy* (Washington: 1986), pp. 259–60.]

But Washington's aversion to an "unconditional surrender" doctrine for the Soviet Union stemmed from yet another less obvious consideration: it had quickly become clear to American policy-makers, after World War II, that insistence on the total defeat of Germany and Japan had profoundly destabilized the postwar balance of power. Only by assuming responsibility for the rehabilitation of these former enemies as well as the countries they had ravaged had the United States been able to restore equilibrium, and even then it had been clear that the American role in this regard would have to be a continuing one. It was no accident that the doctrine of "unconditional surrender" came under severe criticism, after 1945, from a new school of "realist" geopoliticians given to viewing international stability in terms of the wary toleration of adversaries rather than, as a point of principle, their annihilation.[89]

Largely as a result of such reasoning, American officials at no point during the history of the Cold War seriously contemplated, as a deliberate political objective, the elimination of the Soviet Union as a major force in world affairs. By the mid-1950's, it is true, war plans had been devised that, if executed, would have quite indiscriminately annihilated not only the Soviet Union but several of its communist and non-communist neighbors as well.[90] What is significant about those plans, though, is that they reflected the organizational convenience of the military services charged with implementing them, not any conscious policy decisions at the top. Both Eisenhower and Kennedy were appalled on learning of them; both considered them ecologically as well as strategically impossible; and during the Kennedy administration steps were initiated to devise strategies that would leave open the possibility of a surviving political entity in Russia even in the extremity of nuclear war.[91]

All of this would appear to confirm, then, the proposition that systemic interests tend to take precedence over ideological interests.[92] Both the Soviet ideological aversion to capitalism and the American ideological aversion to totalitarianism could have produced policies—and indeed had produced policies in the past—aimed at the complete overthrow of their respective adversaries. That such ideological impulses could be muted to the extent they have been during the past four decades testifies to the stake both Washington and Moscow have developed in preserving the existing international system: the moderation of ideologies must be considered, then, along with nuclear deterrence and reconnaissance, as a major self-regulating mechanism of postwar politics.

# VIII

The question still arises, though: how can order emerge from a system that functions without any superior authority? Even self-regulating mechanisms like automatic pilots or engine governors cannot operate without someone to set them in motion; the prevention of anarchy, it has generally been assumed, requires hierarchy, both at the level of interpersonal and international relations. Certainly the statesmen of World War II expected that some supranational structure would be necessary to sustain a future peace, whether in the form of a new collective security organization to replace the ineffectual League of Nations, or through perpetuation of the great-power consensus that Churchill, Roosevelt, and Stalin sought to forge.[93] All of them would have been surprised by the extent to which order has been maintained since 1945 in the absence of any effective supra-national authority of any kind.*

This experience has forced students of international politics to recognize that their subject bears less resemblance to local, state, or national politics, where order does in fact depend upon legally constituted authority, than it does to the conduct of games, where order evolves from mutual agreement on a set of "rules" defining the range of behavior each side anticipates from the other. The assumption is that the particular "game" being played promises sufficient advantages to each of its "players" to outweigh whatever might be obtained by trying to upset it; in this way, rivalries can be pursued within an orderly framework, even in the absence of a referee. Game theory therefore helps to account for the paradox of order in the absence of hierarchy that characterizes the postwar super-power relationship; through it one can get a sense of how "rules" establish limits of acceptable behavior on the part of nations who acknowledge only themselves as the arbiters of behavior.[94]

These "rules" are, of course, implicit rather than explicit: they grow out of a mixture of custom, precedent, and mutual interest that takes shape quite apart from the realm of public rhetoric, diplomacy, or international law. They require the passage of time to become effective; they depend, for that effectiveness, upon the extent to which successive generations of national leadership on each side find them useful. They certainly do not reflect any agreed-upon standard of international morality: indeed they often violate principles of "justice" adhered to by one side or the other. But these "rules" have played an important role in maintaining the international system that has been in place these past four decades: without them the correlation one would normally anticipate between hostility and instability would have become more exact than it has in fact been since 1945.

No two observers of super-power behavior would express these "rules" in precisely the same way; indeed it may well be that their very vagueness has made them more acceptable than they otherwise might have been to the nations that have followed them. What follows is nothing more than my own list, derived from an attempt to identify *regularities* in the postwar Soviet-American relationship whose pattern neither side could now easily disrupt.

---

* The United Nations, regretfully, cannot be considered an effective supra-national authority.

(1) *Respect spheres of influence.* Neither Russians nor Americans officially admit to having such "spheres," but in fact much of the history of the Cold War can be written in terms of the efforts both have made to consolidate and extend them. One should not, in acknowledging this, fall into so mechanical a comparison of the two spheres as to ignore their obvious differences: the American sphere has been wider in geographical scope than its Soviet counterpart, but it has also been a much looser alignment, participation in which has more often than not been a matter of choice rather than coercion.[95] But what is important from the standpoint of super-power "rules" is the fact that, although neither side has ever publicly endorsed the other's right to a sphere of influence, neither has ever directly challenged it either.*

Thus, despite publicly condemning it, the United States never attempted seriously to undo Soviet control in Eastern Europe; Moscow reciprocated by tolerating, though never openly approving of, Washington's influence in Western Europe, the Mediterranean, the Near East, and Latin America. A similar pattern held up in East Asia, where the Soviet Union took no more action to oppose United States control over occupied Japan than the Truman administration did to repudiate the Yalta agreement, which left the Soviet Union dominant, at least for the moment, on the Northeast Asian mainland.[96]

Where the relation of particular areas to spheres of influence had been left unclear—as had been the case with the Western-occupied zones of Berlin prior to 1948, or with South Korea prior to 1950—or where the resolve of one side to maintain its sphere appeared to have weakened—as in the case of Cuba following the failure of the Bay of Pigs invasion in 1961—attempts by the other to exploit the situation could not be ruled out: the Berlin blockade, the invasion of South Korea, and the decision to place Soviet missiles in Cuba can all be understood in this way.[97] But it appears also to have been understood, in each case, that the resulting probes would be conducted cautiously, and that they would not be pursued to the point of risking war if resistance was encountered.[98]

Defections from one sphere would be exploited by the other only when it was clear that the first either could not or would not reassert control. Hence, the United States took advantage of departures from the Soviet bloc of Yugoslavia and—ultimately—the People's Republic of China; it did not seek to do so in the case of Hungary in 1956, Czechoslovakia in 1968, or (in what was admittedly a more ambiguous situation) Poland in 1981. Similarly, the Soviet Union exploited the defection of Cuba after 1959, but made no attempt to contest the reassertion of American influence in Iran in 1953, Guatemala in 1954, the Dominican Republic in 1965, or Grenada in 1983.[99]

(2) *Avoid direct military confrontation.* It is remarkable, in retrospect,

---

* "In general terms, acquiescence in spheres of influence has taken the form of A disclaiming what B does and in fact disapproving of what B does, but at the same time acquiescing by virtue of effectively doing nothing to oppose B." [Paul Keal, *Unspoken Rules and Superpower Dominance* (New York: 1983), p. 115.]

that at no point during the long history of the Cold War have Soviet and American military forces engaged each other directly in sustained hostilities. The super-powers have fought three major limited wars since 1945, but in no case with each other: the possibility of direct Soviet-American military involvement was greatest—although it never happened—during the Korean War; it was much more remote in Vietnam and has remained so in Afghanistan as well. In those few situations where Soviet and American military units have confronted one another directly—the 1948 Berlin blockade, the construction of the Berlin Wall in 1961, and the Cuban missile crisis the following year—great care was taken on both sides to avoid incidents that might have triggered hostilities.[100]

Where the super-powers have sought to expand or to retain areas of control, they have tended to resort to the use of proxies or other indirect means to accomplish this: examples would include the Soviet Union's decision to sanction a North Korean invasion of South Korea,* and its more recent reliance on Cuban troops to promote its interests in sub-Saharan Africa; on the American side covert intervention has been a convenient (if not invariably successful) means of defending spheres of influence.† In a curious way, clients and proxies have come to serve as buffers, allowing Russians and Americans to pursue their competition behind a façade of "deniability" that minimizes the risks of open—and presumably less manageable—confrontation.

The two super-powers have also been careful not to allow the disputes of third parties to embroil them directly: this pattern has been most evident in the Middle East, which has witnessed no fewer than five wars between Israel and its Arab neighbors since 1948; but it holds as well for the India-Pakistan conflicts of 1965 and 1971, and for the more recent—and much more protracted—struggle between Iran and Iraq. The contrast between this long tradition of restraint and the casualness with which great powers in the past have allowed the quarrels of others to become their own could hardly be more obvious.[101]

(3) *Use nuclear weapons only as an ultimate resort.* One of the most significant—though least often commented upon—of the super-power "rules" has been the tradition that has evolved, since 1945, of maintaining a sharp distinction between conventional and nuclear weapons, and of reserving the military use of the latter only for the extremity of total war. In retrospect, there was nothing at all inevitable about this: the Eisenhower administra-

---

* This analysis assumes, as do most scholarly examinations of the subject, that the North Korean attack could not have taken place without some form of Soviet authorization. The most thorough assessment of this admittedly unclear episode is Robert R. Simmons, *The Strained Alliance: Peking, Pyongyang, Moscow and the Politics of the Korean Civil War* (New York: 1975).

† Which is not to say that the Soviet Union does not engage in covert operations as well; it is, however, somewhat more successful at concealing them. The best recent overview is John Barron, *KGB Today: The Hidden Hand* (New York: 1983).

tion announced quite publicly its willingness to use nuclear weapons in limited war situations;[102] Henry Kissinger's *Nuclear Weapons and Foreign Policy* strongly endorsed such use in 1957 as a way to keep alliance commitments credible;[103*] and Soviet strategists have traditionally insisted as well that in war both nuclear and conventional means would be employed.[104] It is remarkable, given this history, that the world has not seen a single nuclear weapon used in anger since the destruction of Nagasaki more than four decades ago. Rarely has *practice* of nations so conspicuously departed from proclaimed *doctrine;* rarely, as well, has so great a disparity attracted so little public notice.

This pattern of caution in the use of nuclear weapons did not develop solely, as one might have expected, from the prospect of retaliation. As early as 1950, at a time when the Soviet Union had only just tested an atomic bomb and had only the most problematic methods of delivering it, the United States had nonetheless ruled out the use of its own atomic weapons in Korea because of the opposition of its allies, the fear of an adverse reaction in the world at large, and uncertainty as to whether they would produce the desired military effect. And despite his public position favoring such use, Eisenhower would repeatedly, in the years that followed, reject recommendations to resort to them in limited war situations.[105]

It was precisely this sense that nuclear weapons were qualitatively different from other weapons[106] that most effectively deterred their employment by the United States during the first decade of the Cold War, a period in which the tradition of "non-use" had not yet taken hold, within which ample opportunities for their use existed, and during which the possibility of Soviet retaliation could not have been great. The idea of a discrete "threshold" between nuclear and conventional weapons, therefore, may owe more to the moral—and public relations—sensibilities of Washington officials than to any actual fear of escalation. By the time a credible Soviet retaliatory capability was in place, at the end of the 1950s, the "threshold" concept was equally firmly fixed: one simply did not cross it short of all-out war.† Subsequent limited war situations—notably Vietnam for the Americans, and more recently Afghanistan for the Russians—have confirmed the continued effectiveness of this unstated but important "rule" of super-power behavior, as have the quiet but persistent efforts both Washington and Moscow have made to keep nuclear weapons from falling into the hands of others who might not abide by it.[107]

---

* It should be added, in fairness, that Kissinger by 1961 had repudiated his earlier position on this point. See his *The Necessity for Choice: Prospects of American Foreign Policy* (New York: 1961).

† It is interesting to note that John F. Kennedy began his administration with what appeared to be a pledge never to initiate the use of nuclear weapons against the Soviet Union; after protests from NATO allies, though, this was modified into a promise not to initiate hostilities only. See Michael Mandelbaum, *The Nuclear Question: The United States and Nuclear Weapons, 1946–1976* (Cambridge: 1979), p. 75.

(4) *Prefer predictable anomaly over unpredictable rationality.* One of the most curious features of the Cold War has been the extent to which the super-powers—and their respective clients, who have had little choice in the matter—have tolerated a whole series of awkward, artificial, and, on the surface at least, unstable regional arrangements: the division of Germany is, of course, the most obvious example; others would include the Berlin Wall, the position of West Berlin itself within East Germany, the arbitrary and ritualized partition of the Korean peninsula, the existence of an avowed Soviet satellite some ninety miles off the coast of Florida, and, not least, the continued functioning of an important American naval base within it. There is to all of these arrangements an appearance of wildly illogical improvisation: none of them could conceivably have resulted, it seems, from any rational and premeditated design.

And yet, at another level, they have had a kind of logic after all: the fact that these jerry-built but rigidly maintained arrangements have lasted for so long suggests an unwillingness on the part of the super-powers to trade familiarity for unpredictability. To try to rationalize the German, Korean, or Cuban anomalies would, it has long been acknowledged, create the unnerving possibility of an uncertain result; far better, Soviet and American leaders have consistently agreed, to perpetuate the anomalies rather than to risk the possibilities for destabilization inherent in trying to resolve them. For however unnatural and unjust these situations may be for the people whose lives they directly affect, it seems nonetheless incontestable that the super-powers' preference for predictability over rationality has, on the whole, enhanced more than it has reduced prospects for a stable relationship.

(5) *Do not seek to undermine the other side's leadership.* The death of Stalin, in March, 1953, set off a flurry of proposals within the United States government for exploiting vulnerabilities inside the Soviet Union that were thought certain to result, and yet, by the following month President Eisenhower was encouraging Stalin's successors to join in a major new effort to control the arms race and reduce the danger of war.[108] The dilemma here was one that was to recur throughout the Cold War: if what one wanted was stability at the international level, did it make sense to try to destabilize the other side's leadership at the national level?

The answer, it appears, has been no. There have been repeated leadership crises in both the United States and the Soviet Union since Stalin's death: one thinks especially of the decline and ultimate deposition of Khrushchev following the Cuban Missile Crisis, of the Johnson administration's all-consuming fixation with Vietnam, or the collapse of Nixon's authority as a result of Watergate, and of the recent paralysis in the Kremlin brought about by the illness and death of three Soviet leaders within less than three years. And yet, in none of these instances can one discern a concerted effort by the unaffected side to exploit the other's vulnerability; indeed there appears to have existed in several of these situations a sense of frustration, even regret, over the difficulties its rival was undergoing.[109] From the standpoint of game theory, a "rule" that acknowledges legitimacy of leadership on both sides is hardly surprising: there have to be players in order for the game to proceed. But when compared with other historical—and indeed other current—situations in which that reciprocal tolerance has not existed,* its importance as a stabilizing mechanism becomes clear.

Stability, in great power relationships, is not the same thing as politeness. It is worth noting that, despite levels of hostile rhetoric unmatched on both sides since the earliest days of the Cold War, the Soviet Union and the United States have managed to get through the early 1980's without a single significant military confrontation of any kind. Contrast this with the record of Soviet-American relations in the 1970's: an era of far greater politeness in terms of what the two nations *said* about one another, but one marred by potentially dangerous crises over Soviet submarine bases and combat brigades in Cuba, American bombing and mining activities in Vietnam, and a pattern of Soviet interventionism in Angola, Somalia, Ethiopia, South Yemen, and Afghanistan. There was even a major American nuclear alert during the Yom Kippur War in 1973—the only one since the Cuban missile crisis—ironically enough, this occurred at the height of what is now wistfully remembered as the era of "détente."[110]

What stability does require is a sense of caution, maturity, and responsibility on both sides. It requires the ability to distinguish posturing—something in which all political leaders indulge—from provocation, which is something else again. It requires recognition of the fact that competition is a normal rather than an abnormal state of affairs in relations between nations, much as it is in relations between major corporations, but that this need not preclude the identification of certain common—or corporate, or universal—interests as well. It requires, above all, a sense of the relative rather than the absolute nature of security: that one's own security depends not only upon the measures one takes in one's own defense, but also upon the extent to which these create a sense of insecurity in the mind of one's adversary.

It would be foolish to suggest that the Soviet-American relationship today meets all of these prerequisites: the last one especially deserves a good deal more attention than it has heretofore received, on both sides. But to the extent that the relationship has taken on a new maturity—and to see that it has one need only compare the current mood of wary optimism with the almost total lack of communication that existed at the time of the Korean War, or the extreme swings between alarm and amiability that characterized relations in the late 1950's and early 1960's, or the inflated expectations and resulting disillusionments of the 1970's—that maturity would appear to reflect an increasing commitment on the part of both great nations involved to a "game" played "by the rules."

---

* I have in mind here the long history of dynastic struggles in Europe up through the wars of the French Revolution; also, and much more recently, the way in which a refusal to acknowledge leadership legitimacy has perpetuated the Iran-Iraq war.

# I X

History, as anyone who has spent any time at all studying it would surely know, has a habit of making bad prophets out of both those who make and those who chronicle it. It tends to take the expectations of statesmen and turn them upside down; it is not at all tolerant of those who would seek too self-confidently to anticipate its future course. One should be exceedingly wary, therefore, of predicting how long the current era of Soviet-American stability will last. Certainly it is easy to conceive of things that might in one way or another undermine it: domestic developments in either country could affect foreign policy in unpredictable ways; the actions of third parties could embroil the super-powers in conflict with each other against their will; opportunities for miscalculation and accident are always present; incompetent leadership is always a risk. All that one can—or should—say is that the relationship has survived these kinds of disruptions in the past: if history made bad prophets out of the warmakers of 1914 and 1939–41, or the peacemakers of 1919, all of whom approached their tasks with a degree of optimism that seems to us foolish in retrospect, then so too has it made bad prophets out of the peacemakers of 1945, who had so little optimism about the future.

Whether the Soviet-American relationship could survive something more serious is another matter entirely. We know the answer when it comes to nuclear war; recent scientific findings have only confirmed visions of catastrophe we have lived with for decades.[111] But what about a substantial decline in the over-all influence of either great power that did not immediately result in war? Here, it seems to me, is a more probable—if less often discussed—danger. For if history demonstrates anything at all, it is that the condition of being a great power is a transitory one: sooner or later, the effects of exhaustion, overextension, and lack of imagination take their toll among nations, just as surely as does old age itself among individuals. Nor is it often that history arranges for great powers to decline simultaneously and symmetrically. Past experience also suggests that the point at which a great power perceives its decline to be beginning is a perilous one: behavior can become erratic, even desperate, well before physical strength itself has dissipated.[112]*

The Soviet-American relationship has yet to face the test, although there is no reason to think it will escape it indefinitely. When that time comes, the preservation of stability may require something new in international relations: the realization that great nations can have a stake, not just in the survival, but also the success and prosperity of their rivals. International sys-

* Paul M. Kennedy has pointed to the significance of the perception among Germans, after 1900, that British influence in the world was increasing, while their own was not. [*The Rise of the Anglo-German Antagonism, 1860–1914* (Boston: 1980), p. 313.]

tems, like tangoes, require at least two reasonably active and healthy participants; it is always wise, before allowing the dance to end, to consider with what, or with whom, one will replace it.

The Cold War, with all of its rivalries, anxieties, and unquestionable dangers, has produced the longest period of stability in relations among the great powers that the world has known in this century; it now compares favorably as well with some of the longest periods of great power stability in all of modern history. We may argue among ourselves as to whether or not we can legitimately call this "peace": it is not, I daresay, what most of us have in mind when we use that term. But I am not at all certain that the contemporaries of Metternich or Bismarck would have regarded their eras as "peaceful" either, even though historians looking back on those eras today clearly do.

Who is to say, therefore, how the historians a century from now—if there are any left by then—will look back on us? Is it not at least plausible that they will see our era, not as "the Cold War" at all, but rather, like those ages of Metternich and Bismarck, as a rare and fondly remembered "Long Peace"? Wishful thinking? Speculation through a rose-tinted word processor? Perhaps. But would it not behoove us to give at least as much attention to the question of how this might happen—to the elements in the contemporary international system that might make it happen—as we do to the fear that it may not?

# Notes

## 1 Legacies: Russian-American Relations Before the Cold War

1. Foster Rhea Dulles, *The Road to Teheran: The Story of Russia and America, 1781–1943* (Princeton: 1944), p. 261.

2. Thomas A. Bailey, *America Faces Russia: Russian-American Relations from Early Times to Our Own Day* (Ithaca: 1950), p. 355.

3. See, for a recent example, the contrasting viewpoints of Nikolai V. Sivachev and Nikolai N. Yakovlev, *Russia and the United States*, translated by Olga Adler Titelbaum (Chicago: 1979); and John Lewis Gaddis, *Russia, the Soviet Union, and the United States: An Interpretive History* (New York: 1978).

4. N. N. Bolkhovitinov, *The Beginnings of Russian-American Relations: 1775–1815*, translated by Elena Levin (Cambridge, Massachusetts: 1975), p. 355.

5. Sivachev and Yakovlev, *Russia and the United States*, p. 9.

6. Buchanan to Robert Livingston, June 29, 1832, Department of State Records, National Archives microfilm M-35, reel 12.

7. *Ibid.*

8. The best book on this neglected subject is Alan Dowty, *The Limits of American Isolation: The United States and the Crimean War* (New York: 1971). See also Kenneth Bourne, *Britain and the Balance of Power in North America, 1815–1908* (Berkeley: 1967), pp. 170–205.

9. D. P. Crook, *The North, the South, and the Powers, 1861–1865* (New York: 1974), pp. 223–27, 252–53.

10. I base this conclusion also on Hans Rogger, "America Enters the Twentieth Century: The View from Russia, 1895–1915," a paper prepared for the Fifth Colloquium of Soviet and American Historians, Kiev, June, 1984.

11. The classic account, still not superseded, is Edward H. Zabriskie, *American-Russian Rivalry in the Far East: A Study in Diplomacy and Power Politics* (Philadel-

phia: 1946). But see also Pauline Tompkins, *American-Russian Relations in the Far East* (New York: 1949).

12. The conflicting viewpoints are most sharply set forward in George F. Kennan *American Diplomacy, 1900–1950* (Chicago: 1951); and William Appleman Williams, *The Tragedy of American Diplomacy*, Revised Edition (New York: 1962). The most balanced account is Marilyn Blatt Young, *The Rhetoric of Empire: American China Policy, 1895–1901* (Cambridge, Massachusetts: 1968).

13. See, on this point, Raymond A. Esthus, *Theodore Roosevelt and the International Rivalries* (Waltham, Massachusetts: 1970), pp. 28–31.

14. Walter V. and Marie V. Scholes, *The Foreign Policies of the Taft Administration* (Columbia, Missouri: 1970), pp. 109–248.

15. The clearest expression of this tradition occurs in John Quincy Adams's Independence Day address, July 4, 1821, quoted in E. H. Tatum, *The United States and Europe, 1815–1823: A Study in the Background of the Monroe Doctrine* (Berkeley: 1936), pp. 241–45.

16. D. A. Graber, *Crisis Diplomacy: A History of U.S. Intervention Policies and Practices* (Washington: 1959), pp. 51–62. See also Donald S. Spencer, *Louis Kossuth and Young America: A Study of Sectionalism and Foreign Policy, 1848–1852* (Columbia, Missouri: 1977).

17. John Kutolowski, "The Effect of the Polish Insurrection of 1863 on American Civil War Diplomacy," *The Historian*, XXVII (August, 1965), 560–77.

18. See Ann E. Healy, "Tsarist Anti-Semitism and Russian-American Relations, *Slavic Review*, XLII (Fall, 1983), 408–24.

19. Kennan's role is fully discussed in Taylor Stults, "Imperial Russia Through American Eyes, 1894–1904" (Ph.D. Dissertation, University of Missouri, 1970); and in Frederick F. Travis, "George Kennan and Russia, 1865–1905" (Ph.D. Dissertation, Emory University, 1974). There is also a recent Russian biography, E. I. Melamed, *Dzhordzh Kennan protiv tsarizma* (Moscow: 1981).

20. For this series of events, see Gaddis, *Russia, the Soviet Union, and the United States*, pp. 41–54.

21. Norman Saul, "American Perceptions of a Changing Russia, 1890–1914," paper prepared for the Fifth Colloquium of Soviet and American historians, Kiev, June, 1984.

22. Taylor Stults, "Roosevelt, Russian Persecution of Jews, and American Public Opinion," *Jewish Social Studies*, XXIII (January, 1971), 13–22; Philip Ernest Schoenberg, "The American Reaction to the Kishinev Pogrom of 1903," *American Jewish Historical Quarterly*, LXIII (March, 1974), 262–83.

23. Naomi K. Cohen, "The Abrogation of the Russo-American Treaty of 1832," *Jewish Social Studies*, XXV (January, 1963), 3–41; Clifford L. Egan, "Pressure Groups, the Department of State and the Abrogation of the Russian-American Treaty of 1832," *Proceedings of the American Philosophical Society*, CXV (August, 1971), 328–34.

24. Quoted in Zabriskie, *American-Russian Rivalry*, pp. 120–21. See also Gaddis, *Russia, the Soviet Union, and the United States*, p. 41.

25. Sivachev and Yakovlev, *Russia and the United States*, pp. 17–18.

26. Among the works that stress the complexity of Wilson's motives for intervention are John A. White, *The Siberian Intervention* (Princeton: 1950); Betty M. Unterberger, *America's Siberia Expedition, 1918–1920* (Durham: 1956); George F. Kennan, *Soviet-American Relations, 1917–1920: The Decision to Intervene* (Princeton: 1958); and Robert J. Maddox, *The Unknown War with Russia: Wilson's Siberian Intervention* (San Rafael, California: 1977).

27. Works that tend to stress Wilson's anti-Bolshevism include Arno J. Mayer, *The Politics and Diplomacy of Peacemaking: Containment and Counterrevolution at Versailles, 1918–1919* (New York: 1967); N. Gordon Levin, *Woodrow Wilson and World Politics* (New York: 1968); and, on the Soviet side, L. A. Gvishiani, *Sovetskaia Rossiia i SShA, 1917–1920g.* (Moscow: 1970).

28. See, for example, Sivachev and Yakovlev, *Russia and the United States*, pp. 34–36.

29. I detect something of this tone in V. L. Mal'kov, "From Intervention to Recognition: On the History of the Political Struggle in the United States on the Question of Normalizing Soviet-American Relations," paper prepared for the Fifth Colloquium of Soviet and American historians, Kiev, June, 1984, especially pp. 2–15; also Sivachev and Yakovlev, *Russia and the United States*, pp. 62–67, 77–84. For the attitude of Soviet officials at the time, see Gaddis, *Russia, the Soviet Union, and the United States*, pp. 87–93.

30. See, on this point, John Milton Cooper, Jr., *The Warrior and the Priest: Woodrow Wilson and Theodore Roosevelt* (Cambridge, Massachusetts: 1983), p. 268.

31. R. Sh. Ganelin, *Rossiia i SShA, 1914–1917* (Leningrad: 1969).

32. Gaddis, *Russia, the Soviet Union, and the United States*, pp. 50–53. See also Sivachev and Yakovlev, *Russia and the United States*, pp. 25–27, which attributes growing American economic influence inside Russia to the weakness of tsarism, "which no longer had the strength to defend itself against the penetration of Yankee capital."

33. Chicherin report to the Central Executive Committee, January 27, 1922, in Jane Degras, ed., *Soviet Documents on Foreign Policy, 1917–41* (London: 1951–53), I, 291–92.

34. See Lenin's speech in Moscow, November 27, 1920, *ibid.*, pp. 223–24; also Anthony Sutton, *Western Technology and Soviet Economic Development: 1917 to 1930* (Stanford: 1968), pp. 346–48.

35. Joan Hoff Wilson, *Ideology and Economics: United States Relations with the Soviet Union, 1918–1933* (Columbia, Missouri: 1974), p. 48.

36. Quoted in Floyd J. Fithian, "Soviet-American Economic Relations, 1918–1933: American Business in Russia during the Period of Non-recognition" (Ph.D. dissertation, University of Nebraska, 1964), p. 196.

37. The standard accounts are Robert Paul Browder, *The Origins of Soviet-American Diplomacy* (Princeton: 1953); Donald G. Bishop, *The Roosevelt-Litvinov Agreements: The American View* (Syracuse: 1965); and Edward M. Bennett, *Recognition of Russia: An American Foreign Policy Dilemma* (Waltham, Massachusetts: 1970).

38. Wilson, *Ideology and Economics*, pp. 120–30.

39. Litvinov to the Soviet Foreign Ministry, November 8, 17, 1933, *Dokumenty vneshnei politiki SSSR* (Moscow: 1957–    ), XVI, 609, 658–59.

40. See Robert Dallek, *Franklin D. Roosevelt and American Foreign Policy, 1932–1945* (New York: 1979), p. 321.

41. *Ibid.*, p. 68; Wayne S. Cole, *Roosevelt and the Isolationists, 1932–45* (Lincoln, Nebraska: 1983), p. 243.

42. See Thomas R. Maddux, *Years of Estrangement: American Relations with the Soviet Union, 1933–1941* (Tallahassee: 1980), pp. 44–68; and Hugh DeSantis, *The Diplomacy of Silence: The American Foreign Service, the Soviet Union, and the Cold War, 1933–1945* (Chicago: 1980), pp. 11–44.

43. Maddux, *Years of Estrangement*, pp. 69–80.

44. Thomas R. Maddux, "United States–Soviet Naval Relations in the 1930's: The Soviet Union's Efforts to Purchase Naval Vessels," *Naval War College Review*, XXIX (Fall, 1976), 28–37.

45. Gaddis, *Russia, the Soviet Union and the United States*, pp. 138–45.

46. See, on this point, Seweryn Bialer, *The Soviet Paradox: External Expansion, Internal Decline* (New York: 1986), p. 260.

## 2   The Insecurities of Victory: The United States and the Perception of the Soviet Threat After World War II

1. Winston S. Churchill, *The Gathering Storm*, Bantam Edition (Boston: 1948), p. vii.

2. "The 36-Hour War," *Life*, XIX (November 19, 1945), 27–35. For Arnold's complete report, dated November 12, 1945, see *The War Reports of General of the Army George*

*C. Marshall, General of the Army H. H. Arnold, Fleet Admiral Ernest J. King* (Philadelphia: 1947), pp. 419–70, especially pp. 452–70.

3. The most succinct definition of "continentalism" is in Mark A. Stoler, "From Continentalism to Globalism: General Stanley D. Embick, the Joint Strategic Survey Committee, and the Military View of American National Policy during the Second World War," *Diplomatic History,* VI(Summer, 1982), 304. But see also Manfred Jonas, *Isolationism in America, 1935–1941* (Ithaca: 1966), pp. 100–101; and Wayne S. Cole, *Roosevelt and the Isolationists, 1932–45* (Lincoln: 1983), pp. 6–7. For the impact of this thinking on military planning, see Fred Greene, "The Military View of National Policy, 1904–1940," *American Historical Review,* LXVI(January, 1961), 354–77; and Michael S. Sherry, *Preparing for the Next War: American Plans for Postwar Defense, 1941–45* (New Haven: 1977), pp. 27–31.

4. *Ibid.,* pp. 8–12, 113, 243; Robert Dallek, *Franklin D. Roosevelt and American Foreign Policy, 1932–1945* (New York: 1979), pp. 12, 68, 106, 152, 227.

5. Sir Halford Mackinder, "The Geographical Pivot of History," *Geographical Journal,* XXIII(April, 1904), 421–44. See also Mackinder, *Democratic Ideals and Reality: A Study in the Politics of Reconstruction* (New York: 1919).

6. Frederick Sherwood Dunn, "An Introductory Statement," in Nicholas John Spykman, *The Geography of the Peace,* edited by Helen R. Nicholl (New York: 1944), p. x.

7. Nicholas John Spykman, *America's Strategy in World Politics* (New York: 1942), p. 195. See also Spykman, *The Geography of the Peace,* p. 33. Other volumes representative of this line of argument include William T. R. Fox, *The Super-Powers: The United States, Britain, and the Soviet Union—Their Responsibility for Peace* (New York: 1944), and Robert Strausz-Hupé, *The Balance of Tomorrow: Power and Foreign Policy in the United States* (New York: 1945).

8. Walter Lippmann, *U.S. Foreign Policy: Shield of the Republic* (Boston: 1943), especially pp. 49, 94, 105. For the origins and reception of this book, see Ronald Steel, *Walter Lippmann and the American Century* (Boston: 1980), pp. 404–8.

9. The best account of this development is Robert A. Divine, *Second Chance: The Triumph of Internationalism in America During World War II* (New York: 1967).

10. See, for example, Spykman, *The Geography of the Peace,* p. 60; Lippmann, *U.S. Foreign Policy,* pp. 165–68.

11. See, on this point, Strausz-Hupé, *The Balance of Tomorrow,* pp. 275–76; also Divine, *Second Chance,* pp. 297–98.

12. Roosevelt meeting with the Senate Military Affairs Committee, January 31, 1939, as cited in Cole, *Roosevelt and the Isolationists,* p. 304. See also *ibid.,* p. 243; and Dallek, *Franklin D. Roosevelt and American Foreign Policy,* p. 321.

13. See, on this point, John Lewis Gaddis, *The United States and the Origins of the Cold War, 1941–1947* (New York: 1972), pp. 24–25.

14. Roosevelt State of the Union address, January 6, 1945, Samuel I. Rosenman, ed., *The Public Papers and Addresses of Franklin D. Roosevelt* (New York: 1941–50), XIII, 498. See also Roosevelt's fireside chat, December 24, 1943, *ibid.,* XII, 558.

15. Waldo H. Heinrichs, Jr., "The Role of the United States Navy," in Dorothy Borg and Sumpei Okamoto, eds., *Pearl Harbor as History: Japanese-American Relations, 1931–1941* (New York: 1973), pp. 201–4.

16. Jefferson Caffery to Cordell Hull, October 20, 1944, *Foreign Relations of the United States* [hereafter *FR*]: *1944*), III, 743. See also Stoler, "From Continentalism to Globalism," pp. 311, 314.

17. OSS Research and Analysis report #2284, "American Security Interests in the European Settlement," June 29, 1944, Office of Strategic Services Records, Modern Military Records Division, National Archives.

18. *War Reports,* pp. 452–53, 457, 463–64. See also Sherry, *Preparing for the Next War,* pp. 39–42.

19. *Ibid.,* p. 464. For a sampling of civilian assessments of the implications of the

new technology, see Bernard Brodie, ed., *The Absolute Weapon* (New York: 1946);
Dexter Masters and Katharine Way, eds., *One World or None* (New York: 1946);
William Liscum Borden, *There Will Be No Time: The Revolution in Strategy* (New
York: 1946); and B. H. Liddell Hart, *The Revolution in Warfare* (New Haven: 1947).

20. For a persuasive account of Wilson's ability to think in balance of power terms,
see N. Gordon Levin, *Woodrow Wilson and World Politics* (New York: 1968), especially
pp. 8, 36–41. Daniel Yergin provides a succinct characterization of the new "gospel of
national security" in *Shattered Peace: The Origins of the Cold War and the National
Security State* (Boston: 1977), pp. 193–204.

21. *New York Times*, September 9, 1945.

22. H. J. Mackinder, "The Round World and the Winning of the Peace," *Foreign
Affairs*, XXI (July, 1943), 595–605.

23. Spykman, *The Geography of the Peace*, pp. 41–44.

24. Lippmann, *U.S. Foreign Policy*, p. 164. See also Fox, *The Super-Powers*, pp. 103–6.

25. Roosevelt informal remarks to the Advertising War Council Conference, March
8, 1944, Rosenman, ed., *Roosevelt Public Papers*, XIII, 99.

26. See, on these points, Dallek, *Franklin D. Roosevelt and American Foreign Policy*,
pp. 533–34; and John Lewis Gaddis, *Strategies of Containment: A Critical Appraisal of
Postwar American National Security Policy* (New York: 1982), pp. 9–13.

27. Gaddis, *The United States and the Origins of the Cold War*, pp. 206–11. For
Truman's faith in the United Nations, see Robert J. Donovan, *Conflict and Crisis: The
Presidency of Harry S Truman, 1945–1948* (New York: 1977), pp. 49–50.

28. Robert L. Messer, *The End of an Alliance: James F. Byrnes, Roosevelt, Truman,
and the Origins of the Cold War* (Chapel Hill: 1982), pp. 133–34. Truman's complaint
about Churchill is from his appointment sheet, May 19, 1945, as published in Robert H.
Ferrell, ed., *Off the Record: The Private Papers of Harry S. Truman* (New York: 1980),
pp. 31–32.

29. Potsdam Briefing Book Paper, "British Plans for a Western European Bloc," July
4, 1945, *Foreign Relations of the United States: The Conference of Berlin (The Potsdam
Conference) 1945* (Washington: 1960), I, 262–63. For the general State Department
viewpoint, see Hugh DeSantis, *The Diplomacy of Silence: The American Foreign Service,
the Soviet Union, and the Cold War, 1933–1947* (Chicago: 1980), pp. 81–105. For evidence that the Republican Party's chief foreign policy expert shared this viewpoint at
the time, see Ronald W. Pruessen, *John Foster Dulles: The Road to Power* (New York:
1982), pp. 272–76. The American aversion to spheres of influence as a basis for the postwar settlement is discussed in Chapter Three, below.

30. JCS 973/1, "Fundamental Military Factors in Relation to Discussions Concerning
Territorial Trusteeships and Settlements," August 3, 1944, *FR: 1944*, I, 699–703. See also
William D. Leahy to Cordell Hull, May 16, 1944, *Foreign Relations of the United States:
The Conferences at Malta and Yalta, 1945* (Washington: 1955), pp. 106–8. For evaluations of the significance of these documents, see Stoler, "From Continentalism to Globalism," pp. 312–13; Walter S. Poole, "From Conciliation to Containment: The Joint Chiefs
of Staff and the Coming of the Cold War, 1945–1946," *Military Affairs*, XLII (February,
1978), 12; and James F. Schnabel, *The Joint Chiefs of Staff and National Policy, 1945–47*
(Wilmington, Delaware: 1979), pp. 13–16.

31. JIC 250, "Estimate of Soviet Post-War Capabilities and Intentions," January 18,
1945, Army Staff Records, ABC 336 Russia Section 1-A, Record Group 319, National
Archives. See also the following Office of Strategic Services Research and Analysis reports
on Russian intentions: #1337S, "Russian Intentions in the Mediterranean and Danube
Basins," October 20, 1943; #2284, "American Security Interests in the European Settle-
ment," June 29, 1944; #2669, "Capabilities and Intentions of the USSR in the Postwar
Period," January 5, 1945, all in O.S.S. Records; as well as O.S.S. Director William
Donovan's optimistic report of Soviet intentions following the October, 1943, Moscow
Conference of Foreign Ministers, Donovan to Buxton, November 22, 1943, *ibid.*, USSR

Division—1945, Entry 1; also Stephen E. Ambrose, *Eisenhower: Soldier, General of the Army, President-Elect, 1890–1952* (New York: 1983), pp. 399–404.

32. Sherry, *Preparing for the Next War*, pp. 102–3. See also Forrest C. Pogue, *George C. Marshall: Organizer of Victory* (New York: 1973), pp. 574–75.

33. Quoted in Perry McCoy Smith, *The Air Force Plans for Peace, 1943–1945* (Baltimore: 1970), pp. 80–81.

34. *Ibid.*, p. 81.

35. Sherry, *Preparing for the Next War*, pp. 53, 84–87, 168.

36. Smith, *The Air Force Plans for Peace*, pp. 75–83, 111; Sherry, *Preparing for the Next War*, pp. 45–46; Converse, "United States Plans for a Postwar Overseas Military Base System," pp. 143–45, 151–54, 191–234.

37. Hull to Harriman, February 9, 1944, *FR: 1944*, IV, 824–26. For Bohlen's role in drafting this document, see DeSantis, *The Diplomacy of Silence*, p. 111.

38. For the American attitude on these points, see Gaddis, *The United States and the Origins of the Cold War*, pp. 133–73; also Lynn Etheridge Davis, *The Cold War Begins: Soviet-American Conflict Over Eastern Europe* (New York: 1974), especially pp. 369–77.

39. Harriman to Harry Hopkins, September 10, 1944, *FR: 1944*, IV, 989. See also the recollections of American observers to these events in Thomas T. Hammond, ed., *Witnesses to the Origins of the Cold War* (Seattle: 1982).

40. Quoted in W. Averell Harriman and Elie Abel, *Special Envoy to Churchill and Stalin: 1941–1946* (New York: 1975), p. 444. For other evidence of Roosevelt's disillusionment with the Russians during the final months of his life, see Dallek, *Franklin D. Roosevelt and American Foreign Policy*, pp. 523–27.

41. Gaddis, *Strategies of Containment*, pp. 13–15.

42. See William Hillman, ed., *Mr. President* (New York: 1952), p. 153; also Deborah Welch Larson, *Origins of Containment: A Psychological Explanation* (Princeton: 1985), pp. 132–36.

43. Wallace Diary, May 18, 1945, quoted in John Morton Blum, ed., *The Price of Vision: The Diary of Henry A. Wallace, 1942–1946* (Boston: 1973), p. 451. For Truman's April 23, 1945, confrontation with Molotov, see his own account in Harry S. Truman, *Year of Decisions* (Garden City, New York: 1955), pp. 79–82, which should be supplemented with Bohlen's minutes of the meeting, published in *FR: 1945*, V, 256–58.

44. Truman Diary, July 17 and 30, 1945, Ferrell, ed., *Off the Record*, pp. 53, 58. See also the Wallace Diary, October 15, 1945, Blum, ed., *The Price of Vision*, p. 490; and the Stettinius Diary, October 22, 1945, Thomas M. Campbell and George C. Herring, *The Diaries of Edward R. Stettinius, Jr., 1943–1946* (New York: 1975), pp. 439–40. For the Pendergast analogy, see Donovan, *Conflict and Crisis*, p. 75; Jonathan Daniels, *Man of Independence* (Philadelphia: 1950), p. 285.

45. See, for example, Truman's campaign remarks in Eugene, Oregon, June 11, 1948, *Public Papers of the Presidents: Harry S. Truman, 1948* (Washington: 1963), p. 329.

46. For events in Eastern Europe, see Davis, *The Cold War Begins*, pp. 288–334, 358–68; Geir Lundestad, *The American Non-Policy Towards Eastern Europe* (Oslo: 1978), pp. 127–35, 159–64, 205–13, 235–47, 271–78; Richard C. Lukas, *Bitter Legacy: Polish-American Relations in the Wake of World War II* (Lexington, Kentucky: 1982); and Michael M. Boll, *Cold War in the Balkans: American Foreign Policy and the Emergence of Communist Bulgaria, 1943–1947* (Lexington, Kentucky: 1984).

47. Gaddis, *The United States and the Origins of the Cold War*, pp. 325–31.

48. Russell D. Buhite, *Soviet-American Relations in Asia, 1945–1954* (Norman, Oklahoma: 1981), pp. 139–50; Charles M. Dobbs, *The Unwanted Symbol: American Foreign Policy, the Cold War, and Korea, 1945–1950* (Kent, Ohio: 1981), pp. 56–83; James Irving Matray, *The Reluctant Crusade: American Foreign Policy in Korea, 1941–1950* (Honolulu: 1985), pp. 28–98.

49. Alfred E. Eckes, Jr. *A Search for Solvency: Bretton Woods and the International Monetary System, 1941–1971* (Austin: 1975), pp. 205–8.

50. Bruce R. Kuniholm, *The Origins of the Cold War in the Near East: Great Power Conflict and Diplomacy in Iran, Turkey, and Greece* (Princeton: 1980), pp. 270–98. For two contemporary summaries of Russian unilateral actions as of late 1945, see "Summary of Russian Dispatches for the Secretary's Diary," November 26, 1945, James V. Forrestal Papers, Box 100, "Book II, Item 30," Seeley Mudd Library, Princeton University; and a Department of State memorandum, "Foreign Policy of the United States," December 1, 1945, *FR: 1946*, I, 1134–39.

51. Forrestal Diary, December 4, 1945, Walter Millis, ed., *The Forrestal Diaries* (New York: 1951), p. 124.

52. See Truman's press conference comments on October 8, 1945, *Truman Public Papers: 1946*, pp. 384, 387; and the Stettinius Diary, October 22, 1945, Campbell and Herring, eds., *Stettinius Diaries*, p. 437.

53. The best recent account of these developments is Messer, *The End of an Alliance*, pp. 137–66. Truman's controversial memorandum of January 5, 1946, is printed in his *Memoirs: Year of Decisions* (Garden City, New York: 1955), pp. 551–52.

54. Kuniholm, *The Origins of the Cold War in the Near East*, pp. 304–42.

55. Quoted in Hillman, ed., *Mr. President*, p. 107.

56. Truman to Buck, June 15, 1946, Harry S. Truman Papers, OF 220 Miscellaneous, Harry S. Truman Library.

57. Atkinson's articles appeared in the *New York Times* on July 7, 8, and 9, 1946. For his White House visit, see *ibid.*, July 13, 1946.

58. George M. Elsey notes on a Truman conversation with Clark Clifford and Charles G. Ross, July 12, 1946, George M. Elsey Papers, Box 63 "Foreign Relations—Russia 1946—Report—Folder 1," Harry S. Truman Library.

59. The full text of the Clifford report can be found in Arthur Krock, *Memoirs: Sixty Years on the Firing Line* (New York: 1968), pp. 419–82.

60. Truman memorandum, September 19, 1946, quoted in Margaret Truman, *Harry S. Truman* (New York: 1973), pp. 317–18.

61. *Ibid.*, p. 347.

62. Truman to Garner, September 21, 1946, Truman Papers, PSF Box 187, "Russia: 1945–1948."

63. Quoted in *Time*, XLVII (June 17, 1946), 26.

64. Gaddis, *The United States and the Origins of the Cold War*, pp. 32–62. The best overall account of wartime attitudes toward the Soviet Union is Ralph B. Levering, *American Opinion and the Russian Alliance, 1939–1945* (Chapel Hill: 1976).

65. See John Lewis Gaddis, *Russia, the Soviet Union, and the United States: An Interpretive History* (New York: 1978), pp. 27–56; also Chapter One, above.

66. The best discussion is in Levin, *Woodrow Wilson and World Politics*, pp. 37–45. But see also Patrick Devlin, *Too Proud to Fight: Woodrow Wilson's Neutrality* (New York: 1975), pp. 136–39.

67. See, for example, John P. Diggins, *Mussolini and Fascism: The View from America* (Princeton: 1972).

69. Quoted in Millis, ed., *The Forrestal Diaries*, p. 181.

70. Sulzberger to Douglas MacArthur, June 6, 1946, Douglas MacArthur Papers, Record Group 10, Box 9, "Sulzberger" folder, MacArthur Memorial Library, Norfolk, Virginia.

71. Truman letter of November 11, 1946, quoted in Margaret Truman, *Harry S. Truman*, p. 323. See also Truman to Margaret Truman, March 13, 1947, *ibid.*, p. 343.

72. Truman informal remarks to the Association of Radio News Analysts, May 13, 1947, *Truman Public Papers: 1947*, pp. 238–39.

73. Truman speeches at Baylor University, March 6, 1947, Monticello, July 4, 1947, and Rio de Janeiro, September 2, 1947, *ibid.*, pp. 170, 324, 429.

74. Truman speech to Congress on aid to Greece and Turkey, March 12, 1947, *ibid.*,

p. 178. For a further discussion of this point, see Gaddis, *Strategies of Containment*, pp. 65–66.

75. Gaddis, *Russia, the Soviet Union, and the United States*, pp. 65–145; see also Chapter One, above.

76. Division of European Affairs memorandum, "Current Problems in Relations With the Soviet Union," March 24, 1944, *FR: 1944*, IV, 840. See also O. S. S. Research and Analysis report #1552, "The Current Role of the Communist Party in the USSR," June 12, 1944, Office of Intelligence and Research Files, Department of State Records, National Archives.

77. Forrestal Diary, June 30, 1945, Millis, ed., *The Forrestal Diaries*, p. 72.

78. See, on this point, Vojtech Mastny, *Russia's Road to the Cold War: Diplomacy, Warfare, and the Politics of Communism, 1941–1945* (New York: 1979), pp. 194, 231; also William Taubman, *Stalin's American Policy: From Entente to Détente to Cold War* (New York: 1982), pp. 75–82.

79. Inverchapel to Foreign Office, August 31, 1946, Foreign Office Records, FO 371/51609/AN2657, Public Record Office, London.

80. *Newsweek*, XXVIII (September 9, 1946), 27.

81. See sections II and III of this essay, above.

82. See, on this point, Eduard Mark, "American Policy toward Eastern Europe and the Origins of the Cold War: An Alternative Interpretation," *Journal of American History*, LXVIII (September, 1981), 313–36.

83. For the Wallace affair, see Blum, ed., *The Price of Vision*, pp. 589–601, 612–32; also J. Samuel Walker, *Henry A. Wallace and American Foreign Policy* (Westport, Connecticut: 1976), pp. 149–65.

84. The "long telegram" is published in *FR: 1946*, VI, 696–709.

85. See Larson, *Origins of Containment*, pp. 52–57.

86. Kennan's own explanation of his intentions with respect to the "long telegram" and the "X" article are in his *Memoirs: 1925–1950* (Boston: 1967), pp. 292–95, 354–67.

87. "X" [George F. Kennan], "The Sources of Soviet Conduct," *Foreign Affairs*, XXV (July, 1947), 566–82.

88. My argument here follows that of Sherry, *Preparing for the Next War*, p. 215.

89. JCS 1769/1, "United States Assistance to Other Countries from the Standpoint of National Security," April 29, 1947, *FR: 1947*, I, 740.

90. For a sampling of official assessments on this subject, see JIC 250/7, 'Capabilities and Intentions of the U.S.S.R. in the Post-War Period," February 7, 1946, Army Staff Records, ABC 336 Russia 22 Aug 43 Sec 1-B, Modern Military Records Branch, National Archives; Robert Murphy to H. Freeman Matthews, April 3, 1946, Department of State Records, 861.00/4–346, Box 6462, Diplomatic Branch, National Archives; War Department intelligence review, "Soviet Foreign Policy: A Summation," May 2, 1946, Elsey Papers, Box 63, "Foreign Relations—Russia 1946—Report—Folder 3"; Joint Chiefs of Staff to Truman, July 26, 1946, Clark M. Clifford Papers, Box 14, "Russia (folder 3)," Harry S. Truman Library; George F. Kennan lecture to Foreign Service and State Department personnel, September 17, 1946, George F. Kennan Papers, Box 16, Seeley Mudd Library, Princeton University; Joint Chiefs of Staff to Secretaries of Army and Navy, March 13, 1947, *FR: 1947*, V, 111–12.

91. Lincoln executive session testimony, April 2, 1947, U.S. Congress, Senate, Committee on Foreign Relations, *Legislative Origins of the Truman Doctrine* (Washington: 1973), p. 160.

92. State-War-Navy Coordinating Committee "Ad Hoc" Committee report, "Policies, Procedures and Costs of Assistance by the United States to Foreign Countries," April 21, 1947, *FR: 1947*, III, 217.

93. Clayton memorandum, "The European Crisis," May 27, 1947, *ibid.*, p. 231.

94. JCS 1769/1, April 29, 1947, *ibid.*, I, 739.

95. See, for example, Dean Acheson's speech to the Delta Council, Cleveland, Mississippi, May 8, 1947, *Department of State Bulletin*, XVI(May 18, 1947), 991–94. These arguments were not wholly a matter of public rhetoric, though. See Clayton's May 27, 1947, memorandum, *FR: 1947*, III, 231; also Joseph M. Jones to William Benton, February 26, 1947, Joseph M. Jones Papers, Harry S. Truman Library; and the State-War-Navy Coordinating Committee "Ad Hoc" report, April 21, 1947, *FR: 1947*, III, 209–10.

96. See, on these points, Robert A. Pollard, *Economic Security and the Origins of the Cold War, 1945–1950* (New York: 1985), pp. 60–61, 246–52; also Geir Lundestad, *America, Scandinavia, and the Cold War, 1945–1949* (New York: 1980), p. 32.

97. See, for example, Acheson to Marshall, February 21, 1947, *FR: 1947*, V, 30; Report of the Committee Appointed to Study Immediate Aid to Greece and Turkey," February 26, 1947, *ibid.*, pp. 51–52; Clayton memorandum, March 5, 1947, Frederick J. Dobney, ed., *Selected Papers of Will Clayton* (Baltimore: 1971), pp. 198–200; Acheson statement before the Senate Foreign Relations Committee, March 24, 1947, U.S. Congress, Senate, Committee on Foreign Relations, *Assistance to Greece and Turkey* (Washington: 1947), pp. 23–24.

98. Kennan, March 28, 1947, lecture, quoted in Kennan, *Memoirs: 1925–1950*, p. 319.

99. Most excessively, in Gaddis, *Strategies of Containment, passim.*

100. The clearest recent example in English is Nikolai V. Sivachev and Nikolai N. Yakovlev, *Russia and the United States*, translated by Olga Adler Titlebaum (Chicago: 1979), especially Chapter Six.

101. See, for examples of this "revisionism" in its purest form, Gabriel Kolko, *The Politics of War: The World and United States Foreign Policy, 1943–1945* (New York: 1968); and Joyce and Gabriel Kolko, *The Limits of Power: The World and United States Foreign Policy, 1945–1954* (New York: 1972). Other works that stress the "over-reaction" theme in varying degrees include: William A. Williams, *The Tragedy of American Diplomacy*, Revised Edition (New York: 1962); Lloyd C. Gardner, *Architects of Illusion: Men and Ideas in American Foreign Policy, 1941–1949* (Chicago: 1970); Thomas G. Paterson, *Soviet-American Confrontation: Postwar Reconstruction and the Origins of the Cold War* (Baltimore: 1973); and, most recently, Yergin, *Shattered Peace.*

102. Mastny, *Russia's Road to the Cold War*, especially pp. 306–13. Mastny's book is the most prominent example of this new interest in the early Cold War policies of the Soviet Union, but see also Taubman, *Stalin's American Policy, passim.*

103. *Ibid.*, pp. 74, 129.

104. Mastny, *Russia's Road to the Cold War*, pp. 306, 310–11.

105. Lundestad, *America, Scandinavia, and the Cold War*, pp. 32, 335. See also Geir Lundestad, "Empire by Invitation? The United States and Western Europe, 1945–1952," *Journal of Peace Research*, XXIII(1986), 263–77.

106. George Allen to Loy Henderson, July 6, 1946, quoted in Kuniholm, *The Origins of the Cold War in the Near East*, p. 345. Kuniholm's book sees a similar pattern in Turkey and Greece.

107. Terry H. Anderson, *The United States, Great Britain, and the Cold War, 1944–1947* (Columbia, Missouri: 1981); Robert M. Hathaway, *Ambiguous Partnership: Britain and America, 1944–1947* (New York: 1981). The point is also made in Alan Bullock, *Ernest Bevin: Foreign Secretary* (New York: 1983), especially pp. 347–48, 394.

108. J. C. Donnelly minute, March 5, 1946, Foreign Office Records, FO 371/51606/ AN587.

109. See on this point, in addition to the Anderson, Bullock, and Hathaway volumes cited above, Peter G. Boyle, "The British Foreign Office View of Soviet-American Relations, 1945–46," *Diplomatic History*, III(Summer, 1979), 307–20.

110. See the exceptionally perceptive discussion in Bullock, *Ernest Bevin: Foreign Secretary*, pp. 6–12, 105–8, 115–18.

111. *Ibid.*, pp. 529–30; also Timothy Ireland, *Creating the Entangling Alliance: The Origins of the North Atlantic Treaty Organization* (Westport, Connecticut: 1981), pp.

48–79; and Lawrence S. Kaplan, *The United States and NATO: The Formative Years* (Lexington, Kentucky: 1984), pp. 49–64.

112. Bevin to Cabinet, C. P. (48) 72, "The Threat to Western Civilisation," March 3, 1948, Cabinet Records, CAB 129/25, Public Record Office, London.

113. *The Basic Writings of Sigmund Freud*, translated and edited by A. A. Brill (New York: 1938), p. 163.


## 3    Spheres of Influence: The United States and Europe, 1945–1949

1. Kennan to Bohlen, January 26, 1945, Charles E. Bohlen Papers, Box 1, "Personal Correspondence 1944–46," Diplomatic Branch, National Archives. See also Charles E. Bohlen, *Witness to History: 1929–1969* (New York: 1973), pp. 174–76; also Kennan to Harriman, September 18, 1944, George F. Kennan Papers, Box 28, Seeley Mudd Library, Princeton University. This latter memorandum is printed in George F. Kennan, *Memoirs: 1925–1950* (Boston: 1967), pp. 222–23, but under the date of December 16, 1944.

2. Bohlen to Kennan, undated, Kennan Papers, Box 28. See also Bohlen, *Witness to History*, pp. 176–77.

3. See Chapter Two, above.

4. OSS R & A #2284, "American Security Interests in the European Settlement," June 29, 1944, OSS Records, Modern Military Records Branch, National Archives.

5. JCS 973/1, "Fundamental Military Factors in Relation to Discussions Concerning Territorial Trusteeships and Settlements," August 3, 1944, U.S. Department of State, *Foreign Relations of the United States:* [hereafter *FR*] *1944*, I, 699–703. See also Admiral William D. Leahy to Cordell Hull, May 16, 1944, U.S. Department of State, *Foreign Relations of the United States: The Conferences at Malta and Yalta, 1945* [hereafter *FR: Yalta*] (Washington: 1955), pp. 106–8. For evaluations of the significance of these documents, see Mark A. Stoler, "From Continentalism to Globalism: General Stanley D. Embick, the Joint Strategic Survey Committee, and the Military View of American National Policy during the Second World War," *Diplomatic History*, VI(Summer, 1982), 312–13; and James F. Schnabel, *The Joint Chiefs of Staff and National Policy, 1945–1947* (Wilmington, Delaware: 1979), pp. 13–16.

6. OSS R & A #2669, "Capabilities and Intentions of the USSR in the Postwar Period," January 5, 1945, OSS Records.

7. See, on these points, Robert Dallek, *Franklin D. Roosevelt and American Foreign Policy, 1932–1945* (New York: 1979), pp. 389–91, 536–37; and Wm. Roger Louis, *Imperialism at Bay: The United States and the Decolonization of the British Empire, 1941–1945* (New York: 1978), pp. 259–73.

8. Such is the central argument of Geir Lundestad, *The American Non-Policy Towards Eastern Europe, 1943–1947* (New York: 1978).

9. Bohlen minutes, Roosevelt-Churchill-Stalin meeting, February 5, 1945, *FR: Yalta*, p. 617. See also the discussion of American policy regarding postwar overseas military bases in Chapter Two, above.

10. See John Lewis Gaddis, *The United States and the Origins of the Cold War, 1941–1947* (New York: 1972), pp. 206–11.

11. Potsdam briefing book paper, "British Plans for a Western European Bloc," July 4, 1945, U.S. Department of State, *Foreign Relations of the United States: The Conference of Berlin (The Potsdam Conference) 1945* [hereafter *FR: Potsdam*], I, 256–64 [emphasis in original].

12. *Congressional Record*, April 26, 1944, p. 3719.

13. For administration expressions of concern along these lines, see Cordell Hull to W. Averell Harriman, February 9, 1944, *FR: 1944*, IV, 826; a State Department Post-War Programs Committee memorandum, "Policy Toward the Settlement of Territorial Disputes in Europe," July 28, 1944, printed in Harley Notter, *Postwar Foreign Policy Preparation*

(Washington: 1949), p. 593; a State Department briefing book paper prepared for the Yalta Conference, "American Policy Toward Spheres of Influence," undated, *FR: Yalta*, p. 105. For further background, see Gaddis, *The United States and the Origins of the Cold War*, pp. 149–57; and Dallek, *Roosevelt and American Foreign Policy*, p. 536.

14. See, on this point, Robert A. Divine, *Second Chance: The Triumph of Internationalism in America During World War II*, especially pp. 167–74. Two influential wartime best-sellers contributing to the revival of Wilsonianism were Wendell Willkie, *One World* (New York: 1943); and Sumner Welles, *The Time for Decision* (New York: 1944).

15. Concerns about ideology surfaced, for example, in a State Department Division of European Affairs memorandum, "Current Problems in Relations with the Soviet Union," March 24, 1944, *FR: 1944*, IV, 840; in an Office of Strategic Services Research and Analysis report, #1552, "The Current Role of the Communist Party in the USSR," June 12, 1944, OSS Records; in a conversation between Ambassador W. Averell Harriman and Secretary of the Navy James V. Forrestal, April 20, 1945, reported in Walter Millis, ed., *The Forrestal Diaries* (New York: 1951), p. 47; and in a memorandum by Raymond E. Murphy of the State Department's Division of European Affairs, "Possible Resurrection of Communist International, Resumption of Extreme Leftist Activities, Possible Effect on United States," June 2, 1945, *FR: Potsdam*, I, 267–80. See also Chapter Two, above.

16. Such, clearly, was Roosevelt's thinking. See John Lewis Gaddis, *Strategies of Containment: A Critical Appraisal of Postwar American National Security Policy* (New York: 1982), pp. 9–13. For other assessments stressing the probable defensive nature of Soviet expansionism, see the following Office of Strategic Services Research and Analysis reports: #1337S, "Russian Intentions in the Mediterranean and Danube Basins," October 20, 1943; #2284, "American Security Interests in the European Settlement," June 29, 1944; #2669, "Capabilities and Intentions of the USSR in the Postwar Period," January 5, 1945, OSS Records; also JIC 250, "Estimate of Soviet Post-War Capabilities and Intentions," January 18, 1945, Army Staff Records, ABC 336 Russia Section 1-A, Modern Military Records Branch, National Archives.

17. Department of State memorandum, "Foreign Policy of the United States," December 1, 1945, *FR: 1946*, I, 1139. See also OSS Research and Analysis reports 2284 and 2669, cited above; and a draft report by Bohlen and Geroid T. Robinson, "The Capabilities and Intentions of the Soviet Union as Affected by American Policy," December 10, 1945, printed in *Diplomatic History*, I (Fall, 1977), 389–99.

18. Draft report by Bohlen and Robinson, undated but early 1946, Department of State Records, Decimal File 1945–1949, 711.61/2-1446, Diplomatic Branch, National Archives.

19. Bohlen memorandum, March 13, 1946, Bohlen Papers, Box 4, "Memos (CEB) 1946."

20. Bohlen memorandum, October 18, 1945, Bohlen Papers, Box 3, "Memos (CEB) 1945." See also a memorandum by Cloyce K. Huston, Chief of the State Department's Division of Southern European Affairs, "Suggested Extension of American Policy in Eastern Europe," October 24, 1945, Department of State Records, Decimal File 1945–1949, 711.61/10-245.

21. Speech to the New York *Herald Tribune* Forum, October 31, 1945, *Department of State Bulletin*, XIII (November 4, 1945), 709–11.

22. Bohlen memorandum, October 18, 1945, Bohlen Papers, Box 3, "Memos (CEB), 1945."

23. Ethridge memorandum, "Summary Report on Soviet Policy in Rumania and Bulgaria," December 7, 1945, *FR: 1945*, V, 637.

24. For this shift in attitudes toward the Russians, see Gaddis, *The United States and the Origins of the Cold War*, pp. 282–315.

25. For the background of American planning on the postwar treatment of Germany, see *ibid.*, pp. 95–132.

26. See, for example, memoranda on the subject by Llewellyn Thompson and John D. Hickerson, both dated June 22, 1945, *FR: 1945*, III, 528–31.

27. The text of the proposed treaty is in *FR: 1946*, II, 190–93.

28. *New York Times*, May 6, 1946.

29. Kennan to Byrnes, March 6, 1946, *FR: 1946*, V, 519. See also Kennan to Bohlen, January 26, 1945, Bohlen Papers, Box 1, "Personal Correspondence 1944–46"; and Kennan to Carmel Office, May 10, 1946, *ibid.*, pp. 555–56.

30. The Byrnes Stuttgart speech of September 6, 1946, is in the *Department of State Bulletin*, XV (September 15, 1946), 496–501. For reparations and the merger of occupation zones, see John H. Backer, *The Decision to Divide Germany: American Foreign Policy in Transition* (Durham: 1978), pp. 96–101.

31. British notes on a conversation between Marshall and Bevin, London, December 18, 1947, *FR: 1947*, II, 824. For the negotiations on the German peace treaty, see *FR: 1946*, II, 941–65; *FR: 1947*, II, 1–112, 139–502, 676–795.

32. Transcript, Kennan post-lecture question and answer session, Air War College, April 10, 1947, Kennan Papers, Box 17. See also Walter Bedell Smith to Byrnes, January 7, 1947, *FR: 1947*, II, 141; JCS 1769/1, "United States Assistance to Other Countries from the Standpoint of National Security," April 29, 1947, *ibid.*, I, 741; John Balfour to the British Foreign Office, July 20, 1947, Foreign Office Records, FO371/61055/AN2552, Public Record Office, London; W. Averell Harriman to Truman, August 12, 1947, Harry S. Truman Papers, PSF Box 178, "Foreign Affairs: Germany (2)," Harry S. Truman Library; and Robert Murphy to Samuel Reber, November 20, 1947, *FR: 1947*, II, 725.

33. See, for example, Leahy to Hull, May 16, 1944, *FR: Yalta*, pp. 107–8.

34. Truman press conference, April 18, 1946, *Public Papers of the Presidents: Harry S. Truman, 1946* [hereafter *Truman Public Papers*] (Washington: 1962), pp. 211–12.

35. F. B. A. Rundall minute, March 10, 1947, Foreign Office Records, FO 371/61053/AN906.

36. By far the best account of U. S. actions during the Iranian and Turkish crises of 1946, as well as the subsequent Greek crisis, is Bruce R. Kuniholm, *The Origins of the Cold War in the Near East: Great Power Conflict and Diplomacy in Iran, Turkey, and Greece* (Princeton: 1980).

37. "Memorandum Regarding Greece," October 21, 1946, *FR: 1946*, VII, 243 [Emphases in original.]

38. See Joseph M. Jones, *The Fifteen Weeks (February 21–June 5, 1947)* (New York: 1955), p. 141; also p. 36, above.

39. The documentation on these negotiations is in *FR: 1947*, II, 139–471.

40. See, for example, a Joint Chiefs of Staff memorandum to Patterson and Forrestal, March 13, 1947, *FR: 1947*, V, 112; PPS/1, "Policy with Respect to American Aid to Western Europe," May 23, 1947, *ibid.*, III, 224–25; William L. Clayton memorandum, "The European Crisis," May 27, 1947, *ibid.*, 230–32; Kennan National War College lecture, June 18, 1947, quoted in Kennan, *Memoirs: 1925–1950*, p. 351; Burton Y. Berry to Kennan, July 31, 1947, Policy Planning Staff Records, Box 31, "United Nations 1947–1949," Diplomatic Branch, National Archives; Bohlen to Joseph C. Grew, August 2, 1947, Bohlen Papers, Box 1, "Correspondence 1946–1949: G"; Kennan memorandum of a conversation with Clark Clifford, August 19, 1947, Policy Planning Staff Records, Box 33, "Chronological—1947"; CIA 1, "Review of the World Situation as It Relates to the Security of the United States," September 26, 1947, Truman Papers, PSF Box 255, "Central Intelligence Reports—ORE 1948."

41. Minutes, PPS meeting, May 8, 1947, Policy Planning Staff Records, Box 32; Marshall to Jefferson Caffery, June 12, 1947, *FR: 1947*, III, 249; Transcript, Kennan National War College lecture, June 18, 1947, Kennan Papers, Box 17; PPS/4, "Certain Aspects of the European Recovery Program from the United States Standpoint (Preliminary Report), July 23, 1947, printed in Thomas H. Etzold and John Lewis Gaddis, eds., *Containment: Documents on American Policy and Strategy, 1945–1950* (New York: 1978),

p. 113; PPS/5, "Planning With Relation to a United Nations Program at the Forthcoming General Assembly," August 7, 1947, *FR: 1947*, I, 594; Forrestal to Chan Gurney, December 8, 1947, quoted in Millis, ed., *The Forrestal Diaries*, pp. 350–51.

42. Kennan, *Memoirs: 1925–1950*, p. 342.

43. Berry to Kennan, July 31, 1947, Policy Planning Staff Records, Box 31 "United Nations 1947–1949." For evidence that similar thinking was taking place elsewhere within the government, see the draft memorandum of the Executive Committee on the Regulation of Armaments, "Applying the Truman Doctrine to the United Nations," July 30, 1947, *FR: 1947*, I, 577–83.

44. Bohlen memorandum, August 30, 1947, *ibid.*, pp. 763–64. See also Bohlen's notes of Under Secretary of State Lovett's discussion with a group of War Department officials, August 30, 1947, *ibid.*, pp. 762–63; and the Forrestal Diary, August 31, 1947, Millis, ed., *The Forrestal Diaries*, p. 307. For a Policy Planning Staff effort to extend this line of analysis to Japan, see the draft paper "United States Policy Toward a Peace Settlement with Japan," September 17, 1947, Policy Planning Staff Records, Box 32, "Minutes of Meetings—1947."

45. Revised summary of PPS/13, "Résumé of World Situation," November 6, 1947, *FR: 1947*, I, 770n. See also the Forrestal Diary, November 7, 1947, Millis, ed., *The Forrestal Diaries*, p. 341.

46. Inverchapel to Foreign Office, February 9, 1948, Foreign Office Records, FO 371/68013B.

47. Hickerson memorandum of a conversation with Lord Inverchapel, January 21, 1948, *FR: 1948*, III, 11.

48. Inverchapel to Bevin, May 7, 1947, Foreign Office Records, FO 371/61047/AN1751.

49. F. B. A. Rundall minute, May 3, 1947, *ibid.*, FO 371/61054/AN1570.

50. See, on this point, the memorandum of a conversation between William L. Clayton, Lewis Douglas, and British cabinet officials in London, June 25, 1947, *FR: 1947*, III, 281; Lovett to Clayton and Caffery, August 14, 1947, *ibid.*, pp. 356–57; Truman speech at Rio de Janeiro, September 2, 1947, *Truman Public Papers: 1947*, p. 430; Lovett to Inverchapel, February 2, 1948, *FR: 1948*, III, 17–18; Bohlen to Lovett, August 9, 1948, *ibid.*, pp. 208–9; and Marshall to United States embassies in Paris and other capitals, August 27, 1948, *ibid.*, p. 223.

51. Kennan to Cecil B. Lyon, October 13, 1947, Policy Planning Staff Records, Box 33, "Chronological—1947." For Kennan's "five power" concept, see his lectures at the National War College and the Naval War College, September 17 and October 11, 1948, Kennan Papers, Box 17; also Kennan, *Memoirs: 1925–1950*, p. 359.

52. For the Truman administration's response to Kennan's ideas, see Gaddis, *Strategies of Containment*, pp. 55–65.

53. Saltzmann address to the International Council of Women, Philadelphia, September 11, 1947, *Department of State Bulletin*, XVII(September 21, 1947), 595. See also Secretary of State Marshall's testimony before the Senate Foreign Relations Committee, January 8, 1948, U.S. Congress, Senate, Committee on Foreign Relations, *European Recovery Program* (Washington: 1948), p. 13.

54. See, on this point, a draft report by Bohlen and Robinson, undated but early 1946, Department of State Records, Decimal File 1945–1949, 711.61/2–1446; Maxwell M. Hamilton to H. Freeman Matthews, February 14, 1946, *ibid.*; William D. Leahy diary, May 20, 1946, William D. Leahy Papers, Library of Congress; Robert Hooker memorandum, September 20, 1946, Department of State Records, Decimal File 1945–1949, 711.61/9–2046; John Balfour to Nevile Butler, June 9, 1947, Foreign Office Records, FO 371/61048/AN2101; Balfour to Foreign Office, July 20, 1947, *ibid.*, FO 371/61055/AN2552; Harriman to Truman, August 12, 1947, Truman Papers, PSF Box 178, "Foreign Affairs: Germany (2)"; Bohlen to Marshall, March 26, 1948, Bohlen Papers, Box 4, "Memos (CEB) January—June 1948"; Willard Thorp to Marshall, April 7, 1948, *FR: 1948*, I, 558–59; Carlton Savage draft paper, April 26, 1948, filed with PPS minutes, same day, Policy Planning Staff Records, Box 32; and the discussion in Chapter Six, below.

55. Minutes, Cabinet meeting of February 15, 1947, Cabinet Records, CAB 128/9, Public Record Office, London.

56. See, on this point, Kuniholm, *The Origins of the Cold War in the Near East,* pp. 345–46, 381–82.

57. Geir Lundestad, *America, Scandinavia, and the Cold War, 1945–1949* (New York: 1980), p. 194.

58. Marshall speech at Chicago, November 18, 1947, *Department of State Bulletin,* XVII(November 30, 1947), 1025.

59. JCS 1769/1, "United States Assistance to Other Countries from the Standpoint of National Security," April 29, 1947, *FR: 1947,* I, 741. See also an Office of Military Government for Germany memorandum, "A Summarized Analysis of the German Problem," March 5, 1947, *ibid.,* II, 229.

60. Kennan to Marshall, January 20, 1948, *FR: 1948,* III, 7. See also PPS/23, "Review of Current Trends: U. S. Foreign Policy," February 24, 1948, *ibid.,* I, 515–16.

61. Kennan comments at the fifth meeting of the Washington Exploratory Talks on Security, July 9, 1948, *ibid.,* III, 177. See also Kennan to Acheson, May 16, 1947, *FR: 1947,* III, 222.

62. Clayton to Lovett, September 17, 1948, Policy Planning Staff Records, Box 27, "Europe 1947–1948." See also a Clayton memorandum of January 17, 1949, Dean Acheson Papers, Box 64, "Memos—conversations Jan–Feb 49," Harry S. Truman Library.

63. Lovett to Harriman, December 3, 1948, *FR: 1948,* III, 301.

64. Marshall speech at Chicago, November 18, 1947, *Department of State Bulletin,* XVII(November 23, 1947), 1026.

65. Inverchapel to Bevin, May 22, 1947, Foreign Office Records, FO 371/61048/AN1986.

66. Rundall minute, February 23, 1948, *ibid.,* FO 371/68018/AN1702.

67. Kennan to Marshall, January 6, 1948, Policy Planning Staff Records, Box 33, "Chronological: Jan–May 1948" [emphases in original]. See also PPS/13, "Résumé of World Situation," November 6, 1947, *FR: 1947,* I, 776–77; transcripts of Kennan lectures to the Secretary of the Navy's Council and the National War College, December 3 and 18, 1947, Kennan Papers, Box 17; Kennan to Marshall, February 3, 1948, Policy Planning Staff Records, Box 33 "Chronological Jan–May 1948." See also a Moscow Embassy staff report, "Evaluation of Present Kremlin International Policies," November 5, 1947, *FR: 1947* IV, 606–12; and Walter Bedell Smith to Marshall, December 30, 1947, *ibid.,* II, 908. See also David Mayers, "Containment and the Primacy of Diplomacy: George Kennan's Views, 1947–1948," *International Security,* XI(Summer, 1986), 124–62.

68. JIC 380/2, "Estimate of the Intentions and Capabilities of the USSR Against the Continental United States and the Approaches Thereto, 1948–1957," February 16, 1948, Army Staff Records, ABC 381, USSR 2 Mar 46 Sec 5–B. On the deterrent effect of the atomic bomb, see Forrestal to Chan Gurney, December 8, 1947, quoted in Millis, ed., *The Forrestal Diaries,* pp. 349–51; and NSC 30, "United States Policy on Atomic Weapons," September 10, 1948, *FR: 1948,* I, 626–27.

69. "Summary of a Memorandum Representing Mr. Bevin's Views on the Formation of a Western Union," enclosed in Inverchapel to Marshall, January 13, 1948, *ibid.,* III, 4–6. See also the minutes of the British Cabinet meeting of January 8, 1948, Cabinet Records, CAB 128/12; C. P. (48)6, "The First Aim of British Foreign Policy," January 4, 1948, *ibid.,* CAB 129/23; and C. P. 48(72), "The Threat to Western Civilisation," March 3, 1948, *ibid.,* CAB 129/25. See also Alan Bullock, *Ernest Bevin: Foreign Secretary* (New York: 1983), pp. 513–25.

70. Marshall to Truman, March 12, 1948, *FR: 1948,* III, 49–50. For expressions of concern from other foreign leaders, see *ibid.,* pp. 6–7, 29–30, 34–35, 52–53.

71. See, on this point, the memoranda of conversations between Lovett and Inverchapel, January 27 and February 7, 1948, *ibid.,* pp. 12–13, 21–23.

72. Memorandum by George Butler, "Points for Discussion at S/P Meeting," March

19, 1948, Policy Planning Staff Records, Box 33, "Chronological Jan–May 1948"; John Hickerson comments at the second meeting of the US–UK–Canada security conversations, March 23, 1948, *FR: 1948*, III, 65; Inverchapel to Foreign Office, April 30, 1948, Foreign Office Records, FO 371/71671/N5183.

73. Kennan unsent letter to Walter Lippmann, April 6, 1948, Kennan Papers, Box 17.

74. State Department publication 3462, "The North Atlantic Pact: Collective Defense and the Preservation of Peace, Security and Freedom in the North Atlantic Community," printed in the *Department of State Bulletin*, XX(March 20, 1949), 342–50. See also Lovett's executive session testimony before the Senate Foreign Relations Committee, May 11, 1948, U.S. Congress, Senate, Committee on Foreign Relations, *Historical Series: The Vandenberg Resolution and the North Atlantic Treaty* (Washington: 1973), p. 9; and Acheson's memorandum of a conversation with the Danish foreign minister, March 11, 1949, *FR: 1949*, IV, 194.

75. Lovett comments, third meeting, Washington exploratory talks, July 7, 1948, *FR: 1948*, III, 157; Hickerson to William J. McWilliams, November 27, 1948, Policy Planning Staff Records, Box 27, "Europe 1947–1948"; Bohlen memoranda of conversations with the Norwegian and Danish foreign ministers, February 8 and March 12, 1949, *FR: 1949*, IV, 70–71, 198–99; Acheson statement to the House Foreign Affairs Committee, July 28, 1949, *Department of State Bulletin*, XXI(August 8, 1949), 193. For Johnson's suggestion, see his executive session testimony before the Senate Foreign Relations Committee, April 21, 1949, *The Vandenberg Resolution and the North Atlantic Treaty*, p. 228.

76. Hickerson to McWilliams, November 27, 1948, Policy Planning Staff Records, Box 27, "Europe 1947–1948." See also, on the "arsenal" concept, Willard Thorp to Marshall, April 7, 1948, *FR: 1948*, I, 560. For the question of ground troops, see Bohlen to Marshall S. Carter, November 7, 1948, *ibid.*, p. 654n; Marshall to Forrestal, November 8, 1948, *ibid.*, p. 655; Acheson and Johnson executive session testimony before the Senate Foreign Relations Committee, April 21, 1949, *The Vandenberg Resolution and the North Atlantic Treaty*, pp. 216, 235.

77. See, for example, *Department of State Bulletin*, XXX(March 20, 1949), 342–50.

78. Kennan draft memorandum for Marshall and Lovett, September 26, 1948, Policy Planning Staff Records, Box 27, "Europe 1947–1948." See also the transcripts of Kennan's lectures at the National War College, the Naval War College, and the Pentagon Joint Orientation Conference, September 17, October 11, and November 8, 1948, all in the Kennan Papers, Box 17; and PPS/43, "Considerations Affecting the Conclusion of a North Atlantic Security Pact," November 23, 1948, *FR: 1948*, III, 283–89.

79. Bohlen to Acheson, February 8, 1949, Bohlen Papers, Box 4, "Memos (CEB) 1949."

80. Minutes, Policy Planning Staff meeting, June 14, 1949, Policy Planning Staff Records, Box 32.

81. London Conference communique, June 7, 1948, *FR: 1948*, II, 315. For documentation on the London Conference, see *ibid.*, pp. 1–374.

82. State Department policy statement, "Germany," August 26, 1948, *ibid.*, p. 1298.

83. See note 32, above.

84. For the most comprehensive statement of Kennan's position, see PPS 37/1, "Position to be Taken by the U.S. at a CFM Meeting," November 15, 1948, *FR: 1948*, II, 1320–38. See also Kennan's memorandum of March 8, 1949, *FR: 1949*, III, 96–102; and his *Memoirs: 1925–1950*, pp. 415–48.

85. Minutes, Acheson-Kennan discussion, March 9, 1949, *FR: 1949*, III, 102–3. For the formation of the NSC steering group, see the minutes of the Policy Planning Staff meeting of January 28, 1949, Policy Planning Staff Records, Box 32. See also, on the reception of "Program A," Wilson D. Miscamble, "George F. Kennan, the Policy Planning Staff and American Foreign Policy, 1947–1950" (Ph.D. Dissertation, University of Notre Dame, 1979), pp. 134–72.

86. Bohlen to Kennan, October 25, 1948, Bohlen Papers, Box 4, "Memos (CEB)

July–December 1948." See also Hickerson to McWilliams, November 23, 1948, Policy Planning Staff Records, Box 27, "Europe 1947–1948"; Robert Murphy to Jacob Beam, December 7, 1948, *FR: 1948*, II, 1320n; Murphy to Marshall S. Carter, January 14, 1949, Policy Planning Staff Records, Box 15, "Germany 1947–8."

87. Bruce to Acheson, May 14, 1949, *FR: 1949*, III, 878. See also Kennan, *Memoirs: 1925–1950*, p. 445.

88. Kennan to Acheson, March 29, 1949 (unsent), Kennan Papers, Box 23.

89. Acheson memorandum of conversation with Senators Tom Connally and Arthur Vandenberg, February 14, 1949, *FR: 1949*, IV, 109. See also a message from Bevin read to the National Security Council on May 20, 1948, *FR: 1948*, III, 122, and Timothy P. Ireland, *Creating the Entangling Alliance: The Origins of the North Atlantic Treaty Organization* (Westport, Connecticut: 1981), especially pp. 4–8, 137–41.

90. Secret conclusions, Cabinet meeting of March 5, 1948, Cabinet Records, CAB 128/14. See also the minutes of the meeting of March 8, 1948, *ibid.*, CAB 128/12.

91. Lovett to Harriman, December 3, 1948, *FR: 1948*, III, 303.

92. Jebb to Kennan, April 7, 1949, *FR: 1949*, IV, 289–91.

93. PPS minutes, meeting of May 18, 1949, Policy Planning Staff Records, Box 32.

94. Kennan notes for introductory meeting, June 6, 1949, *ibid.*, Box 27, "Europe 1949."

95. Kennan, *Memoirs: 1925–1950*, pp. 462–64.

96. See Kennan's comments as reported in the minutes of the PPS meeting of June 3, 1949, Policy Planning Staff Records, Box 32.

97. PPS 55, "Outline: Study of U.S. Stance Toward Question of European Union," July 7, 1949, *ibid.*, Box 27, "Europe 1949"; Kennan to Acheson and Webb, August 22, 1949, *ibid.*, Box 33, "Chronological 1949."

98. See the comments of Kennan, Niebuhr, and Smith, as reported in the minutes of the PPS meetings of June 13 and 14, 1949, *ibid.*, Box 32.

99. PPS minutes, meeting of October 18, 1949, *ibid.*

100. Bohlen to Kennan, October 6, 1949, Bohlen Papers, Box 1, "Correspondence 1946–49: K."

101. David Bruce to Acheson, October 22, 1949, *FR: 1949*, IV, 343.

102. C.P. (49) 208, "European Policy: Memorandum by the Secretary of State for Foreign Affairs," October 18, 1949, Cabinet Records, CAB 129/37.

103. Kennan to Bohlen, November 7, 1949, Kennan Papers, Box 28.

104. Bohlen to Kennan, undated but November, 1949, *ibid.*; Kennan to Bohlen, November 17, 1949, *ibid.*

105. Kennan, *Memoirs: 1925–1950*, p. 464.

106. See, on this point, A. W. DePorte, *Europe Between the Super-Powers: The Enduring Balance* (New Haven: 1979).

## 4   Drawing Lines: The Defensive Perimeter Strategy in East Asia, 1947–1951

1. J. Lawton Collins, *War in Peacetime: The History and Lessons of Korea* (Boston: 1969), p. 31. Acheson's speech, entitled "Crisis in Asia—An Examination of U.S. Policy," is printed in the *Department of State Bulletin* XXII(January 23, 1950), 111–18. See also Dean Acheson, *Present at the Creation: My Years in the State Department* (New York: 1969), pp. 358, 691.

2. For the best available evidence on this question, see Robert R. Simmons, *The Strained Alliance: Peking, P'yongyang, Moscow and the Politics of the Korean Civil War* (New York: 1975); and Masao Okonogi, "The Domestic Roots of the Korean War," in Yonosuke Nagai and Akira Iriye, eds., *The Origins of the Cold War in Asia* (New York: 1977), pp. 299–320. A useful recent summary of what is known can be found in Burton I. Kaufman, *The Korean War: Challenges in Crisis, Credibility, and Command* (New York: 1986), especially pp. 31–33.

3. Kennan to Marshall, March 14, 1948, U.S. Department of State, *Foreign Relations of the United States* [hereafter *FR*]: *1948*, I, 531–38.

4. Kennan notes, conversations with MacArthur, March 5 and 21, 1948, enclosed in PPS/28, "Recommendations with Respect to U.S. Policy Toward Japan," March 25, 1948, *ibid.*, VI, 700–701, 709.

5. See MacArthur to Albert C. Wedemeyer, C–65590, November 20, 1948, Joint Chiefs of Staff Records, William D. Leahy Papers, File 9, "China—1948" folder, Modern Military Records Branch, National Archives; Fayette J. Flexner notes, conversation with MacArthur, December 6, 1948, *FR: 1949*, IX, 263–65; *New York Times*, March 2, 1949; Max W. Bishop to W. Walton Butterworth, April 1, 1949, *FR: 1949*, VII, 695; William R. Mathews account of interview with MacArthur, August 5, 1949, enclosed in Mathews to John Foster Dulles, June 5, 1950, John Foster Dulles Papers, Box 49, "Mathews" folder, Seeley Mudd Library, Princeton University; William J. Sebald to Acheson, September 9, 1949, *FR: 1949*, VII, 857; H. Alexander Smith Diary, October 10, 1949, H. Alexander Smith Papers, Box 282, Seeley Mudd Library, Princeton University; MacArthur to Arthur Hayes Sulzberger, October 28, 1949, Douglas MacArthur Papers, Record Group 5, Box 1A, File #4, MacArthur Memorial, Norfolk, Virginia. See also D. Clayton James, *The Years of MacArthur: Triumph and Disaster, 1945–1964* (Boston: 1985), pp. 401–2.

6. CIA ORE 17–49, "The Strategic Importance of the Far East to the US and the USSR," May 4, 1949, Harry S. Truman Papers, PSF, Box 256, "CIA Reports—ORE 49."

7. NSC 49, "Strategic Evaluation of United States Security Needs in Japan," June 9, 1949, *FR: 1949*, VII, 774–75.

8. State Department Consultants Report, "Outline of Far Eastern and Asian Policy for Review with the President," enclosed in Philip C. Jessup to Acheson, November 16, 1949, *ibid.*, pp. 1211–12.

9. NSC 48/1, "The Position of the United States with Respect to Asia," December 23, 1949, U.S. Department of Defense, *United States–Vietnam Relations, 1945–67* [hereafter cited as *Pentagon Papers*] (Washington: 1971), VIII, 257.

10. Acheson, *Present at the Creation*, p. 357. For the quote from the Press Club speech, see the *Department of State Bulletin*, XXII (January 23, 1950), 116.

11. See, for example, Marshall to John Leighton Stuart, February 9, 1948, *FR: 1948*, VIII, 13–14; and Butterworth to Lewis Clark, March 8, 1948, *ibid.*, pp. 30–31.

12. See, on this point, Tang Tsou, *America's Failure in China, 1941–50* (Chicago: 1963), p. 446; and William Whitney Stueck, Jr., *The Road to Confrontation: American Policy Toward China and Korea, 1947–1950* (Chapel Hill: 1981), pp. 52–54.

13. U.S. Department of State, *United States Relations with China, with Special Reference to the Period 1944–1949* [hereafter *China White Paper*] (Washington: 1949), p. xvi.

14. *Department of State Bulletin*, XXII (January 23, 1950), 116–17. See also Acheson's speeches to the Commonwealth Club, San Francisco, March 15, 1950, and to the Harvard Alumni Association, Cambridge, Massachusetts, June 22, 1950, *ibid.*, XXII (March 27, 1950), 470–71, and XXIII (July 3, 1950), 16.

15. See John Lewis Gaddis, *Strategies of Containment: A Critical Appraisal of Postwar American National Security Policy* (New York: 1982), pp. 58–59.

16. Kennan National War College lecture, "Contemporary Problems of Foreign Policy," September 17, 1948, George F. Kennan Papers, Box 17, Seeley Mudd Library, Princeton University. See also Kennan's *Memoirs: 1925–1950* (Boston: 1967), p. 359.

17. Kennan Naval War College lecture, October 11, 1948, Kennan Papers, Box 17. For other expressions of this point of view, see CIA ORE 17–49, May 4, 1949, Truman Papers, PSF, Box 256, "CIA Reports—ORE 49"; and NSC 48/1, December 23, 1949, *Pentagon Papers*, VIII, 228–39 [error in page numbering in original].

18. Acheson executive session testimony, May 1, 1950, U.S. Congress, Senate Committee on Foreign Relations, *Historical Series: Reviews of the World Situation, 1949–1950* (Washington: 1974), p. 292.

19. See the *Department of State Bulletin* XXII (January 23, 1950), 112–13, for the expression of this theme in Acheson's National Press Club speech; see also Acheson's executive session testimony before the Senate Foreign Relations Committee on October 12, 1949, and May 1, 1950, *Reviews of the World Situation*, pp. 87, 291–92; and NSC 48/1, December 23, 1949, *Pentagon Papers*, VIII, 226–27.

20. See, for example, two memoranda by O. Edmund Clubb, August 3 and 28, 1947, *FR: 1947*, VII, 266, 701; Joseph E. Jacobs to Marshall, September 19, 1947, *ibid.*, VI, 803–7; and PPS/13, "Résumé of World Situation," *ibid.*, I, 776.

21. *Department of State Bulletin*, XXII (January 23, 1950), 115. See also Acheson's remarks to the Advertising Council, Washington, February 16, 1950, and his Commonwealth Club speech, San Francisco, March 15, 1950, *ibid.*, XXII (March 20 and 27, 1950), 428, 468, 472.

22. For details, see Chapter Six, below.

23. Charlton Ogburn, Jr., memorandum, "Decisions Reached by Consensus at the Meetings with the Secretary and the Consultants on the Far East," November 2, 1949, *FR: 1949*, IX, 160–61.

24. SM–8388, "Study of the Military Aspects of United States Policy Toward China," June 9, 1947, *FR: 1947*, VII, 843. See also JCS 1721/5, "United States Policy Toward China," June 9, 1947, Joint Chiefs of Staff Records, CCS 452 China (4–3–45), sec. 7, pt. 1; NSC 6, "The Position of the United States Regarding Short-Term Assistance to China," March 26, 1948, *FR: 1948*, VIII, 47–50; William D. Leahy to James V. Forrestal, April 1, 1948, Joint Chiefs of Staff Records, CCS 452 China (4–3–45), sec. 7, pt. 2; NSC 22, "Possible Courses of Action for the U.S. with Respect to the Critical Situation in China," July 26, 1948, *FR: 1948*, VIII, 118–22.

25. Wedemeyer to Truman, September 19, 1947, *China White Paper*, p. 814; Badger to Louis Denfeld, July 16, 1948, *FR: 1948*, VIII, 171–72. See also Badger's executive session testimony before the Senate Foreign Relations and Armed Services Committees, September 8, 1949, U.S. Congress, Senate Committee on Foreign Relations, *Historical Series: Military Assistance Program, 1949* (Washington: 1974), p. 541; and William Stueck, *The Wedemeyer Mission: American Politics and Foreign Policy during the Cold War* (Athens, Georgia: 1984).

26. SM–8388, June 9, 1947, *FR: 1947*, VII, 840. See also Robert P. Patterson to Marshall, February 26, 1947, *ibid.*, p. 800. For evidence that Admiral Badger may not have shared this view, see DeWitt C. Ramsey to Denfeld, February 18, 1949, Records of the Immediate Office of the Chief of Naval Operations [hereafter CNO Immediate Office Records], Box 1, Folder A8–2, Operational Archives, Naval Historical Center, Washington.

27. See Wedemeyer to Truman, September 19, 1947, *China White Paper*, pp. 809–10; also Wedemeyer to Forrestal, March 29, 1948, Joint Chiefs of Staff Records, CCS 452 China (4–3–45), sec. 7, pt. 2.

28. NSC 22/1, "Possible Courses of Action for the U.S. with Respect to the Critical Situation in China," August 6, 1948, *FR: 1948*, VIII, 133. This language also appears in SM–8388, June 9, 1947, *FR: 1947*, VII, 844.

29. JCS 1769/1, "United States Assistance to Other Countries from the Standpoint of National Security," April 29, 1947, *ibid.*, I, 746.

30. SANACC 360/11, August 18, 1948, enclosed in Rusk to Acheson, March 16, 1949, *FR: 1949*, I, 262.

31. Joint Chiefs of Staff to Forrestal, November 2, 1948, enclosed in NSC 35, "Existing Commitments Involving the Possible Use of Armed Forces," November 17, 1948, *FR: 1948*, I, 661. See also a Joint Chiefs of Staff undated comment, enclosed in SANA–6333, March 16, 1949, *FR: 1949*, I, 258.

32. Marshall testimony, May 10, 1951, U.S. Congress, Senate Committees on Armed Services and Foreign Relations, *Military Situation in the Far East* (Washington: 1951), p. 465.

33. JPS 633/4, "United States Post-War Military Policy and Strategic Plan," Army Staff Records, ABC 092 (18 July 45), sec. 1–A, Modern Military Records Branch, National Archives.

34. JCS 1769/1, April 29, 1947, *FR: 1947*, I, 745.

35. JWPC 476/1, "The Soviet Threat in the Far East and the Means Required to Oppose It: Short Title, MOONRISE," June 16, 1947, Joint Chiefs of Staff Records, 381 USSR (3–2–46), sec. 5; JWPC 476/2, August 29, 1947, *ibid.*, sec. 6.

36. *Ibid.*

37. JSPC 877/72, "The Impact of Current Far Eastern Developments on Emergency War Planning," September 14, 1949, Army Staff Records, P & O 1949–50, 381 TS, sec. 3, case 56.

38. NSC 48/1, December 23, 1949, *Pentagon Papers*, VIII, 256–57.

39. MacArthur to Charles A. Eaton, March 3, 1948, MacArthur Papers, Record Group 6, Box 2, "FECOM: Formosa" file.

40. Mathews account, interview with MacArthur, August 5, 1949, Dulles Papers, Box 49, "Mathews" folder. See also Kennan's notes of a conversation with MacArthur, March 21, 1948, *FR: 1948*, VI, 711–12.

41. MacArthur to Eaton, March 3, 1948, MacArthur Papers, Record Group 6, Box 2, "FECOM: Formosa" file.

42. Smith notes of conversation with MacArthur, September 27, 1949, Smith Papers, Box 98, "Far East Trip, 1949" folder.

43. MacArthur to Wedemeyer, C–65590, November 20, 1948, Leahy Papers, File 9, "China—1948" folder.

44. Max W. Bishop memorandum, conversation with MacArthur, February 16, 1949, *FR: 1949*, VII, 656; Ramsey to Denfeld, February 18, 1949, CNO Immediate Office Records, Box 1, Folder A8–2; MacArthur to Kennan, June 16, 1949, MacArthur Papers, Record Group 5, Box 1A, File 5; Jessup memorandum, conversation with MacArthur, January 8, 1950, *FR: 1950*, VI, 1111; MacArthur to Robert C. Richardson, June 9, 1950, MacArthur Papers, Record Group 5, Box 49.

45. Briefing by Maj. Gen. Charles W. Willoughby, "Relation of World-Wide Political Situation to CINCFE Missions," October 1, 1949, MacArthur Papers, Record Group 6, Box 83, "RMAP" folder.

46. Douglas MacArthur, *Reminiscences* (New York: 1964), p. 389. See also a memorandum by John Foster Dulles of a conversation with MacArthur, July 1, 1950, Dulles Papers, Box 47, "Acheson" folder.

47. MacArthur to Roy Howard, April 24, 1947, and to Robert A. Taft, March 23, 1950, MacArthur Papers, Record Group 5, Boxes 28 and 56. See also Michael Schaller, *The American Occupation of Japan: The Origins of the Cold War in Asia* (New York: 1985), pp. 60–61.

48. Leahy to Forrestal, November 24, 1948, enclosed in NSC 37, "The Strategic Importance of Formosa," December 1, 1948, *FR: 1949*, IX, 261–62. See also Denfeld to Forrestal, February 10, 1949, enclosed in NSC 37/3, "The Strategic Importance of Formosa," February 11, 1949, *ibid.*, p. 285.

49. State Department draft report, NSC 37/1, "The Position of the United States with Respect to Formosa," January 19, 1949, *ibid.*, p. 274. See also Robert Lovett to Truman, January 14, 1949, *ibid.*, p. 266.

50. Bishop memorandum, conversation with MacArthur, February 16, 1949, *ibid.*, VII, 656–57. See also Flexner notes, conversation with MacArthur, December 6, 1948, *ibid.*, IX, 263–64.

51. Denfeld to Forrestal, February 10, 1949, enclosed in NSC 37/3, February 11, 1949, *ibid.*, p. 285.

52. Flexner notes, conversation with MacArthur, December 6, 1948, *ibid.*, p. 265; Kenneth Krentz to Butterworth, April 25, 1949, *ibid.*, p. 317.

53. Acheson statement at National Security Council meeting, March 1, 1949, *ibid.*,

p. 295. See also NSC 11/2, "U.S. Naval Forces at Tsingtao," *FR: 1948*, VIII, 341; NSC 37/1, January 19, 1949, *FR: 1949*, IX, 272–73; and Livingston Merchant to Acheson, March 23, 1949, *ibid.*, pp. 302–3.

54. NSC 37/2, "The Current Position of the United States with Respect to Formosa," February 3, 1949, *ibid.*, pp. 280–82. See also Lovett to Truman, January 14, 1949, *ibid.*, pp. 302–3; and Russell D. Buhite, *Soviet-American Relations in Asia, 1945–1950* (Norman, Oklahoma: 1981), pp. 92–95.

55. Acheson statement at National Security Council meeting, March 1, 1949, *ibid.*, p. 295. See also Acheson to Merchant, February 14, 1949, *ibid.*, pp. 287–88; and NSC 37/4, "The Current Position of the United States with Respect to Formosa," February 18, 1949, *ibid.*, pp. 288–89.

56. Merchant to Acheson, March 23, 1949, *ibid.*, pp. 302–3; Allen Griffith to Harlan Cleveland, April 14, 1949, enclosed in Cleveland to Butterworth, April 29, 1949, *ibid.*; Merchant to Acheson, May 4, 1949, *ibid.*, pp. 324–25; Merchant to Butterworth, May 24, 1949, *ibid.*, pp. 346–50.

57. Acheson statement to the National Security Council, March 1, 1949, *ibid.*, p. 296.

58. JCS 1966/11, "The Strategic Importance of Formosa," March 22, 1949, Joint Chiefs of Staff Records, 381 Formosa (11–8–48), sec. 1. See also Louis Johnson to Sidney Souers, April 2, 1949, *FR: 1949*, IX, 307–8; and Omar Bradley to Johnson, August 17, 1949, enclosed in NSC 37/7, "The Position of the United States with Respect to Formosa," August 22, 1949, *ibid.*, pp. 377–78.

59. JCS 1844/46, "Joint Oßutline Emergency War Plan OFFTACKLE," approved December 8, 1949, Joint Chiefs of Staff Records, 381 USSR (3–2–46), sec. 41. For preliminary versions of this plan, see JSPC 877/58, May 10, 1949, JSPC 877/59, May 29, 1949, and JSPC 877/66, August 2, 1949, all in *ibid.*, secs. 32 and 36.

60. Robert M. Blum, *Drawing the Line: The Origin of the American Containment Policy in East Asia* (New York: 1982), pp. 131–44.

61. Smith Diary, October 13–18, Smith Papers, Box 282.

62. Blum, *Drawing the Line*, pp. 178–79.

63. Sebald to Acheson, September 9, 1949, *FR: 1949*, VII, 875; Willoughby briefing, "Relation of World-Wide Political Situation to CINCFE Missions," October 1, 1949, MacArthur Papers, Record Group 6, Box 83, "RMAP" folder; MacArthur to Sulzberger, October 28, 1949, *ibid.*, Record Group 5, Box 1A, File 4.

64. Bradley to Johnson, December 23, 1949, enclosed in NSC 37/9, "Possible United States Military Action Toward Taiwan Not Involving Major Military Forces," December 27, 1949, *FR: 1949*, IX, 460–61. See also J. Lawton Collins to the Joint Chiefs of Staff, JCS 1966/22, December 7, 1949, Joint Chiefs of Staff Records, 381 Formosa (11–8–48), sec. 2; and Tracy Voorhees draft, Johnson to Truman, December 15, 1949, copy in MacArthur Papers, Record Group 6, Box 2, "Formosa" folder.

65. Ogburn memorandum, November 2, 1949, *FR: 1949*, IX, 161. See also NSC 37/8, "The Position of the United States with Respect to Formosa," October 6, 1949, *ibid.*, pp. 392–97; and Acheson to John J. MacDonald, November 18, 1949, *ibid.*, pp. 428–29.

66. Merchant to Butterworth, December 1, 1949, *ibid.*, pp. 431–33; "Policy Information Paper—Formosa," December 23, 1949, printed in *Military Situation in the Far East*, pp. 667–69.

67. NSC 48/2, "The Position of the United States with Respect to Asia," December 30, 1949, *FR: 1949*, VII, 1219–20. See also NSC 48/1, December 23, 1949, *Pentagon Papers*, VIII, 244–46; Butterworth to Acheson, December 28, 1949, *FR: 1949*, IX, 461–63; and Acheson's memorandum of a conversation with the Joint Chiefs of Staff, December 29, 1949, *ibid.*, pp. 463–67.

68. *Public Papers of the Presidents: Harry S. Truman, 1950* [hereafter cited as *Truman Public Papers*] (Washington: 1965), pp. 11–12. See also Acheson's press conference statement, January 5, 1950, *Department of State Bulletin*, XXII (January 16, 1950), 80–81.

69. Acheson memorandum, meeting with Knowland and Smith, January 5, 1950, *FR: 1950*, VI, 263.

70. Senate Foreign Relations Committee executive session, January 13, 1950, *Reviews of the World Situation*, pp. 184–85.

71. Smith Diary, January 20, 1950, Smith Papers, Box 282.

72. Dulles speech, "The Importance of Spiritual Resources," January 27, 1950, Cold Spring Harbor, Long Island, copy in Dulles Papers, Box 48, "Liberation Policy" folder. See also Dulles to Vandenberg, January 6, 1950, *ibid.*, "Formosa" folder.

73. Acheson press conference, January 5, 1950, *Department of State Bulletin*, XXII (January 16, 1950), 81.

74. Bradley's executive session testimony is in *Reviews of the World Situation*, pp. 239–45.

75. JCS 1844/53, January 26, 1950, Joint Chiefs of Staff Records, 381 USSR (3-2-46), sec. 44. See also James F. Schnabel, *Policy and Direction: The First Year* [*United States Army in the Korean War* series] (Washington: 1972), pp. 50–51.

76. JCS 2109, "Notes on Visit of the Joint Chiefs of Staff to Alaska, the Far East, and the Pacific," March 13, 1950, Joint Chiefs of Staff Records, 333.1 Far East (1–13–50).

77. Donovan address, New York City, February 16, 1950, copy in Dwight D. Eisenhower Papers, 1916–52 File, Box 32, Dwight D. Eisenhower Library.

78. "Report on Formosa," May, 1950, copy in Smith Papers, Box 100, "Twitchell Report" folder. See also Smith to Twitchell, June 3, 1950, *ibid.*

79. Knowland to Johnson, May 15, 1950, copy in *ibid.*, Box 100, "Foreign Relations" folder.

80. Smith Diary, May 24, 1950, Box 282. For the circumstances surrounding Dulles's appointment, see Ronald W. Pruessen, *John Foster Dulles: The Road to Power* (New York: 1982), pp. 432–36.

81. Dulles memorandum of May 18, 1950, *FR: 1950*, I, 314–16. Dulles also submitted copies of this memorandum to Paul Nitze, Director of the State Department Policy Planning Staff, and to Under Secretary of State James Webb.

82. Smith Diary, May 14, 1950, Smith Papers, Box 282. See also Warren I. Cohen, *Dean Rusk* (Totowa, New Jersey: 1980), pp. 46–47.

83. J. H. Burns to Director, Joint Staff, and others, May 29, 1950, Joint Chiefs of Staff Records, 381 Formosa (11–8–48), sec. 3. See also Burns to Rusk, May 29, 1950, *FR: 1950*, VI, 346–47.

84. W. Park Armstrong memorandum of Rusk-Nitze-Jessup-Merchant-Sprouse conversation, May 31, 1950, *ibid.*, pp. 347–49.

85. Rusk draft memorandum to Acheson, May 30, 1950, *ibid.*, pp. 349–51. There is no indication whether this memorandum was actually sent.

86. Cooke to MacArthur, May 2, 1950, MacArthur Papers, Record Group 10, Box 3. See also Cooke to Knowland, April 10, 1950, copy in Smith Papers, Box 100, "Foreign Relations Committee" folder; Cooke to Sherman, April 14, 1950, Forrest P. Sherman Papers, Folder 1, in CNO Immediate Office Records; Cooke to MacArthur, April 27, 1950, MacArthur Papers, Record Group 10, Box 3; Cooke to Sherman, May 23, 1950, Sherman Papers, Folder 1.

87. MacArthur to Department of the Army, C–56410, May 29, 1950, MacArthur Papers, Record Group 6, Box 2, "Formosa" folder.

88. S. G. Kelly to Vice Admiral Duncan, June 9, 1950, Joint Chiefs of Staff Records, 381 Formosa (11–8–48), sec. 3.

89. MacArthur "Memorandum on Formosa," June 14, 1950, *FR: 1950*, VII, 161–65. See also, on pre-Korean War rethinking of Taiwan policy, Buhite, *Soviet-American Relations in Asia*, pp. 99–101.

90. Bradley to the Joint Chiefs, June 25, 1950, Joint Chiefs of Staff Records, 381

Formosa (11–8–48), sec. 3. See also a Bradley draft memorandum for Johnson to Truman, June 25, 1950, *ibid.*

91. Jessup notes, Blair House meetings of June 25 and 26, 1950, *FR: 1950*, VII, 157–58, 179–80.

92. Smith Diary, June 28, 1950, Smith Papers, Box 282. For Truman's June 27 announcement, see the *Truman Public Papers:* 1950, p. 492.

93. Joint Chiefs of Staff to MacArthur, JCS–84681, June 29, 1950, *FR: 1950*, VII, 240–41; Acheson to the United States mission at the United Nations, July 1, 1950, *ibid.*, p. 276; Acheson to Lewis Douglas, July 28, 1950, *ibid.*, VI, 397; Rusk to Karl L. Rankin, August 14, 1950, *ibid.*, p. 438; Truman radio-television address, September 1, 1950, *Truman Public Papers: 1950*, p. 613; Acheson to Loy Henderson, September 1, 1950, *FR: 1950*, VI, 478–80; and Acheson's executive session testimony before the Senate Foreign Relations Committee, July 24 and September 11, 1950, *Reviews of the World Situation*, pp. 316, 354.

94. The text of MacArthur's message is in *FR: 1950*, VI, 453. For the events surrounding its recall, see James, *MacArthur: Triumph and Disaster*, pp. 460–64. The Chinese troop offer and its subsequent rejection are documented in *FR: 1950*, VII, 239, 262–63, 269, 276–77.

95. Acheson to Rankin, September 4, 1950, *ibid.*, VI, 485.

96. Joint Chiefs of Staff to Johnson, July 27, 1950, *ibid.*, p. 392.

97. NSC 37/10, "Immediate United States Courses of Action with Respect to Formosa," August 3, 1950, *ibid.*, pp. 413–14; Truman to Acheson, August 25, 1950, cited in *ibid.*, p. 414n.

98. John Allison memorandum, Dulles-Acheson conversation October 23, 1950, *ibid.*, pp. 534–36. See also Dulles's memorandum of a conversation with Tingfu F. Tsiang, October 27, 1950, *ibid.*, pp. 542–44.

99. Acheson to Marshall, November 11, 1950, *ibid.*, p. 555.

100. Dulles to Acheson, November 15, 1950, *ibid.*, pp. 572–73. See also minutes of discussions of the Taiwan issue in the U.S. delegation to the U.N., November 14 and 15, 1950, *ibid.*, pp. 556–72.

101. Jessup notes, Acheson-Franks conversation, December 7, 1950, *ibid.*, VII, 1437; minutes, Truman-Attlee meeting, December 7, 1950, *ibid.*, pp. 1452–53, 1455–56.

102. PPS/51, "United States Policy Toward Southeast Asia," March 29, 1949, later circulated to the National Security Council as NSC 51, July 1, 1949, *FR: 1949*, VII, 1129. See also Michael Schaller, "Securing the Great Crescent: Occupied Japan and the Origins of Containment in Southeast Asia," *Journal of American History*, LXIX (September, 1982), 392–414.

103. NSC 48/1, December 23, 1949, *Pentagon Papers*, VIII, 248.

104. Joint Chiefs of Staff to Johnson, undated, enclosed in Johnson to Acheson, April 14, 1950, *FR: 1950*, VI, 781.

105. Acheson executive session testimony, October 12, 1949, *Reviews of the World Situation*, p. 90. See also Acheson's memorandum of a conversation with Carlos P. Romulo, March 10, 1950, *FR: 1950*, VI, 753; and his Senate Foreign Relations Committee testimony of May 1, 1950, *Reviews of the World Situation*, p. 306.

106. See Acheson to the Consulate General, Saigon, May 10, 1949, *FR: 1949*, VII, 23–25; Butterworth to Jessup, January 20, 1950, *FR: 1950*, VI, 698–700; and Acheson to Truman, February 2, 1950, *ibid.*, pp. 716–17. See also Gary R. Hess, "The First American Commitment in Indochina: The Acceptance of the 'Bao Dai Solution,' 1950," *Diplomatic History*, II (Fall, 1978), 331–50.

107. NSC 64, "The Position of the United States with Respect to Indochina," February 27, 1950, *FR: 1950*, VI, 747; James S. Lay, Jr., to the National Security Council, April 24, 1950, *ibid.*, p. 787n.

108. Marshall to U.S. Embassy, Paris, February 3, 1947, *FR: 1947*, VI, 68; Acheson to U.S. Consulate, Hanoi, April 14, 1947, *ibid.*, p. 85; Marshall to U.S. Consulate General, Saigon, July 17, 1947, *ibid.*, pp. 117–18; Jefferson Caffery to Marshall, July 31, 1947,

*ibid.,* pp. 127–28; Marshall to U.S. Embassy, Paris, July 3, 1948, *ibid.,* p. 30; Marshall to U.S. Embassy, Nanjing, July 7, 1948, *FR: 1948,* VI, 28.

109. Charles S. Reed to Marshall, July 11, 1947, *FR: 1947,* VI, 114; James L. O'Sullivan to Marshall, July 19, 1947, *ibid.,* p. 120; O'Sullivan to Marshall, July 21, 1947, *ibid.,* pp. 121–23; Reed to Marshall, July 24, 1947, *ibid.,* pp. 123–27; O'Sullivan to Marshall, September 15, 1947, *ibid.,* pp. 136–37; Department of State Policy State-ment on Indochina, September 27, 1948, *FR: 1948,* VI, 48; George M. Abbott to Mar-shall, November 5, 1948, *ibid.,* pp. 54–55.

110. Acheson to U.S. Consulate General, Hanoi, May 20, 1949, *FR: 1949,* VII, 29.

111. Acheson press conference statement, February 1, 1950, *Department of State Bulletin,* XXII(February 13, 1950), 244. See also Loy Henderson's address to the Indian Council on World Affairs, New Delhi, March 27, 1950, *ibid.,* XXII(April 10, 1950), 565.

112. I am indebted to Professor John Cady of the Ohio University History Depart-ment for this suggestion, which is based on his personal experiences in the State De-partment during the period in question. See also Hugh DeSantis, *The Diplomacy of Silence: The American Foreign Service, the Soviet Union, and the Cold War, 1933–1947* (Chicago: 1980), pp. 108–9.

113. Department of State memorandum, "Basic Factors in Soviet Far Eastern Policy," enclosed in Department circular telegram, October 12, 1948, *FR: 1948,* I, 644.

114. Yost to George W. Perkins, January 31, 1950, *FR: 1950,* VI, 710.

115. Weekly Intelligence Report, Department of the Army, March 17, 1950, quoted in Schabel, *Policy and Direction,* p. 63.

116. Gullion to Acheson, May 6, 1950, *FR: 1950,* VI, 803.

117. NSC 48/1, December 23, 1949, *Pentagon Papers,* VII, 258–59. See also CIA ORE 17–49, May 4, 1949, Truman Papers, PSF, Box 256, "CIA Reports—ORE 49." Schaller, *The American Occupation of Japan,* especially pp. 137–38, 205–25, documents the relationship of Southeast Asia to the economic rehabilitation of Japan.

118. Joint Chiefs of Staff to Johnson, no date, enclosed in Johnson to Acheson, April 14, 1950, *FR: 1950,* VI, 781.

119. State Department working group paper, "Military Aid for Indochina," Feb-ruary 1, 1950, *ibid.,* p. 714. See also Yost to Perkins, January 31, 1950, *ibid.,* pp. 710–11; NSC 64, February 27, 1950, *ibid.,* p. 747; and Johnson to Truman, March 6, 1950, *Penta-gon Papers,* II, A–17.

120. Merchant to Butterworth, March 7, 1950, *FR: 1950,* VI, 750.

121. Joint Chiefs of Staff to Johnson, no date, enclosed in Johnson to Acheson, April 14, 1950, *ibid.,* p. 781.

122. Jessup notes, Blair House meeting, June 26, 1950, *ibid.,* VII, 180. See also Truman's public announcement on June 27, *Truman Public Papers: 1950,* p. 492.

123. Joint Chiefs of Staff to Marshall, November 28, 1950, enclosed in NSC 64/1, "The Position of the United States with Respect to Indochina," December 21, 1950, *FR: 1950,* VI, 946. See also John F. Melby and G. B. Erskine to the Foreign Assistance Coordinating Committee, August 6, 1950, *ibid.,* p. 844; and Southeast Asia Aid Policy Committee to Acheson and Marshall, October 11, 1950, *ibid.,* p. 888.

124. See, for example, Melby and Erskine to FACC, August 6, 1950, *ibid.,* p. 842; Melby to Rusk and Lacy, August 7, 1950, *ibid.,* pp. 845–48; Policy Planning Staff memo-randum, "United States Policy Toward Indochina in the Light of Recent Developments," August 16, 1950, *ibid.,* pp. 857–58.

125. Ogburn to Rusk, August 18, 1950, *ibid.,* p. 863.

126. Ohly to Acheson, November 20, 1950, *ibid.,* pp. 929–30.

127. Joint Strategic Survey Comittee analysis, November 17, 1950, enclosed in Joint Chiefs to Marshall, November 28, 1950, *ibid.,* pp. 949–51.

128. Joint Chiefs of Staff to Marshall, November 28, 1950, *ibid.,* pp. 947–48.

129. NSC Staff Study, enclosed in NSC 48/5, "United States Objectives, Policies and Courses of Action in Asia," May 17, 1951, *FR: 1951,* VI, 59.

130. James Irving Matray, *The Reluctant Crusade: American Foreign Policy in Korea,*

*1941–1950* (Honolulu: 1985), pp. 106–10; Charles M. Dobbs, *The Unwanted Symbol: American Foreign Policy, the Cold War, and Korea, 1945–1950* (Kent, Ohio: 1981), pp. 91–93; John Lewis Gaddis, "Korea in American Politics, Strategy, and Diplomacy, 1945–50," in Nagai and Iriye, *Origins of the Cold War in Asia*, pp. 277–78.

131. JWPC 476/1, June 16, 1947, Joint Chiefs of Staff Records, 381 USSR (3-2-46), sec. 5.

132. Forrestal to Marshall, September 29, 1947, *FR: 1947*, VI, 818.

133. JCS1769/1, April 29, 1947, *ibid.*, I, 744.

134. SWNCC 176/30, "United States Policy in Korea," August 4, 1947, *ibid.*, VI, 738.

135. Wedemeyer report, September 19, 1947, *ibid.*, p. 803. See also Francis B. Stevens to Kennan and John M. Allison, September 9, 1947, *ibid.*, p. 784.

136. Butterworth to Lovett, October 1, 1947, *ibid.*, p. 820. See also PPS/13, November 6, 1947, *ibid.*, I, 776.

137. NSC 8, "The Position of the United States with Respect to Korea," approved by Truman, April 8, 1948, *FR: 1948*, VI, 1167; NSC 8/2, "The Position of the United States with Respect to Korea," approved by Truman, March 23, 1949, *FR: 1949*, VII, 975.

138. CIA ORE 3-49, "Consequences of US Troop Withdrawal from Korea in Spring, 1949," February 28, 1949, Army Staff Records, P & O 350.05 TS 28 Feb 49.

139. Schnabel, *Policy and Direction*, pp. 30, 35, 50–51. See also Kenneth C. Royall to Acheson, January 25, 1949, *FR: 1949*, VII, 945–46; and Johnson to Acheson, May 4, 1949, *ibid.*, p. 1007.

140. See Everett F. Drumwright to Acheson, March 15, 1949, *ibid.*, p. 966; Acheson to U.S. mission in Korea, April 13, 1949, *ibid.*, pp. 987–88; John J. Muccio to Acheson, May 9, 1949, *ibid.*, p. 1013; and two Acheson telegrams to the U.S. Embassy in Seoul, both dated May 9, 1949, *ibid.*, pp. 1014–16. See also Schnabel, *Policy and Direction*, pp. 34–35.

141. Butterworth to Ray T. Maddocks, May 13, 1949, *FR: 1949*, VII, 1022–23. See also Schnabel, *Policy and Direction*, p. 30.

142. Department of the Army memorandum, "Implications of a Possible Full Scale Invasion from North Korea Subsequent to Withdrawal of United States Troops from South Korea," June 27, 1949, *FR: 1949*, VII, 1054–56.

143. Acheson testimony, January 13, 1950, *Reviews of the World Situation*, p. 191. See also Acheson, *Present at the Creation*, p. 357.

144. See, on this point, Schnabel, *Policy and Direction*, pp. 35–36.

145. Allison memorandum, Dulles-Rhee conversation, June 19, 1950, *FR: 1950*, VII, 108.

146. Allison account, meetings with MacArthur on June 25 and 26, 1950, *ibid.*, pp. 140n, 141n.

147. Jessup notes, Blair House meetings, June 25 and 26, 1950, *ibid.*, pp. 159–60, 183; Charles L. Bolte to Pace, June 28, 1950, Army Staff Records, G-3, 901 Korea TS sec. 2, case 25. See also Schnabel, *Policy and Direction*, p. 79.

148. Dulles memorandum of conversations with Acheson, Pace and others, July 1, 1950, Dulles Papers, Box 47, "Acheson" folder [emphasis in original].

149. Bohlen to Kennan, June 26, 1950, *FR: 1950*, VII, 174–75.

150. Kennan memorandum prepared for Acheson, "Possible Further Communist Initiatives in the Light of the Korean Situation" (not sent), June 26, 1950, Kennan Papers, Box 24.

151. Philip C. Jessup, *The Birth of Nations* (New York: 1974), p. 10.

152. Kennan background press conference, Department of State, August 22, 1950, transcript in Kennan Papers, Box 18.

153. For the debate over crossing the 38th parallel, see Kaufman, *The Korean War*, pp. 57–60; Rosemary Foot, *The Wrong War: American Policy and the Dimensions of the Korean Conflict, 1950–1953* (Ithaca: 1985), pp. 67–74; and James I. Matray, "Tru-

man's Plan for Victory: National Self-Determination and the Thirty-Eighth Parallel Decision in Korea," *Journal of American History*, LXVI (September, 1979), 314–33.

154. Kennan Diary, July 21, 1950, quoted in Kennan, *Memoirs: 1925–1950*, p. 488.

155. Kennan press conference, August 22, 1950, Kennan Papers, Box 18.

156. Frederick E. Nolting notes, Bohlen meeting with State Department officials, June 30, 1950, *FR: 1950*, VII, 258. See also Alan G. Kirk to Acheson, July 27, 1950, *ibid.*, pp. 483–85.

157. George H. Butler draft, untitled Policy Planning Staff paper, July 22, 1950, *ibid.*, pp. 449–54; Butler draft memorandum, July 25, 1950, *ibid.*, pp. 469–73; Central Intelligence Agency memorandum, "Factors Affecting the Desirability of a UN Military Conquest of All of Korea," August 18, 1950. *ibid.*, pp. 600–603.

158. Allison to Rusk, July 1, 1950, *ibid.*, 272. Rusk noted on his copy of this memorandum, "Agree DR."

159. Allison to Paul Nitze, July 24, 1950, *ibid.*, pp. 460–61. See also Allison to Rusk, July 15, 1950, *ibid.*, pp. 393–95.

160. Dulles to Nitze, July 14, 1950. *ibid.*, pp. 386–87; Dulles to William R. Mathews, July 24, 1950, Dulles Papers, Box 49, "Mathews" folder; Dulles to Nitze, August 1, 1950, *FR: 1950*, VII, 514.

161. Defense Department draft memorandum, "U.S. Courses of Action in Korea," July 31, 1950, *ibid.*, 502–3, 506; revised version, same memorandum, August 7, 1950, *ibid.*, pp. 528–29, 532–33; Allison draft memorandum, "U.S. Courses of Action in Korea," August 12, 1950, *ibid.*, pp. 569–70. See also p. 169, above.

162. Allison to Rusk, July 13, 1950, *ibid.*, p. 373; Butler draft memorandum for Policy Planning Staff, July 25, 1950, *ibid.*, p. 472.

163. Kennan press conference, August 22, 1950, Kennan Papers, Box 18.

164. NSC 81/1, "United States Courses of Action with Respect to Korea," September 9, 1950, *FR: 1950*, VII, 712–21.

165. Harding F. Bancroft notes, Rusk meeting with Warren R. Austin, September 23, 1950.

166. MacArthur to Robert C. Richardson, March 20, 1951, MacArthur Papers, Record Group 5, Box 49. See also MacArthur to the Joint Chiefs of Staff, November 7 and 29, December 3 and 30, 1950, *FR: 1950*, VII, 1077n, 1253n, 1320–22, 1630–33; and Collins to the Joint Chiefs, December 7, 1950, summarized in *ibid.*, p. 1469n. For a sympathetic account of MacArthur's position, see Kaufman, *The Korean War*, pp. 118–20.

167. See, on these points, Jessup to Acheson, November 20, 1950, *FR: 1950*, VII, 1193–96; Jessup speech to the Philadelphia World Affairs Council, November 24, 1950, *Department of State Bulletin*, XXIII (December 4, 1950), 885; Jessup notes, National Security Council meeting, November 28, 1950, *FR: 1950*, VII, 1242–49; Jessup notes, meeting of State Department, Defense Department, and Central Intelligence Agency representatives, December 1, 1950, *ibid.*, pp. 1276–81; Lucius W. Battle notes, Truman meeting with Acheson, Marshall and Bradley, December 2, 1950, *ibid.*, pp. 1310–12; Jessup notes, Acheson-Marshall-Joint Chiefs of Staff meeting, December 3, 1950, *ibid.*, pp. 1323–24; minutes, Truman-Attlee meeting, December 5, 1950, *ibid.*, p. 1395. See also George F. Kennan, *Memoirs: 1950–1963* (Boston: 1972), pp. 32–33.

168. Acheson to U.S. Embassy, London, November 28, 1950, *FR: 1950*, VII, 1251.

169. See, on this point, Joint Chiefs of Staff to Marshall, November 9, 1950, *ibid.*, pp. 1119–20; Marshall to Acheson, November 10, 1950, *ibid.*, p. 1126; Acheson to U.S. embassies in Great Britain, Australia, Canada, and France, November 13, 1950, *ibid.*, pp. 1144–45; Rusk briefing for ambassadors of nations contributing troops in Korea, November 30, 1950, *ibid.*, p. 1264; Battle memorandum, Acheson briefing on Truman statement, December 6, 1950, *ibid.*, p. 1431. See also Foot, *The Wrong War*, pp. 113–23.

170. NSC 48/5, "United States Objectives, Policies, and Courses of Action in Asia," approved by Truman on May 17, 1951, *FR: 1951*, VI, 37.

171. See, on this point, Edward N. Luttwak, *The Grand Strategy of the Roman Empire* (Baltimore: 1977), p. 61.

## 5  The Origins of Self-Deterrence: The United States and the Non-Use of Nuclear Weapons, 1945–1958

1. For the history of the B-36 program, see Norman Polmar, ed., *Strategic Air Command: People, Aircraft, and Missiles* (Annapolis: 1979), pp. 154–59. According to figures provided by the Air Force Museum, the B-36 cost approximately $3.7 million per plane.

2. Robert Jervis, *The Illogic of American Nuclear Strategy* (Ithaca: 1984), p. 12.

3. Stephen E. Ambrose, *Eisenhower: The President* (New York: 1984), p. 229.

4. Harold D. Smith Diary, October 5, 1945, Harold D. Smith Papers, Harry S. Truman Library.

5. Bernard Brodie, "War in the Atomic Age," in Brodie, ed., *The Absolute Weapon: Atomic Power and World Order* (New York: 1946), pp. 33–34.

6. David E. Lilienthal Journal, July 21, 1948, quoted in *The Journals of David E. Lilienthal: The Atomic Energy Years, 1945–1950* (New York: 1964), p. 391.

7. Lilienthal Journal, February 14, 1949, *ibid.*, p. 474. For other representative Truman pronouncements on the atomic bomb, see his press conference, August 14, 1947, *Public Papers of the Presidents: Harry S. Truman: 1947* (Washington: 1963), p. 381; and Truman to Mary Truman, April 12, 1948, quoted in Margaret Truman, *Harry S. Truman* (New York: 1973), pp. 5–6.

8. Lilienthal Journal, February 14, 1949, *Lilienthal Journals: Atomic Energy Years*, p. 474.

9. See, on this point, Peter Wyden, *Day One: Before Hiroshima and After* (New York: 1984), p. 292.

10. James V. Forrestal Diary, July 15, 1948, quoted in Walter Millis, ed., *The Forrestal Diaries* (New York: 1951), p. 458. For a good recent discussion of the custody dispute, see Steven L. Rearden, *History of the Office of the Secretary of Defense:* Volume I: *The Formative Years, 1947–1950* (Washington: 1984), pp. 425–31.

11. NSC 30, "United States Policy on Atomic Weapons," September 10, 1948, *Foreign Relations of the United States* [hereafter *FR*]: *1948*, I, 624–28. See also Rearden, *The Formative Years*, pp. 432–36.

12. *Ibid.*, pp. 426–27.

13. For the problems of war planning, see David Alan Rosenberg, "American Atomic Strategy and the Hydrogen Bomb Decision," *Journal of American History*, LXVI(June, 1979), 63–71; Gregg Herken, *The Winning Weapon: The Atomic Bomb in the Cold War* (New York: 1980), pp. 218–36; Harry R. Borowski, *A Hollow Threat: Strategic Air Power and Containment Before Korea* (Westport, Connecticut: 1982), pp. 101–7; and Rosenberg, "The Origins of Overkill: Nuclear Weapons and American Strategy, 1945–1960," *International Security*, VII(Spring, 1983), 11–16.

14. For early production difficulties, see the Atomic Energy Commission's report to Truman, April 3, 1947, Harry S. Truman Papers, PSF, Box 200, "NSC—Atomic energy; annual reports," Harry S. Truman Library; also Rosenberg, "American Atomic Strategy and the Hydrogen Bomb Decision," pp. 65–66.

15. See, on this point, Robert L. Messer, *The End of an Alliance: James F. Byrnes, Roosevelt, Truman, and the Origins of the Cold War* (Chapel Hill: 1982), pp. 88–92, 114.

16. Stimson memorandum, "Reflections on the Basic Problems Which Confront Us," July 19, 1945, *Foreign Relations of the United States: The Conference of Berlin (The Potsdam Conference)* (Washington: 1960), II, 1155–57. See also Henry L. Stimson and McGeorge Bundy, *On Active Service in Peace and War* (New York: 1948), pp. 637–41.

17. Quoted in David Holloway, *The Soviet Union and the Arms Race* (New Haven: 1983), p. 27.

18. For the pressures that led the Truman administration to seek international con-

trol, see John Lewis Gaddis, *The United States and the Origins of the Cold War, 1941–1947* (New York: 1972), pp. 247–54, 268–73.

19. JIC 250/6, "Soviet Capabilities," November 29, 1945, Army Staff Records, ABC 336, Russia 22 Aug 43 Sec. 1-A, Modern Military Records Branch, National Archives.

20. Department of State Interim Research and Analysis Service report #3430, "Soviet Capabilities and the Atomic Bomb," November 9, 1945, Office of Strategic Services Records, USSR Division—1945, Entry 1, Modern Military Records Branch, National Archives.

21. SM4810, "Guidance as to the Military Implications of a United Nations Commission on Atomic Energy," January 23, 1946, *FR: 1946*, I, 748.

22. Bernard Brodie, "Implications for Military Policy," in Brodie, ed., *The Absolute Weapon*, p. 76.

23. Lilienthal Journal, May 18, 1948, *Lilienthal Journals: Atomic Energy Years*, p. 342.

24. Douglas to Lovett, April 17, 1948, *FR: 1948*, III, 90.

25. For atomic bomb stockpile figures, see David Alan Rosenberg, "U.S. Nuclear Stockpile, 1945 to 1950," *Bulletin of the Atomic Scientists*, XXXVIII(May, 1982), 25–30; also Rearden, *The Formative Years*, p. 439; Rosenberg, "The Origins of Overkill," pp. 14–15; and Borowski, *A Hollow Threat*, pp. 99–100.

26. Marshall memorandum of conversation with the Norwegian foreign minister, Paris, November 20, 1948, *FR: 1948*, III, 281.

27. For the B-29 deployment, see Herken, *The Winning Weapon*, pp. 257–60; Borowski, *A Hollow Threat*, pp. 125–28; Daniel F. Harrington, "American Policy in the Berlin Crisis of 1948–49" (Ph.D. Dissertation, Indiana University: 1979), pp. 110–14; and Avi Shlaim, *The United States and the Berlin Blockade, 1948–1949: A Study in Crisis Decision-Making* (Berkeley: 1983), pp. 234–40.

28. Marshall memorandum, November 28, 1948, *FR:1948*, III, 281. For other American expressions of confidence that the atomic deterrent was working, see General Omar Bradley's executive session testimony before the Senate Foreign Relations Committee, August 10, 1949, U.S. Congress, Senate Committee on Foreign Relations, *Historical Series: Military Assistance Act of 1949* (Washington: 1974), p. 92; and his statement to the House Armed Services Committee, October 19, 1949, U.S. Congress, House of Representatives, *Hearings on Unification and Strategy* (Washington: 1949), pp. 523, 525–26.

29. Lilienthal Journal, February 9, 1949, *Lilienthal Journals: Atomic Energy Years*, p. 464.

30. Lilienthal Journal, June 28, 1947, *ibid.*, p. 215.

31. NSC 30, "United States Policy on Atomic Weapons," September 10, 1948, *FR: 1948*, I, 626. President Truman formally approved this document on September 16, 1948.

32. British minutes, Attlee-Pleven conversations, December 2, 1950, Foreign Office Records, FO 371/83019/F1027/6G, Public Record Office, London.

33. Rosenberg, "American Atomic Strategy and the Hydrogen Bomb Decision," pp. 69–70; Borowski, *A Hollow Threat*, pp. 138, 150–51, 156.

34. Forrestal Diary, September 13, 1948, Millis, ed., *The Forrestal Diaries*, p. 487.

35. Forrestal Diary, October 10, 1948, *ibid.*, p. 488.

36. NSC 20/1, "U.S. Objectives with Respect to Russia," August 18, 1948, in Thomas H. Etzold and John Lewis Gaddis, eds., *Containment: Documents on American Policy and Strategy, 1945–1950* (New York: 1978), p. 193. See also the briefer final version of this document, NSC 20/4, "U.S. Objectives with Respect to the USSR To Counter Soviet Threats to U.S. Security," November 23, 1948, *FR: 1948*, I, 667.

37. Rosenberg, "American Atomic Strategy and the Hydrogen Bomb Decision," pp. 70–71. See also JCS 1952/1, "Evaluation of Current Strategic Air Offensive Plans," December 21, 1948, in Etzold and Gaddis, eds., *Containment*, pp. 357–60.

38. Pace to Truman, April 5, 1949, Truman Papers, PSF Box 200, "NSC—Atomic energy—budget."

39. "Evaluation of Effect on Soviet War Effort Resulting from Strategic Air Offensive," May 11, 1949, in Etzold and Gaddis, eds., *Containment*, pp. 362–63.

40. Rosenberg, "American Atomic Strategy and the Hydrogen Bomb Decision," pp. 76–77.

41. Minutes, Policy Planning Staff meeting, December 16, 1949, *FR: 1949*, I, 415–16. See also comments on the probable ineffectiveness of an air-atomic offensive by James B. Conant at a meeting of the State Department–Defense Department Policy Review Group, March 2, 1950, *FR: 1950*, I, 180–81; and by Vannevar Bush in a memorandum to General Omar Bradley, April 13, 1950, *ibid.*, pp. 228–29.

42. Minutes, Policy Planning Staff meeting, October 11, 1949, *FR: 1949*, I, 403.

43. Kennan paper on "International Control of Atomic Energy," January 20, 1950, *FR: 1950*, I, 39. For background on this document, see George F. Kennan, *Memoirs: 1925–1950* (Boston: 1967), pp. 471–76; also Kennan's draft memorandum to Acheson (not sent), February 17, 1950, *FR: 1950*, I, 164–65.

44. R. Gordon Arneson notes, conversation between Kennan, Acheson, and Dean Rusk, August 2, 1949, *FR: 1949*, I, 507. See also Kennan to Rusk, September 7, 1949, *ibid.*, pp. 382–83.

45. "Report to the President by the Special Committee of the National Security Council on the Proposed Acceleration of the Atomic Energy Program," October 10, 1949, *ibid.*, pp. 559–64.

46. See, on this point, Rosenberg, "American Atomic Strategy and the Hydrogen Bomb Decision," pp. 79–83.

47. Minutes, Policy Planning Staff meetings of October 11 and December 16, 1949, *FR: 1949*, I, 402–3, 414. See also Nitze's memorandum, "Recent Soviet Moves," February 8, 1950, *FR: 1950*, I, 145–46.

48. See, on this point, Steven L. Rearden, *The Evolution of American Strategic Doctrine: Paul H. Nitze and the Soviet Challenge* (Boulder, Colorado: 1984), p. 7.

49. NSC 68, "United States Objectives and Programs for National Security," April 14, 1950, *FR: 1950*, I, 235–92. The term "scare campaign" was used by Assistant Secretary of State for Public Affairs Edward W. Barrett in a memorandum to Acheson, April 6, 1950, *ibid.*, p. 226. For an over-all assessment of NSC 68, see Samuel F. Wells, Jr., "Sounding the Tocsin: NSC 68 and the Soviet Threat," *International Security*, IV (Fall, 1979), 116–58.

50. NSC 68, April 14, 1950, *FR: 1950*, I, 264–68; see also pp. 277–78.

51. Bohlen to Nitze, April 5, 1950, *ibid.*, p. 223.

52. Charles E. Bohlen, *Witness to History: 1929–1969* (New York: 1973), p. 290.

53. See Chapter Four.

54. Lovett-Acheson telephone conversation, December 2, 1950, Acheson Papers, Box 66, "Memos—conversations Dec 50."

55. Nitze memorandum, November 4, 1950, *FR: 1950*, VII, 1042.

56. James F. Schnabel, *United States Army in the Korean War: Policy and Direction: The First Year* (Washington: 1972), pp. 283–84, 320n; D. Clayton James, *The Years of MacArthur: Triumph and Disaster, 1945–1964* (Boston: 1985), pp. 578–81. See also Walter G. Hermes, *United States Army in the Korean War: Truce Tent and Fighting Front* (Washington: 1966), p. 332.

57. Carlton Savage memorandum, "Circumstances Under Which the United States Would Be at War with the Soviet Union: Use of Atomic Weapons," April 12, 1951, *FR: 1951*, I, 819. For the possibility of military action against Chinese targets in the event of aggression elsewhere in Asia, see NSC 48/5, "United States Objectives, Policies and Courses of Action in Asia," *ibid.*, VI, 37; and NSC 124/2, "United States Objectives and Courses of Action with Respect to Southeast Asia," June 25, 1952, *FR: 1952–54*, XII, 132.

58. Acheson memorandum, conversation with Bradley, Winston Churchill and Anthony Eden, January 6, 1952, *FR: 1952–54*, VI, 745.

59. NSC 73/4, "The Position and Actions of the United States with Respect to Possible Further Soviet Moves in the Light of the Korean Situation," August 25, 1950, *FR: 1950*, I, 377; Carlton Savage memorandum, "Possibilities of War with the Soviet Union, 1951–52: Use of Atomic Weapons," May 23, 1951, *FR: 1951*, I, 836.

60. Henry Koch to John H. Ferguson, August 24, 1951, *ibid.*, p. 168. See also Harry H. Schwartz to Bohlen, May 12, 1952, *FR: 1952–54*, II, 12–17.

61. NSC 114/2, "United States Programs for National Security," October 12, 1951, *FR: 1951*, I, 188. See also CIA NIE-25, "Probable Soviet Courses of Action to Mid-1951," August 2, 1951, *ibid.*, pp. 120–27; and CIA SE-13, "Probable Developments in the World Situation Through Mid-1953," September 24, 1951, *ibid.*, pp. 193–207.

62. See, for example, O. Edmund Clubb to Dean Rusk, November 1, 4, 17 and December 1, 1950, *FR: 1950*, VII, 1024, 1039–40, 1169, 1292; John Paton Davies memorandum, "Chinese Communist Intervention in Korea," November 7, 1950, *ibid.*, pp. 1084–85; CIA NIE-2/1, "Chinese Communist Intervention in Korea," November 24, 1950, *ibid.*, p. 1222; Central Intelligence Agency memorandum, "Soviet Intentions in the Current Situation," December 2, 1950, ibid., p. 1309; and a Carlton Savage memorandum of April 12, 1951, *FR: 1951*, I, 819. See also Foot, *The Wrong War*, pp. 123–27.

63. Nitze memorandum, November 4, 1950, *FR: 1950*, VII, 1042.

64. R. Gordon Arneson memorandum, Acheson conversation with Nitze and Hume Wrong, May 25, 1951, *FR: 1951*, I, 841. See also Arneson's memorandum of an Acheson-Lester Pearson meeting on June 14, 1951, *ibid.*, p. 849; and John H. Ferguson's notes of a conversation between Acheson, Lovett, and the Joint Chiefs of Staff, August 6, 1951, *ibid.*, p. 878.

65. See NSC 48/5, May 17, 1951, *ibid.*, VI, 37–38; also Hermes, *Truce Tent and Fighting Front*, pp. 56–58.

66. Rosenberg, "The Origins of Overkill," pp. 18–25.

67. See, on this point, Robert R. Simmons, *The Strained Alliance: Peking, P'yongyang, Moscow and the Politics of the Korean Civil War* (New York: 1975), pp. 137–68.

68. Emmerson to Rusk, November 8, 1950, *FR: 1950*, VII, 1098–1100.

69. Truman press conference, November 30, 1950, *Truman Public Papers: 1950*, p. 727. See also Dean Acheson, *Present at the Creation: My Years in the State Department* (New York: 1969), pp. 478–79.

70. Julius Holmes to Acheson, December 1, 1950, *FR: 1950*, VII, 1296–97.

71. British minutes, Attlee-René Pleven conversation, December 2, 1950, Foreign Office Records, FO371/83019/F1027/6G.

72. Chiefs of Staff to Bouchier, December 7, 1950, *ibid.*, FO371/84108/FK1022/584.

73. Philip Jessup notes, meeting of State Department, Defense Department, and Central Intelligence Agency representatives, December 1, 1950, *FR: 1950*, VII, 1279.

74. Austin to Acheson, December 1, 1950, *ibid.*, p. 1300.

75. John D. Hickerson memorandum, December 3, 1950, *ibid.*, p. 1334.

76. Minutes, Attlee-Pleven conversation, December 2, 1950, Foreign Office Records, FO371/83019/F1027/6G.

77. Symington to Truman, undated but clearly January, 1951, *FR: 1951*, I, 22–25.

78. NSC 100, "Recommended Policies and Actions in Light of the Grave World Situation," January 11, 1951, *ibid.*, pp. 8, 10.

79. *Ibid.*, p. 33n.

80. Joint Strategic Survey Committee—State Department paper, "United States Position on Considerations Under Which the United States Will Accept War and on Atomic Warfare," August 3, 1951, *ibid.*, p. 874.

81. Arneson notes, Acheson-Pearson meeting, June 14, 1951, *ibid.*, p. 851.

82. JSSC-State Department paper, August 3, 1951, *ibid.*, p. 871.

83. John H. Ferguson notes, Acheson meeting with Lovett and Joint Chiefs of Staff, August 6, 1951, *ibid.*, pp. 878–80.

84. J. Kenneth Mansfield to Senator Brien McMahon, August 15, 1951, *ibid.*, pp. 158, 161. See also David C. Elliott, "Project Vista and Nuclear Weapons in Europe," *International Security*, XI(Summer, 1986), 163–83.

85. L vett to James S. Lay, Jr., December 11, 1951, enclosed in Lay to Acheson and others, December 13, 1951, Truman Papers, PSF Box 200, "NSC Atomic energy—expansion."

86. Lovett to Lay, May 16, 1952, *FR: 1952–54*, II, 934–35 [emphases added].

87. Acheson to Lay, May 14, 1952, *ibid.*, p. 934.

88. Nitze memorandum, January 12, 1953, *ibid.*, 204.

89. NSC 141, January 19, 1953, p. 73. This portion is not printed in *FR*, but is available in the NSC series at the Modern Military Records Branch, National Archives.

90. Nitze memorandum, January 12, 1953, *FR: 1952–54*, II, 203–4.

91. Dulles memorandum, June 25, 1952, John Foster Dulles Papers, Box 57, "Baldwin" folder, Seeley Mudd Library, Princeton University.

92. Eisenhower speech to the New York State Republican dinner, New York, May 7, 1953, *Public Papers of the Presidents: Dwight D. Eisenhower, 1953* (Washington: 1960), p. 265.

93. Minutes, National Security Council meeting, March 25, 1953, *FR: 1952–54*, II, 260.

94. NSC 162/2, "Basic National Security Policy," October 30, 1953, *ibid.*, p. 593.

95. Eisenhower speech to the United Nations, December 8, 1953, *Eisenhower Public Papers: 1953*, p. 815.

96. James, *MacArthur: Triumph and Disaster*, p. 654. See also Ambrose, *Eisenhower: The President*, pp. 34–35.

97. Minutes, NSC meeting, February 11, 1953, *FR: 1952–54*, XV, 769–70.

98. Robert Cutler to Charles E. Wilson, March 21, 1953, *ibid.*, p. 815.

99. Minutes, meeting of State and Defense Department representatives, March 27, 1953, *ibid.*, pp. 817–18.

100. NSC 147, "Analysis of Possible Courses of Action in Korea," April 2, 1953, *ibid.*, pp. 845–48. See also SE-41, "Probable Communist Reactions to Certain Possible US/UN Military Courses of Action with Respect to the Korean War," April 8, 1953, *ibid.*, pp. 886–92.

101. Minutes, NSC meeting, May 6, 1953, *ibid.*, p. 977. See also minutes of the NSC meetings of March 31 and May 13, 1953, *ibid.*, pp. 826, 1014.

102. Minutes, NSC meetings of March 31, April 8, and May 20, 1953, *ibid.*, pp. 827, 894, 1065–66.

103. Joseph B. Phillips to Jesse M. MacKnight, September 3, 1952, forwarded with the approval of Deputy Under Secretary of State for Political Affairs H. Freeman Matthews to the Central Intelligence Agency, same date, *ibid.*, p. 484.

104. *New York Times*, December 15, 1952.

105. Dulles speech to New York State Republican dinner, New York, May 7, 1953, *Department of State Bulletin*, XXVIII(May 18, 1953), 706.

106. Dulles memorandum of conversation with Nehru, May 21, 1953, *FR: 1952–54*, XV, 1068.

107. See Foot, *The Wrong War*, p. 230.

108. Minutes, Eisenhower-Churchill-Bidault meeting, Bermuda, December 7, 1953, *FR: 1952–54*, V, 1811.

109. Sherman Adams, *Firsthand Report* (New York: 1961), pp. 48–49. See also Ambrose, *Eisenhower: The President*, p. 658.

110. "Sixteen-Nation Declaration on Korea," July 27, 1953, *Department of State Bulletin*, XXIX(August 24, 1953), 247.

111. Minutes, NSC meeting, December 3, 1953, *FR: 1952–54*, XV, 1638.

112. James C. Hagerty Diary, January 5, 1954, Robert H. Ferrell, ed., *The Diary of James C. Hagerty: Eisenhower in Mid-Course, 1954–1955* (Bloomington: 1983), p. 3. See

also L. Arthur Minnich, Jr., notes, Eisenhower meeting with legislative leaders, January 5, 1954, Dwight D. Eisenhower Papers, Ann Whitman File: DDE Diaries, Box 3, "Staff Notes, Jan-Dec. 54," Dwight D. Eisenhower Library.

113. Minutes, NSC meeting, January 8, 1954, *FR: 1952–54*, XV, 1709.

114. Minutes, NSC meeting, October 7, 1953, *ibid.*, II, 532–33.

115. Minutes, NSC meeting, October 13, 1953, *ibid.*, pp. 546–47.

116. NSC 167, "U.S. Courses of Action in Korea in the Absence of an Acceptable Political Settlement," October 22, 1953, *ibid.*, XV, 1554.

117. Joint Chiefs of Staff to Wilson, November 27, 1953, *ibid.*, p. 1628.

118. NSC 166/1, U.S. Policy Toward Communist China," November 6, 1953, *ibid.*, XIV, 280–81.

119. Minutes, NSC meeting, December 3, 1953, *ibid.*, XV, 1639–41. See also Walter Bedell Smith to Eisenhower, December 3, 1953, *ibid.*, II, 607–8.

120. Minutes, NSC meeting, January 8, 1954, *ibid.*, XV, 1705.

121. NIE 10-2-54, "Communist Courses of Action in Asia Through Mid-1955," March 15, 1954, *ibid.*, XIV, 389, 395. See also SNIE 100-2-54, "Probable Reactions of Communist China, the USSR, and the Free World to Certain US Courses of Action in Korea," March 5, 1954, *ibid.*, XV, 1758–62.

122. Hagerty Diary, July 27, 1954, *ibid.*, pp. 1841, 1844-45.

123. Minutes, NSC meeting, July 2, 1953, *ibid.*, p. 1307 [emphasis in original].

124. Dulles speech to American Legion convention, St. Louis, September 2, 1953, *Department of State Bulletin*, XXIX (September 14, 1953), 342.

125. Hagerty Diary, March 26, 1954, *FR: 1952–54*, XIII, 1173. See also Dulles's speech to the Overseas Press Club, New York, March 29, 1954, *Department of State Bulletin*, XXX (April 12, 1954), 540.

126. Minutes, NSC meeting, January 8, 1954, *FR: 1952–54*, XIII, 949.

127. Dulles memorandum of conversation with Eisenhower, March 24, 1954, *ibid.*, p. 1150. See also minutes of the NSC meeting of January 8, 1954, *ibid.*, pp. 951–53.

128. Hagerty Diary, April 1, 1954, *ibid.*, p. 1204.

129. Douglas MacArthur II to Dulles, April 7, 1954, *ibid.*, pp. 1270–72.

130. *Ibid.*, pp. 1271–72.

131. See, on this point, George C. Herring and Richard H. Immerman, "Eisenhower, Dulles, and Dienbienphu: 'The Day We Didn't Go to War' Revisited," *Journal of American History*, LXXI (September, 1984), 351–53.

132. Dulles to Eisenhower, April 29, 1954, *FR: 1952–54*, XVI, 607. See also Admiral Radford's report on his conversations with Churchill, delivered at the NSC meeting of April 29, 1954, and Dulles's briefing for members of Congress, May 5, 1954. [*Ibid.*, pp. 1437, 1474.]

133. Minutes, NSC meeting, April 29, 1954, *ibid.*, pp. 1440–41.

134. Cutler to Smith, April 30, 1954, *ibid.*, p. 1448 [emphases in original]. See also *ibid.*, p. 1443; and, for a slightly different version, Richard M. Nixon, *RN: The Memoirs of Richard Nixon* (New York: 1978), p. 154.

135. Radford (for the JCS) to Wilson, May 20, 1954, *FR: 1952–54*, XIII, 1591.

136. Bowie to Dulles, May 27, 1954, *ibid.*, p. 1625. See also Everett F. Drumwright to Douglas MacArthur II, May 24, 1954, *ibid.*, p. 1606.

137. SNIE 10–4–54, "Communist Reactions to Certain US Courses of Action with Respect to Indochina," June 15, 1954, *ibid.*, p. 1704.

138. Radford (for the JCS) to Wilson, June 23, 1954, *ibid.*, II, 684–85.

139. Minutes, NSC meeting, June 24, 1954, *ibid.*, II, 694–96.

140. Minutes, NSC meeting, August 5, 1954, *ibid.*, pp. 707–9.

141. Eisenhower State of the Union address, February 2, 1953, *Eisenhower Public Papers: 1953*, pp. 16–17. For background on the Taiwan Strait crisis, see Alexander L. George and Richard Smoke, *Deterrence in American Foreign Policy: Theory and Practice* (New York: 1974), pp. 267–72.

142. See, for example, the minutes of the NSC meeting of August 18, 1954, *FR: 1952–54*, XIV, 536–38; also a memorandum by Morris Draper, Jr., on a Dulles meeting with State Department advisers, August 31, 1954, *ibid.*, pp. 554–55.

143. Minutes, NSC meeting, August 5, 1954, *ibid.*, p. 519.

144. Dulles to John M. Allison, August 20, 1954, *ibid.*, pp. 545–46.

145. Dulles memorandum, September 12, 1954, *ibid.*, p. 611.

146. Minutes, NSC meeting, September 12, 1954, *ibid.*, p. 619.

147. *Ibid.*

148. Minutes, NSC meeting, November 2, 1954, *ibid.*, p. 831.

149. "Basic National Security Policy (Suggestions of the Secretary of State)," November 15, 1954, *ibid.*, II, 774–75.

150. Dulles speech to the National 4-H Clubs Congress, Chicago, November 29, 1954, *Department of State Bulletin*, XXXI(December 13, 1954), 892.

151. These discussions are documented in *FR: 1952–54*, XIV, 490–553.

152. Dulles to Walter Robertson, October 8, 1954, *ibid.*, p. 709.

153. Minutes, NSC meeting of November 2, 1954, *ibid.*, pp. 828–29.

154. "Mutual Defense Treaty Between the United Sttates and the Republic of China," December 2, 1954, U.S. Department of State, *American Foreign Policy, 1950–1955: Basic Documents* (Washington: 1957), pp. 945–47.

155. Walter P. McConaughy memorandum, Robertson conversation with Chinese Foreign Minister George K. C. Yeh, November 6, 1954, *FR: 1952–54*, XIV, 870–71.

156. "Congressional Authorization for the President to Employ the Armed Forces of the United States to Protect Formosa, the Pescadores, and Related Positions and Territories of That Area," January 29, 1955, *American Foreign Policy, 1950–1955: Basic Documents*, pp. 2486–87.

157. Dulles memorandum of conversation with Eisenhower, January 19, 1955, *FR: 1955–57*, II, 42.

158. Eisenhower to Churchill, January 25, 1955, Eisenhower Papers, Whitman File, DDE Diary, Box 5, "January, 1955 (1)." See also Eisenhower to General Alfred M. Gruenther, February 1, 1955, *FR: 1955–57*, II, 191–92.

159. Dulles memoranda of conversations with Eisenhower, March 6, 1955, *ibid.*, pp. 336–37.

160. Minutes, NSC meeting, March 10, 1955, *ibid.*, p. 347. See also a separate set of notes on this meeting in the Dulles Papers, Box 2 "Memoranda—1955—Formosa Straits (2)."

161. Eisenhower press conference, March 16, 1955, *Eisenhower Public Papers: 1955*, p. 332.

162. Dwight D. Eisenhower, *The White House Years: Mandate for Change, 1953–1956* (Garden City, New York: 1963), p. 477.

163. Robert Cutler memorandum, Eisenhower meeting with Dulles and other advisers, March 11, 1955, *FR: 1955–57*, II, 358–60.

164. NIE 100–4–55, "Communist Capabilities and Intentions with Respect to the Offshore Islands and Taiwan Through 1955, and Communist and Non-Communist Reactions with Respect to the Defense of Taiwan," March 16, 1955, *ibid.*, p. 379.

165. J. W. Hanes, Jr., notes, Dulles meeting with advisers, March 28, 1955, *ibid.*, pp. 410, 413.

166. Hagerty Diary, March 29 and April 4, 1955, Ferrell, ed., *Hagerty Diary*, pp. 220, 224.

167. Eisenhower to Churchill, March 29, 1955, *FR: 1955–57*, II, 420 [Emphasis in original].

168. Herbert Hoover, Jr., notes, Eisenhower meeting with advisers, April 1, 1955, *ibid.*, pp. 439–41; Dulles notes, conversation with Eisenhower, April 4, 1955, *ibid.*, pp. 444–45; Eisenhower to Dulles, April 5, 1955, *ibid.*, pp. 445–50.

169. Dulles memorandum of conversation with Eisenhower, April 17, 1955, *ibid.*, p 492. See also "Annex E," attached to this document, *ibid.*, p. 495.

170. Robertson to Dulles, April 25, 1955, *ibid.*, pp. 510, 512, 516.

171. Dulles to Eisenhower, May 18, 1955, *ibid.*, pp. 566–67. See also Dulles's notes of a conversation with Eisenhower, April 27, 1955, Dulles Papers, Box 3, "Meetings with the President, 1955 (4)."

172. Dulles memorandum of conversation with Eisenhower, August 5, 1955, *ibid.*, Box 3, "Meetings with the President, 1955 (3)."

173. See McConaughy's notes of a conversation between Dulles and Chinese Nationalist Foreign Minister George Yeh, January 19, 1955, *FR: 1955–57*, II, 47.

174. Dulles press conference, January 17, 1956, *Department of State Bulletin*, XXXIV (January 30, 1956), 156.

175. James Shepley, "How Dulles Averted War," *Life*, XL (January 16, 1956), 70–80.

176. See footnotes 113, 114, and 140, above.

177. See, on this point, Foot, *The Wrong War*, pp. 204–5.

178. Quoted in Ambrose, *Eisenhower: The President*, p. 184.

179. Minutes, NSC meeting, June 4, 1953, *FR: 1952–54*, II, 369. See also minutes of the NCS meeting of November 19, 1953, *ibid.*, p. 601; also the Hagerty Diary, February 8, 1955, Ferrell, ed., *Hagerty Diary*, p. 188.

180. Minnich notes, Eisenhower meeting with legislative leaders, December 14, 1954, *ibid.*, p. 825.

181. Minutes, NSC meeting, January 12, 1956, Eisenhower Papers, Whitman NSC Series, Box 7.

182. NSC 5602, "Basic National Security Policy," February 8, 1956, Modern Military Records Branch, National Archives.

183. "A Report to the President and the National Security Council by the Panel on The Human Effects of Nuclear Weapons Development," November 21, 1956, Eisenhower Papers, White House Office Files, NSC Assistant, NSC Series, Subject Subseries, Box 6, "Nuclear Testing (2)" (Nov. 56–June 57). See also Wm. F. Vandercook, "Making the Very Best of the Very Worst: The 'Human Effects of Nuclear Weapons' Report of 1956," *International Security*, XI (Summer, 1986), 184–95.

184. Eisenhower telephone conversation with Styles Bridges, May 21, 1957, Eisenhower Papers, Whitman DDE Diary, Box 13, "May 57 Misc (2)."

185. NSC 5440, "Basic National Security Policy," December 13, 1954, *FR: 1952–54*, II, 815.

186. Dulles draft memorandum, January 28, 1956, Dulles Papers, Subject Series, Box 4, "Paper on Nuclear Weapons 1/56 (1)."

187. Andrew J. Goodpaster memorandum, Eisenhower-Taylor conversation, May 24, 1956, Eisenhower Papers, Whitman DDE Diaries, Box 8, "May 56 Goodpaster." See also Goodpaster's memorandum of an Eisenhower conversation with Radford, May 14, 1956, *ibid.*

188. Eisenhower press conferences, February 6 and April 17, 1957, *Eisenhower Public Papers: 1957*, pp. 130, 287.

189. Goodpaster memorandum, Eisenhower conversation with John McCone and Edward Teller, August 14, 1958, Eisenhower Papers, Whitman Files, DDE Diary, Box 22, "Aug 58 Staff Notes."

190. Dulles to Eisenhower, September 4, 1958, Dulles Papers, White House memoranda, Box 7, "Meetings with the President, July–December, 58 (7)." Eisenhower made a point of publishing this candid memorandum in his memoirs. See Dwight D. Eisenhower, *White House Years: Waging Peace* (Garden City, New York: 1965), pp. 691–93.

191. Dulles memorandum, conversation with Eisenhower, September 4, 1958, Dulles Papers, White House memoranda, Box 7, "Meetings with the President, July–December 58 (7)."

192. Dulles to Macmillan, September 4, 1958, *ibid.*, "Meetings with the President, July–December 58 (6)."

193. Phyllis Bernau to Dulles, summarizing telephone message from Ann Whitman,

September 10, 1958, *ibid.*, Box 8, "Correspondence with the President, Personal, 1954–1958."

194. *New York Times*, September 20, 1958. The Russians subsequently made the text of Khrushchev's letter available to the press.

195. Eisenhower, *White House Years: Waging Peace*, p. 293. Eisenhower does not specifically mention Khrushchev's note.

196. Dulles notes, conversation with Eisenhower, September 23, 1958, Dulles Papers, White House Memoranda, Box 7, "Meetings with the President, July–December 58 (6)."

197. For the problem of disproportionality, see Jervis, *The Illogic of American Nuclear Strategy*, pp. 22–26; also Michael Mandelbaum, *The Nuclear Revolution: International Politics Before and After Hiroshima* (Cambridge: 1981), p. 4.

## 6  Dividing Adversaries: The United States and International Communism, 1945–1958

1. David Hackett Fischer, *Historians' Fallacies: Toward a Logic of Historical Thought* (New York: 1970), p. 109.

2. John Lewis Gaddis, *Russia, the Soviet Union, and the United States: An Interpretive History* (New York: 1978), pp. 222, 224.

3. Memorandum of Eisenhower-Churchill-Bidault meeting, December 7, 1953, Dwight D. Eisenhower Papers, Ann Whitman File, International Meetings Series, Box 1, "Bermuda—State Department Report," Dwight D. Eisenhower Library. This document has since been published in U.S. Department of State, *Foreign Relations of the United States* [hereafter *FR*]: *1952–54*, V, 1808–18.

4. See, on this point, Donald S. Zagoria, *The Sino-Soviet Conflict, 1956–1961* (Princeton: 1962), pp. 152–221; and John Gittings, *Survey of the Sino-Soviet Dispute, 1963–1967* (London: 1968), pp. 20–26, 89–109.

5. For an attempt to make amends, see John Lewis Gaddis, *Strategies of Containment: A Critical Appraisal of Postwar American National Security Policy* (New York: 1982), pp. 136–45, 181–82.

6. See Gaddis, *Russia, the Soviet Union, and the United States,* pp. 105–11; also Peter G. Filene, *Americans and the Soviet Experiment, 1917–1933* (Cambridge, Massachusetts: 1967), especially pp. 282–84. For some possible psychological explanations of this attitude, see Robert Jervis, *Perception and Misperception in International Politics* (Princeton: 1976), pp. 319–26; and Deborah Welch Larson, *Origins of Containment: A Psychological Explanation* (Princeton: 1985), pp. 50–57.

7. Raymond E. Murphy memorandum, "Possible Resurgence of Communist International Resumption of Extreme Leftist Activities, Possible Effect on United States," June 2, 1945, U.S. Department of State, *Foreign Relations of the United States: The Conference of Berlin (The Potsdam Conference), 1945* (Washington: 1960), I, 272. This document was subsequently included in the briefing book prepared for President Truman's use at the Potsdam Conference.

8. Wallace Diary, June 18, 1945, John Morton Blum, ed., *The Price of Vision: The Diary of Henry A. Wallace, 1942–1946* (Boston: 1973), p. 462.

9. Clark Kerr to Foreign Office, November 30, 1945, enclosed in John Paton Davies to the State Department, December 13, 1945, Department of State Records, 861.00/12–1345, Box 6461, Diplomatic Branch, National Archives.

10. Office of Strategic Services Research and Analysis report 2669, "Capabilities and Intentions of the USSR in the Postwar Period," Office of Strategic Services Records, Modern Military Records Branch, National Archives. See also JIC 250, "Estimate of Soviet Post-War Capabilities and Intentions," January 18, 1945, Army Staff Records, ABC Russia Section 1-A, Modern Military Records Branch, National Archives.

11. Undated "Draft," apparently prepared by Bohlen in February, 1946, Department of State Records, 711.61/2–1446, Box 3428. For the origins of this document, see Robert

L. Messer, "Paths Not Taken: The United States Department of State and Alternatives to Containment," *Diplomatic History* I(Fall, 1977), 311n. See also Bohlen's memorandum of March 13, 1946, Charles E. Bohlen Papers, Box 4, "Memos (CEB) 1946," Diplomatic Branch, National Archives; and Hugh DeSantis, *The Diplomacy of Silence: The American Foreign Service, the Soviet Union, and the Cold War, 1933–1947* (Chicago: 1980), p. 111.

12. Kennan post-lecture comment, meeting of Foreign Service and State Department personnel, Washington, September 17, 1946, George F. Kennan Papers, Box 16, Seeley Mudd Library, Princeton University. See also Kennan's lecture at the National War College, "Contemporary Problems of Foreign Policy," September 17, 1948, *ibid.*, Box 17.

13. Kennan papers, "The Soviet Way of Thought and Its Effect on Foreign Policy," January 24, 1947, *ibid.*

14. Kennan lecture at the University of Virginia, February 20, 1947, *ibid.*

15. See, for example, Walter Bedell Smith to Secretary of State Marshall, January 27, 1947, *FR: 1947*, IV, 524–25; also John Lewis Gaddis, *The United States and the Origins of the Cold War, 1941–1947* (New York: 1972), pp. 318–22.

16. See, on this point, DeSantis, *The Diplomacy of Silence*, p. 188.

17. Gaddis, *The United States and the Origins of the Cold War*, p. 352. For Truman's loyalty program, see Richard M. Freeland, *The Truman Doctrine and the Origins of McCarthyism: Foreign Policy, Domestic Politics, and Internal Security, 1946–1948* (New York: 1972).

18. See, on this point, William Taubman, *Stalin's America Policy: From Entente to Détente to Cold War* (New York: 1982), pp. 175–77.

19. Kennan National War College lecture, May 6, 1947, Kennan Papers, Box 17.

20. Truman speech to Congress, March 12, 1947, *Public Papers of the Presidents: Harry S. Truman, 1947* (Washington: 1963), pp. 178–79.

21. Kennan National War College post-lecture comment, May 6, 1947, Kennan Papers, Box 17.

22. Kennan to Acheson, May 23, 1947, *FR: 1947*, III, 229.

23. Joseph M. Jones to Acheson, May 20, 1947, *ibid.*, p. 233n.

24. Bohlen to Marshall S. Carter, May 29, 1947, Bohlen Papers, Box 4, "Memos 1947."

25. J. C. Drier memorandum, August 11, 1947, *ibid.*, Box 4, "Memos (CEB) 1947." Further documentation on the Argentine proposal is in *FR: 1947*, VIII, 5, 42–44.

26. Kennan talk to the Board of Advisers of the Federal Reserve System, December 1, 1947, and to the Secretary of the Navy's Council, December 3, 1947, Kennan Papers, Box 17. See also Kennan's lecture at the National War College, December 18, 1947, *ibid.*, and James Edward Miller, *The United States and Italy, 1940–1950: The Politics and Diplomacy of Stabilization* (Chapel Hill: 1986), pp. 236–42.

27. Kennan National War College lecture, May 6, 1947, Kennan Papers, Box 17.

28. Kennan to Acheson, May 23, 1947, *FR: 1947*, III, 224–25.

29. See, on these points, Miller, *The United States and Italy*, pp. 243–49; Robert A. Pollard, *Economic Security and the Origins of the Cold War, 1945–1950* (New York: 1985), especially pp. 3–5, 244–47; and Hadley Arkes, *Bureaucracy, the Marshall Plan, and the National Interest* (Princeton: 1972), pp. 299–300.

30. NSC 7, "The Position of the United States with Respect to Soviet-Directed World Communism," March 30, 1948, *FR: 1948*, I, 545–50.

31. Thorp to Marshall, April 7, 1948, *ibid.*, pp. 558–59.

32. Butler draft speech for Robert Lovett, April 12, 1948, Policy Planning Staff Records, Box 33, "Chronological Jan–May, 1948." See also a draft paper by Carlton Savage, April 26, 1948, *ibid.*, Box 32, "Minutes of Meetings—1948."

33. Truman speech to the Swedish Pioneer Centennial Association, Chicago, June 4, 1948, *Truman Public Papers: 1948*, pp. 289–90.

34. Kennan to Acheson, May 23, 1947, *FR: 1947*, III, 228.

35. See George F. Kennan, *Memoirs: 1925–1950* (Boston: 1967), pp. 342–43.

36. Walter Millis, ed., *The Forrestal Diaries* (New York: 1951), p. 279.

37. Maurice Peterson memorandum of conversation between Bevin and William Clayton, London, June 24, 1947, *FR: 1947*, III, 268. See also Bevin's comments on the following day, *ibid.*, p. 277; and Alan Bullock, *Ernest Bevin: Foreign Secretary, 1945–1951* (New York: 1983), pp. 414–15.

38. Kennan notes for conversation with Marshall, July 21, 1947, *FR: 1947*, III, 335.

39. Kennan to Lovett, October 6, 1947, Policy Planning Staff Records, Box 33, "Chronological—1947." See also PPS/13, "Résumé of World Situation," November 6, 1947, *FR: 1947*, I, 770–77.

40. Kennan talk to selected industrial leaders, Washington, January 14, 1948, Kennan Papers, Box 17.

41. See PPS/13, November 6, 1947, *FR: 1947*, I, 773; also Kennan's January 14, 1948, talk, cited above; and his *Memoirs: 1925–1950*, p. 379.

42. For an excellent recent assessment of the Czech coup's impact, see Bullock, *Ernest Bevin: Foreign Secretary*, pp. 528–31.

43. Norman to Ministry of External Affairs, Ottawa, March 6, 1948, copy in British Foreign Office Records, F0371/71671, Public Record Office, London.

44. Sir Charles Peake to Foreign Office, June 18, 1948, *ibid.*, F0371/72630/R7301.

45. Robert R. Reams to Marshall, June 18, 1948, *FR: 1948*, IV, 1073.

46. PPS/35, "The Attitude of This Government Toward Events in Yugoslavia," June 30, 1948, *ibid.*, p. 1079.

47. *Ibid.*, p. 1080.

48. Frank G. Wisner to W. Averell Harriman, July 22, 1948, *ibid.*, p. 1096. See also Bohlen to Isaiah Berlin, July 31, 1948, Bohlen Papers, Box 1, "Correspondence, 1946–49; B"; and a Central Intelligence Agency assessment, ORE 49–48, "The Trend of Soviet-Yugoslav Relations," November 18, 1948, Harry S. Truman Papers, President's Secretary's File, Box 255, "CIA Reports ORE 1948."

49. PPS/35, June 30, 1948, *FR: 1948*, IV, 1079–80.

50. PPS 60, "Yugoslav-Moscow Controversy as Related to U.S. Foreign Policy Objectives," September 12, 1949, *FR: 1949*, V, 947–54. President Truman approved a subsequent draft of this document as NSC 18/4, "United States Policy Toward the Conflict Between the USSR and Yugoslavia," November 17, 1949, published in an unfortunately sanitized version in *FR: 1950*, IV, 1341–48. See also Lorraine M. Lees, "The American Decision to Aid Tito, 1948–1949," *Diplomatic History*, II (Fall, 1978), 407–22.

51. Eban A. Ayres Diary, September 14, 1949, Eban A. Ayers Papers, Harry S. Truman Library, Box 27.

52. NSC 20/4, "U.S. Objectives with Respect to the USSR to Counter Soviet Threats to U.S. Security," November 23, 1948, *FR: 1948*, I, 668. For an earlier and more detailed version of this document, see NSC 20/1, "U.S. Objectives with Respect to Russia," August 18, 1948, in Thomas H. Etzold and John Lewis Gaddis, eds., *Containment: Documents on American Policy and Strategy, 1945–1950* (New York: 1978), pp. 173–211.

53. Policy Planning Staff minutes, September 26, 1949, Policy Planning Staff Records, Box 32.

54. NSC 58/2, "United States Policy Toward the Soviet Satellite States of Eastern Europe," December 8, 1949, *FR: 1949*, V, 42–54. President Truman approved this document on December 13, 1949.

55. Kohler to Acheson, February 24, 1949, *ibid.*, p. 231. For documentation on the human rights campaign in the United Nations, see *ibid.*, pp. 223–76; also Richard P. Stebbins, *The United States in World Affairs: 1949* (New York: 1950), pp. 246–50.

56. George W. Perkins to Acheson, October 25, 1949, *FR: 1949*, V, 161–62. See also the "Conclusions and Recommendations" of the London Conference of United States Chiefs of Mission to the Satellite States," October 24–26, 1949, *ibid.*, pp. 31–32; and summaries of dispatches from Paul R. Porter and the American Embassy in London to the State Department, June 8 and August 18, 1949, *ibid.*, pp. 124–25, 137.

57. There is thin but suggestive documentation on these activities in *FR: 1949*, V, 277–97.

58. Kennan to Acheson, April 19, 1949 (drafted by Robert Joyce), Policy Planning Staff Records, Box 33 "Chronological 1949." See also Joyce's notes of a Policy Planning Staff meeting, April 1, 1949, *FR: 1949*, V, 12; and Acheson to certain diplomatic posts, June 21, 1949, *ibid.*, pp. 289–90. On CIA funding for the National Committee on Free Europe and Radio Free Europe, see Anne Karalekas, "History of the Central Intelligence Agency," in U.S. Congress, Senate, Select Committee to Study Governmental Operations with Respect to Intelligence Activities, *Supplementary Reports on Foreign and Military Intelligence* (Washington: 1976), p. 36.

59. The story is effectively told in Nicholas Bethell, *Betrayed* (New York: 1984). There is also incomplete documentation on these efforts in *FR: 1949*, V, 298–325.

60. See, on this episode, Thomas Powers, *The Man Who Kept the Secrets: Richard Helms and the CIA* (New York: 1979), pp. 49–52; and John Ranelagh, *The Agency: The Rise and Decline of the CIA* (New York: 1986), pp. 226–28.

61. Thomas W. Wolfe, *Soviet Power and Europe: 1945–1970* (Baltimore: 1970), pp. 303–8.

62. Kennan summary of comments made orally to Marshall, September 8, 1948, Policy Planning Staff Records, Box 33 "Chronological July–December, 1948." See also, on this point, Cavendish Cannon to Acheson, April 25, 1949 (drafted by William K. K. Leonhart), *FR: 1949*, V, 888–89.

63. Kennan lecture at Pentagon Joint Orientation Conference, November 8, 1948, Kennan Papers, Box 17.

64. Minutes, Washington Explanatory Talks on Security, July 7, 1948, *FR: 1948*, III, 157. See also Kennan to Walter Bedell Smith, August 20, 1948, Kennan Papers, Box 28; and Kennan's lecture at the Pentagon Joint Orientation Conference, November 8, 1948, *ibid.*, Box 17.

65. CIA ORE 22–48 (Addendum), "Possibility of Direct Soviet Military Action During 1948–49," September 16, 1948, Truman Papers, PSF Box 255, "Central Intelligence Reports, ORE 1948." For similar conclusions, see NSC 20/2, "Factors Affecting the Nature of the U.S. Defense Arrangements in the Light of Soviet Policies," August 25, 1948, *FR: 1948*, I, 618–19; and NSC 58/2, "United States Policy Toward the Soviet Satellite States in Eastern Europe," December 8, 1949, *FR: 1949*, V, 53–54.

66. Minutes, Policy Planning Staff meeting, March 1, 1949, *ibid.*, p. 10.

67. Kennan Naval War College lecture, October 11, 1948, Kennan Papers, Box 17.

68. For Roosevelt's views on China, see Michael Schaller, *The U.S. Crusade in China, 1938–1945* (New York: 1979), pp. 90–91, 98–99, 156–57, 177–78, 197; also Robert Dallek, *Franklin D. Roosevelt and American Foreign Policy, 1932–1945* (New York: 1979), pp. 328–30, 389–91, 429.

69. See Steven I. Levine, "A New Look at American Mediation in the Chinese Civil War: The Marshall Mission and Manchuria," *Diplomatic History*, III(Fall, 1979), especially 373–74.

70. For these contacts, see Schaller, *The U.S. Crusade in China*, pp. 177–90; also Kenneth E. Shewmaker, *Americans and Chinese Communists, 1927–1945: A Persuading Encounter* (Ithaca: 1971), especially pp. 186–256.

71. See Steven M. Goldstein, "Chinese Communist Policy Toward the United States: Opportunities and Constraints, 1944–1950," in Dorothy Borg and Waldo Heinrichs, eds., *Uncertain Years: Chinese-Americans Relations, 1947–1950* (New York: 1980), pp. 248–53.

72. Schaller, *The U.S. Crusade in China*, pp. 222–29; William Whitney Stueck, Jr., *The Road to Confrontation: American Policy Toward China and Korea, 1947–1950* (Chapel Hill: 1981), pp. 15–16; Russell D. Buhite, *Soviet-American Relations in Asia, 1945–1950* (Norman, Oklahoma: 1981), pp. 32–36.

73. See Kennan's lecture at the University of Virginia, February 20, 1947, Kennan Papers, Box 16; John Carter Vincent to Marshall, June 20, 1947, *FR: 1947*, VII, 849; and O. Edmund Clubb to Marshall, August 28, 1947, *ibid.*, pp. 263–66.

74. See, on this point, Stueck, *The Road to Confrontation*, pp. 56–57; also Chapter Four, above.

75. Kennan to Marshall, "The Situation in China and U.S. Policy," November 3, 1947, Policy Planning Staff Records, Box 13 "China 1947–8."

76. See, on this point, Kennan's Naval War College lecture, October 11, 1948, Kennan Papers, Box 17; John Hickerson memorandum, "Pattern of Soviet Policy in Far East and Southeast Asia," October 13, 1948, *FR: 1948*, I, 638–39; CIA ORE 27–48, "Possible Developments in China," November 3, 1948, Army Staff Records, P. & O. Division, Decimal File, 1946–48 (TS) 091 China, Modern Military Records Division, National Archives. For the over-all effect of Tito's defection on American thinking about communism in China, see Robert M. Blum, *Drawing the Line: The Origin of the American Containment Policy in East Asia* (New York: 1982), pp. 10–13; and Nancy Bernkopf Tucker, *Patterns in the Dust: Chinese-American Relations and the Recognition Controversy, 1949–1950* (New York: 1983), pp. 27–32.

77. John Paton Davies, Jr., *Dragon by the Tail: American, British, Japanese and Russian Encounters with China and One Another* (New York: 1972), pp. 272–73. See also Schaller, *The U.S. Crusade in China*, pp. 156–57. For the influence of Davies on Kennan, see Blum, *Drawing the Line*, pp. 15–16; and David Allan Mayers, *Cracking the Monolith: U.S. Policy Against the Sino-Soviet Alliance, 1949–1955* (Baton Rouge: 1986), pp. 18–19.

78. Davies to Kennan, December 15, 1947, Policy Planning Staff Records, Box 8 "Communism 1947–51."

79. PPS/39, "United States Policy Toward China," September 7, 1948, *FR: 1948*, VIII, 148.

80. NSC 34/2, "U.S. Policy Toward China," February 28, 1949, *FR: 1949*, IX, 494–95. For Truman's approval of this document, see *ibid.*, p. 499.

81. NSC 41, "United States Policy Regarding Trade with China," February 28, 1949, approved by Truman March 3, 1949, *ibid.*, pp. 826–34.

82. Blum, *Drawing the Line*, pp. 30–35.

83. NSC 34/2, *FR: 1949*, IX, 494.

84. NSC 37/5, "Supplementary Measures with Respect to Formosa," March 1, 1949, approved by Truman March 3, 1949, *ibid.*, pp. 290–92. See also Secretary of State Acheson's explanatory statement to the National Security Council on the Taiwan question, March 3, 1949, *ibid.*, pp. 294–96; and Chapter Four, above.

85. Blum, *Drawing the Line*, pp. 35–37. See also the executive session testimony of Acheson and W. Walton Butterworth before the Senate Foreign Relations Committee, March 18, 1949, U.S. Congress, Senate Committee on Foreign Relations, *Historical Series: Economic Assistance to China and Korea* (Washington: 1974), pp. 33–36; and Acheson's memorandum of a conversation with Truman, November 17, 1949, Dean Acheson Papers, Box 64, "Memoranda of Conversations, Oct.-Nov. 1949," Harry S. Truman Library.

86. Kennan lecture to the 4th Joint Orientation Conference, the Pentagon, September 19, 1949, Kennan Papers, Box 17. See also two memoranda by Charles Yost, "Current Objectives of Soviet Foreign Policy," November 22, 1949, and "United States Policy vis-à-vis the Soviet Union," December 5, 1949, Department of State Records, 711.61/12–1349, Box 3431.

87. David Lilienthal account of a conversation with Truman, May 11, 1949, *The Journals of David E. Lilienthal: The Atomic Energy Years, 1945–1950* (New York: 1964), p. 525.

88. *Time*, LIII (March 7, 1949), 25. See also Blum, *Drawing the Line*, pp. 40–41.

89. Acheson executive session testimony, October 12, 1949, U.S. Congress, Senate Committee on Foreign Relations, *Historical Series: Reviews of the World Situation, 1949–1950* (Washington: 1974), p. 87.

90. Acheson executive session testimony, March 29, 1950, *ibid.*, p. 273.

91. Acheson National Press Club speech, January 12, 1950, *Department of State Bulletin*, XXII (January 23, 1950), 115. The China "White Paper" was published as U.S. Department of State, *United States Relations with China with Special Reference to*

*the Period 1944–1949* (Washington: 1949). For the January 5, 1950, statement on Taiwan, see the *Truman Public Papers: 1950*, pp. 11–12.

92. See, on this point, Acheson to David Bruce, January 25, 1950, *FR: 1950*, VI, 294–96; also C. L. Sulzberger, *A Long Row of Candles: Memoirs and Diaries, 1943–1954* (New York: 1969), pp. 492, 495.

93. Acheson executive session testimony, March 18, 1949, *Economic Assistance to China and Korea*, p. 34. See also CIA ORE 29–49, "Prospects for Soviet Control of a Communist China," April 15, 1949, Truman Papers, PSF Box 256, "Central Intelligence Reports—ORE 1949."

94. For the effect of the "lean to one side" speech and the Sino-Soviet Treaty, see Blum, *Drawing the Line*, pp. 63, 192; Mayers, *Cracking the Monolith*, pp. 46–49, 65–70.

95. Acheson executive session testimony, March 18, 1949, *Economic Assistance to China and Korea*, p. 34.

96. Tucker, *Patterns in the Dust*, pp. 42–53, provides a sophisticated and balanced assessment of Chinese Communist attitudes toward the United States. See also Blum, *Drawing the Line*, pp. 80–84; and Michael Hunt, "Mao Tse-tung and the Issue of Accommodation with the United States," in Borg and Heinrichs, eds., *Uncertain Years*, pp. 210–24, 231–32.

97. For the debate, see Thomas C. Reeves, "McCarthyism: Interpretations Since Hofstadter," *Wisconsin Magazine of History*, LX (Autumn, 1976), 42–54.

98. Johnson to Sidney Souers, June 10, 1949, U.S. Department of Defense, *United States—Vietnam Relations, 1945–1967* (Washington: 1971), VIII, 218.

99. See Chapter Four, above.

100. Lucius D. Battle memorandum, Acheson-Dewey telephone conversation, April 10, 1950, Acheson Papers, Box 65, "Memoranda of conversations: April 1950."

101. For the administration's intentions in this regard, see Rosemary Foot, *The Wrong War: American Policy and the Dimensions of the Korean Conflict, 1950–1953* (Ithaca: 1985), pp. 66–67, 105–6, 118–20, 128–30; also Mayers, *Cracking the Monolith*, pp. 81–82; and Chapter Four, above.

102. Foot, *The Wrong War*, pp. 65–66; Hunt, "Mao Tse-tung and the Issue of Accommodation with the United States," pp. 231–32.

103. Allen to State Department, July 6, 1950, *FR: 1950*, VII, 319.

104. Franks to Bevin, August 30, 1950, Foreign Office Records, FO371/81616.

105. See, on United States policy toward Korea prior to the outbreak of the Korean conflict, the relevant chapters in Stueck, *The Road to Confrontation*; also Charles M. Dobbs, *The Unwanted Symbol: American Foreign Policy, the Cold War, and Korea, 1945–1950* (Kent, Ohio: 1981); James I. Matray, *The Reluctant Crusade: American Foreign Policy in Korea, 1941–1950* (Honolulu: 1985); and Chapter Four, above.

106. Foot, *The Wrong War*, pp. 59–60.

107. Office of Intelligence Research Intelligence Estimate, "Korea (Preliminary Version)," June 25, 1950, *FR: 1950*, VII, 152–53.

108. Defense Department draft memorandum, "U.S. Courses of Action in Korea," July 31, 1950, *ibid.*, p. 506; John M. Allison draft memorandum, "U.S. Courses of Action in Korea," August 12, 1950, *ibid.*, pp. 569–70; also p. 99, above.

109. Merchant to Dean Rusk, November 27, 1950, *FR: 1950*, VI, 581. See also a draft memorandum by John Paton Davies, July 31, 1950, Policy Planning Staff Records, Box 36, "Record Copies, 1947–1951"; and a memorandum by Robert Tufts, "On the Development of the Relationship between the U.S. and the U.S.S.R.," October 13, 1950, *ibid.*, Box 23, "USSR 1946–1950."

110. Minutes, Bohlen meeting with British and French representatives, Paris, August 4, 1950, *FR: 1950*, VI, 420.

111. Joint executive session, Senate Foreign Relations Committee and House Foreign Affairs Committee, September 11, 1950, *Reviews of the World Situation*, p. 366.

112. Minutes, Truman-Attlee meeting, December 5, 1950, *FR: 1950*, VII, 1397–1402.

There is a somewhat less detailed British account of this meeting in Franks to the Foreign Office, December 5, 1950, Foreign Office Records, FO371/84105/FK1022/548.

113. Minutes, Truman-Attlee meeting, December 4, 1950, *FR: 1950*, VII, 1368–69.

114. There is extensive documentation on this initiative, primarily undertaken by Marshall, in *FR: 1951*, VII, 1476–1503, 1519–20, 1530–35, 1542–52, 1557–62, 1583–84, 1607–8, 1652–64, 1667–71, 1697–98, 1711–12, 1716, although the names of most of the Chinese participants have been deleted and in some instances were not included in the original documentation. The Marshall quote is from p. 1480. There is also a brief discussion in Dean Acheson, *Present at the Creation: My Years in the State Department* (New York: 1969), p. 532.

115. See Foot, *The Wrong War*, pp. 132–33.

116. See, on this point, the State Department's "Report on the Effect Within China and Other Eastern Countries of United States Backing of Chiang Kai-shek," February 9, 1951, *FR: 1951*, VII, 1574–78.

117. Allen B. Morehead memorandum of conversation with McCormack, April 14, 1951, *ibid.*, p. 1630.

118. Marshall to Kenneth C. Krentz, June 4, 1951, *ibid.*, pp. 1697–98.

119. Foot, *The Wrong War*, pp. 157–58.

120. NSC 48/5, "United States Objectives, Policies and Courses of Action in Asia," May 17, 1951, *FR: 1951*, VI, 35, 37.

121. Acheson memorandum of conversation with Truman, May 21, 1951, *ibid.*, VII, 1672. For Rusk's speech, delivered to the China Institute in America on May 18, 1951, see the *Department of State Bulletin*, XXIV(May 28, 1951), 843–48; also the perceptive analysis of it in Warren I. Cohen, *Dean Rusk* (Totowa, New Jersey: 1980), pp. 62–67.

122. Davies memorandum, "Negotiated Settlement of the Korean Conflict," March 24, 1951, *FR: 1951*, VII, 1607.

123. Acheson memorandum, conversation with Churchill and Anthony Eden, January 6, 1952, *FR: 1952–54*, VI, 743–44" [emphasis added]. See also Acheson's notes of a meeting with Lester Pearson, June 14, 1951, *FR: 1951*, I, 852.

124. NSC 48/5, May 17, 1951, *ibid.*, VI, 33–63, is the most comprehensive presidentially approved statement of United States policy in Asia during the final years of the Truman administration. For the sections on Taiwan, see pp. 38, 55–57.

125. State Department position paper, "Formosa," November 21, 1951, *ibid.*, VII, 1861.

126. Dulles untitled memorandum, June 16, 1949, John Foster Dulles Papers, Box 40, "Council of Foreign Ministers" folder, Seeley Mudd Library, Princeton University.

127. Dulles to Homer Ferguson, June 28, 1949, *ibid.*, Box 41, "Ferguson" folder.

128. Dulles to Acheson, November 30, 1950, *ibid.*, Box 48, "Korea" folder.

129. NSC 48/2, "The Position of the United States with Respect to Asia," December 30, 1949, *FR: 1949*, VII, 1215–20, and NSC 58/2, "United States Policy Toward the Soviet Satellite States in Eastern Europe," December 8, 1949, *ibid.*, V, 42–52, provide the clearest expositions of the Truman administration's strategy for exploiting differences within the international communist movement. See also, on this point, Gaddis, *Strategies of Containment*, pp. 42–48, 65–71.

130. Dulles memorandum of conversation with Ales Bebler, June 24, 1952, enclosed in Dulles to Eisenhower, June 25, 1952, Dulles Papers, Box 57, "Bebler" folder; and Dulles to the editors of *Commonweal*, September 5, 1952, *ibid.*, Box 59, "Containment" folder, both stress that the exploitation of Soviet-satellite differences is to take place by peaceful means. For Dulles's campaign rhetoric, see Robert A. Divine, *Foreign Policy and U.S. Presidential Elections: 1952–1960* (New York: 1974), pp. 50–56.

131. My thinking on this point has been influenced by the work of one of my students, Zhai Qiang, "American Policy Toward Sino-Soviet Relations, 1952–1954," seminar paper, Ohio University, March, 1986. See also Mayers, *Cracking the Monolith*, pp. 119–20.

132. Dulles to Bowles, March 25, 1952, Dulles Papers, Box 58, "Bowles" folder.

133. Dulles memorandum of conversation with Bebler, enclosed in Dulles to Eisenhower, June 25, 1952, *ibid.,* Box 57, "Bebler" folder.

134. Dulles to the editors of *Commonweal,* September 5, 1952, *ibid.,* Box 59, "Containment" folder.

135. John Foster Dulles, *War or Peace* (New York: 1950), p. 242. See also Walter McConaughy's notes of a conversation between Dulles and Chinese Nationalist Foreign Minister George Yeh, October 27, 1954, *FR: 1952–54,* XIV, 801.

136. Dulles radio-television address, January 27, 1953, *Department of State Bulletin,* XXVIII(February 9, 1953), 215.

137. Cutler memorandum, "Some Major Questions Raised by a Review of Approved National Security Policies," enclosed in James S. Lay to the National Security Council, February 6, 1953, *FR: 1952–54,* II, 231.

138. See the memorandum of Dulles's conversation with John Selwyn Lloyd, December 26, 1952, *ibid.,* XIV, 129n; also Peter Lyon, *Eisenhower: Portrait of the Hero* (Boston: 1974), p. 520.

139. Minutes, legislative leadership meeting, February 16, 1953, Eisenhower Papers, Whitman File, DDE Diary, Box 2, "Staff Notes, Jan-Dec 53." See also Dulles's public explanations of the "Captive Nations Resolution" in his press conference of February 18, 1953, and in testimony before the House Foreign Affairs Committee, February 26, 1953, *Department of State Bulletin,* XXVIII(March 2 and March 9, 1953), 330, 372.

140. Dulles comments to Boy's Nation, Washington, July 27, 1953, *ibid.,* XXVIX(August 10, 1953), 176. See also Assistant Secretary of State Walter S. Robertson's address to the Virginia Society of Baltimore, January 22, 1954, *ibid.,* XXX(February 1, 1954), 151.

141. Dulles to certain diplomatic posts, March 6, 1953, *FR: 1952–54,* II, 1684–85. See also Dulles's circular telegram of the previous day, *ibid.,* pp. 1681–84, suggesting how this might be done.

142. Minutes, National Security Council meeting, March 12, 1953, Eisenhower Papers, Whitman File, NSC series, Box 4.

143. Minutes, NSC meeting, March 31, 1953, *FR: 1952–54,* II, 267–68.

144. Minutes, NSC meeting, March 12, 1953, Eisenhower Papers, Whitman File, NSC series, Box 4.

145. NSC 153/1, "Restatement of Basic National Security Policy," approved by Eisenhower June 10, 1953, *FR: 1952–54,* II, 385. See also, for a much more detailed explication of this strategy, the Report of the President's Committee on International Information Activities, June 30, 1953, *ibid.,* pp. 1795–1899.

146. Ranelagh, *The Agency,* pp. 258–59.

147. Dulles press conference statement, June 30, 1953, *Department of State Bulletin,* XXIX(July 13, 1953), 40. See also Dulles's speech to the United Nations General Assembly, September 17, 1953, *ibid.,* XXIX(September 28, 1953), 406.

148. Eisenhower press conference, July 1, 1953, *Public Papers of the Presidents: Dwight D. Eisenhower, 1953* (Washington: 1960), p. 468.

149. Minutes, NSC meeting of July 30, 1953, *FR: 1952–54,* II, 439.

150. Cutler memorandum of conversation with Eisenhower, September 3, 1953, *ibid.,* p. 457.

151. NSC 162/2, "Basic National Security Policy," approved by Eisenhower October 30, 1953, *ibid.,* p. 580.

152. Minutes, NSC meeting, March 4, 1953, Eisenhower Papers, Whitman File, NSC series, Box 4.

153. Bohlen memorandum, March 7, 1953, and memorandum of conversation between Bohlen, C. D. Jackson, Emmett John Hughes, and Paul Nitze, same date, Policy Planning Staff Records, Box 72, "Eisenhower 1953."

154. NSC Staff Study, "Basic U.S. Objectives Toward Communist China," April 6, 1953, *FR: 1952–54,* XIV, 175–77.

155. Notes, Eisenhower meeting with legislative leaders, May 19, 1953, Eisenhower Papers, Whitman File, DDE Diary, Box 2, "Staff Notes, Jan-Dec 53."

156. Dwight D. Eisenhower, *The White House Years: Mandate for Change, 1953–1956* (Garden City, New York: 1963), p. 214. See also Eisenhower's press conference, August 4, 1954, *Eisenhower Public Papers: 1954*, p. 686.

157. Eisenhower to Dulles, June 2, 1953, Eisenhower Papers, Whitman File, DDE Diary, Box 2, "Dec. 52-July 53 (2)."

158. Minutes, NSC meeting, June 18, 1953, *FR: 1952–54*, XIV, 204–5.

159. Minutes, NSC meeting, November 5, 1953, *ibid.*, pp. 268–72. See also Eisenhower's press conference June 16, 1954, *Eisenhower Public Papers: 1954*, pp. 570–71; and the James C. Hagerty Diary, June 21, 1954, Robert H. Ferrell, ed., *The Diary of James C. Hagerty: Eisenhower in Mid-Course, 1954–1955* (Bloomington: 1983), p. 70.

160. NSC 166/1, "U.S. Policy Towards Communist China," November 6, 1953, *FR: 1952–54*, XIV, 281, 297–98.

161. Charlton Ogburn, Jr., to McConaughy, October 30, 1953, *ibid.*, pp. 257–59. Ogburn's memorandum was written as a comment on NSC 146/1, which dealt with United States policy toward Taiwan but complemented the strategy enunciated in NSC 166/1.

162. Minutes, Eisenhower-Churchill-Bidault meeting, December 7, 1953, *ibid.*, V, 1814.

163. Ridgway comment, enclosed in Nathan Twining to Charles E. Wilson, August 11, 1954, *ibid.*, XII, 723.

164. Minutes, NSC meeting, August 18, 1954 *FR: 1952–54*, XIV, 533–36.

165. For traditional interpretations of the Quemoy-Matsu crises, see Foster Rhea Dulles, *American Policy Toward Communist China, 1949–1969* (New York: 1972), pp. 164–67, 183–84; J. H. Kalicki, *The Pattern of Sino-American Crises: Political-Military Interactions in the 1950s* (Cambridge: 1975), pp. 123–27; and Townsend Hoopes, *The Devil and John Foster Dulles* (Boston: 1973), pp. 262–63, 419–23. A recent study of domestic constraints that does take into account the "wedge" strategy is Leonard A. Kusnitz, *Public Opinion and Foreign Policy: America's China Policy, 1949–1979* (Westport, Connecticut: 1984), especially pp. 23–94.

166. Dulles memorandum, September 12, 1954, *FR: 1952–54*, XIV, 611–13.

167. Minutes, NSC meeting, September 12, 1954, *ibid.*, p. 617.

168. Minutes, NSC meeting, November 2, 1954, *ibid.*, p. 831.

169. Minutes, NSC meeting, December 21, 1954, *ibid.*, p. 841.

170. Livingston Merchant notes, Dulles-Makins conversation, February 7, 1955, *FR: 1955–57*, II, 236.

171. McConaughy notes, Dulles-Yeh conversation, February 10, 1955, *ibid.*, pp. 253–55, 257–58. See also Dulles's report of a conversation with Chiang Kai-shek, March 4, 1955, *ibid.*, p. 323; and with Australian Prime Minister Robert Menzies, March 14, 1955, *ibid.*, p. 369.

172. Minutes, NSC meeting, February 26, 1954, *FR: 1952–54*, XIV, 366.

173. Bohlen to State Department, October 2, 1954, *ibid.*, p. 674. See also Bohlen's cables of October 9, 1954, *ibid.*, pp. 720–71; January 27, 1955, *FR: 1955–57*, II, 147–48; February 4, 1955, *ibid.*, pp. 211–12; February 18, 1955, *ibid.*, pp. 289–91; and June 6, 1955, *ibid.*, pp. 587–88.

174. Minutes, NSC meeting, October 6, 1954, *FR: 1952–54*, XIV, 690. See also Dulles's briefing for the National Security Council, February 3, 1955, *FR: 1955–57*, II, 199; and Special National Intelligence Estimate 11–4–55, "Review of Current Communist Attitudes Toward General War," February 15, 1955, *ibid.*, pp. 275–76.

175. Hagerty Diary, February 3, 1955, *ibid.*, p. 203. See also Eisenhower's conversation with Chinese Foreign Minister Yeh, December 20, 1954, *FR: 1952–54*, XIV, 1041; Eisenhower to Alfred Gruenther, February 1, 1955, *FR: 1955–57*, II, 192–93; and the Hagerty Diary, April 4, 1955, quoted in Ferrell, ed., *The Diary of James C. Hagerty* p. 224.

176. See the transcript of a Dulles-Hagerty telephone conversation, July 7, 1954, John

Foster Dulles Papers, Telephone Calls, Box 10, "July-October 1954 (2)," Dwight D. Eisenhower Library; also the Hagerty Diary, July 7, 1954, James C. Hagerty Papers, Box 1, Dwight D. Eisenhower Library.

177. NSC 5429/3, "Current U.S. Policy in the Far East," November 19, 1954, *FR: 1952–54*, XIV, 918.

178. Dulles notes, conversation with Eisenhower, December 22, 1954, *ibid.*, p. 1048. See also the minutes of the NSC meeting of December 1, 1954, *ibid.*, pp. 968–77.

179. For these negotiations, see Kenneth T. Young, *Negotiating with the Chinese Communists: The United States Experience, 1953–1967* (New York: 1968).

180. Minutes, NSC meeting, December 1, 1954, *FR: 1952–54*, XIV, 973.

181. Dulles report, conversation with Chiang Kai-shek, March 4, 1955, *FR: 1955–57*, II, 326.

182. Young, *Negotiating with the Chinese Communists*, pp. 91–128.

183. Dulles San Francisco speech, June 28, 1957, *Department of State Bulletin*, XXXVII (July 15, 1957), 94. See also the State Department press release of August 11, 1958, *ibid.*, XXXIX (September 8, 1958), 385–90.

184. Dulles notes, conversation with Eisenhower, August 12, 1958, Dulles Papers (Eisenhower Library), White House Memoranda, Box 7, "Meetings with the President, July-December 1958 (8)"; Andrew J. Goodpaster notes, Eisenhower-Dulles conversation, August 14, 1958, Eisenhower Papers, Whitman File, DDE Diary, Box 22, "Aug 58 Staff Notes (2)"; Dulles memorandum, September 4, 1958, published in Dwight D. Eisenhower, *The White House Years: Waging Peace, 1956—1961* (Garden City, New York: 1965), 691–93; Dulles to Harold Macmillan, September 4, 1958, Dulles Papers (Eisenhower Library, White House Memoranda, Box 7, "Meetings with the President, July-December 1958 (6)"; Eisenhower, *Waging Peace*, p. 293.

185. Gray notes, Eisenhower meeting with United States delegation to Geneva technical military conference on surprise attack, November 5, 1958, Eisenhower Papers, Whitman File, DDE Diary, Box 23, "Staff Notes—Nov. 58."

186. Dulles notes, conversation with Eisenhower, November 18, 1958, Dulles Papers (Eisenhower Library), Box 7, "Meetings with the President, July-December 1958 (3)."

187. Dulles executive session testimony, January 14, 1959, U.S. Congress, Senate Committee on Foreign Relations, *Historical Series: Eighty-Sixth Congress, First Session, 1959* (Washington: 1982), p. 8.

188. See, on this point, Gaddis, *Strategies of Containment*, pp. viii–ix.

189. See, for example, NSC 5913/1, "U.S. Policy in the Far East," September 25, 1959, reviewed and reapproved without changes by the National Security Council Planning Board, November 10, 1960, Eisenhower Papers, White House Office Files, NSC Assistant: NSC Subseries: Policy Paper subseries, Box 27.

190. See NIE 13–54, "Communist China's Power Potential Through 1957," June 3, 1954, *FR: 1952–54*, XIV, 445–61; and NIE 11–4–54, "Soviet Capabilities and Probable Courses of Action Through Mid-1959," August 28, 1954, Eisenhower Papers, White House Office Files, NSC Assistant, Subject Subseries, Box 10.

191. Allen Dulles memorandum, prepared for NSC discussion, November 18, 1954, *FR: 1952–54*, II, 777–78.

192. John W. Hanes, Jr., to Ann Whitman, March 3, 1954, Dulles Papers (Eisenhower Library), White House Memoranda, Box 1, "Correspondence 1954 (4)."

193. Minutes, NSC meeting, August 5, 1954, *FR: 1952–54*, II, 711.

194. Eisenhower press conference, June 29, 1955, *Eisenhower Public Papers: 1955*, p. 650.

195. Dulles memorandum, conversation with Eisenhower, August 11, 1955, Dulles Papers (Eisenhower Library), White House Memoranda, Box 3, "Meetings with the President, 1955 (2)." See also Dulles's memorandum of a telephone conversation with Eisenhower on the same day regarding the possibility of a Tito visit to the United States, Dulles Papers (Eisenhower Library), Telephone Conversations, Box 10, "March 7–Aug. 29, 1955

(1)"; Dulles's press conference, April 24, 1956, *Department of State Bulletin* XXXIV (May 7, 1956), 752; and Dulles's executive session testimony before the Senate Foreign Relations Committee, January 6 and June 26, 1956, U.S. Congress, Senate, Committee on Foreign Relations, *Historical Series: Eighty-Fourth Congress, Second Session, 1956* (Washington: 1978), pp. 17, 520.

196. Eisenhower press conference, June 6, 1956, *Eisenhower Public Papers: 1956,* p. 558.

197. See Dulles's speech to the *Philadelphia Bulletin* Forum, February 26, 1956, *Department of State Bulletin*, XXXIV (March 5, 1956), 363–67; Eisenhower's press conference of March 21 and April 4, 1956, *Eisenhower Public Papers: 1956,* pp. 330, 370–71; and Dulles's press conference, April 3, 1956, *Department of State Bulletin*, XXXIV (April 16, 1956), 642.

198. Allen Dulles speech to the Los Angeles World Aaffirs Council, April 13, 1956, *ibid.*, XXXIV (May 7, 1956), 761.

199. Eisenhower informal remarks to the American Society of Newspaper Editors, April 21, 1956, *Eisenhower Public Papers: 1956,* p. 423.

200. Dulles press conference, April 24, 1956, *Department of State Bulletin*, XXXIV (May 7, 1956), 752.

201. For the CIA's acquisition of the Khrushchev speech and the decision to make it public see Ranelagh, *The Agency*, pp. 285–88.

202. Dulles speech to Kiwanis International, San Francisco, June 21, 1956, *Department of State Bulletin*, XXXV (July 2, 1956), 4. See also Dulles's press conference, June 27, 1956, *ibid.*, XXXV (July 9, 1956), 47, 52.

203. Dulles memorandum, conversation with Eisenhower, July 13, 1956, Dulles Papers (Eisenhower Library), White House memoranda, Box 4, "Meetings with the President, January-July, 1956 (1)."

204. Dulles executive session testimony, June 26, 1956, *Historical Series: Eighty-Fourth Congress, Second Session, 1956,* pp. 501, 503.

205. Dulles to Eisenhower, September 5, 1956, Dulles Papers (Eisenhower Library), White House Memoranda, Box 3, "Correspondence—General 1956 (2)."

206. Goodpaster notes, Eisenhower conversation with Sherman Adams and others, November 7, 1956, Dulles Papers (Eisenhower Library), White House Memoranda, Box 4, "Meetings with the President, August-December, 1956 (3)." See also Dulles's notes of a conversation with Eisenhower, December 22, 1956, *ibid.*, Box 4, "Meetings with the President, August-December 1956 (1)."

207. Eisenhower to C. D. Jackson, November 19, 1956, quoted in Ambrose, *Eisenhower: The President*, p. 372.

208. See, on this point, Ranelagh, *The Agency*, pp. 287, 306–9; Powers, *The Man Who Kept the Secrets*, pp. 93–94; and Leonard Mosley, *Dulles: A Biography of Eleanor, Allen, and John Foster Dulles and Their Family Network* (New York: 1978), pp. 452–53.

209. L. Arthur Minnich, Jr., notes, Eisenhower and Allen Dulles meeting with legislative leaders, November 9, 1956, *ibid.*, Whitman File, DDE Diary, Box 11, "Nov. 56 Misc (3)." See also Goodpaster's notes of a John Foster Dulles meeting wtih Eisenhower, December 15, 1956, Dulles Papers (Eisenhower Library), White House Memoranda, Box 4, "Meetings with the President, August-December, 1956 (2)."

210. Minnich notes, bipartisan meeting of legislative leaders, January 1, 1957, Eisenhower Papers, Whitman File, DDE Diary, Box 12, "January 1957 Misc (4)."

211. Eisenhower press conference, April 3, 1957, *Eisenhower Public Papers: 1957,* p. 247.

212. See, on these points, Ranelagh, *The Agency*, pp. 237–46; also Gaddis, *Strategies of Containment*, pp. 157–59, 161; and Ambrose, *Eisenhower: The President*, pp. 110–11.

213. NSC 5412, "Covert Operations," March 15, 1954, Eisenhower Papers, White House Office Files, Office of the Special Assistant for National Security Affairs, Box 7, "NSC 5412/2."

214. These activties are described in Ranelagh, *The Agency*, pp. 246–52, 259–68, 332–36, 353–60.

215. Eisenhower Diary, March 8, 1956, Robert H. Ferrell, ed., *The Eisenhower Diaries* (New York: 1981), p. 319.

216. Dulles executive session testimony, Senate Foreign Relations Committee, June 26, 1956, *Historical Series: Eighty-Fourth Congress, Second Session, 1956*, p. 515.

217. Dulles memorandum, conversation with Eisenhower, September 17, 1956, Dulles Papers (Eisenhower Library), White House Memoranda, Box 4, "Meetings with the President, August-December, 1956 (5)."

218. Eisenhower press conference, August 21, 1957, *Eisenhower Public Papers, 1957*, p. 625.

219. Eisenhower speech to the United Nations General Assembly, August 13, 1958, *Eisenhower Public Papers, 1958*, p. 616.

220. Eisenhower press conference, August 20, 1958, *ibid.*, pp. 630–31.

221. See p. 182, above.

222. See, on these points, Gaddis, *Strategies of Containment*, pp. 143–45, 181–82, 238–43.

## 7 Learning to Live with Transparency: The Emergence of a Reconnaissance Satellite Regime

1. For two early journalistic accounts, see Philip J. Klass, *Secret Sentries in Space* (New York: 1971); and John W. R. Taylor and David Mondley, *Spies in the Sky* (New York: 1972). John Newhouse provided the first good discussion of the importance of satellite reconnaissance in verifying the SALT I agreement in *Cold Dawn: The Story of SALT* (New York: 1973), especially pp. 14–17.

2. See, for example, D. L. Hafner, "Anti-Satellite Weapons: The Prospects for Arms Control," in Bhupendra Jasani, *Outer Space—A New Dimension of the Arms Race* (London: 1982), pp. 311–23; also the special supplement on "Space Weapons" in the *Bulletin of the Atomic Scientists*, XL(May, 1984), pp. 1S–15S.

3. There are now two important books on this subject, based on access to U.S. official sources. They are Gerald M. Steinberg, *Satellite Reconnaissance: The Role of Informal Bargaining* (New York: 1983); and Paul B. Stares, *The Militarization of Space: U.S. Policy, 1945–84* (Ithaca: 1985). The following essay relies heavily upon them. Two other recent accounts that deal extensively with this topic are John Prados, *The Soviet Estimate: U.S. Intelligence Analysis and Russian Military Strength* (New York: 1982); and Walter McDougall, *The Heavens and the Earth: A Political History of the Space Age* (New York: 1985).

4. L. T. C. Rolt, *The Aeronauts: A History of Ballooning, 1783–1903* (New York: 1966), p. 162.

5. Taylor and Mondley, *Spies in the Sky*, p. 22. See also Christopher Andrew, *Her Majesty's Secret Service: The Making of the British Intelligence Community* (New York: 1986), pp. 133, 136–37.

6. Taylor and Mondley, *Spies in the Sky*, pp. 56–59.

7. The best account of the U-2 incident is now Michael Beschloss, *Mayday: Eisenhower, Khrushchev and the U-2 Affair* (New York: 1986).

8. The magazine *Aviation Week and Space Technology* has long been an important source of information on new U.S. military technologies. For some examples of its role in this regard in the 1950's, see Prados, *The Soviet Estimate*, pp. 36–37, 105. See also, on the question of U.S. anxieties about the difficulty of penetrating Soviet secrecy, Harry Rositzke, *The CIA's Secret Operations: Espionage, Counterespionage, and Covert Action* (New York: 1977), pp. 13–17; and W. W. Rostow, *Open Skies: Eisenhower's Proposal of July 21, 1955* (Austin: 1982), p. 12.

9. Almost no documentary evidence has been declassified concerning these efforts, but

their general outlines have been reconstructed in Rositzke, *The CIA's Secret Operations*, pp. 18–100; Prados, *The Soviet Estimate*, pp. 24–30; Thomas Powers, *The Man Who Kept the Secrets: Richard Helms and the CIA* (New York: 1979), pp. 42–58; James Bamford, *The Puzzle Palace: A Report on America's Most Secret Agency* (New York: 1982), pp. 181–83, 232–39; John Ranelagh, *The Agency: The Rise and Decline of the CIA* (New York: 1986), pp. 135–42, 226–28; and David Alan Rosenberg, "The Origins of Overkill: Nuclear Weapons and American Strategy, 1945–1960," *International Security*, VII (Spring, 1983), 15.

10. Minutes, National Security Council meeting, March 31, 1953, U.S. Department of State, *Foreign Relations of the United States: 1952–54*, II, 268.

11. James R. Killian, Jr., *Sputnik, Scientists, and Eisenhower: A Memoir of the First Special Assistant to the President for Science and Technology* (Cambridge, Massachusetts, 1977), pp. 79–85.

12. Eisenhower statement, July 21, 1955, *Public Papers of the Presidents: Dwight D. Eisenhower, 1955* (Washington: 1959), pp. 715–16.

13. Rostow, *Open Skies*, pp. 26–56.

14. For the relationship between the Killian Committee report and the "Open Skies" proposal, see *ibid.*, p. 10; also Stephen Ambrose, *Eisenhower: The President* (New York: 1984), p. 258; and Ray S. Cline, *Secrets, Spies, and Scholars: The Essential CIA* (Washington: 1976), pp. 158–59.

15. See, on this point, Stephen E. Ambrose, *Ike's Spies: Eisenhower and the Intelligence Establishment* (Garden City, New York: 1981), p. 267.

16. Andrew J. Goodpaster notes, Eisenhower conversation with Radford, Nathan Twining, Herbert Hoover, Jr., and Allen Dulles, May 28, 1956, Dwight D. Eisenhower Papers, Ann Whitman File, DDE Diary, Box 8, "May 56 Goodpaster," Dwight D. Eisenhower Library. For other Eisenhower expressions of concern about overflights, see the transcript of an Eisenhower telephone conversation with John Foster Dulles, December 18, 1956, Eisenhower Papers, Whitman File, DDE Diary, Box 11, "Dec. 56 Phone Calls"; and Dulles notes, conversations with Eisenhower, January 22 and March 7, 1958, John Foster Dulles Papers, White House Memoranda, Box 6, "Meetings with the President, January–June, 1958 (6, 7)," Dwight D. Eisenhower Library.

17. Goodpaster notes, Eisenhower conversation with Donald Quarles and other advisers, October 8, 1957, Eisenhower Papers, Whitman File, DDE Diary, Box 16, "Oct. 57 Staff Notes (2)." See also Quarles's comment at the cabinet meeting of October 18, 1957, L. L. Minnich notes, *ibid.*, "Oct. 57 Staff Notes (1)."

18. See John Lewis Gaddis, *The United States and the Origins of the Cold War, 1941–1947* (New York: 1972), pp. 81–86.

19. See, on this point, McDougall, *The Heavens and the Earth*, p. 109; also Irvin L. White, *Decision-Making for Space: Law and Politics in Air, Sea, and Outer Space* (West Lafayette, Indiana: 1970), pp. 102–11.

20. Allen S. Krass, "The Soviet View of Verification," in William C. Potter, ed., *Verification and Arms Control* (Lexington, Massachusetts: 1985), pp. 37–39.

21. *Department of State Bulletin*, XXXII (May 30, 1955), 900–905.

22. Dwight D. Eisenhower, *White House Years: Mandate for Change, 1953–1956* (Garden City, New York: 1963), p. 521.

23. See Rostow, *Open Skies*, pp. 79–83.

24. *Ibid.*, pp. 63–64.

25. A. A. Gromyko and B. N. Ponomarev, eds., *Soviet Foreign Policy, 1945–1980*, Fourth Edition (Moscow: 1981), II, 234.

26. McDougall, *The Heavens and the Earth*, p. 258.

27. *Ibid.*, pp. 258–61; Steinberg, *Satellite Reconnaissance*, pp. 27–28; Stuart A. Cohen, "The Evolution of Soviet Views on SALT Verification: Implications for the Future," in William C. Potter, ed., *Verification and SALT: The Challenge of Strategic Deception* (Boulder, Colorado: 1980), pp. 56–58.

28. George B. Kistiakowsky, *A Scientist at the White House: The Private Diary of President Eisenhower's Special Assistant for Science and Technology* (Cambridge, Massachusetts: 1976), pp. 229–30; also Steinberg, *Satellite Reconnaissance*, pp. 31–35; and Stares, *The Militarization of Space*, pp. 49–54.

29. Steinberg, *Satellite Reconnaissance*, p. 24. See also Dwight D. Eisenhower, *White House Years: 1956–1961* (Garden City, New York: 1965), p. 259n.

30. *Ibid.*, pp. 40–42.

31. See Stares, *The Militarization of Space*, pp. 62–65; Steinberg, *Satellite Reconnaissance*, pp. 30–31, 44–45.

32. For the Gilpatric speech, see the *New York Times*, October 22, 1961. Its background is best discussed in Roger Hilsman, *To Move a Nation: The Politics of Foreign Policy in the Administration of John F. Kennedy* (New York: 1967), pp. 163–64, although Hilsman mistakenly dates the speech as November, 1961.

33. Steinberg, *Satellite Reconnaissance*, pp. 50–51. Prados suggests, unfortunately without providing a source, that Kennedy actually showed Gromyko satellite reconnaissance photographs in September, 1961. [*The Soviet Estimate*, p. 122.] The best discussion of Khrushchev's "strategic deception" strategy, which he followed from 1957 to 1961, is Arnold Horelick and Myron Rush, *Strategic Power and Soviet Foreign Policy* (Chicago: 1966).

34. Steinberg, *Satellite Reconnaissance*, pp. 83–84. For details on the SAINT system, see Stares, *The Militarization of Space*, pp. 112–17.

35. Steinberg, *Satellite Reconnaissance*, p. 85; Stares, *The Militarization of Space*, pp. 80–82, 117–28.

36. Quoted in *ibid.*, p. 69. For the Soviet diplomatic offensive of 1962 on this subject, see Steinberg, *Satellite Reconnaissance*, pp. 54–55.

37. *Ibid.*, pp. 56–62.

38. Quoted in Stares, *The Militarization of Space*, p. 71.

39. *New York Times*, July 15, 1963. The report was by C. L. Sulzberger, but curiously Sulzberger does not mention the comment about satellites in his July 11, 1963, diary entry about the Spaak-Khrushchev picnic. [C. L. Sulzberger, *The Last of the Giants* (New York: 1970), pp. 994–95.] For a similar Khrushchev offer to William Benton in May, 1964, see Klass, *Secret Sentries in Space*, p. 127n.

40. Steinberg, *Satellite Reconnaissance*, pp. 64–65; Klass, *Secret Sentries in Space*, pp. 127–29. For the General Assembly resolutions, see Jenks, *Space Law*, pp. 317–19, 326–27.

41. Klass, *Secret Sentries in Space*, pp. 119–22.

42. See footnote 39, above.

43. Klass, *Secret Sentries in Space*, pp. 120–22; Stares, *The Militarization of Space*, p. 238.

44. See Rostow, *Open Skies*, pp. 82–83.

45. Taylor and Mondley, *Spies in the Sky*, pp. 72–79.

46. See, on this point, Glenn T. Seaborg, *Kennedy, Khrushchev, and the Test Ban* (Berkeley: 1981), pp. 226–28.

47. Quoted in Klass, *Secret Sentries in Space*, p. 217. For a discussion of the "Gilpatric principle," see *ibid.*, pp. 216–18.

48. Steinberg, *Satellite Reconnaissance*, pp. 71–87.

49. Stares, *The Militarization of Space*, pp. 116–17.

50. *Ibid.*, pp. 50–53, 127.

51. For the Soviet anti-satellite program that began in 1976, and its effect in stimulating comparable U.S. programs, see Stares, *The Militarization of Space*, pp. 176, 187–92, 243.

52. See Hilsman, *To Move a Nation*, p. 224.

53. David Hafemeister, Joseph J. Romm, and Kosta Tsipis, "The Verification of Compliance with Arms-Control Agreements," *Scientific American*, CCLIII(March, 1985), 40–

41. For technical details, see Bhupendra Jasani, "Military Space Technology and Its Implications," in Jasani, ed., *Outer Space*, pp. 43–50; T. Sakata and H. Shimoda, "Image Analysis and Sensor Technology for Satellite Monitoring," *ibid.*, pp. 197–214; also T. Orhaug and G. Forssell, "Information Extraction from Images," *ibid.*, pp. 215–27.

54. B. G. Blair, "Reconnaissance Satellites," *ibid.*, pp. 125–30.

55. Jasani, "Military Space Technology," *ibid.*, pp. 54–56; Blair, "Reconnaissance Satellites," *ibid.*, pp. 132–33. See also Charles Elachi, "Radar Images of the Earth from Space," *Scientific American*, CCXLVII (December, 1982), 54–61.

56. Jasani, "Military Space Technology," in Jasani, ed., *Outer Space*, pp. 50–54. See also Bamford, *The Puzzle Palace*, pp. 252–55.

57. See Prados, *The Soviet Estimate*, pp. 3–4, 290.

58. See footnote 33, above.

59. U.S. Arms Control and Disarmament Agency, *Arms Control and Disarmament Agreements* (Washington: 1982), pp. 141, 151.

60. *Ibid.*, pp. 249, 261.

61. K. Santhanam, "Use of Satellites in Crisis Monitoring," in Jasani, ed., *Outer Space*, pp. 269–71. For the Falklands conflict, see "America's Falklands War," *Economist*, CCXC (March 3, 1984), 30–31.

62. Santhanam, "Use of Satellites in Crisis Monitoring," p. 271; Stares, *The Militarization of Space*, pp. 140–41; Raymond Garthoff, *Détente and Confrontation: American-Soviet Relations from Nixon to Reagan* (Washington: 1985), p. 763.

63. For some dramatic examples, see Nicholas M. Short, *et al.*, *Mission to Earth: Landsat Views the World* (Washington: 1976).

64. See Stares, *The Militarization of Space*, p. 49.

65. *Ibid.*, pp. 120–29, 201–2. On the danger to other satellites of nuclear explosions in outer space, see *ibid.*, p. 108.

66. *Ibid.*, pp. 136–46.

67. Stares, *The Militarization of Space*, pp. 146–56. See also Richard L. Garwin and John Pike, "Space Weapons: History and Current Debate," *Bulletin of the Atomic Scientists*, XL (May, 1984), 2S–3S.

68. Stares, *The Militarization of Space*, pp. 162–66.

69. These events are most fully discussed in Garthoff, *Détente and Confrontation*, pp. 360–537.

70. Stares, *The Militarization of Space*, pp. 145–46.

71. Prados, *The Soviet Estimate*, pp. 245–57.

72. Stares, *The Militarization of Space*, pp. 168–71.

73. For recent American anti-satellite weapons, development, see *ibid.*, pp. 206–9; also Garwin and Pike, "Space Weapons," 3S–4S.

74. On the anti-satellite implications of SDI, see *ibid.*, pp. 2S–9S.

75. For discussions on an anti-satellite weapons ban during the Carter and Reagan administrations, see Stares, *The Militarization of Space*, pp. 181–87, 192–99, 216–20, 229–35; and National Academy of Sciences, Committee on International Security and Arms Control, *Nuclear Arms Control: Background and Issues* (Washington: 1985), pp. 159–86.

76. The discussion that follows owes much to Steinberg, *Satellite Reconnaissance*, especially pp. 99–101, 111–12, 116–19, 122–24, 129–35, 166–67.

77. See, on this question, David B. Rivkin, Jr., "Star Wars: The Nagging Questions: What Does Moscow Think?" *Foreign Policy*, #59 (Summer, 1985), 85–105.

78. Two recent discussions of the impact of domestic politics on recent American foreign policy are Joseph S. Nye, Jr., *The Making of America's Soviet Policy* (New Haven: 1984); and I. M. Destler, Leslie H. Gelb, and Anthony Lake, *Our Own Worst Enemy: The Unmaking of American Foreign Policy* (New York: 1984). There is also a fine brief case study of the Soviet "combat brigade" controversy in Richard E. Neustadt and Ernest R. May, *Thinking in Time: The Uses of History for Decision-Makers* (New York: 1986), pp. 92–96.

79. For some possibilities, see Ashton B. Carter, "Satellites and Anti-Satellites: The Limits of the Possible," *International Security*, X (Spring, 1986), 73–88.

80. See Alexander L. George and Richard Smoke, *Deterrence in American Foreign Policy: Theory and Practice* (New York: 1974), pp. 527–30, 565.

81. See, on this point, Robert Jervis, Richard Ned Lebow, and Janice Gross Stein, *Psychology and Deterrence* (Baltimore: 1985), pp. 15–18; also Deborah Welch Larson, *Origins of Containment: A Psychological Explanation* (Princeton: 1985), pp. 34–42.

82. Prados, *The Soviet Estimate*, pp. 278–82.

83. See William M. Arkin, "Waging Secrecy," *Bulletin of the Atomic Scientists*, XLI (March, 1985), 5–6.

## 8 The Long Peace: Elements of Stability in the Postwar International System

1. Geoffrey Blainey, *The Causes of War* (London: 1973), p. 3.

2. Jack S. Levy, *War in the Modern Great Power System, 1495–1975* (Lexington, Kentucky: 1983), p. 1. Other standard works on this subject, in addition to Blainey, cited above, include: Lewis F. Richardson, *Arms and Insecurity: A Mathematical Study of the Causes and Origins of War* (Pittsburgh: 1960); Quincy Wright, *A Study of War*, Second Edition (Chicago: 1965); Kenneth N. Waltz, *Man, the State and War: A Theoretical Analysis* (New York: 1959); Kenneth Boulding, *Conflict and Defense: A General Theory* (New York: 1962); Raymond Aron, *Peace and War: A Theory of International Relations*, translated by Richard Howard and Annette Baker Fox (New York: 1966); Robert Gilpin, *War and Change in World Politics* (New York: 1981); Melvin Small and J. David Singer, *Resort to Arms: International and Civil Wars, 1816–1980* (Beverly Hills, California: 1982); and Michael Howard, *The Causes of Wars*, Second Edition (Cambridge, Massachusetts: 1984). A valuable overview of conflicting explanations is Keith Nelson and Spencer C. Olin, Jr., *Why War? Ideology, Theory, and History* (Berkeley: 1979).

3. The classic example of such abstract conceptualization is Morton A. Kaplan, *System and Process in International Politics* (New York: 1957). For the argument that 1945 marks the transition from a "multipolar" to a "bipolar" international system, see Glenn H. Snyder and Paul Diesing, *Conflict Among Nations: Bargaining, Decision Making, and System Structure in International Crises* (Princeton: 1977), pp. 419–20; and Kenneth Waltz, *Theory of International Politics* (Reading, Massachusetts: 1979), pp. 161–63.

4. I have followed here the definition of Robert Jervis, "Systems Theories and Diplomatic History," in Paul Gordon Lauren, ed., *Diplomacy: New Approaches in History, Theory, and Policy* (New York: 1979), p. 212. For a more rigorous discussion of the requirements of systems theory, and a critique of some of its major practioners, see Waltz, *Theory of International Politics*, pp. 38–78. Akira Iriye is one of the few historians who have sought to apply systems theory to the study of international relations. See his *After Imperialism: The Search for a New Order in the Far East, 1921–1931* (Cambridge, Massachusetts: 1965); and *The Cold War in Asia: A Historical Introduction* (Englewood Cliffs, New Jersey: 1974).

5. See, on this point, Robert Jervis, *Perception and Misperception in International Politics* (Princeton: 1976), pp. 58–62.

6. For other early expressions of pessimism about the stability of the postwar international system, see Walter Lippmann, *The Cold War: A Study in U.S. Foreign Policy* (New York: 1947), pp. 26–28, 37–39, 60–62.

7. Karl W. Deutsch and J. David Singer, "Multipolar Power Systems and International Stability," in James N. Rosenau, ed., *International Politics and Foreign Policy: A Reader in Research and Theory*, Revised Edition (New York: 1969), pp. 315–17. Deutsch and Singer equate "self-regulation" with "negative feedback": "By negative—as distinguished from positive or amplifying—feedback, we refer to the phenomenon of self-

correction: as stimuli in one particular direction increase, the system exhibits a decreasing response to those stimuli, and increasingly exhibits the tendencies that counteract them." See also Jervis, "Systems Theories and Diplomatic History," p. 220. For Kaplan's more abstract definition of stability, see his *System and Process in International Politics*, p. 8. The concept of "stability" in international systems owes a good deal to "functionalist" theory; see, on this point, Charles Reynolds, *Theory and Explanation in International Politics* (London: 1973), p. 30.

8. I have followed here, in slightly modified form, criteria provided in Gordon A. Craig and Alexander L. George, *Force and Statecraft: Diplomatic Problems of Our Time* (New York: 1983), p. x, a book that provides an excellent discussion of how international systems have evolved since the beginning of the 18th century. But see also Gilpin, *War and Change in World Politics*, pp. 50–105.

9. See, on this point, Waltz, *Theory of International Politics*, pp. 180–81; also DePorte, *Europe Between the Super-Powers*, p. 167.

10. Waltz, *Theory of International Politics*, pp. 73–78; Gilpin, *War and Change in World Politics*, pp. 85–88.

11. Harold Nicolson, *Peacemaking 1919* (New York: 1965), pp. 30–31.

12. Bernadotte E. Schmitt and Harold Vedeler, *The World in the Crucible: 1914–1919* (New York: 1984), p. 470.

13. Nicolson, *Peacemaking 1919*, pp. 26–29. See also Lawrence E. Gelfand, *The Inquiry: American Preparations for Peace, 1917–1919* (New Haven: 1963).

14. Quoted in John Morton Blum, *Woodrow Wilson and the Politics of Morality* (Boston: 1956), p. 161. The most convenient overview of Wilson's ideas regarding the peace settlement can be found in N. Gordon Levin, Jr., *Woodrow Wilson and World Politics: America's Response to War and Revolution* (New York: 1968), especially pp. 123–251; and Arthur S. Link, *Woodrow Wilson: Revolution, War, and Peace* (Arlington Heights, Illinois: 1979), pp. 72–103.

15. See, on this point, Gelfand, *The Inquiry*, pp. 323–26; Schmitt and Vedeler, *The World in the Crucible*, pp. 474–75; and Klaus Schwabe, *Woodrow Wilson, Revolutionary Germany, and Peacemaking, 1918–1919: Missionary Diplomacy and the Realities of Power* (Chapel Hill: 1985), pp. 395–402.

16. Winston Churchill's is the classic indictment of this decision. See his *The Gathering Storm*, Bantam Edition (New York: 1961), pp. 9–10.

17. Craig and George, *Force and Statecraft*, pp. 87–100; see also Howard, *The Causes of Wars*, pp. 163–64.

18. See, on Germany, Tony Sharp, *The Wartime Alliance and the Zonal Division of Germany* (Oxford: 1975), and John H. Backer, *The Decision to Divide Germany: American Foreign Policy in Transition* (Durham: 1978); on Austria, William Bader, *Austria Between East and West, 1945–1955* (Stanford: 1966), and Sven Allard, *Russia and the Austrian State Treaty: A Case Study of Soviet Policy in Europe* (University Park, Pennsylvania: 1970); on Korea, Charles M. Dobbs, *The Unwanted Symbol: American Foreign Policy, the Cold War, and Korea, 1945–1950* (Kent, Ohio: 1981), and Bruce Cumings, *The Origins of the Korean War: Liberation and the Emergence of Separate Regimes, 1945–1947* (Princeton: 1981). For useful comparative perspectives on the issue of partition, see Thomas E. Hachey, ed., *The Problem of Partition: Peril to World Peace* (Chicago: 1972).

19. Lynn Etheridge Davis, *The Cold War Begins: Soviet-American Conflict Over Eastern Europe* (Princeton: 1974); Eduard Mark, "American Policy toward Eastern Europe and the Origins of the Cold War, 1941–1946: An Alternative Interpretation," *Journal of American History*, LXVIII (September, 1981), 313–36. For a valuable series of first-person accounts by American diplomats, see Thomas T. Hammond, ed., *Witnesses to the Origins of the Cold War* (Seattle: 1982).

20. See, on this point, John Lewis Gaddis, "The Emerging Post-Revisionist Synthesis on the Origins of the Cold War," *Diplomatic History*, VII (Summer, 1983), 181–83. For

a perceptive discussion of post-World War II American "imperial" expansion, see Tony Smith, *The Pattern of Imperialism: The United States, Great Britain, and the Late-Industrializing World since 1815* (Cambridge: 1981), pp. 182–202.

21. Robert H. Ferrell, ed., *The Autobiography of Harry S. Truman* (Boulder, Colorado: 1980), p. 120; David McLellan, *Dean Acheson: The State Department Years* (New York: 1976), p. 116.

22. Hans J. Morgenthau, *Politics Among Nations: The Struggle for Power and Peace* (New York: 1949), p. 285. For the transition from bipolarity to multipolarity, see the 1973 edition of *Politics Among Nations*, pp. 338–42; also Waltz, *Theory of International Politics*, p. 162. For an eloquent history of the Cold War that views it as the product of the polarization of world politics, see Louis J. Halle, *The Cold War as History* (New York: 1967).

23. Among those who have emphasized the instability of bipolar systems, are Morgenthau, *Politics Among Nations*, pp. 350–54; Wright, *A Study of War*, pp. 763–64. See also Blainey, *The Causes of War*, pp. 110–11.

24. Henry Kissinger has written two classic accounts dealing with the importance of individual leadership in sustaining international systems. See his *A World Restored* (New York: 1957), on Metternich; and, on Bismarck, "The White Revolutionary: Reflections on Bismarck," *Daedalus*, XCVII (Summer, 1968), 888–924. For a somewhat different perspective on Bismarck's role, see George F. Kennan, *The Decline of Bismarck's European Order: Franco-Russian Relations, 1875–1890* (Princeton: 1979), especially pp. 421–22.

25. Waltz, *Theory of International Politics*, p. 176. On the tendency of unstable systemic structures to induce irresponsible leadership, see Ludwig Dehio, *The Precarious Balance: Four Centuries of the European Power Struggle*, translated by Charles Fullman (New York: 1962), pp. 257–58.

26. See, on this point, Roger V. Dingman, "Theories of, and Approaches to, Alliance Politics," in Lauren, ed., *Diplomacy*, pp. 246–47.

27. My argument here follows that of Snyder and Diesing, *Conflict Among Nations*, pp. 429–45.

28. Waltz, *Theory of International Politics*, pp. 167–69.

29. Foster Rhea Dulles, *The Road to Teheran: The Story of Russia and America, 1781–1943* (Princeton: 1944), p. 8.

30. See, for example, Thomas A. Bailey, *America Faces Russia: Russian-American Relations from Early Times to Our Day* (Ithaca: 1950), pp. 347–49. A more recent discussion of these developments is in John Lewis Gaddis, *Russia, the Soviet Union, and the United States: An Interpretive History* (New York: 1978), pp. 27–56; see also Chapter One, above.

31. The argument is succinctly summarized in Nelson and Olin, *Why War?*, pp. 35–43.

32. Waltz, *Theory of International Politics*, p. 138. For Waltz's general argument against interdependence as a necessary cause of peace, see *ibid.*, pp. 138–60.

33. Small and Singer, *Resort to Arms*, p. 102. The one questionable case is the Crimean War, which pitted Britain and France against Russia, but that conflict began as a dispute between Russia and Turkey.

34. See, on this point, Herbert S. Dinerstein, *The Making of a Missile Crisis, October, 1962* (Baltimore: 1976), especially pp. 230–38.

35. See footnote 33, above.

36. Zbigniew Brzezinski and Samuel P. Huntington, *Political Power: USA/USSR* (New York: 1964), pp. 90–104. For a more recent assessment of the extent of public participation in the Soviet political system, see Jerry F. Hough and Merle Fainsod, *How the Soviet Union Is Governed* (Cambridge, Massachusetts: 1979), pp. 314–19.

37. For a useful brief review of this literature, see Nelson and Olin, *Why War?*, pp. 58–84; also Richard J. Barnet, *Roots of War* (New York: 1972), pp. 208–14.

38. See, most recently, Arno J. Mayer, *The Persistence of the Old Regime: Europe to the Great War* (New York: 1981), especially pp. 304–23; and Paul M. Kennedy, *The*

*Rise of the Anglo-German Antagonism, 1869–1914* (Boston: 1980), especially pp. 465–66.

39. Examples include Charles S. Maier, *Recasting Bourgeois Europe: Stabilization in France, Germany, and Italy in the Decade After World War I* (Princeton: 1975); Stephen A. Schuker, *The End of French Predominance in Europe: The Financial Crisis of 1924 and the Adoption of the Dawes Plan* (Chapel Hill: 1976); Michael J. Hogan, *Informal Entente: The Private Structure of Cooperation in Anglo-American Economic Diplomacy, 1918–1928* (Columbia, Missouri: 1977); Melvyn P. Leffler, *The Elusive Quest: America's Pursuit of European Stability and French Security, 1919–1933* (Chapel Hill: 1979); Frank Costigliola, *Awkward Dominion: American Political, Economic, and Cultural Relations with Europe, 1919–1933* (Ithaca: 1984).

40. For some recent—and sometimes contradictory—attempts to come to grips with this question, see John Lewis Gaddis, *Strategies of Containment: A Critical Appraisal of Postwar American National Security Policy* (New York: 1982), pp. 352–57; Ralph B. Levering, *The Public and American Foreign Policy, 1918–1978* (New York: 1978); William Appleman Williams, *Empire as a Way of Life* (New York: 1980); Cecil V. Crabb, Jr., *The Doctrines of American Foreign Policy: Their Meaning, Role, and Future* (Baton Rouge: 1982), pp. 371–86; Robert Dallek, *The American Style of Foreign Policy: Cultural Politics and Foreign Affairs* (New York: 1983), pp. xi–xx; and Lloyd C. Gardner, *A Covenant with Power: America and World Order from Wilson to Reagan* (New York: 1984).

41. William Appleman Williams, *The Tragedy of American Diplomacy*, Revised Edition (New York: 1962). See also Charles A. Beard, *The Idea of National Interest: An Analytical Study in American Foreign Policy* (New York: 1934), and *The Open Door at Home: A Trial Philosophy of National Interest* (New York: 1934). Other important expressions of the Beard/Williams thesis include Gabriel Kolko, *The Roots of American Foreign Policy: An Analysis of Power and Purpose* (Boston: 1969); and Harry Magdoff, *The Age of Imperialism: The Economics of U.S. Foreign Policy* (New York: 1969).

42. Charles S. Maier, "The Two Postwar Eras and the Conditions for Stability in Twentieth-Century Western Europe," *American Historical Review*, LXXXVI(April, 1981), 327–52; Robert Griffith, "Dwight D. Eisenhower and the Corporate Commonwealth," *ibid.*, LXXXVII(February, 1982), 87–122; Michael J. Hogan, "American Marshall Planners and the Search for a European Neocapitalism," *ibid.*, XC(February, 1985), 44–72.

43. The best critiques of the "open door" model are Robert W. Tucker, *The Radical Left and American Foreign Policy* (Baltimore: 1971); Charles S. Maier, "Revisionism and the Interpretation of Cold War Origins," *Perspectives in American History*, IV(1970), 313–47; Richard A. Melanson, "Revisionism Subdued? Robert James Maddox and the Origins of the Cold War," *Political Science Reviewer*, VII(1977), 229–71, and "The Social and Political Thought of William Appleman Williams," *Western Political Quarterly*, XXXI(1978), 392–409. Kenneth Waltz provides an effective theoretical critique of "reductionism" in his *Theory of International Politics*, pp. 60–67. There is as yet no substantial published critique of "corporatism," although the present author has attempted an insubstantial one, "The Corporatist Synthesis: A Skeptical View," *Diplomatic History*, X(Fall, 1986), 357–62.

44. Williams, *The Tragedy of American Diplomacy*, pp. 43, 49 [emphasis in original]. See also Levin's elaboration of this key point in *Woodrow Wilson and World Politics*, pp. 2–5.

45. Maier, "The Two Postwar Eras and the Conditions for Stability in Twentieth-Century Western Europe"; Hogan, "American Marshall Planners and the Search for a European Neocapitalism."

46. C. Wright Mills, *The Power Elite* (New York: 1956), p. 360.

47. Eisenhower "farewell address," January 17, 1961, *Public Papers of the Presidents of the United States: Dwight D. Eisenhower, 1960–61* [hereafter *Eisenhower Public Papers*] (Washington: 1961), p. 1038.

48. Fred J. Cook, *The Warfare State* (New York: 1962); W. Carroll Pursell, Jr., ed., *The Military-Industrial Complex* (New York: 1972); Bruce M. Russett and Alfred Stepan,

*Military Force and American Society* (New York: 1973) ; Seymour Melman, *The Permanent War Economy: American Capitalism in Decline* (New York: 1974).

49. See, on the immediate postwar period, Warner R. Schilling, "The Politics of National Defense: Fiscal 1950," in Warner R. Schilling, Paul Y. Hammond, and Glenn H. Snyder, *Strategy, Politics, and Defense Budgets* (New York: 1962), pp. 1–266; on the 1970's, Lawrence J. Korb, *The Fall and Rise of the Pentagon: American Defense Policies in the 1970's* (Westport, Connecticut: 1979).

50. Vernon V. Asparturian, "The Soviet Military-Industrial Complex—Does It Exist?" *Journal of International Affairs*, XXVI(1972), 1–28; William T. Lee, "The 'Politico-Military-Industrial Complex' of the U.S.S.R.," *ibid.*, pp. 73–86; Andrew Cockburn, *The Threat: Inside the Soviet Military Machine* (New York: 1983), pp. 120–49.

51. Joseph S. Nye, Jr., ed., *The Making of America's Soviet Policy* (New Haven: 1984) ; I. M. Destler, Leslie H. Gelb, and Anthony Lake, *Our Own Worst Enemy: The Unmaking of American Foreign Policy* (New York: 1984).

52. See, on this point, Seyom Brown, *The Faces of Power: Constancy and Change in United States Foreign Policy from Truman to Reagan* (New York: 1983), pp. 7–14.

53. The quotation appears in Kennan to State Department, March 20, 1946, U.S. Department of State, *Foreign Relations of the United States* [hereafter *FR*]: *1946*, VI, 721. For Kennan's famous "long telegram" of February 22, 1946, see *ibid.*, pp. 696–709; the equally influential "Mr. X" article is "The Sources of Soviet Conduct," *Foreign Affairs*, XXV(July, 1947), 566–82. The circumstances surrounding the drafting of these documents are discussed in George F. Kennan, *Memoirs: 1925–1950* (Boston: 1967), pp. 292–95, 354–57.

54. See, for example, Taubman, *Stalin's American Policy*, pp. 243–55; Vernon V. Asparturian, "Internal Politics and Foreign Policy in the Soviet System," in Asparturian, ed., *Process and Power in Soviet Foreign Policy* (Boston: 1971), pp. 491–551; Seweryn Bialer, "The Political System," in Robert F. Byrnes, ed., *After Brezhnev: Sources of Soviet Conduct in the 1980s* (Bloomington: 1983), pp. 10–11, 35–36, 51, 55; Adam Ulam, "The World Outside," in *ibid.*, pp. 345–48; and Seweryn Bialer, *The Soviet Paradox: External Expansion, Internal Decline* (New York: 1986), pp. 38–40, 198–200, 350.

55. On this point, see Gaddis, *Strategies of Containment*, pp. 34–35, 62, 74, 83–84.

56. Alexander L. George and Richard Smoke, *Deterrence in American Foreign Policy: Theory and Practice* (New York: 1974), pp. 527–30; also Patrick M. Morgan, *Deterrence: A Conceptual Analysis* (Beverly Hills: 1977), pp. 205–7.

57. Blainey, *The Causes of War*, p. 53. See also Howard, *The Causes of Wars*, pp. 14–15; Paul M. Kennedy, *Strategy and Diplomacy: 1870–1945* (London: 1983), pp. 163–77; and Richard Smoke's perceptive discussion on the role of expectations in escalation in *War: Controlling Escalation* (Cambridge, Massachusetts: 1977), pp. 268–77.

58. Kennan, *The Decline of Bismarck's European Order*, pp. 3–4.

59. See Michael Howard's observations on the absence of a "bellicist" mentality among the great powers in the postwar era, in his *The Causes of War*, pp. 271–73.

60. Small and Singer, *Resort to Arms*, pp. 167, 169.

61. For a persuasive elaboration of this argument, with an intriguing comparison of the post-1945 "nuclear" system to the post-1815 "Vienna" system, see Michael Mandelbaum, *The Nuclear Revolution: International Politics Before and After Hiroshima* (New York: 1981), pp. 58–77; also Morgan, *Deterrence*, p. 208; Craig and George, *Force and Statecraft*, pp. 117–20; Howard, *The Causes of War*, pp. 22, 278–79.

62. See, on this point, Mandelbaum, *The Nuclear Revolution*, p. 109; also the discussion of the "crystal ball effect" in Albert Carnesale, *et al.*, *Living with Nuclear Weapons* (New York: 1983), p. 44.

63. For a brief review of the literature on crisis management, together with an illustrative comparison of the July, 1914, crisis with the Cuban missile crisis, see Ole R. Holsti, "Theories of Crisis Decision Making," in Lauren, ed., *Diplomacy*, pp. 99–136; also Craig and George, *Force and Statecraft*, pp. 205–19.

64. Gilpin, *War and Change in World Politics*, pp. 202–3.

65. For the historical evolution of reconnaissance satellites, see Chapter Seven, above.

66. The most recent assessment, but one whose analysis does not take into account examples prior to 1940, is Richard K. Betts, *Surprise Attack: Lessons for Defense Planning* (Washington: 1982). See also, on the problem of assessing adversary intentions, Ernest R. May, ed., *Knowing One's Enemies: Intelligence Assessment Before the Two World Wars* (Princeton: 1984).

67. For a summary of what the open literature reveals about the difficulties faced by American intelligence in the first decade after World War II, see Thomas Powers, *The Man Who Kept the Secrets: Richard Helms and the CIA* (New York: 1979), pp. 43–58; and John Prados, *The Soviet Estimate: U.S. Intelligence and Russian Military Strength* (New York: 1982), pp. 24–30.

68. On this point, see Michael Krepon, *Arms Control: Verification and Compliance* (New York: 1984), especially pp. 8–13.

69. Prados, *The Soviet Estimate*, pp. 30–35, 96–110; also Michael R. Beschloss, *Mayday: Eisenhower, Khrushchev and the U-2 Affair* (New York: 1986), pp. 85–112; and John Ranelagh, *The Agency: The Rise and Decline of the CIA* (New York: 1986), pp. 310–28.

70. See, on this point, Wright, *A Study of War*, pp. 1290–91; Aron, *Peace and War*, pp. 64–69; Reynolds, *Theory and Explanation in International Politics*, p. 176; also Murray Edelman, *Politics as Symbolic Action: Mass Arousal and Quiescence* (Chicago: 1971), pp. 53–64.

71. Norman Rich, *Hitler's War Aims: Ideology, the Nazi State, and the Course of Expansion* (New York: 1973), pp. xxxvi–xxxvii, xlii–xliii, 3–10.

72. On the recent resurgence of religion as an influence on world politics, see Paul Johnson, *Modern Times: The World from the Twenties to the Eighties* (New York: 1983), pp. 698–710.

73. See, on this point, Halle, *The Cold War as History*, 157–60.

74. Adam B. Ulam, *Expansion and Coexistence: The History of Soviet Foreign Policy, 1917–73*, Second Edition (New York: 1974), pp. 130–31.

75. See, on this point, E. H. Carr, *The Bolshevik Revolution, 1917–1923* (New York: 1953), pp. 549–66; and Marshall D. Shulman, *Stalin's Foreign Policy Reappraised* (New York: 1969), p. 82.

76. For Stalin's mixed record on this issue, see Shulman, *Stalin's Foreign Policy Reappraised, passim.*; also Taubman, *Stalin's American Policy*, pp. 128–227; and Adam B. Ulam, *Stalin: The Man and His Era* (New York: 1973), especially pp. 641–43, 654.

77. Herbert Dinerstein, *War and the Soviet Union: Nuclear Weapons and the Revolution in Soviet Military and Political Thinking* (New York: 1959), pp. 65–90; William Zimmerman, *Soviet Perspectives on International Relations, 1956–1967* (Princeton: 1969), pp. 251–52.

78. Nikita S. Khrushchev, *Khrushchev Remembers: The Last Testament*, translated and edited by Strobe Talbott (Boston: 1974), p. 529.

79. Zimmerman, *Soviet Perspectives on International Relations*, pp. 252–55.

80. *Ibid.*, pp. 5, 255–59. See also *Khrushchev Remembers*, p. 530; and Bialer, *The Soviet Paradox*, pp. 270–71.

81. John Lewis Gaddis, *The United States and the Origins of the Cold War, 1941–1947* (New York: 1972), pp. 56–62, 133–75.

82. See, on this point, Michael S. Sherry, *Preparing for the Next War: American Plans for Postwar Defense, 1941–45* (New Haven: 1977), pp. 52–53; Eduard Maximilian Mark, "The Interpretation of Soviet Foreign Policy in the United States, 1928–1947" (Ph.D. Dissertation, University of Connecticut, 1978), pp. 95–96, 326–29; and, for the Wilsonian background of this idea, see Levin, *Woodrow Wilson and World Politics*, pp. 37–45. The "totalitarian" threat is discussed at greater length in Chapter Two, above. For the ideological roots of "unconditional surrender," see Anne Armstrong, *Unconditional Surrender: The Impact of the Casablanca Policy Upon World War II* (New Brunswick: 1961), pp. 250–53.

83. See, for example, Hannah Arendt, *The Origins of Totalitarianism* (New York: 1951), and Carl Friedrich and Zbigniew Brzezinski, *Totalitarian Dictatorship and Autocracy* (Cambridge, Massachusetts: 1956); also Les K. Adler and Thomas G. Paterson, "Red Fascism: The Merger of Nazi Germany and Soviet Russia in the American Image of Totalitarianism, 1930's–1950's," *American Historical Review*, LXXV(April, 1970), 1046–64. For a good historiographical assessment of the "totalitarianism school" in American Soviet studies, see Stephen F. Cohen, *Rethinking the Soviet Experience: Politics and History Since 1917* (New York: 1985), pp. 20–27.

84. The best brief review of early American war plans is in Gregg Herken, *The Winning Weapon: The Atomic Bomb in the Cold War, 1945–1950* (New York: 1980), pp. 195–303. A selection from these plans has been published in Thomas H. Etzold and John Lewis Gaddis, eds., *Containment: Documents on American Policy and Strategy, 1945–1950* (New York: 1978), pp. 277–381. The Soviet Union has yet to make any comparable selection of its postwar documents available.

85. NSC 20/4, "U.S. Objectives with Respect to the USSR to Counter Soviet Threats to U.S. Security," November 23, 1948, *FR: 1948*, I, 668–69.

86. NSC 68, "United States Objectives and Programs for National Security," *FR: 1950*, I, 242.

87. Kennan made the point explicitly in NSC 20/1, "U.S. Objectives with Respect to Russia," August 18, 1948, in Etzold and Gaddis, eds., *Containment*, p. 191; also in *The Realities of American Foreign Policy* (Princeton: 1954), p. 80.

88. On changing Soviet psychology as the ultimate goal of containment, see Gaddis, *Strategies of Containment*, pp. 48–51, 71–83, 98–99, 102–6.

89. See, for example, Hans J. Morgenthau, *In Defense of the National Interest: A Critical Examination of American Foreign Policy* (New York: 1951), pp. 31–33, 142–46. The critique of "unconditional surrender" can best be followed in Armstrong, *Unconditional Surrender*, pp. 248–62; and in Hanson W. Baldwin, *Great Mistakes of the War* (New York: 1950), pp. 14–25.

90. David Alan Rosenberg, "'A Smoking, Radiating Ruin at the End of Two Hours': Documents on American Plans for Nuclear War with the Soviet Union, 1954–55," *International Security*, VI(Winter, 1981/82), 3–38, and "The Origins of Overkill: Nuclear Weapons and American Strategy, 1945–1960," *ibid.*, VII(Spring, 1983), 3–71. For more general accounts, see Fred Kaplan, *The Wizards of Armageddon* (New York: 1983), especially pp. 263–70; and Gregg Herken, *Counsels of War* (New York: 1985), pp. 137–40.

91. Rosenberg, "The Origins of Overkill," pp. 8, 69–71; Kaplan, *Wizards of Armageddon*, pp. 268–85; Herken, *Counsels of War*, pp. 140–65; Stephen E. Ambrose, *Eisenhower: The President* (New York: 1984), pp. 494, 523, 564.

92. See, on this point, John Spanier, *Games Nations Play: Analyzing International Politics*, Fifth Edition (New York: 1984), p. 91.

93. Gaddis, *The United States and the Origins of the Cold War*, pp. 23–31.

94. My definition here is based on Paul Keal, *Unspoken Rules and Superpower Dominance* (New York: 1983), pp. 2–3. Other more generalized studies dealing with theories of games and bargaining include Snyder and Diesing, *Conflict Among Nations*, especially pp. 33–182; Anatol Rapaport, *Fights, Games, and Debates* (Ann Arbor: 1960); Charles Lockhart, *Bargaining in International Conflicts* (New York: 1979); and Friedrich V. Kratochwil, *International Order and Foreign Policy: A Theoretical Sketch of Post-War International Politics* (Boulder, Colorado: 1978), *passim*.

95. On this point, see Geir Lundestad, *America, Scandinavia, and the Cold War, 1945–1949* (New York: 1980), especially pp. 327–38. For the formation of spheres of influence, see Keal, *Unspoken Rules and Superpower Dominance*, pp. 66–71, 80–84, 90–98; also Chapter Three, above.

96. For a good overview of this process of consolidation, see Keal, *Unspoken Rules and Superpower Dominance*, pp. 87–115.

97. George and Smoke, *Deterrence in American Foreign Policy*, pp. 523–26, 557–60.

98. *Ibid.*, pp. 536–43.

99. For a discussion of the Hungarian, Czech, Cuban, and Dominican Republic episodes, see Keal, *Unspoken Rules and Superpower Dominance*, pp. 116–58. There is no adequate comparative analysis of how the United States responded to the defections of Yugoslavia and China.

100. Coral Bell, *The Conventions of Crisis: A Study in Diplomatic Management* (London: 1971) : Phil Williams, *Crisis Management: Confrontation and Diplomacy in the Nuclear Age* (New York: 1976). They have also managed successfully to control incidents at sea; see Sean M. Lynn-Jones, "A Quiet Success for Arms Control: Preventing Incidents at Sea," *International Security*, IX (Spring, 1985), 154–84.

101. The classic case, of course, is the amply documented July, 1914, crisis, the implications of which have most recently been reassessed in a special edition of *International Security*, IX (Summer, 1984). But see also Richard Smoke's essays on how the Seven Years War and the Crimean War grew out of a comparable failure of the major powers to limit the escalation of quarrels they did not initiate, in *War: Controlling Escalation*, pp. 147–236; also Richard Ned Lebow, *Between Peace and War: The Nature of International Crisis* (Baltimore: 1981).

102. See Chapter Five, above.

103. Henry A. Kissinger, *Nuclear Weapons and Foreign Policy* (New York: 1957).

104. For a summary of Soviet thinking on the subject, see Harriet Fast Scott and William F. Scott, *The Armed Forces of the USSR* (Boulder, Colorado: 1979), especially pp. 55–56, 61–62.

105. These points are more fully developed in Chapter Five, but see also Richard Ned Lebow, "Windows of Opportunity: Do States Jump Through Them?" *International Security*, IX (Summer, 1984), 147–86.

106. For the importance of this distinction, see Thomas C. Schelling, *Arms and Influence* (New Haven: 1966), pp. 132–34.

107. A good recent review of non-proliferation efforts is in the National Academy of Sciences study, *Nuclear Arms Control: Background and Issues* (Washington: 1985), pp. 224–73.

108. Eisenhower speech to the American Society of Newspaper Editors, April 16, 1953, *Eisenhower Public Papers: 1953* (Washington: 1960), pp. 179–88. For the origins of this speech, see Emmet John Hughes, *The Ordeal of Power: A Political Memoir of the Eisenhower Years* (New York: 1963), pp. 100–112. Efforts to exploit vulnerabilities arising from Stalin's death are discussed in Chapter Six, above.

109. See, for example, Lyndon B. Johnson, *The Vantage Point: Perspectives of the Presidency, 1963–1969* (New York: 1971), pp. 468–69; also Henry Kissinger, *Years of Upheaval* (Boston: 1982), pp. 287–88.

110. I am indebted to Ambassador Jack Matlock for suggesting this point.

111. See Carl Sagan, "Nuclear War and Climatic Catastrophe: Some Policy Implications," *Foreign Affairs*, LXII (Winter, 1983/84), 257–92. Subsequent reassessments suggesting that Sagan and his colleagues may have overestimated the consequences of a "nuclear winter" [see Starley L. Thompson and Stephen H. Schneider, "Nuclear Winter Reappraised," *ibid.*, LXIV (Summer, 1986), 981–1006] do not make that phenomenon any more palatable.

112. See, on this point, Gilpin, *War and Change in World Politics*, pp. 156–210.

# Bibliography

**Manuscript Sources**

Acheson, Dean. Papers. Harry S. Truman Library.
Bohlen, Charles E. Papers. Diplomatic Blanch, National Archives.
Clifford, Clark M. Papers. Harry S. Truman Library.
Davies, Joseph E. Papers. Library of Congress.
Dulles, John Foster. Papers. Dwight D. Eisenhower Library.
———. Papers. Seeley Mudd Library, Princeton University.
Eisenhower, Dwight D. Papers. Dwight D. Eisenhower Library.
Elsey, George M. Papers. Harry S. Truman Library.
Forrestal, James V. Papers. Seeley Mudd Library, Princeton University.
Great Britain. Cabinet Records. Public Record Office, London.
———. Combined Chiefs of Staff Records. Public Record Office, London.
———. Foreign Office Records. Public Record Office, London.
Hagerty, James C. Papers. Dwight D. Eisenhower Library.
Jones, Joseph M. Papers. Harry S. Truman Library.
Kennan, George F. Papers. Seeley Mudd Library, Princeton University.
Leahy, William D. Papers. Modern Military Records Branch, National Archives.
MacArthur, Douglas. Papers. MacArthur Memorial Library, Norfolk, Virginia.
Patterson, Robert P. Papers. Library of Congress.
Smith, H. Alexander. Papers. Seeley Mudd Library, Princeton University.
Smith, Harold D. Papers. Harry S. Truman Library.
Stimson, Henry L. Papers. Yale University Library.
Truman, Harry S. Papers. Harry S. Truman Library.
U.S. Army. Staff Records. Modern Military Records Branch, National Archives.
U.S. Department of State. Records, 1871–1929. National Archives Microfilm.
———. Decimal Files. Diplomatic Branch, National Archives.
———. Office of Intelligence and Research Records. Diplomatic Branch, National Archives.
———. Policy Planning Staff Records. Diplomatic Branch, National Archives.

U.S. Joint Chiefs of Staff. Records. Modern Military Records Branch, National Archives.
U.S. Navy. Immediate Office of the Chief of Naval Operations. Records. Operational Archives, Naval Historical Center.
U.S. Office of Strategic Services. Records. Modern Military Records Branch, National Archives.

### Unpublished Materials

Boe, Jonathan Evers. "American Business: The Response to the Soviet Union, 1933–1947" (Ph.D. Dissertation, Stanford University, 1979).
Converse, Elliott Vanveltner, III. "United States Plans for a Postwar Overseas Military Base System, 1942–1948" (Ph.D. dissertation, Princeton University, 1984).
Fithian, Floyd J. "Soviet-American Economic Relations, 1918–1933: American Business in Russia during the Period of Non-recognition" (Ph.D. dissertation, University of Nebraska, 1964).
Harrington, Daniel F. "American Policy in the Berlin Crisis of 1948–49" (Ph.D. Dissertation, Indiana University: 1979).
Mal'kov, V. L. "From Intervention to Recognition: On the History of the Political Struggle in the United States on the Question of Normalizing Soviet-American Relations," paper prepared for the Fifth Colloquium of Soviet and American Historians, Kiev, June, 1984.
Mark, Eduard Maximilian. "The Interpretation of Soviet Foreign Policy in the United States, 1928–1947" (Ph.D. Dissertation, University of Connecticut, 1978).
Miscamble, Wilson D. "George F. Kennan, the Policy Planning Staff and American Foreign Policy, 1947–1950" (Ph.D. Dissertation, University of Notre Dame, 1979).
Rogger, Hans. "America Enters the Twentieth Century: The View from Russia, 1895–1915," paper prepared for the Fifth Colloquium of Soviet and American Historians, Kiev, June, 1984.
Saul, Norman. "American Perceptions of a Changing Russia, 1890–1914," paper prepared for the Fifth Colloquium of Soviet and American Historians, Kiev, June, 1984.
Stults, Taylor. "Imperial Russia Through American Eyes, 1894–1904" (Ph.D. Dissertation, University of Missouri, 1970).
Travis, Frederick F. "George Kennan and Russia, 1865–1905" (Ph.D. Dissertation, Emory University, 1974).
Zhai Qiang, "American Policy Toward Sino-Soviet Relations, 1952–1954," seminar paper, Ohio University, March, 1986.

### Newspapers and Periodicals

*Aviation Week and Space Technology*
*Life.*
*New York Times.*
*Newsweek.*
*Time.*

### Published Documents

Blum, John Morton, ed. *The Price of Vision: The Diary of Henry A. Wallace, 1942–1946* (Boston: 1973).
Campbell, Thomas M., and George C. Herring. *The Diaries of Edward R. Stettinius, Jr., 1943–1946* (New York: 1975).
Degras, Jane, ed. *Soviet Documents on Foreign Policy, 1917–41* (London: 1951–53).
Dobney, Frederick J., ed. *Selected Papers of Will Clayton* (Baltimore: 1971).
Etzold, Thomas H., and John Lewis Gaddis, eds. *Containment: Documents on American Policy and Strategy, 1945–1950* (New York: 1978).

Ferrell, Robert H., ed. *The Autobiography of Harry S. Truman* (Boulder: 1980).

——, ed. *The Diary of James C. Hagerty: Eisenhower in Mid-Course, 1954–1955* (Bloomington: 1983).

——, ed. *The Eisenhower Diaries* (New York: 1981).

——, ed. *Off the Record: The Private Papers of Harry S. Truman* (New York: 1980).

Millis, Walter, ed. *The Forrestal Diaries* (New York: 1951).

*Public Papers of the Presidents: Dwight D. Eisenhower, 1953–1961* (Washington: 1960–61).

*Public Papers of the Presidents: Harry S. Truman, 1945–1953* (Washington: 1961–66).

*Public Papers of the Presidents: Jimmy Carter, 1977–1981* (Washington: 1978–82).

Rosenman, Samuel I., ed. *The Public Papers and Addresses of Franklin D. Roosevelt* (New York: 1941–50).

U.S. Arms Control and Disarmament Agency. *Arms Control and Disarmament Agreements* (Washington: 1982).

U.S. Congress. *Congressional Record.*

——. House of Representatives, *Committee on Armed Services, Unification nad Strategy* (Washington: 1949).

——. Senate. Committees on Armed Services and Foreign Relations, *Military Situation in the Far East* (Washington: 1951).

——. ——. Committee on Foreign Relations. *Assistance to Greece and Turkey* (Washington: 1947).

——. ——. *European Recovery Program* (Washington: 1948).

——. ——. *Historical Series: Economic Assistance to China and Korea* (Washington: 1974).

——. ——. *Historical Series: Eighty-fourth Congress, Second Session, 1956* (Washington: 1978).

——. ——. *Historical Series: Eighty-sixth Congress, First Session, 1959* (Washington: 1982).

——. ——. *Historical Series: Legislative Origins of the Truman Doctrine* (Washington: 1973).

——. ——. *Historical Series: Military Assistance Program, 1949* (Washington: 1974).

——. ——. *Historical Series: Reviews of the World Situation, 1949–1950* (Washington: 1974).

——. ——. *Historical Series: The Vandenberg Resolution and the North Atlantic Treaty* (Washington: 1973).

——. ——. Select Committee to Study Governmental Operations with Respect to Intelligence Activities, *Supplementary Reports on Foreign and Military Intelligence* (Washington: 1976).

U.S. Department of Commerce. *Statistical Abstract of the United States.*

U.S. Department of Defense. *United States-Vietnam Relations, 1945–67* [Pentagon Papers] (Washington: 1971).

U.S. Department of State. *American Foreign Policy, 1950–1955: Basic Documents* (Washington: 1957).

——. *Department of State Bulletin.*

——. *Foreign Relations of the United States.*

——. *Foreign Relations of the United States: The Conference of Berlin (The Potsdam Conference) 1945* (Washington: 1960).

——. *Foreign Relations of the United States: The Conferences at Malta and Yalta, 1945* (Washington: 1955).

——. *United States Relations with China, with Special Reference to the Period 1944–1949* [*China White Paper*] (Washington: 1949).

U.S. Office of the President. *Weekly Compilation of Presidential Documents.*

U.S.S.R. Ministerstvo innostrannykh del. *Dokumenty vneshnei politiki SSSR.*

**Books**

Acheson, Dean. *Present at the Creation: My Years in the State Department* (New York: 1969).

Adams, Sherman. *Firsthand Report* (New York: 1961).

Allard, Sven. *Russia and the Austrian State Treaty: A Case Study of Soviet Policy in Europe* (University Park, Pennsylvania: 1970).

Allison, John M. *Ambassador from the Prairie* (Boston: 1973).

Ambrose, Stephen E. *Eisenhower: The President* (New York: 1984).

———. *Eisenhower: Soldier, General of the Army, President-Elect, 1890–1952* (New York: 1983).

———. *Ike's Spies: Eisenhower and the Intelligence Establishment* (Garden City, New York: 1981).

Anderson, Terry H. *The United States, Great Britain, and the Cold War, 1944–1947* Columbia, Missouri: 1981).

Andrew, Christopher. *Her Majesty's Secret Service: The Making of the British Intelligence Community* (New York: 1986).

Arendt, Hannah. *The Origins of Totalitarianism* (New York: 1951).

Arkes, Hadley. *Bureaucracy, the Marshall Plan, and the National Interest* (Princeton: 1972).

Armstrong, Anne. *Unconditional Surrender: The Impact of the Casablanca Policy Upon World War II* (New Brunswick: 1961).

Aron, Raymond Aron. *Peace and War: A Theory of International Relations*, translated by Richard Howard and Annette Baker Fox (New York: 1966).

Aspaturian, Vernon V., ed. *Process and Power in Soviet Foreign Policy* (Boston: 1971).

Backer, John H. *The Decision to Divide Germany: American Foreign Policy in Transition* (Durham: 1978).

Bader, William. *Austria Between East and West, 1945–1955* (Stanford: 1966).

Bailey, Thomas A. *America Faces Russia: Russian-American Relations From Early Times to Our Own Day* (Ithaca: 1950).

Baldwin, Hanson W. *Great Mistakes of the War* (New York: 1950).

Bamford, James. *The Puzzle Palace: A Report on America's Most Secret Agency* (New York: 1982).

Barron, John. *KGB Today: The Hidden Hand* (New York: 1983).

Beard, Charles A. *The Idea of National Interest: An Analytical Study in American Foreign Policy* (New York: 1934).

———. *The Open Door at Home: A Trial Philosophy of National Interest* (New York: 1934).

Beckman, Peter H. *World Politics in the Twentieth Century* (Englewood Cliffs, New Jersey: 1984).

Bell, Coral. *The Conventions of Crisis: A Study in Diplomatic Management* (London: 1971).

Bennett, Edward M. *Recognition of Russia: An American Foreign Policy Dilemma* (Waltham, Massachusetts: 1970).

Beschloss, Michael. *Mayday: Eisenhower, Khrushchev and the U-2 Affair* (New York: 1986).

Bethell, Nicholas. *Betrayed* (New York: 1984).

Betts, Richard K. *Surprise Attack: Lessons for Defense Planning* (Washington: 1982).

Bialer, Seweryn. *The Soviet Paradox: External Expansion, Internal Decline* (New York: 1986).

Bishop, Donald G. *The Roosevelt-Litvinov Agreements: The American View* (Syracuse: 1965).

Blainey, Geoffrey. *The Causes of War* (London: 1973).

Blum, John Morton. *Woodrow Wilson and the Politics of Morality* (Boston: 1956).

Blum, Robert M. *Drawing the Line: The Origin of the American Containment Policy in East Asia* (New York: 1982).

Bohlen, Charles E. *Witness to History: 1929–1969* (New York: 1973).

Bolkhovitinov, N. N. *The Beginnings of Russian-American Relations: 1775–1815*, translated by Elena Levin (Cambridge, Massachusetts: 1975).

Boll, Michael M. *Cold War in the Balkans: American Foreign Policy and the Emergence of Communist Bulgaria, 1943–1947* (Lexington, Kentucky: 1984).

Borden, William Liscum. *There Will Be No Time: The Revolution in Strategy* (New York: 1946).

Borg, Dorothy, and Shumpei Okamoto, eds. *Pearl Harbor as History: Japanese-American Relations, 1931–1941* (New York: 1973).

———, and Waldo Heinrichs, eds. *Uncertain Years: Chinese-American Relations, 1947–1950* (New York: 1980).

Borowski, Harry R. *A Hollow Threat: Strategic Air Power and Containment Before Korea* (Westport, Connecticut: 1982).

Boulding, Kenneth. *Conflict and Defense: A General Theory* (New York: 1962).

Bourne, Kenneth. *Britain and the Balance of Power in North America, 1815–1908* (Berkeley: 1967).

Brodie, Bernard, ed. *The Absolute Weapon* (New York: 1946).

Browder, Robert Paul. *The Origins of Soviet-American Diplomacy* (Princeton: 1953).

Brown, Seyom. *The Faces of Power: Constancy and Change in United States Foreign Policy from Truman to Reagan* (New York: 1983).

Brzezinski, Zbigniew, and Samuel P. Huntington. *Political Power: USA/USSR* (New York: 1964).

Buhite, Russell D. *Soviet-American Relations in Asia, 1945–1954* (Norman: 1981).

Bullock, Alan. *Ernest Bevin: Foreign Secretary* (New York: 1983).

Carnesale, Albert, et al. *Living with Nuclear Weapons* (New York: 1983).

Carr, E. H. *The Bolshevik Revolution, 1917–1923* (New York: 1953).

Churchill, Winston S. *The Gathering Storm*, Bantam Edition (Boston: 1948).

Clausewitz, Carl von. *On War*, edited and translated by Peter Paret and Michael Howard (Princeton: 1976).

Cline, Ray S. *Secrets, Spies, and Scholars: The Essential CIA* (Washington: 1976).

Cockburn, Andrew. *The Threat: Inside the Soviet Military Machine* (New York: 1983).

Cohen, Stephen F. *Rethinking the Soviet Experience: Politics and History Since 1917* (New York: 1985).

Cohen, Warren I. *Dean Rusk* (Totowa, New Jersey: 1980).

Cole, Wayne S. *Roosevelt & the Isolationists, 1932–45* (Lincoln, Nebraska: 1983).

Collins, J. Lawton. *War in Peacetime: The History and Lessons of Korea* (Boston: 1969).

Cook, Fred J. *The Warfare State* (New York: 1962).

Cooper, John Milton, Jr. *The Warrior and the Priest: Woodrow Wilson and Theodore Roosevelt* (Cambridge, Massachusetts: 1983).

Costigliola, Frank. *Awkward Dominion: American Political, Economic, and Cultural Relations with Europe, 1919–1933* (Ithaca: 1984).

Crabb, Cecil V., Jr. *The Doctrines of American Foreign Policy: Their Meaning, Role, and Future* (Baton Rouge: 1982).

Craig, Gordon A., and Alexander L. George. *Force and Statecraft: Diplomatic Problems of Our Time* (New York: 1983).

Crook, D. P. *The North, the South, and the Powers, 1861–1865* (New York: 1974).

Cumings, Bruce. *The Origins of the Korean War: Liberation and the Emergence of Separate Regimes, 1945–1947* (Princeton: 1981).

Dallek, Robert. *The American Style of Foreign Policy: Cultural Politics and Foreign Affairs* (New York: 1983).

———. *Franklin D. Roosevelt and American Foreign Policy, 1932–1945* (New York: 1979).

Daniels, Jonathan. *Man of Independence* (Philadelphia: 1950).

Davies, John Paton, Jr. *Dragon by the Tail: American, British, Japanese and Russian Encounters with China and One Another* (New York: 1972).

Davis, Lynn Etheridge. *The Cold War Begins: Soviet-American Conflict Over Eastern Europe* (New York: 1974).

Dehio, Ludwig. *The Precarious Balance: Four Centuries of the European Power Struggle*, translated by Charles Fullman (New York: 1962).

Deibel, Terry L., and John Lewis Gaddis, eds. *Containment: Concept and Policy* (Washington: 1986).

DePorte, A. W. *Europe Between the Super-Powers: The Enduring Balance* (New Haven: 1979).

Devlin, Patrick. *Too Proud to Fight: Woodrow Wilson's Neutrality* (New York: 1975).

DeSantis, Hugh. *The Diplomacy of Silence: The American Foreign Service, the Soviet Union, and the Cold War, 1933–1945* (Chicago: 1980).

Destler, I. M., with Leslie H. Gelb and Anthony Lake. *Our Own Worst Enemy: The Unmaking of American Foreign Policy* (New York: 1984).

Diggins, John P. *Mussolini and Fascism: The View from America* (Princeton: 1972).

Dinerstein, Herbert S. *The Making of a Missile Crisis, October, 1962* (Baltimore: 1976).

———. *War and the Soviet Union: Nuclear Weapons and the Revolution in Soviet Military and Political Thinking* (New York: 1959).

Divine, Robert A. *Foreign Policy and U.S. Presidential Elections: 1952–1960* (New York: 1974).

———. *Second Chance: The Triumph of Internationalism in America During World War II* (New York: 1967).

Dobbs, Charles M. *The Unwanted Symbol: American Foreign Policy, the Cold War, and Korea, 1945–1950* (Kent, Ohio: 1981).

Donovan, Robert J. *Conflict and Crisis: The Presidency of Harry S. Truman, 1945–1948* (New York: 1977).

Dowty, Alan. *The Limits of American Isolation: The United States and the Crimean War* (New York: 1971).

Drew, Elizabeth. *Portrait of an Election: The 1980 Presidential Campaign* (New York: 1981).

Dulles, Foster Rhea. *American Policy Toward Communist China, 1949–1969* (New York: 1972).

———. *The Road to Teheran: The Story of Russia and America, 1781–1943* (Princeton: 1944).

Dulles, John Foster. *War or Peace* (New York: 1950).

Eckes, Alfred E., Jr. *A Search for Solvency: Bretton Woods and the International Monetary System, 1941–1971* (Austin: 1975).

Edelman, Murray. *Politics as Symbolic Action: Mass Arousal and Quiescence* (Chicago: 1971).

Eisenhower, Dwight D. *The White House Years: Mandate for Change, 1953–1956* (Garden City, New York: 1963).

———. *The White House Years: Waging Peace, 1957–1961* (Garden City, New York: 1965.

Esthus, Raymond A. *Theodore Roosevelt and the International Rivalries* (Waltham, Massachusetts: 1970).

Fawcett, J. E. S. *Outer Space: New Challenges to Law and Policy* (Oxford: 1984).

Filene, Peter G. *Americans and the Soviet Experiment, 1917–1933* (Cambridge, Massachusetts: 1967).

Fischer, David Hackett. *Historians' Fallacies: Toward a Logic of Historical Thought* (New York: 1970).

Foot, Rosemary. *The Wrong War: American Policy and the Dimensions of the Korean Conflict, 1950–1953* (Ithaca: 1985).

Fox, William T. R. *The Super-Powers: The United States, Britain, and the Soviet Union—Their Responsibility for Peace* (New York: 1944).

Freeland, Richard M. *The Truman Doctrine and the Origins of McCarthyism: Foreign Policy, Domestic Politics, and Internal Security, 1946–1948* (New York: 1972).

Freud, Sigmund. *The Basic Writings of Sigmund Freud*, translated and edited by A. A. Brill (New York: 1938).

Friedrich, Carl, and Zbigniew Brzezinski. *Totalitarian Dictatorship and Autocracy* (Cambridge, Massachusetts: 1956).

Gaddis, John Lewis. *Russia, the Soviet Union, and the United States: An Interpretive History* (New York: 1978).

————. *Strategies of Containment: A Critical Appraisal of Postwar American National Security Policy* (New York: 1982).

————. *The United States and the Origins of the Cold War, 1941–1947* (New York: 1972).

Ganelin, R. Sh. *Rossiia i SShA, 1914–1917* (Leningrad: 1969).

Gardner, Lloyd C. *Architects of Illusion: Men and Ideas in American Foreign Policy, 1941–1949* (Chicago: 1970).

————. *A Covenant with Power: America and World Order from Wilson to Reagan* (New York: 1984).

Garthoff, Raymond. *Detente and Confrontation: American-Soviet Relations from Nixon to Reagan* (Washington: 1985).

Gelfand, Lawrence E. *The Inquiry: American Preparations for Peace, 1917–1919* (New Haven: 1963).

George, Alexander L., and Richard Smoke. *Deterrence in American Foreign Policy: Theory and Practice* (New York: 1974).

Gilpin, Robert. *War and Change in World Politics* (New York: 1981).

Gittings, John. *Survey of the Sino-Soviet Dispute, 1963–1967* (London: 1968).

Graber, D. A. *Crisis Diplomacy: A History of U.S. Intervention Policies and Practices* (Washington: 1959).

Grew, Joseph C. *Turbulent Era: A Diplomatic Record of Forty Years, 1904–1945* (Boston: 1952).

Gromyko, A. A., and B. N. Ponomarev, eds. *Soviet Foreign Policy, 1945–1980*, Fourth Edition (Moscow: 1981).

Gvishiani, L. A. *Sovetskaia Rossiia i SShA, 1917–1920g* (Moscow: 1970).

Hachey, Thomas E., ed. *The Problem of Partition: Peril to World Peace* (Chicago: 1972).

Halle, Louis J. *The Cold War as History* (New York: 1967).

Hammond, Thomas T., ed. *Witnesses to the Origins of the Cold War* (Seattle: 1982).

Harriman, W. Averell, and Elie Abel. *Special Envoy to Churchill and Stalin: 1941–1946* (New York: 1975).

Hathaway, Robert M. *Ambiguous Partnership: Britain and America, 1944–1947* (New York: 1981).

Herken, Gregg. *Counsels of War* (New York: 1985).

————. *The Winning Weapon: The Atomic Bomb in the Cold War* (New York: 1980).

Hermes, Walter G. *United States Army in the Korean War: Truce Tent and Fighting Front [United States Army in the Korean War]* (Washington: 1966).

Hewlett, Richard G., and Oscar E. Anderson, Jr. *A History of the United States Atomic Energy Commission: Volume 1: The New World, 1939/1946* (University Park, Pennsylvania: 1962).

Hillman, William, ed. *Mr. President* (New York: 1952).

Hilsman, Roger. *To Move a Nation: The Politics of Foreign Policy in the Administration of John F. Kennedy* (New York: 1967).

Hoff Wilson, Joan. *Ideology and Economics: United States Relations with the Soviet Union, 1918–1933* (Columbia, Missouri: 1974).

Hogan, Michael J. *Informal Entente: The Private Structure of Cooperation in Anglo-American Economic Diplomacy, 1918–1928* (Columbia, Missouri: 1977).

Holloway, David. *The Soviet Union and the Arms Race* (New Haven: 1983).

Hoopes, Townsend. *The Devil and John Foster Dulles* (Boston: 1973).

Horelick, Arnold, and Myron Rush. *Strategic Power and Soviet Foreign Policy* (Chicago: 1966).

Hough, Jerry F., and Merle Fainsod. *How the Soviet Union Is Governed* (Cambridge, Massachusetts: 1979).

Howard, Michael. *The Causes of Wars*, Second Edition (Cambridge, Massachusetts: 1984).

———. *Studies in War and Peace* (New York: 1970).

Hughes, Emmet John. *The Ordeal of Power: A Political Memoir of the Eisenhower Years* (New York: 1963).

Ireland, Timothy. *Creating the Entangling Alliance: The Origins of the North Atlantic Treaty Organization* (Westport, Connecticut: 1981).

Iriye, Akira. *After Imperialism: The Search for a New Order in the Far East, 1921–1931* (Cambridge, Massachusetts: 1965).

———. *The Cold War in Asia: A Historical Introduction* (Englewood Cliffs, New Jersey: 1974).

James, D. Clayton. *The Years of MacArthur: Triumph and Disaster, 1945–1964* (Boston: 1985).

Jasani, Bhupendra, ed. *Outer Space—A New Dimension of the Arms Race* (London: 1982).

Jenks, C. Wilfred. *Space Law* (New York: 1965).

Jervis, Robert. *The Illogic of American Nuclear Strategy* (Ithaca: 1984).

———. *Perception and Misperception in International Politics* (Princeton: 1976).

———, with Richard Ned Lebow and Janice Gross Stein. *Psychology and Deterrence* (Baltimore: 1985).

Jessup, Philip C. *The Birth of Nations* (New York: 1974).

Johnson, Lyndon B. *The Vantage Point: Perspectives of the Presidency, 1963–1969* (New York: 1971).

Johnson, Paul. *Modern Times: The World from the Twenties to the Eighties* (New York: 1983).

Jonas, Manfred. *Isolationism in America, 1935–1941* (Ithaca: 1966).

Jones, Joseph M. *The Fifteen Weeks (February 21–June 5, 1947)* (New York: 1955).

Jones, R. V. *The Wizard War: British Scientific Intelligence, 1939–1945* (New York: 1978).

Kahn, E. J., Jr. *The China Hands: America's Foreign Service Officers and What Befell Them* (New York: 1975).

Kalicki, J. H. *The Pattern of Sino-American Crises: Political-Military Interactions in the 1920s* (Cambridge: 1975).

Kaplan, Fred. *The Wizards of Armageddon* (New York: 1983).

Kaplan, Lawrence S. *The United States and NATO: The Formative Years* (Lexington: 1984).

Kaplan, Morton A. *System and Process in International Politics* (New York: 1957).

Kaufman, Burton I. *The Korean War: Challenges in Crisis, Credibility, and Command* (New York: 1986).

Keal, Paul. *Unspoken Rules and Superpower Dominance* (New York: 1983).

Kennan, George F. *American Diplomacy, 1900–1950* (Chicago: 1951).

———. *The Decline of Bismarck's European Order: Franco-Russian Relations, 1875–1890* (Princeton: 1979).

———. *Memoirs: 1925–1950* (Boston: 1967).

———. *Memoirs: 1950–1963* (Boston: 1972).

———. *The Realities of American Foreign Policy* (Princeton: 1954).

——. *Soviet-American Relations, 1917–1920: The Decision to Intervene* (Princeton: 1958).

Kennedy, Paul M. *The Rise of the Anglo-German Antagonism, 1869–1914* (Boston: 1980).

——. *Strategy and Diplomacy: 1870–1945* (London: 1983).

Khrushchev, Nikita S. *Khrushchev Remembers: The Last Testament,* translated and edited by Strobe Talbott (Boston: 1974).

Killian, James R., Jr. *Sputnik, Scientists, and Eisenhower: A Memoir of the First Special Assistant to the President for Science and Technology* (Cambridge, Massachusetts, 1977).

Kissinger, Henry A. *A World Restored* (New York: 1957).

——. *The Necessity for Choice: Prospects of American Foreign Policy* (New York: 1961).

——. *Nuclear Weapons and Foreign Policy* (New York: 1957).

——. *Years of Upheaval* (Boston: 1982).

Kistiakowsky, George B. *A Scientist at the White House: The Private Diary of President Eisenhower's Special Assistant for Science and Technology* (Cambridge, Massachusetts, 1976).

Klass, Philip J. *Secret Sentries in Space* (New York: 1971).

Kolko, Gabriel. *The Politics of War: The World and United States Foreign Policy, 1943–1945* (New York: 1968).

——. *The Roots of American Foreign Policy: An Analysis of Power and Purpose* (Boston: 1969).

Kolko, Joyce, and Gabriel Kolko. *The Limits of Power: The World and United States Foreign Policy, 1945–1954* (New York: 1972).

Korb, Lawrence J. *The Fall and Rise of the Pentagon: American Defense Policies in the 1970's* (Westport, Connecticut: 1979).

Kratochwil, Friedrich V. *International Order and Foreign Policy: A Theoretical Sketch of Post-War International Politics* (Boulder: 1978).

Krepon, Michael. *Arms Control: Verification and Compliance* (New York: 1984).

Krock, Arthur. *Memoirs: Sixty Years on the Firing Line* (New York: 1968).

Kuniholm, Bruce R. *The Origins of the Cold War in the Near East: Great Power Conflict and Diplomacy in Iran, Turkey, and Greece* (Princeton: 1980).

Kusnitz, Leonard A. *Public Opinion and Foreign Policy: America's China Policy, 1949–1979* (Westport, Connecticut: 1984).

Larson, Deborah Welch. *Origins of Containment: A Psychological Explanation* (Princeton: 1985).

Lash, Joseph P. *Eleanor: The Years Alone* (New York: 1972).

Lauren, Paul Gordon, ed. *Diplomacy: New Approaches in History, Theory, and Policy* (New York: 1979).

Lebow, Richard Ned. *Between Peace and War: The Nature of International Crisis* (Baltimore: 1981).

Leffler, Melvin P. *The Elusive Quest: America's Pursuit of European Stability and French Security, 1919–1933* (Chapel Hill: 1979).

Levering, Ralph B. *American Opinion and the Russian Alliance, 1939–1945* (Chapel Hill: 1976).

——. *The Public and American Foreign Policy, 1918–1978* (New York: 1978).

Levin, N. Gordon. *Woodrow Wilson and World Politics* (New York: 1968).

Levy, Jack S. *War in the Modern Great Power System, 1495–1975* (Lexington, Kentucky: 1983).

Liddell Hart, B. H. *The Revolution in Warfare* (New Haven: 1947).

Lilienthal, David E. *The Journals of David E. Lilienthal: The Atomic Energy Years, 1945–1950* (New York: 1964).

Link, Arthur S. *Woodrow Wilson: Revolution, War, and Peace* (Arlington Heights, Illinois: 1979).

Lippmann, Walter. *The Cold War: A Study in U. S. Foreign Policy* (New York: 1947).
———. *U.S. Foreign Policy: Shield of the Republic* (Boston: 1943).
Lockhart, Charles. *Bargaining in International Conflicts* (New York: 1979).
Louis, Wm. Roger. *The British Empire in the Middle East, 1945–1951* (Oxford: 1984).
———. *Imperialism at Bay: The United States and the Decolonization of the British Empire, 1941–1945* (New York: 1978).
Lukas, Richard C. *Bitter Legacy: Polish-American Relations in the Wake of World War II* (Lexington, Kentucky: 1982).
Lundestad, Geir. *America, Scandinavia, and the Cold War, 1945–1949* (New York: 1980).
———. *The American Non-Policy Towards Eastern Europe, 1943–1947* (Oslo: 1978).
Luttwak, Edward N. *The Grand Strategy of the Roman Empire* (Baltimore: 1977).
Lyon, Peter. *Eisenhower: Portrait of the Hero* (Boston: 1974).
MacArthur, Douglas. *Reminiscences* (New York: 1964).
Mackinder, Halford. *Democratic Ideals and Reality: A Study in the Politics of Reconstruction* (New York: 1919).
Maddox, Robert J. *The Unknown War with Russia: Wilson's Siberian Intervention* (San Rafael, California: 1977).
Maddux, Thomas R. *Years of Estrangement: American Relations with the Soviet Union, 1933–1941* (Tallahassee: 1980).
Magdoff, Harry. *The Age of Imperialism: The Economics of U.S. Foreign Policy* (New York: 1969).
Maier, Charles S. *Recasting Bourgeois Europe: Stabilization in France, Germany, and Italy in the Decade After World War I* (Princeton: 1975).
Mandelbaum, Michael. *The Nuclear Question: The United States and Nuclear Weapons, 1946–1976* (Cambridge: 1979).
———. *The Nuclear Revolution: International Politics Before and After Hiroshima* (Cambridge: 1981).
Masters, Dexter, and Katharine Way, eds. *One World or None* (New York: 1946).
Mastny, Vojtech. *Russia's Road to the Cold War: Diplomacy, Warfare, and the Politics of Communism, 1941–1945* (New York: 1979).
Matray, James Irving. *The Reluctant Crusade: American Foreign Policy in Korea, 1941–1950* (Honolulu: 1985).
May, Ernest R., ed. *Knowing One's Enemies: Intelligence Assessment Before the Two World Wars* (Princeton: 1984).
Mayer, Arno J. *The Persistence of the Old Regime: Europe to the Great War* (New York: 1981).
———. *The Politics and Diplomacy of Peacemaking: Containment and Counterrevolution at Versailles, 1918–1919* (New York: 1967).
Mayers, David Allan. *Cracking the Monolith: U.S. Policy Against the Sino-Soviet Alliance, 1949–1955* (Baton Rouge: 1986).
McDougall, Walter. *The Heavens and the Earth: A Political History of the Space Age* (New York: 1985).
McLellan, David S. *Dean Acheson: The State Department Years* (New York: 1976).
McNeill, William Hardy. *America, Britain & Russia: Their Cooperation and Conflict, 1941–1946* (London: 1955).
Melamed, E. I. *Dzhordzh Kennan protiv tsarizma* (Moscow: 1981).
Melman, Seymour. *The Permanent War Economy: American Capitalism in Decline* (New York: 1974).
Messer, Robert L. *The End of an Alliance: James F. Byrnes, Roosevelt, Truman, and the Origins of the Cold War* (Chapel Hill: 1982).
Miller, James Edward. *The United States and Italy, 1940–1950: The Politics and Diplomacy of Stabilization* (Chapel Hill: 1986).
Mills, C. Wright. *The Power Elite* (New York: 1956).
Morgan, Patrick M. *Deterrence: A Conceptual Analysis* (Beverly Hills: 1977).

Morgenthau, Hans J. *In Defense of the National Interest: A Critical Examination of American Foreign Policy* (New York: 1951).

————. *Politics Among Nations: The Struggle for Power and Peace* (New York: 1949).

Mosley, Leonard. *Dulles: A Biography of Eleanor, Allen, and John Foster Dulles and Their Family Network* (New York: 1978).

Nagai, Yonosuke, and Akira Iriye, eds. *The Origins of the Cold War in Asia* (Tokyo: 1977).

National Academy of Sciences, Committee on International Security and Arms Control. *Nuclear Arms Control: Background and Issues* (Washington: 1985).

Nelson, Keith, and Spencer C. Olin, Jr. *Why War? Ideology, Theory, and History* (Berkeley: 1979).

Neustadt, Richard E., and Ernest R. May. *Thinking in Time: The Uses of History for Decision-Makers* (New York: 1986).

Newhouse, John. *Cold Dawn: The Story of SALT* (New York: 1973).

Nicolson, Harold. *Peacemaking 1919* (New York: 1965).

Nixon, Richard M. *RN: The Memoirs of Richard Nixon* (New York: 1978).

Notter, Harley. *Postwar Foreign Policy Preparation* (Washington: 1949).

Nye, Joseph S., Jr. *The Making of America's Soviet Policy* (New Haven: 1984).

Østerud, Øyvind, ed. *Studies of War and Peace* (Oslo: 1986).

Paterson, Thomas G. *Soviet-American Confrontation: Postwar Reconstruction and the Origins of the Cold War* (Baltimore: 1973).

Pogue, Forrest C. *George C. Marshall: Organizer of Victory* (New York: 1973).

Pollard, Robert A. *Economic Security and the Origins of the Cold War, 1945–1950* (New York: 1985).

Polmar, Norman, ed. *Strategic Air Command: People, Aircraft, and Missiles* (Annapolis: 1979).

Potter, William C., ed. *Verification and Arms Control* (Lexington, Massachusetts: 1985).

————, ed. *Verification and SALT: The Challenge of Strategic Deception* (Boulder: 1980).

Powers, Thomas. *The Man Who Kept the Secrets: Richard Helms and the CIA* (New York: 1979).

Prados, John. *The Soviet Estimate: U.S. Intelligence Analysis and Russian Military Strength* (New York: 1982).

Pruessen, Ronald W. *John Foster Dulles: The Road to Power* (New York: 1982).

Pursell, W. Carroll, Jr., ed. *The Military-Industrial Complex* (New York: 1972).

Ranelagh, John. *The Agency: The Rise and Decline of the CIA* (New York: 1986).

Rapaport, Anatol. *Fights, Games, and Debates* (Ann Arbor: 1960).

Rearden, Steven L. *The Evolution of American Strategic Doctrine: Paul H. Nitze and the Soviet Challenge* (Boulder: 1984).

————. *History of the Office of the Secretary of Defense: Volume I: The Formative Years, 1947–1950* (Washington: 1984).

Reynolds, Charles. *Theory and Explanation in International Politics* (London: 1973).

Rich, Norman. *Hitler's War Aims: Ideology, the Nazi State, and the Course of Expansion* (New York: 1973).

Richardson, Lewis F. *Arms and Insecurity: A Mathematical Study of the Causes and Origins of War* (Pittsburgh: 1960).

Riste, Olav, ed. *Western Security: The Formative Years: European and Atlantic Defence, 1947–1953* (Oslo: 1985).

Rolt, L. T. C. *The Aeronauts: A History of Ballooning, 1783–1903* (New York: 1966).

Rosenau, James N., ed. *International Politics and Foreign Policy: A Reader in Research and Theory, Revised Edition* (New York: 1969).

Rositzke, Harry. *The CIA's Secret Operations: Espionage, Counterespionage, and Covert Action* (New York: 1977).

Rostow, W. W. *Open Skies: Eisenhower's Proposal of July 21, 1955* (Austin: 1982).

Russett, Bruce M., and Alfred Stepan. *Military Force and American Society* (New York: 1973).

Schaller, Michael. *The American Occupation of Japan: The Origins of the Cold War in Asia* (New York: 1985).

———. *The U.S. Crusade in China, 1938–1945* (New York: 1979).

Schelling, Thomas C. *Arms and Influence* (New Haven: 1966).

Schilling, Warner R., with Paul Y. Hammond and Glenn H. Snyder. *Strategy, Politics, and Defense Budgets* (New York: 1962).

Schmitt, Bernadotte E., and Harold C. Vedeler. *The World in the Crucible: 1914–1919* (New York: 1984).

Schnabel, James F. *The Joint Chiefs of Staff and National Policy, 1945–47* (Wilmington, Delaware: 1979).

———. *Policy and Direction: The First Year* [United States Army in the Korean War] (Washington: 1972).

Scholes, Walter V. and Marie V. *The Foreign Policies of the Taft Administration* (Columbia, Missouri: 1970).

Schuker, Stephen A. *The End of French Predominance in Europe: The Financial Crisis of 1924 and the Adoption of the Dawes Plan* (Chapel Hill: 1976).

Schwabe, Klaus. *Woodrow Wilson, Revolutionary Germany, and Peacemaking, 1918–1919: Missionary Diplomacy and the Realities of Power* (Chapel Hill: 1985).

Scott, Harriet Fast, and William F. Scott. *The Armed Forces of the USSR* (Boulder: 1979).

Seaborg, Glenn T. *Kennedy, Khrushchev, and the Test Ban* (Berkeley: 1981).

Sharp, Tony. *The Wartime Alliance and the Zonal Division of Germany* (Oxford: 1975).

Sherry, Michael S. *Preparing for the Next War: American Plans for Postwar Defense, 1941–45* (New Haven: 1977).

Shewmaker, Kenneth E. *Americans and Chinese Communists, 1927–1945: A Persuading Encounter* (Ithaca: 1971).

Shlaim, Avi. *The United States and the Berlin Blockade, 1948–1949: A Study in Crisis Decision-Making* (Berkeley: 1983).

Shulman, Marshall D. *Stalin's Foreign Policy Reappraised* (New York: 1969).

Short, Nicholas M., *et al. Mission to Earth: Landsat Views the World* (Washington: 1976).

Simmons, Robert R. *The Strained Alliance: Peking, P'yongyang, Moscow and the Politics of the Korean Civil War* (New York: 1975).

Sivachev, Nikolai V., and Nikolai N. Yakovlev. *Russia and the United States*, translated by Olga Adler Titelbaum (Chicago: 1979).

Small, Melvin, and J. David Singer, *Resort to Arms: International and Civil Wars, 1816–1980* (Beverly Hills: 1982).

Smith, Perry McCoy. *The Air Force Plans for Peace, 1943–1945* (Baltimore: 1970).

Smith, Tony. *The Pattern of Imperialism: The United States, Great Britain, and the Late-Industrializing World since 1815* (Cambridge: 1981).

Smoke, Richard. *War: Controlling Escalation* (Cambridge, Massachusetts: 1977).

Snyder, Glenn H., and Paul Diesing. *Conflict Among Nations: Bargaining, Decision Making, and System Structure in International Crises* (Princeton: 1977).

Spanier, John. *Games Nations Play: Analyzing International Politics*, Fifth Edition (New York: 1984).

Spencer, Donald S. *Louis Kossuth and Young America: A Study of Sectionalism and Foreign Policy, 1848–1852* (Columbia, Missouri: 1977).

Spykman, Nicholas John. *America's Strategy in World Politics* (New York: 1942).

———. *The Geography of the Peace*, edited by Helen R. Nicoll (New York: 1944).

Stares, Paul B. *The Militarization of Space: U.S. Policy, 1945–84* (Ithaca: 1985).

Stebbins, Richard P. *The United States in World Affairs: 1949* (New York: 1950).

Steel, Ronald. *Walter Lippmann and the American Century* (Boston: 1980).

Stimson, Henry L., and McGeorge Bundy. *On Active Service in Peace and War* (New York: 1948).

Strausz-Hupé, Robert. *The Balance of Tomorrow: Power and Foreign Policy in the United States* (New York: 1945).

Stein, Harold, ed. *American Civil-Military Decisions* (Birmingham, Alabama: 1963).

Steinberg, Gerald M. *Satellite Reconnaissance: The Role of Informal Bargaining* (New York: 1983).

Stueck, William Whitney, Jr. *The Road to Confrontation: American Policy Toward China and Korea, 1947–1950* (Chapel Hill: 1981).

———. *The Wedemeyer Mission: American Politics and Foreign Policy During the Cold War* (Athens, Georgia: 1984).

Sulzberger, C. L. *A Long Row of Candles: Memoirs and Diaries, 1943–1954* (New York: 1969).

———. *The Last of the Giants* (New York: 1970).

Sutton, Anthony. *Western Technology and Soviet Economic Development: 1917 to 1930* (Stanford: 1968).

Talbott, Strobe. *Deadly Gambits: The Reagan Administration and the Stalemate in Nuclear Arms Control* (New York: 1984).

Tang Tsou, *America's Failure in China, 1941–50* (Chicago: 1963).

Tatum, E. H. *The United States and Europe, 1815–1823: A Study in the Background of the Monroe Doctrine* (Berkeley: 1936).

Taubman, William. *Stalin's American Policy: From Entente to Detente to Cold War* (New York: 1982).

Taylor, John W. R., and David Mondley. *Spies in the Sky* (New York: 1972).

Tompkins, Pauline. *American-Russian Relations in the Far East* (New York: 1949).

Tucker, Robert W. *The Radical Left and American Foreign Policy* (Baltimore: 1971).

Truman, Harry S. *Memoirs: Year of Decisions* (Garden City, New York: 1955).

Truman, Margaret. *Harry S. Truman* (New York: 1973).

Tucker, Nancy Bernkopf. *Patterns in the Dust: Chinese-American Relations and the Recognition Controversy, 1949–1950* (New York: 1983).

Ulam, Adam B. *Expansion and Coexistence: The History of Soviet Foreign Policy, 1917–73*, Second Edition (New York: 1974).

———. *Stalin: The Man and His Era* (New York: 1973).

Unterberger, Betty M. *America's Siberia Expedition, 1918–1920* (Durham: 1956).

Walker, J. Samuel. *Henry A. Wallace and American Foreign Policy* (Westport, Connecticut: 1976).

Waltz, Kenneth N. *Man, the State and War: A Theoretical Analysis* (New York: 1959).

———. *Theory of International Politics* (Reading, Massachusetts: 1979).

*The War Reports of General of the Army George C. Marshall, General of the Army H. H. Arnold, Fleet Admiral Ernest J. King* (Philadelphia: 1947).

Welles, Sumner. *The Time for Decision* (New York: 1944).

White, Irvin L. *Decision-Making for Space: Law and Politics in Air, Sea, and Outer Space* (West Lafayette, Indiana: 1970).

White, John A. *The Siberian Intervention* (Princeton: 1950).

Williams, Phil. *Crisis Management: Confrontation and Diplomacy in the Nuclear Age* (New York: 1976).

Williams, William Appleman. *Empire as a Way of Life* (New York: 1980).

———. *The Tragedy of American Diplomacy*, Revised Edition (New York: 1962).

Willkie, Wendell. *One World* (New York: 1943).

Wolfe, Thomas W. *Soviet Power and Europe: 1945–1970* (Baltimore: 1970).

Wright, Quincy. *A Study of War*, Second Edition (Chicago: 1965).

Wyden, Peter. *Day One: Before Hiroshima and After* (New York: 1984).

Yergin, Daniel. *Shattered Peace: The Origins of the Cold War and the National Security State* (Boston: 1977).

Young, Kenneth T. *Negotiating with the Chinese Communists: The United States Experience, 1953–1967* (New York: 1968).

Young, Marilyn Blatt. *The Rhetoric of Empire: American China Policy, 1895–1901* (Cambridge, Massachusetts: 1968).

Zabriskie, Edward H. *American-Russian Rivalry in the Far East: A Study in Diplomacy and Power Politics* (Philadelphia: 1946).

Zagoria, Donald S. *The Sino-Soviet Conflict, 1956–1961* (Princeton: 1962).

Zimmerman, William. *Soviet Perspectives on International Relations, 1956–1967* (Princeton: 1969).


## Articles

Adler, Les K., and Thomas G. Paterson. "Red Fascism: The Merger of Nazi Germany and Soviet Russia in the American Image of Totalitarianism, 1930's–1950's," *American Historical Review,* LXXV (April 1970), 1046–64.

"America's Falklands War," *Economist,* CCXC (March 3, 1984), 30–31.

Arkin, William M. "Waging Secrecy," *Bulletin of the Atomic Scientists,* XLI (March 1985), 5–6.

Aspaturian, Vernon V. "Internal Politics and Foreign Policy in the Soviet System," in Vernon V. Aspaturian, ed., *Process and Power in Soviet Foreign Policy* (Boston: 1971), pp. 491–551.

———. "The Soviet Military-Industrial Complex—Does It Exist?" *Journal of International Affairs,* XXVI (1972), 1–28.

Bialer, Seweryn. "The Political System," in Robert F. Byrnes, ed., *After Brezhnev: Sources of Soviet Conduct in the 1980s* (Bloomington: 1983), pp. 1–67.

Blair, B. G. "Reconnaissance Satellites," in Bhupendra Jasani, ed., *Outer Space—A New Dimension of the Arms Race* (London: 1982), pp. 125–34.

Boyle, Peter G. "The British Foreign Office View of Soviet-American Relations, 1945–46," *Diplomatic History,* III (Summer 1979), 307–20.

Brodie, Bernard. "War in the Atomic Age," in Brodie, ed., *The Absolute Weapon: Atomic Power and World Order* (New York: 1046), pp. 21–69.

Bundy, McGeorge, with George F. Kennan, Robert S. McNamara, and Gerard Smith. "Nuclear Weapons and the Atlantic Alliance," *Foreign Affairs,* LX (Spring 1982), 753–68.

Carter, Ashton B. "Satellites and Anti-Satellites: The Limits of the Possible," *International Security,* X (Spring 1986), 46–98.

Clifford, J. Garry. "President Truman and Peter the Great's Will," *Diplomatic History,* IV (Fall 1980), 371–85.

Cohen, Naomi W. "The Abrogation of the Russo-American Treaty of 1832," *Jewish Social Studies,* XXV (January 1963), 3–41.

Cohen, Stuart A. "The Evolution of Soviet Views on SALT Verification: Implications for the Future," in William C. Potter, ed., *Verification and SALT: The Challenge of Strategic Deception* (Boulder: 1980), pp. 55–72.

Deutsch. Karl W., and J. David Singer. "Multipolar Power Systems and International Stability," in James N. Rosenau, ed., *International Politics and Foreign Policy: A Reader in Research and Theory,* Revised Edition (New York: 1969), pp. 315–24.

Dingman, Roger V. "Theories of, and Approaches to, Alliance Politics," in Paul Gordon Lauren, ed., *Diplomacy: New Approaches in History, Theory, and Policy* (New York: 1979), pp. 245–68.

Dunn, Frederick Sherwood. "An Introductory Statement," in Nicholas John Spykman,

*The Geography of the Peace*, edited by Helen R. Nicholl (New York: 1944), pp. ix–xii.

Edwards, D. D. "Making Remote Sense Out of Space Commercialization," *Science News* CXXVII (December 21 and 28, 1985), 393.

Egan, Clifford L. "Pressure Groups, the Department of State and the Abrogation of the Russian-American Treaty of 1832," *Proceedings of the American Philosophical Society*, CXV (August 1971), 328–34.

Elachi, Charles. "Radar Images of the Earth from Space," *Scientific American*, CCXLVII (December 1982), 54–61.

Elliott, David C. "Project Vista and Nuclear Weapons in Europe," *International Security*, XI (Summer 1986), 163–83.

Feiveson, Harold A., with Richard H. Ullmann and Frank von Hippel. "Reducing U.S. and Soviet Nuclear Arsenals," *Bulletin of the Atomic Scientists*, XLI (August 1985), 144–53.

Gaddis, John Lewis. "The Corporatist Synthesis: A Skeptical View," *Diplomatic History*, X (Fall 1986), 357–62.

———. "The Emerging Post-Revisionist Synthesis on the Origins of the Cold War," *Diplomatic History*, VII (Summer 1983), 171–90.

———. "Korea in American Politics, Strategy, and Diplomacy, 1945–50," in Yonosuke Nagai and Akira Iriye, eds., *The Origins of the Cold War in Asia* (Tokyo: 1977), pp. 227–98.

Garwin, Richard L., and John Pike. "Space Weapons: History and Current Debate," *Bulletin of the Atomic Scientists*, XL (May 1984), 2S–3S.

Goldstein, Steven M. "Chinese Communist Policy Toward the United States: Opportunities and Constraints, 1944–1950," in Dorothy Borg and Waldo Heinrichs, eds., *Uncertain Years: Chinese-American Relations, 1947–1950* (New York: 1980), pp. 235–78.

Greene, Fred. "The Military View of National Policy, 1904–1940," *American Historical Review*, LXVI (January 1961), 354–77.

Griffith, Robert. "Dwight D. Eisenhower and the Corporate Commonwealth," *American Historical Review*, LXXXVII (February 1982), 87–122.

Hafemeister, David, Joseph J. Romm, and Kosta Tsipis. "The Verification of Compliance with Arms-Control Agreements," *Scientific American*, CCLIII (March 1985), 38–45.

Hafner, D. L. "Anti-Satellite Weapons: The Prospects for Arms Control," in Bhupendra Jasani, ed., *Outer Space—A New Dimension of the Arms Race* (London: 1982), pp. 311–23.

Hammond, Paul Y. "Super Carriers and B-36 Bombers: Appropriations, Strategy and Politics," in Harold Stein, ed., *American Civil-Military Decisions* (Birmingham, Alabama: 1963), pp. 465–568.

Healy, Ann E. "Tsarist Anti-Semitism and Russian-American Relations, *Slavic Review*, XLII (Fall 1983), 408–24.

Heinrichs, Waldo H., Jr. "The Role of the United States Navy," in Dorothy Borg and Shumpei Okamoto, eds., *Pearl Harbor as History: Japanese-American Relations, 1931–1941* (New York: 1973), pp. 197–224.

Herring, George C., and Richard H. Immerman. "Eisenhower, Dulles, and Dienbienphu: 'The Day We Didn't Go to War' Revisited," *Journal of American History*, LXXI (September 1984), 343–63.

Hess, Gary R. "The First American Commitment in Indochina: The Acceptance of the 'Bao Dai Solution,' 1950," *Diplomatic History*, II (Fall 1978), 331–50.

Hogan, Michael J. "American Marshall Planners and the Search for a European Neocapitalism," *American Historical Review*, XC (February 1985), 44–72.

Holsti, Ole R. "Theories of Crisis Decision Making," in Paul Gordon Lauren, ed., *Diplomacy: New Approaches in History, Theory, and Policy* (New York: 1979), pp. 99–136.

Hunt, Michael. "Mao Tse-tung and the Issue of Accommodation with the United States," in Dorothy Borg and Waldo Heinrichs, eds., *Uncertain Years: Chinese-American Relations, 1947–1950* (New York: 1980), pp. 185–234.

Jasani, Bhupendra. "Military Space Technology and Its Implications," in Bhupendra Jasani, ed., *Outer Space—A New Dimension of the Arms Race* (London: 1982), pp. 43–50.

Jervis, Robert. "Systems Theories and Diplomatic History," in Paul Gordon Lauren, ed., *Diplomacy: New Approaches in History, Theory, and Policy* (New York: 1979), pp. 212–44.

Kennan, George F. "Letter to a Russian," *New Yorker*, LX (September 24, 1984), 55–73.

[Kennan, George F.]. "The Sources of Soviet Conduct," *Foreign Affairs*, XXV (July 1947), 566–82.

Kissinger, Henry A. "The White Revolutionary: Reflections on Bismarck," *Daedalus*, XCVII (Summer 1968), 888–924.

Krass, Allen S. "The Soviet View of Verification," in William C. Potter, ed., *Verification and Arms Control* (Lexington, Massachusetts: 1985), pp. 35–54.

Kutolowski, John. "The Effect of the Polish Insurrection of 1863 on American Civil War Diplomacy," *The Historian*, XXVII (August 1965), 560–77.

Lebow, Richard Ned. "Windows of Opportunity: Do States Jump Through Them?" *International Security*, IX (Summer 1984), 147–86.

Lee, William T. "The 'Politico-Military-Industrial Complex' of the U.S.S.R.," *Journal of International Affairs*, XXVI (1972), 73–86.

Lees, Lorraine M. "The American Decision to Aid Tito, 1948–1949," *Diplomatic History*, II (Fall 1978), 407–22.

Leffler, Melvyn P. "Adherence to Agreements: Yalta and the Experience of the Early Cold War," *International Security*, XI (Summer 1986), 88–123.

Levine, Steven I. "A New Look at American Mediation in the Chinese Civil War: The Marshall Mission and Manchuria," *Diplomatic History*, III (Fall 1979), 349–76.

Lundestad, Geir. "Empire by Invitation? The United States and Western Europe, 1945–1952," *Journal of Peace Research*, XXIII (1986), 263–77.

Lynn-Jones, Sean. "A Quiet Success for Arms Control: Preventing Incidents at Sea," *International Security*, IX (Spring 1985), 154–84.

Mackinder, Halford. "The Geographical Pivot of History," *Geographical Journal*, XXIII (April 1904), 421–44.

———. "The Round World and the Winning of the Peace," *Foreign Affairs*, XXI (July 1943), 595–605.

Maddux, Thomas R. "United States–Soviet Naval Relations in the 1930's: The Soviet Union's Efforts to Purchase Naval Vessels," *Naval War College Review*, XXIX (Fall 1976), 28–37.

Maier, Charles S. "The Two Postwar Eras and the Conditions for Stability in Twentieth-Century Western Europe," *American Historical Review*, LXXXVI (April 1981), 327–52.

———. "Revisionism and the Interpretation of Cold War Origins," *Perspectives in American History*, IV (1970), 313–47.

Mark, Eduard. "American Policy toward Eastern Europe and the Origins of the Cold War: An Alternative Interpretation," *Journal of American History*, LXVIII (September 1981), 313–36.

Matray, James I. "Truman's Plan for Victory: National Self-Determination and the Thirty-Eighth Parallel Decision in Korea," *Journal of American History*, LXVI (September 1979), 314–33.

Mayers, David. "Containment and the Primacy of Diplomacy: George Kennan's Views, 1947–1948," *International Security*, XI (Summer 1986), 124–62.

Melanson, Richard A. "Revisionism Subdued? Robert James Maddox and the Origins of the Cold War," *Political Science Reviewer*, VII (1977), 229–71.

————. "The Social and Political Thought of William Appleman Williams," *Western Political Quarterly*, XXXI(1978), 392–409.

Messer, Robert L. "Paths Not Taken: The United States Department of State and Alternatives to Containment," *Diplomatic History* I(Fall 1977), 297–320.

Okonogi, Masao. "The Domestic Roots of the Korean War," in Yonosuke Nagai and Akira Iriye, eds., *The Origins of the Cold War in Asia* (New York: 1977), pp. 299–320.

Orhaug, T., and G. Forssell. "Information Extraction from Images," in Bhupendra Jasani, ed., *Outer Space—A New Dimension of the Arms Race* (London: 1982), pp. 215–27.

Perry, G. E. "Identification of Military Components Within the Soviet Space Programme," in Bhupendra Jasani, ed., *Outer Space—A New Dimension of the Arms Race* (London: 1982), pp. 135–54.

Poole, Walter S. "From Conciliation to Containment: The Joint Chiefs of Staff and the Coming of the Cold War, 1945–1946," *Military Affairs*, XLII(February 1978), 12–16.

Quester, George H. "The Impact of the Strategic Balance on Containment," in Terry L. Deibel and John Lewis Gaddis, eds., *Containment: Concept and Policy* (Washington: 1986), pp. 255–86.

Reeves, Thomas C. "McCarthyism: Interpretations since Hofstadter," *Wisconsin Magazine of History*, LX(Autumn 1976), 42–54.

Rivkin, David B., Jr. "Star Wars: The Nagging Questions: What Does Moscow Think?" *Foreign Policy*, #59(Summer 1985), 85–105.

Rosenberg, David Alan. "American Atomic Strategy and the Hydrogen Bomb Decision," *Journal of American History*, LXVI(June 1979), 62–87.

————. "The Origins of Overkill: Nuclear Weapons and American Strategy, 1945–1960," *International Security*, VII(Spring 1983), 3–71.

————. " 'A Smoking, Radiating Ruin at the End of Two Hours': Documents on American Plans for Nuclear War with the Soviet Union, 1954–55," *International Security*, VI(Winter 1981/82), 3–38.

————. "U.S. Nuclear Stockpile, 1945 to 1950," *Bulletin of the Atomic Scientists*, XXXVIII(May 1982), 25–30.

Sagan, Carl. "Nuclear War and Climatic Catastrophe: Some Policy Implications," *Foreign Affairs*, LXII(Winter 1983/84), 257–92.

Sakata, T., and H. Shimoda. "Image Analysis and Sensor Technology for Satellite Monitoring," in Bhupendra Jasani, ed., *Outer Space—A New Dimension of the Arms Race* (London: 1982), pp. 197–214.

Santhanam, K. "Use of Satellites in Crisis Monitoring," in Bhupendra Jasani, ed., *Outer Space—A New Dimension of the Arms Race* (London: 1982), pp. 265–74.

Schaller, Michael. "Securing the Great Crescent: Occupied Japan and the Origins of Containment in Southeast Asia," *Journal of American History*, LXIX(September 1982), 392–414.

Schilling, Warner R. "The Politics of National Defense: Fiscal 1950," in Warner R. Schilling, Paul Y. Hammond, and Glenn H. Snyder, *Strategy, Politics, and Defense Budgets* (New York: 1962), pp. 1–266.

Schoenberg, Philip Ernest. "The American Reaction to the Kishinev Pogrom of 1903," *American Jewish Historical Quarterly*, LXIII(March 1974), 262–83.

Shepley, James. "How Dulles Averted War," *Life*, XL(January 16, 1956), 70–80.

"Space Weapons," *Bulletin of the Atomic Scientists*, XL(May 1984), pp. 1S–15S.

Stoler, Mark A. "From Continentalism to Globalism: General Stanley D. Embick, the Joint Strategic Survey Committee, and the Military View of American National Policy during the Second World War," *Diplomatic History*, VI(Summer 1982), 303–21.

Stults, Taylor. "Roosevelt, Russian Persecution of Jews, and American Public Opinion," *Jewish Social Studies*, XXIII(January 1971), 13–22.

"The 36-Hour War," *Life*, XIX (November 19, 1945), 27–35.

Thompson, Starley L., and Stephen H. Schneider. "Nuclear Winter Reappraised," *Foreign Affairs*, LXIV (Summer 1986), 981–1006.

Trofimenko, G. A. "Uroki mirnogo sosushestvovaniia," *Voprosy istorii*, #11 (November 1983), 3–28.

Ulam, Adam. "The World Outside," in Robert F. Byrnes, ed., *After Brezhnev: Sources of Soviet Conduct in the 1980s* (Bloomington: 1983), pp. 345–422.

Vandercook, Wm. F. "Making the Very Best of the Very Worst: The 'Human Effects of Nuclear Weapons' Report of 1956," *International Security*. XI (Summer 1986), 184–95.

Walzer, Michael. "The Reform of the International System," in Øyvind Østerud, ed., *Studies of War and Peace* (Oslo: 1986), pp. 227–39.

Wells, Samuel F., Jr. "Sounding the Tocsin: NSC 68 and the Soviet Threat," *International Security*, IV (Fall 1979), 116–58.

# Index

Acheson, Dean G.: and Germany, 65–66; and Kennan, 65, 69; and NATO, 66; and "defensive perimeter" strategy, 72–75, 102–3; and China, 74, 82–88, 90, 99, 102, 165; and balance of power in Europe, 76; and Sino-Soviet differences, 76, 81, 102, 166–73, 182, 194; and Taiwan, 82–88; and Korea, 88, 96–100; and Indochina, 89–90; and international communism, 90, 160, 174; and United Nations, 93n; and Soviet Union, 110; and nuclear weapons, 112, 117, 121–22; and Great Britain, 121; and Yugoslavia, 158–59; and nationalism, 165; mentioned, 64

Afghanistan, 109, 131, 193, 208, 211, 230–32, 240–41

Africa, 193, 210, 234n, 240

Air Force, Soviet, 28, 41, 125

Air Force, U.S., 28n, 111–13n, 201–2. See also Strategic Air Command

Air War College, 55

Alaska, 4, 6

Albania, 160, 177, 222

Aleutian Islands, 73–75

Alexander II (Tsar), 8

Algeria, 234n

Allen, George V., 168

Allied Control Commissions, 30

Allison, John M., 98–99

Alsace-Lorraine, 225

Anderson, Terry, 45

Angola, 243

Anti-ballistic missile system, 105, 196n, 208, 233

Anti-Comintern Pact (1936), 154n

Arab-Israeli War (1973), 208, 230, 243

Argentina, 154, 218n, 232

Arms control, 196, 199–200, 203–5, 208. See also Strategic Arms Limitation Agreements

Army, Soviet, 65, 109, 112, 119, 154

Army, U.S., 24, 91, 96, 107, 125, 202

Army Air Force, U.S., 21, 24, 28

Arnold, Henry H., 21, 24–25, 28

"Arsenal of democracy" concept, 63

Asia, East: 6–9, 22, 24, 28, 35, 50, 72–103, 112, 115, 119–20, 167, 239. See also Individual countries; Southeast Asia Treaty Organization

Asia, Southeast, 74, 89–90, 92–94, 184. See also individual countries

Aswan Dam, 192

Atkinson, Brooks, 32

Atlantic Charter, 25, 36, 51

Atomic Energy Act (1946), 107n

Atomic Energy Commission, 107, 113